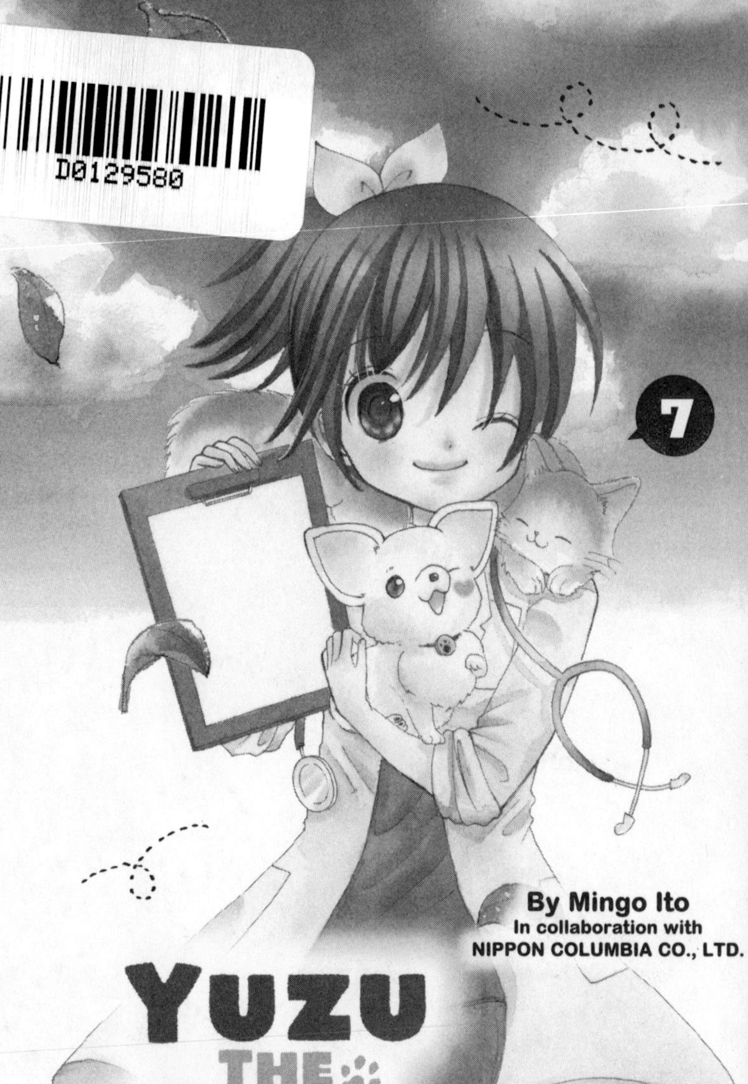

7

By Mingo Ito
In collaboration with
NIPPON COLUMBIA CO., LTD.

# YUZU THE PET VET

## Welcome to the Bow Meow Animal Hospital

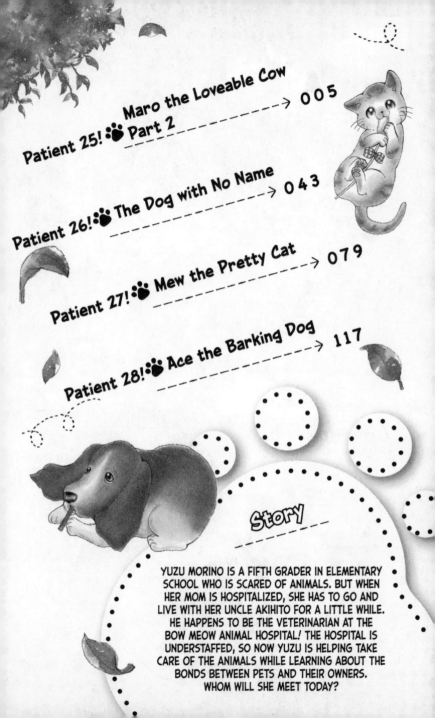

Patient 25! 🐾 Maro the Loveable Cow Part 2 ----→ 005

Patient 26! 🐾 The Dog with No Name ----→ 043

Patient 27! 🐾 Mew the Pretty Cat ----→ 079

Patient 28! 🐾 Ace the Barking Dog ----→ 117

### Story

YUZU MORINO IS A FIFTH GRADER IN ELEMENTARY SCHOOL WHO IS SCARED OF ANIMALS. BUT WHEN HER MOM IS HOSPITALIZED, SHE HAS TO GO AND LIVE WITH HER UNCLE AKIHITO FOR A LITTLE WHILE. HE HAPPENS TO BE THE VETERINARIAN AT THE BOW MEOW ANIMAL HOSPITAL! THE HOSPITAL IS UNDERSTAFFED, SO NOW YUZU IS HELPING TAKE CARE OF THE ANIMALS WHILE LEARNING ABOUT THE BONDS BETWEEN PETS AND THEIR OWNERS. WHOM WILL SHE MEET TODAY?

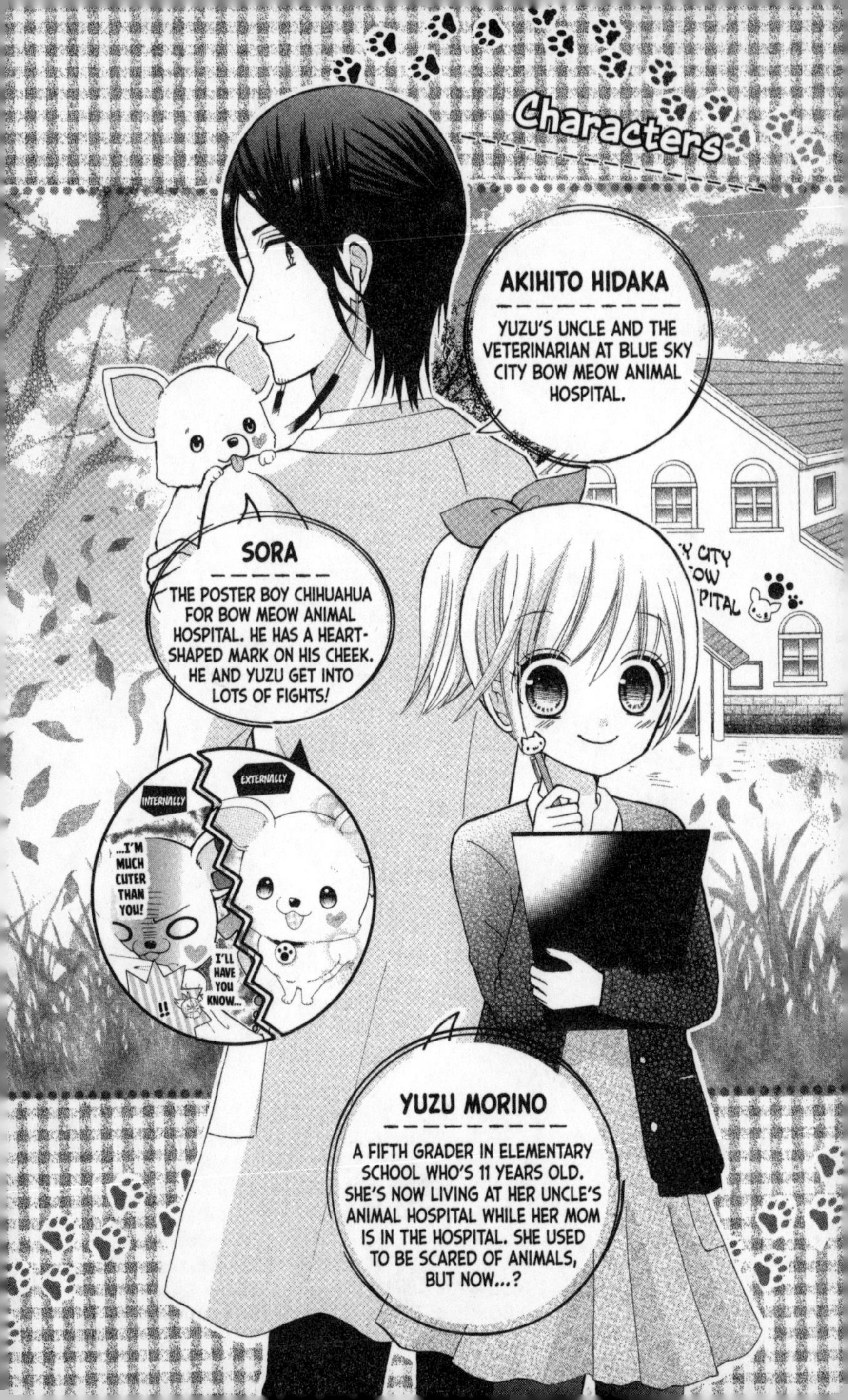
Characters
AKIHITO HIDAKA
YUZU'S UNCLE AND THE VETERINARIAN AT BLUE SKY CITY BOW MEOW ANIMAL HOSPITAL.
SORA
THE POSTER BOY CHIHUAHUA FOR BOW MEOW ANIMAL HOSPITAL. HE HAS A HEART-SHAPED MARK ON HIS CHEEK. HE AND YUZU GET INTO LOTS OF FIGHTS!
EXTERNALLY
INTERNALLY
...I'M MUCH CUTER THAN YOU!
I'LL HAVE YOU KNOW...
!!
YUZU MORINO
A FIFTH GRADER IN ELEMENTARY SCHOOL WHO'S 11 YEARS OLD. SHE'S NOW LIVING AT HER UNCLE'S ANIMAL HOSPITAL WHILE HER MOM IS IN THE HOSPITAL. SHE USED TO BE SCARED OF ANIMALS, BUT NOW...?

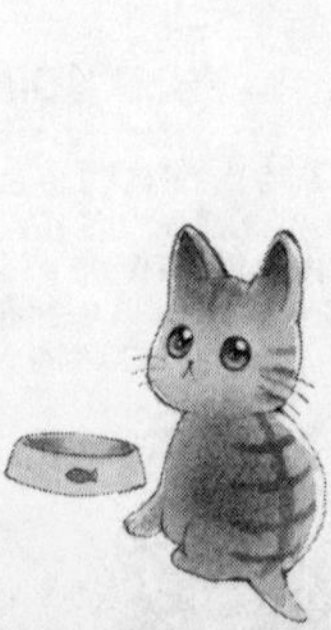

YUZU THE PET VET

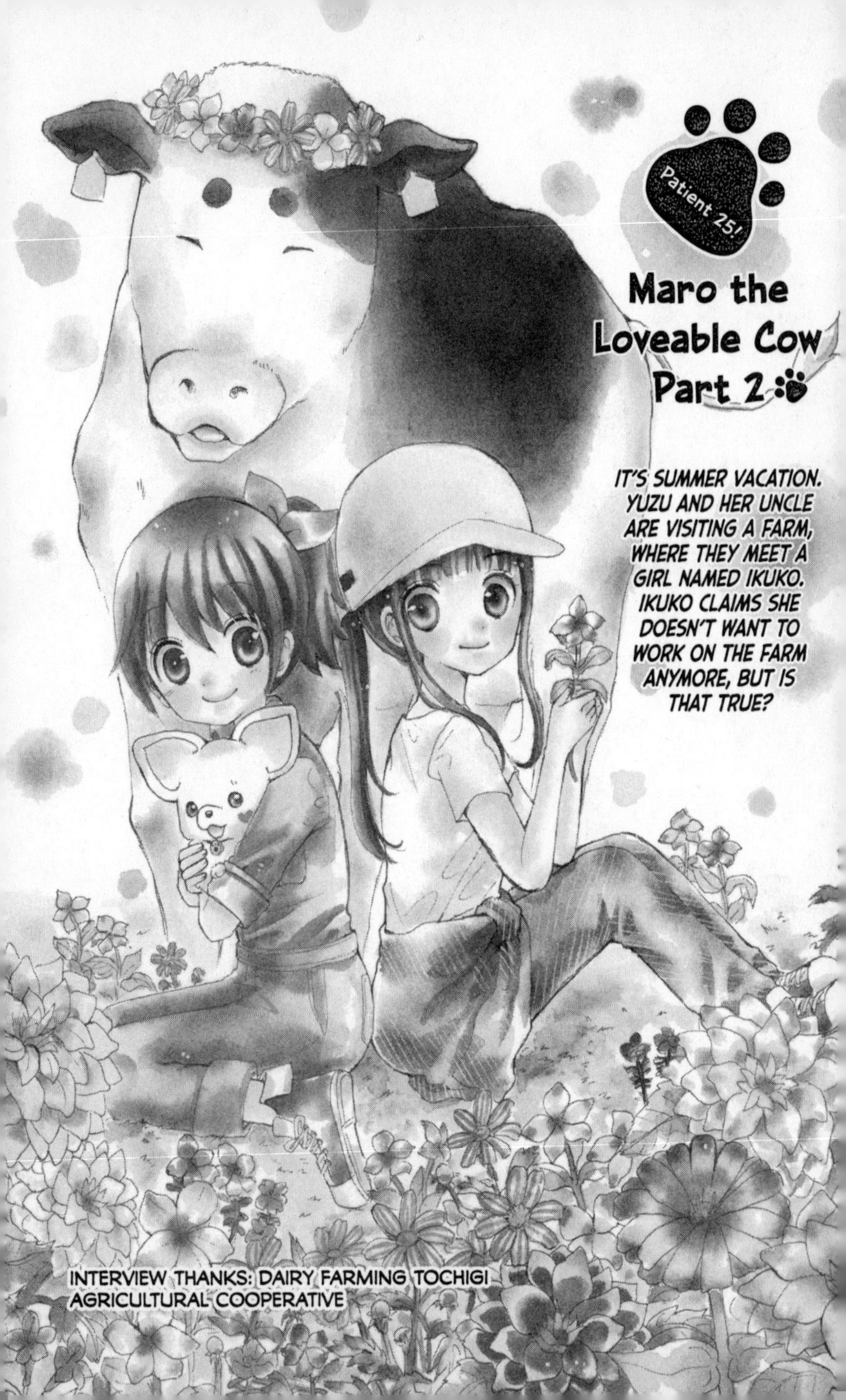
Patient 25!
Maro the Loveable Cow Part 2
IT'S SUMMER VACATION. YUZU AND HER UNCLE ARE VISITING A FARM, WHERE THEY MEET A GIRL NAMED IKUKO. IKUKO CLAIMS SHE DOESN'T WANT TO WORK ON THE FARM ANYMORE, BUT IS THAT TRUE?
INTERVIEW THANKS: DAIRY FARMING TOCHIGI AGRICULTURAL COOPERATIVE

YUZU THE PET VET

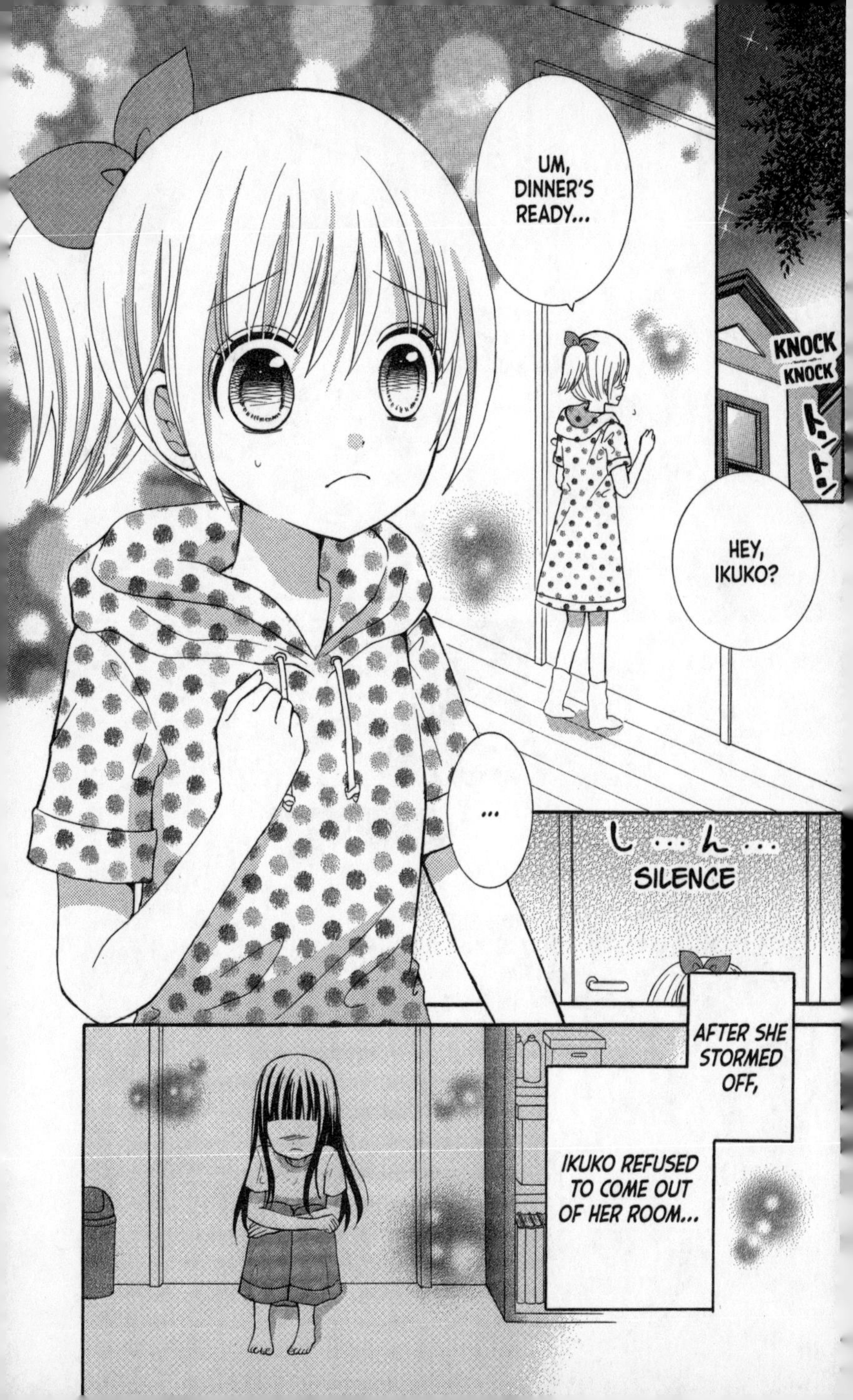

KNOCK KNOCK
HEY, IKUKO?
UM, DINNER'S READY...
...
し…ん…
SILENCE
AFTER SHE STORMED OFF,
IKUKO REFUSED TO COME OUT OF HER ROOM...

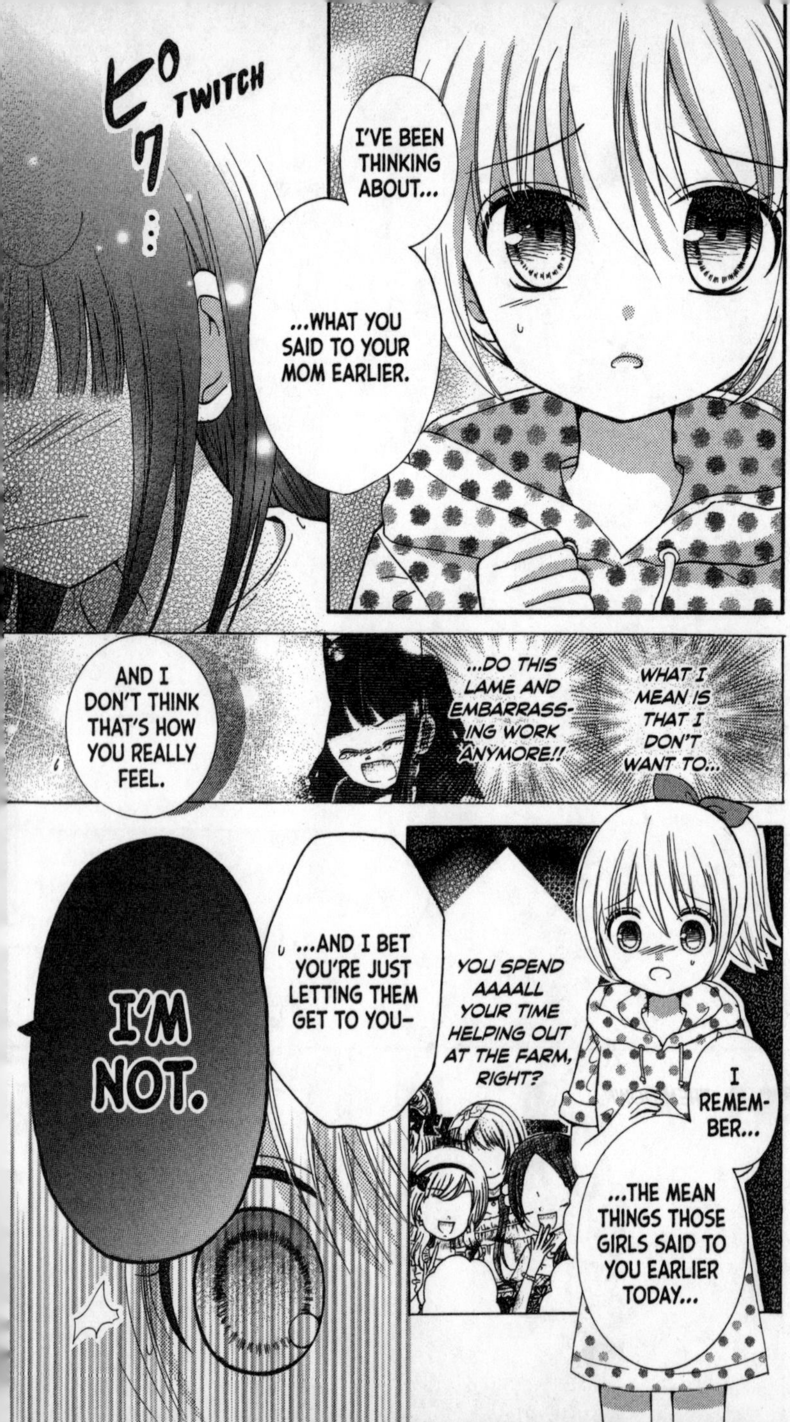
I'VE BEEN THINKING ABOUT...
...WHAT YOU SAID TO YOUR MOM EARLIER.
ピク TWITCH
WHAT I MEAN IS THAT I DON'T WANT TO...
...DO THIS LAME AND EMBARRASS-ING WORK ANYMORE!!
AND I DON'T THINK THAT'S HOW YOU REALLY FEEL.
I REMEM-BER...
...THE MEAN THINGS THOSE GIRLS SAID TO YOU EARLIER TODAY...
YOU SPEND AAAALL YOUR TIME HELPING OUT AT THE FARM, RIGHT?
...AND I BET YOU'RE JUST LETTING THEM GET TO YOU–
I'M NOT.

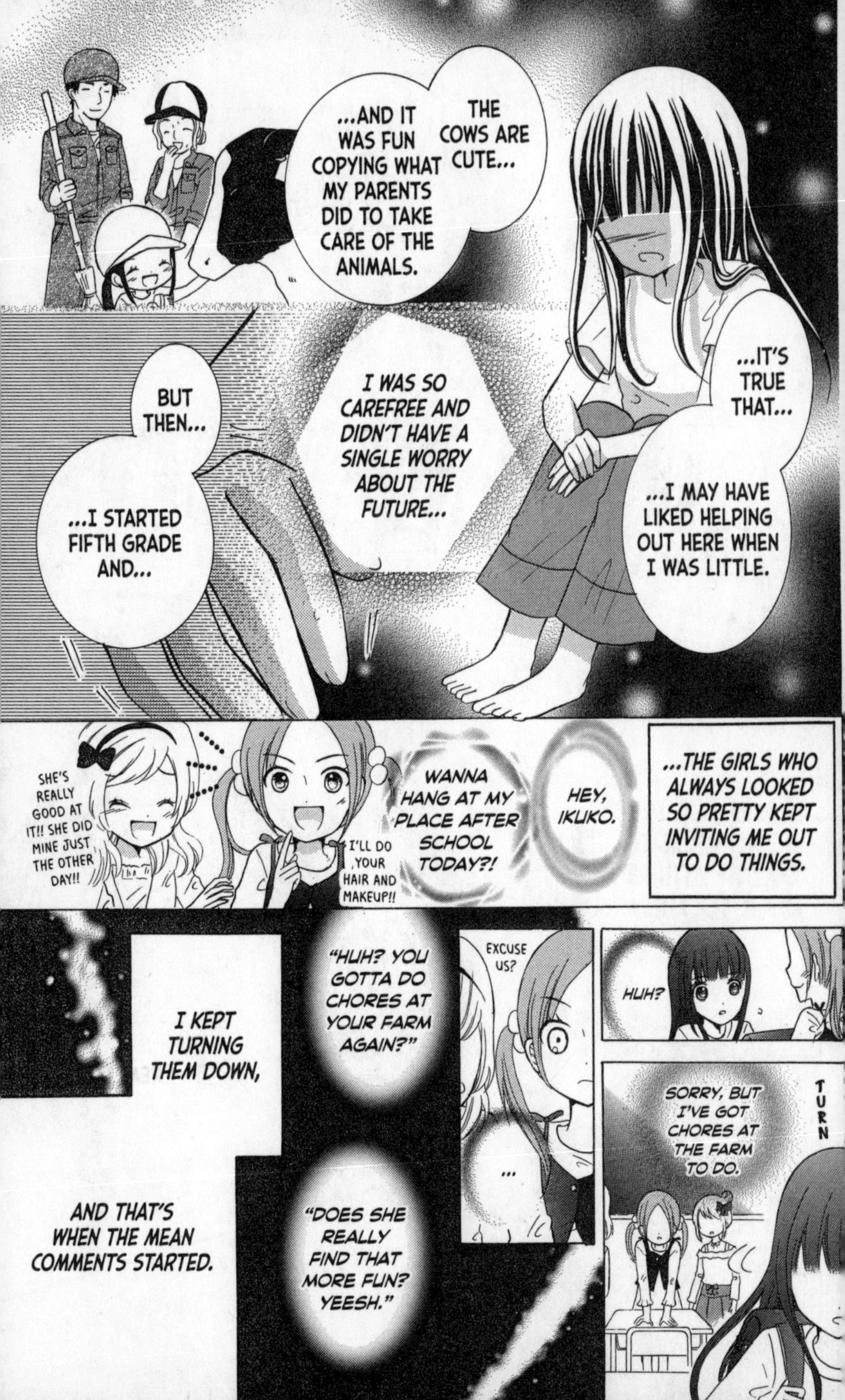
...IT'S TRUE THAT...
...I MAY HAVE LIKED HELPING OUT HERE WHEN I WAS LITTLE.
THE COWS ARE CUTE...
...AND IT WAS FUN COPYING WHAT MY PARENTS DID TO TAKE CARE OF THE ANIMALS.
I WAS SO CAREFREE AND DIDN'T HAVE A SINGLE WORRY ABOUT THE FUTURE...
BUT THEN...
...I STARTED FIFTH GRADE AND...
...THE GIRLS WHO ALWAYS LOOKED SO PRETTY KEPT INVITING ME OUT TO DO THINGS.
HEY, IKUKO.
WANNA HANG AT MY PLACE AFTER SCHOOL TODAY?!
I'LL DO YOUR HAIR AND MAKEUP!!
SHE'S REALLY GOOD AT IT!! SHE DID MINE JUST THE OTHER DAY!!
HUH?
SORRY, BUT I'VE GOT CHORES AT THE FARM TO DO.
TURN
EXCUSE US?
...
I KEPT TURNING THEM DOWN,
"HUH? YOU GOTTA DO CHORES AT YOUR FARM AGAIN?"
"DOES SHE REALLY FIND THAT MORE FUN? YEESH."
AND THAT'S WHEN THE MEAN COMMENTS STARTED.

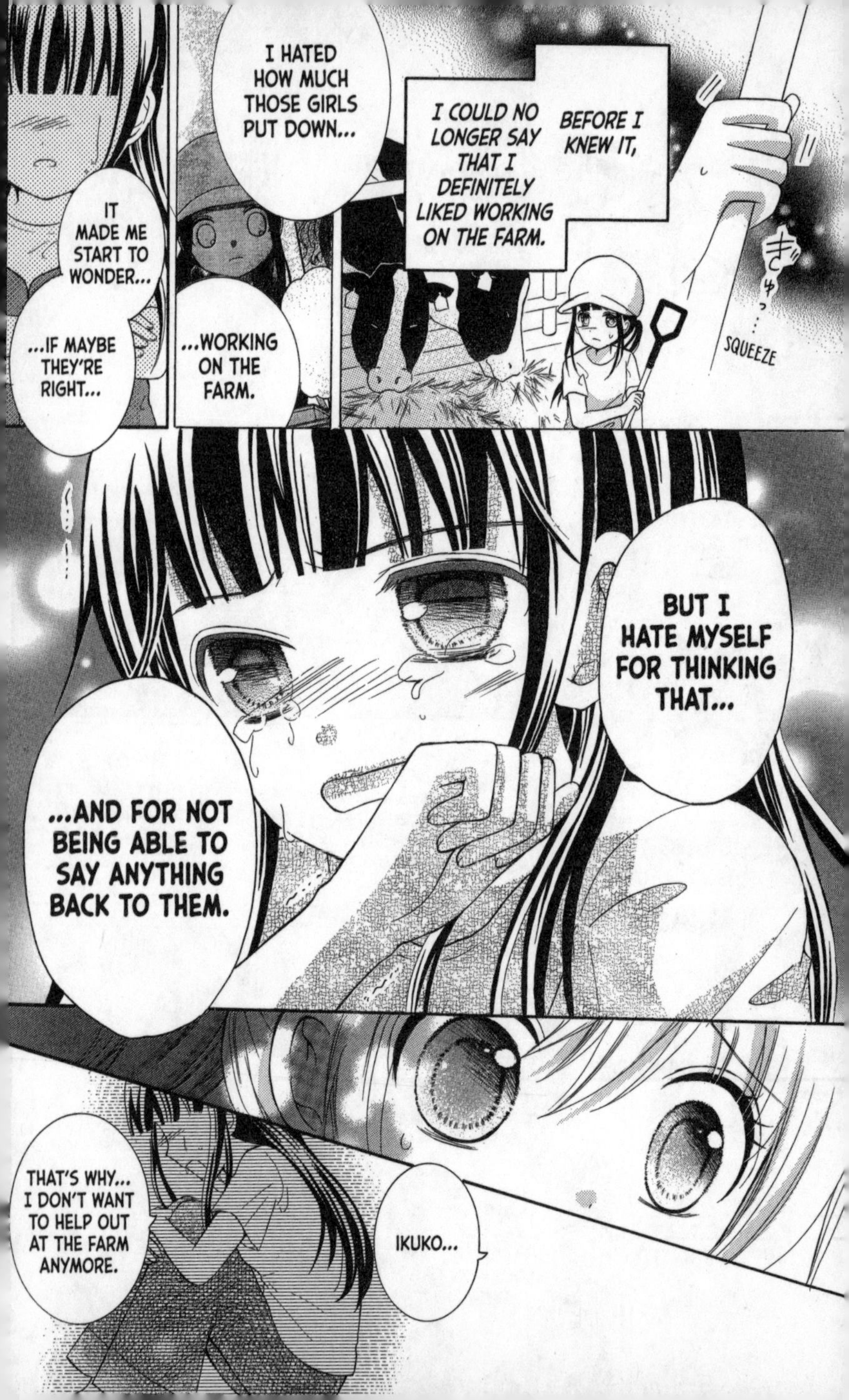
BEFORE I KNEW IT,
I COULD NO LONGER SAY THAT I DEFINITELY LIKED WORKING ON THE FARM.
ぎゅっ…
SQUEEZE
I HATED HOW MUCH THOSE GIRLS PUT DOWN...
...WORKING ON THE FARM.
IT MADE ME START TO WONDER...
...IF MAYBE THEY'RE RIGHT...
BUT I HATE MYSELF FOR THINKING THAT...
...AND FOR NOT BEING ABLE TO SAY ANYTHING BACK TO THEM.
THAT'S WHY... I DON'T WANT TO HELP OUT AT THE FARM ANYMORE.
IKUKO...

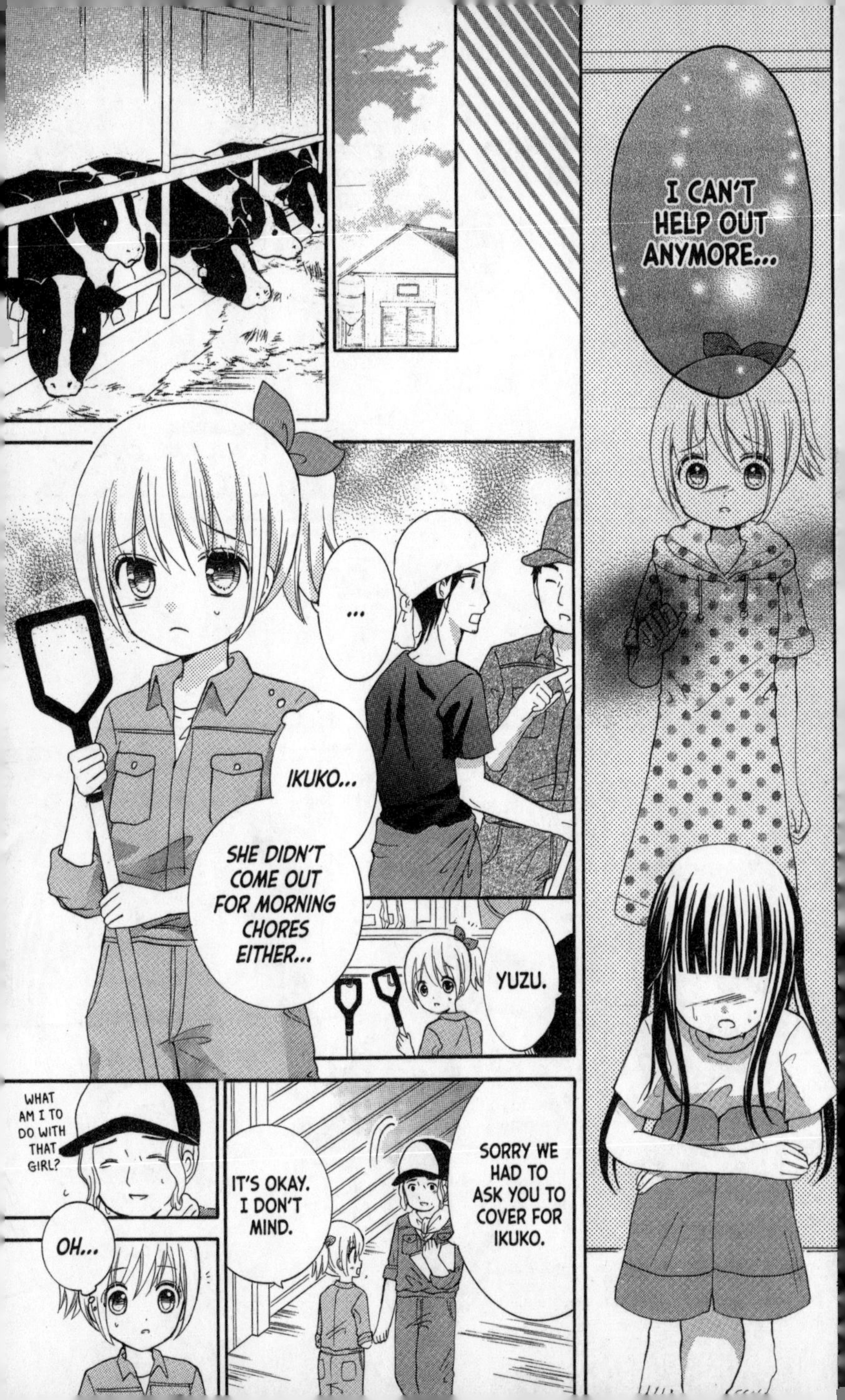
I CAN'T HELP OUT ANYMORE...
...
IKUKO...
SHE DIDN'T COME OUT FOR MORNING CHORES EITHER...
YUZU.
SORRY WE HAD TO ASK YOU TO COVER FOR IKUKO.
IT'S OKAY. I DON'T MIND.
WHAT AM I TO DO WITH THAT GIRL?
OH...

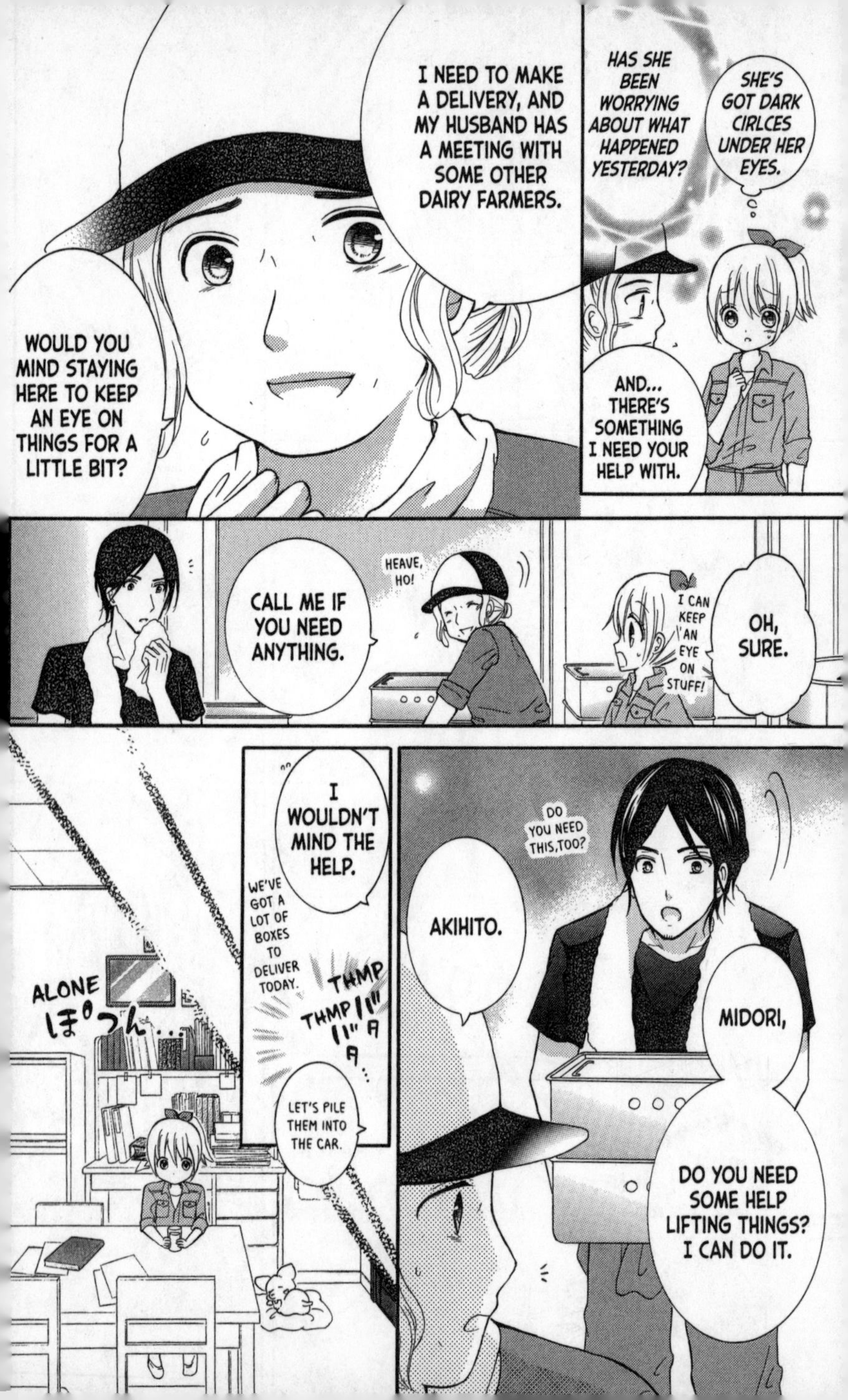
SHE'S GOT DARK CIRLCES UNDER HER EYES.
HAS SHE BEEN WORRYING ABOUT WHAT HAPPENED YESTERDAY?
AND... THERE'S SOMETHING I NEED YOUR HELP WITH.
I NEED TO MAKE A DELIVERY, AND MY HUSBAND HAS A MEETING WITH SOME OTHER DAIRY FARMERS.
WOULD YOU MIND STAYING HERE TO KEEP AN EYE ON THINGS FOR A LITTLE BIT?
OH, SURE.
I CAN KEEP AN EYE ON STUFF!
HEAVE, HO!
CALL ME IF YOU NEED ANYTHING.
MIDORI,
DO YOU NEED SOME HELP LIFTING THINGS? I CAN DO IT.
DO YOU NEED THIS,TOO?
AKIHITO.
I WOULDN'T MIND THE HELP.
WE'VE GOT A LOT OF BOXES TO DELIVER TODAY.
THMP THMP バタバタ...
LET'S PILE THEM INTO THE CAR.
ALONE ぽつん...

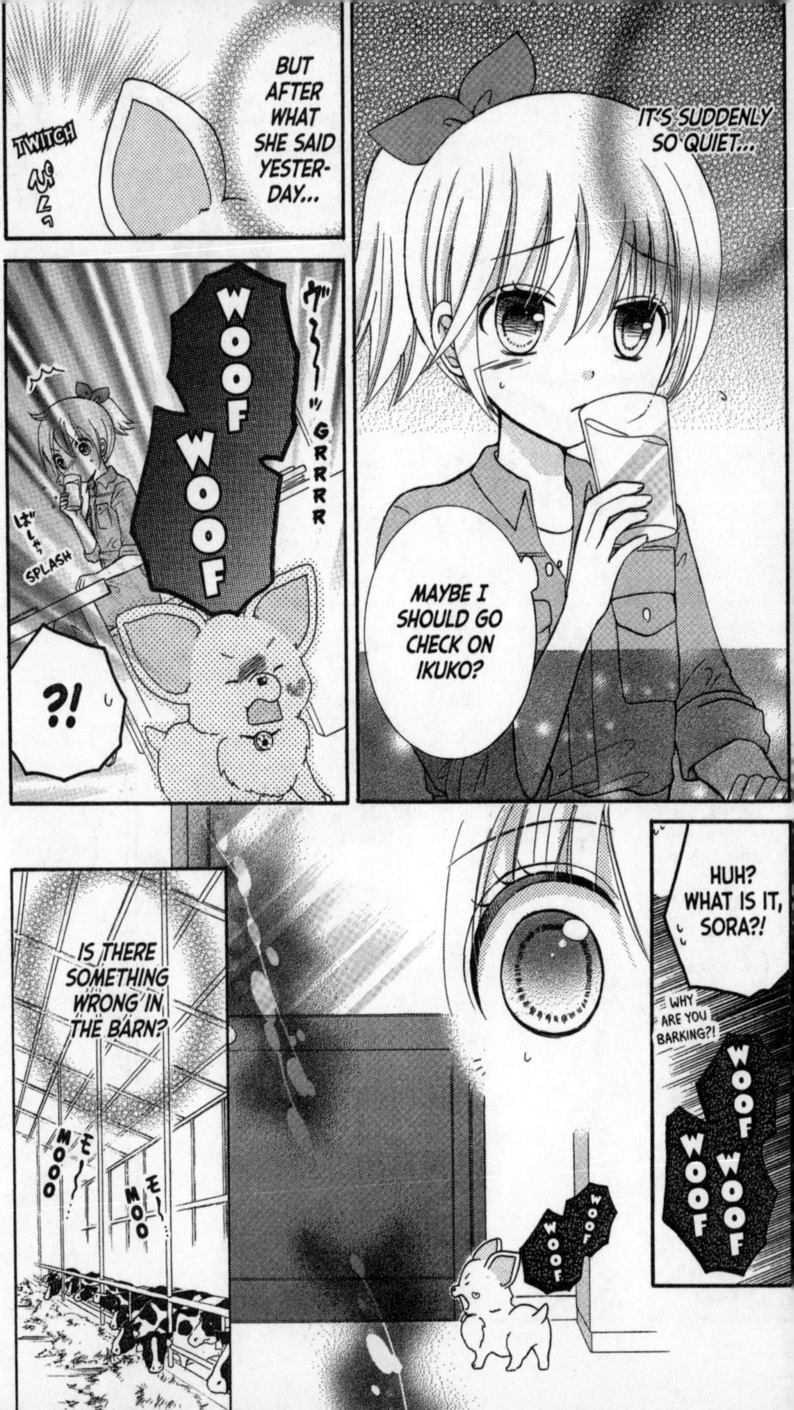
IT'S SUDDENLY SO QUIET...
MAYBE I SHOULD GO CHECK ON IKUKO?
BUT AFTER WHAT SHE SAID YESTER-DAY...
TWITCH
WOOF WOOF WOOF WOOF
GRRRR
ばしゃっ
SPLASH
?!
HUH? WHAT IS IT, SORA?!
WHY ARE YOU BARKING?!
WOOF WOOF WOOF WOOF
WOOF WOOF
IS THERE SOMETHING WRONG IN THE BARN?
MOOO
MOO

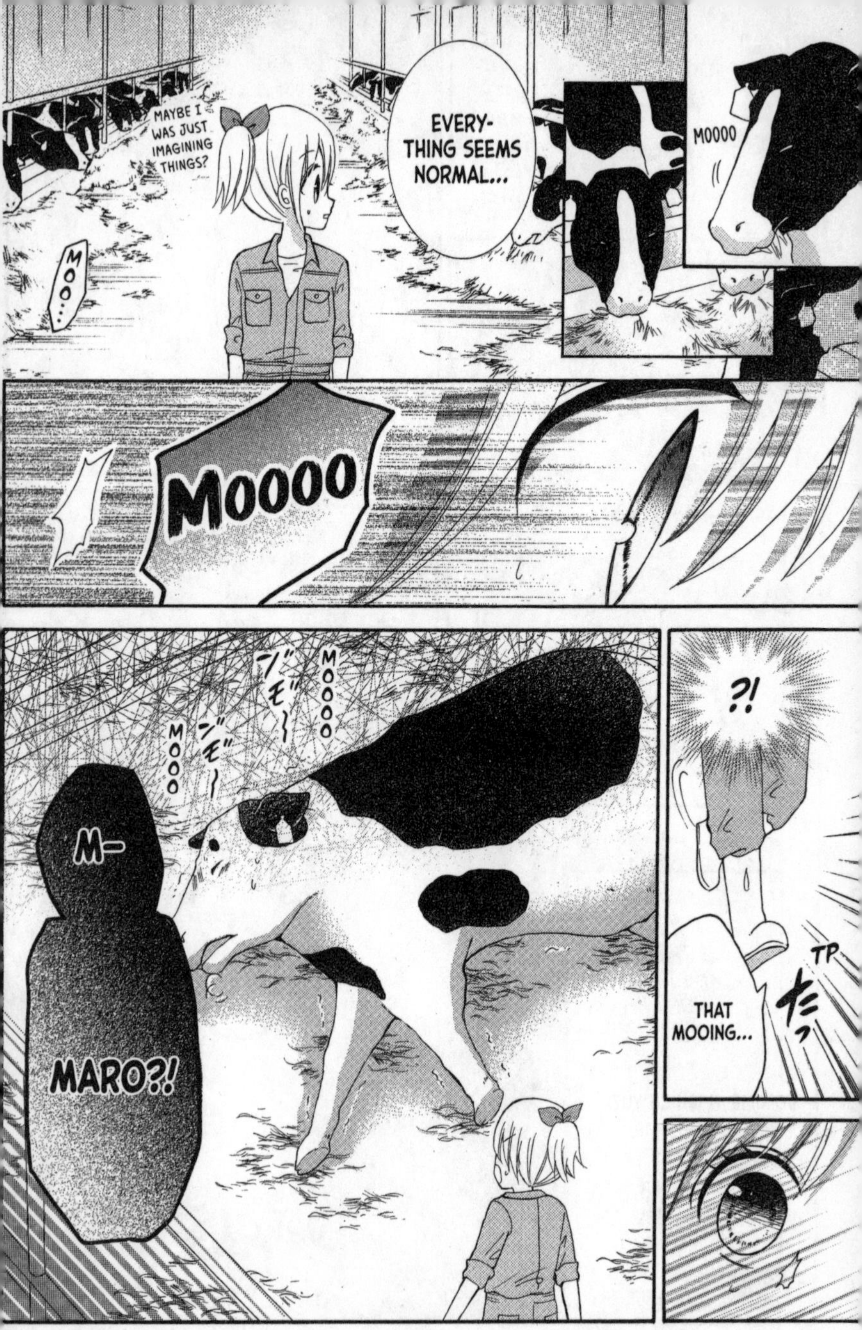
MOOOO
EVERY-THING SEEMS NORMAL...
MAYBE I WAS JUST IMAGINING THINGS?
MOO...
MOOOO
?!
TP
THAT MOOING...
MOOOOO
ンモ〜
MOOO
ンモ〜
M-
MARO?!

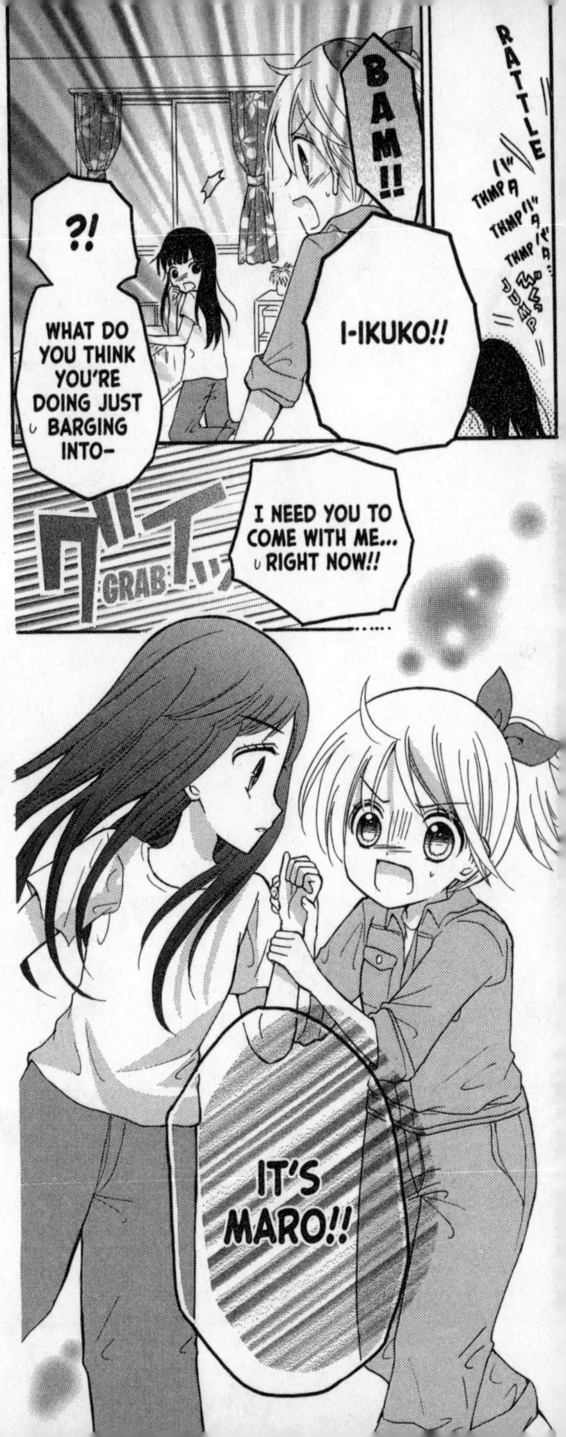
RATTLE
BAM!!
THMP
THMP
THMP
I-IKUKO!!
?!
WHAT DO YOU THINK YOU'RE DOING JUST BARGING INTO-
I NEED YOU TO COME WITH ME... RIGHT NOW!!
GRAB
IT'S MARO!!

## GREETINGS

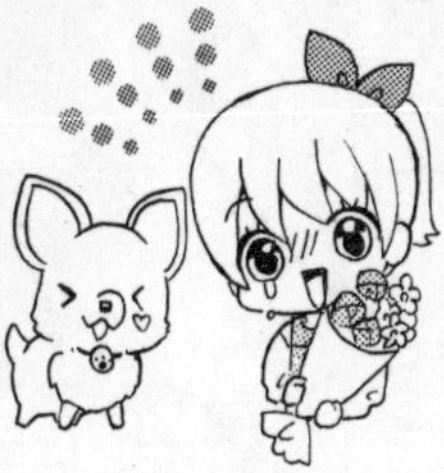

THANK YOU SO MUCH FOR BUYING VOLUME SEVEN OF YUZU *THE PET VET!*

I STILL CAN'T BELIEVE I'VE BEEN ABLE TO DRAW SO MUCH OF YUZU, SORA, AND ALL OF THE OTHER ANIMALS!

THIS IS THE FINAL VOLUME IN WHICH YUZU IS AN ELEMENTARY SCHOOLER, BUT THE STORY'S NOT OVER YET. IT WOULD MAKE ME SO HAPPY IF YOU'D READ THE CONTINUATION OF *YUZU THE PET VET*, TOO!

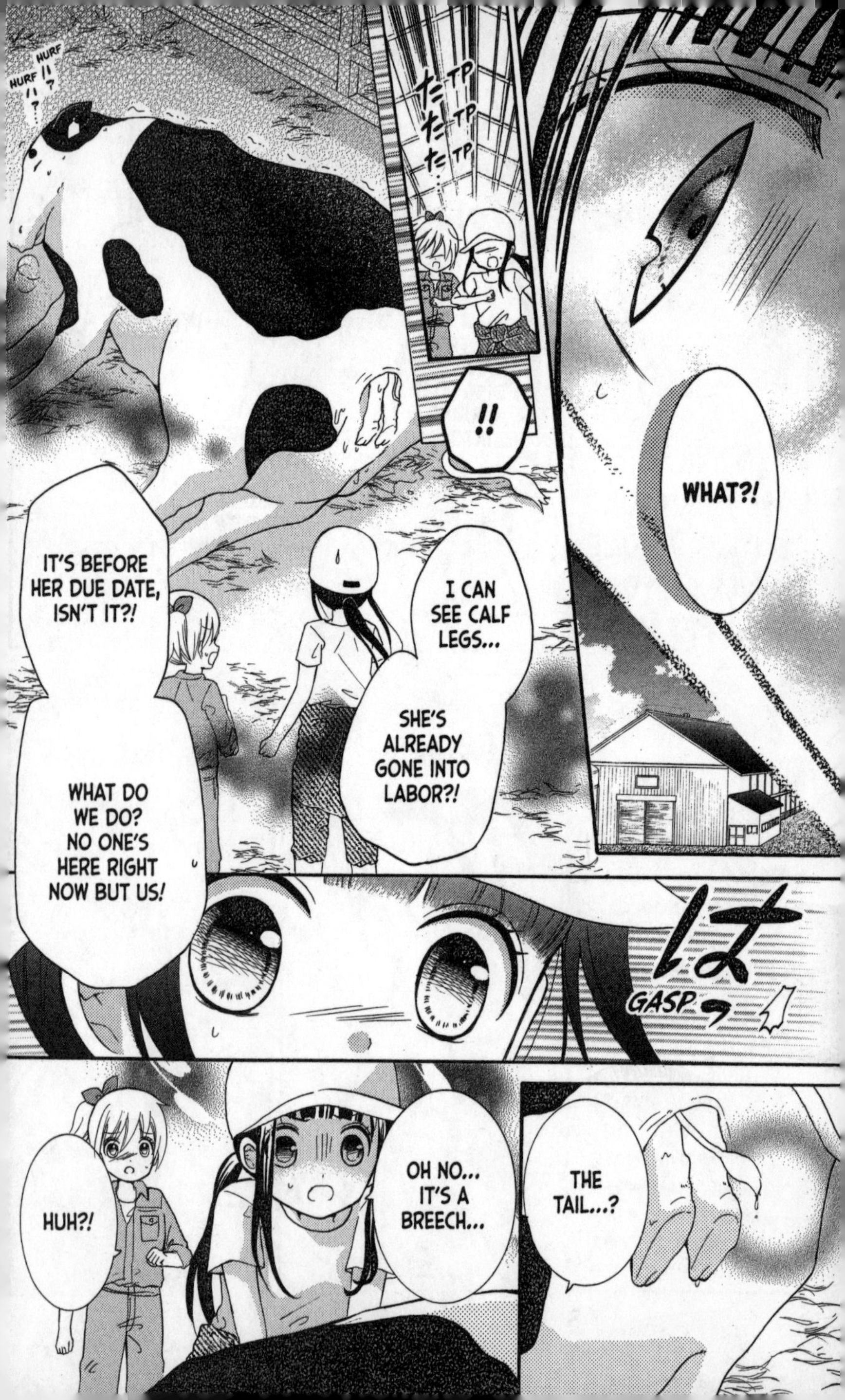

WHAT?!
たたた
TP TP TP
!!
ハァ ハァ
HURF HURF
I CAN SEE CALF LEGS...
SHE'S ALREADY GONE INTO LABOR?!
IT'S BEFORE HER DUE DATE, ISN'T IT?!
WHAT DO WE DO? NO ONE'S HERE RIGHT NOW BUT US!
は
GASP
THE TAIL...?
OH NO... IT'S A BREECH...
HUH?!

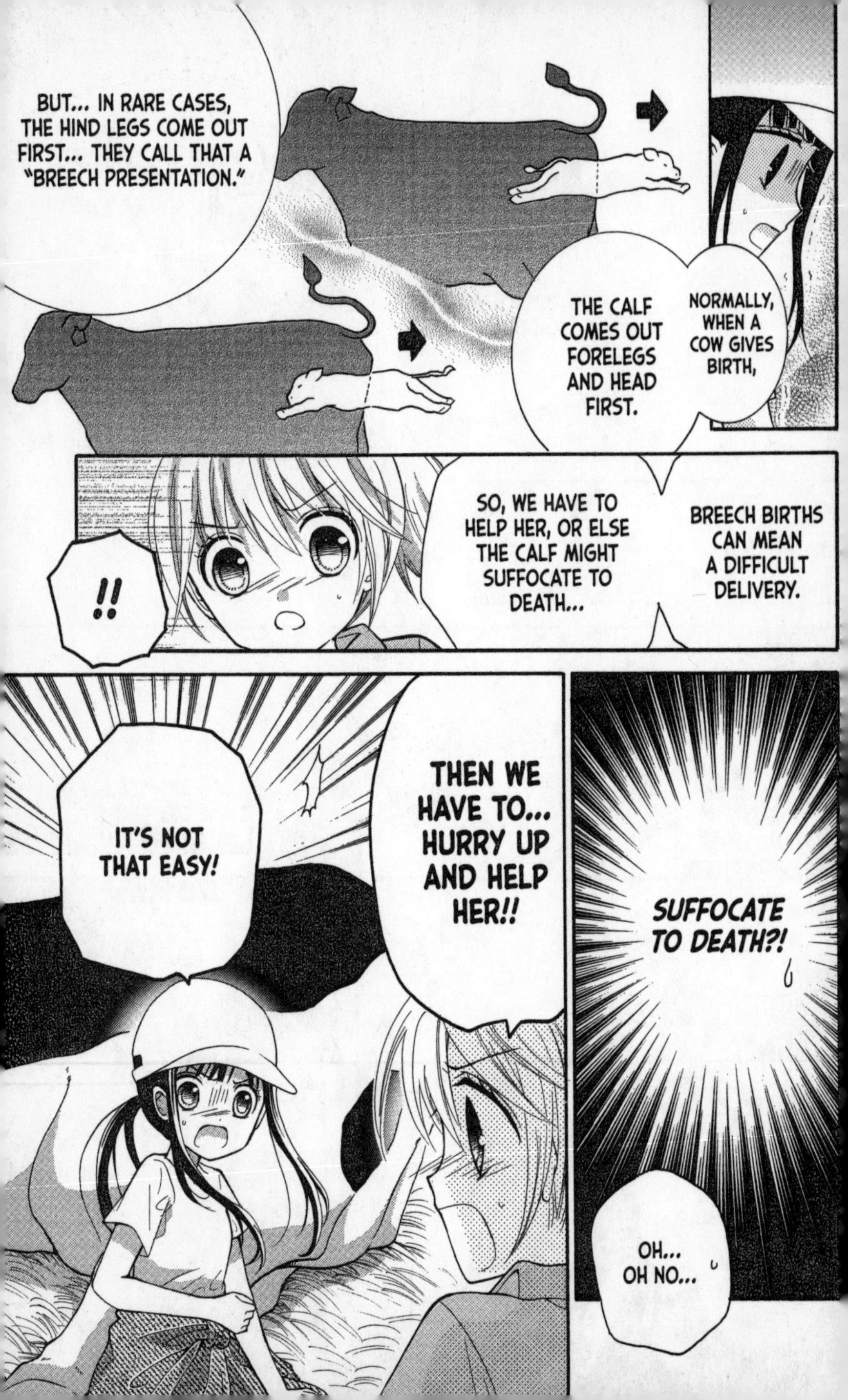
NORMALLY, WHEN A COW GIVES BIRTH,
THE CALF COMES OUT FORELEGS AND HEAD FIRST.
BUT... IN RARE CASES, THE HIND LEGS COME OUT FIRST... THEY CALL THAT A "BREECH PRESENTATION."
BREECH BIRTHS CAN MEAN A DIFFICULT DELIVERY.
SO, WE HAVE TO HELP HER, OR ELSE THE CALF MIGHT SUFFOCATE TO DEATH...
!!
SUFFOCATE TO DEATH?!
OH... OH NO...
THEN WE HAVE TO... HURRY UP AND HELP HER!!
IT'S NOT THAT EASY!

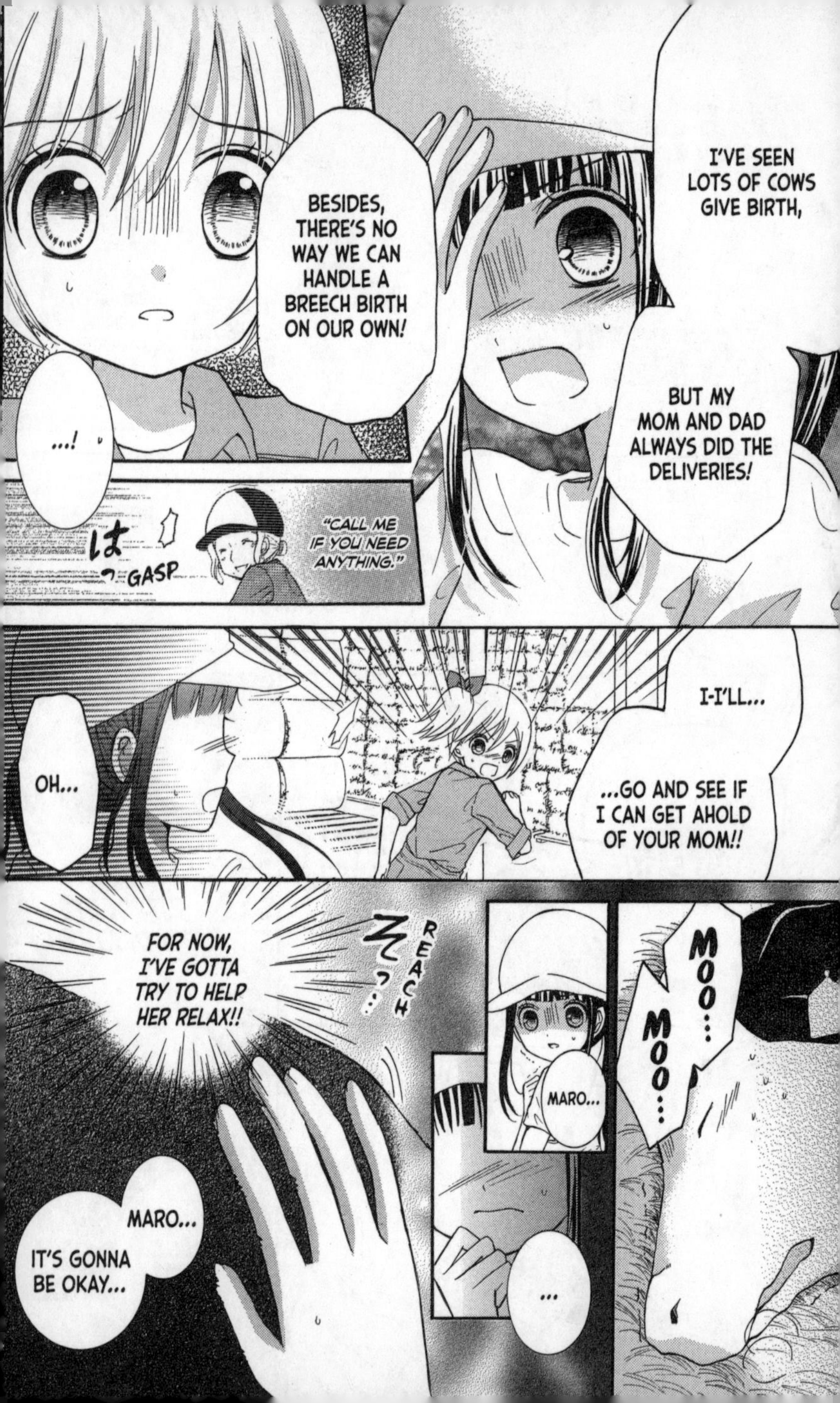

I'VE SEEN LOTS OF COWS GIVE BIRTH,
BUT MY MOM AND DAD ALWAYS DID THE DELIVERIES!
BESIDES, THERE'S NO WAY WE CAN HANDLE A BREECH BIRTH ON OUR OWN!
...!
"CALL ME IF YOU NEED ANYTHING."
GASP
I-I'LL...
...GO AND SEE IF I CAN GET AHOLD OF YOUR MOM!!
OH...
MOO...
MOO...
MARO...
...
FOR NOW, I'VE GOTTA TRY TO HELP HER RELAX!!
REACH
MARO...
IT'S GONNA BE OKAY...

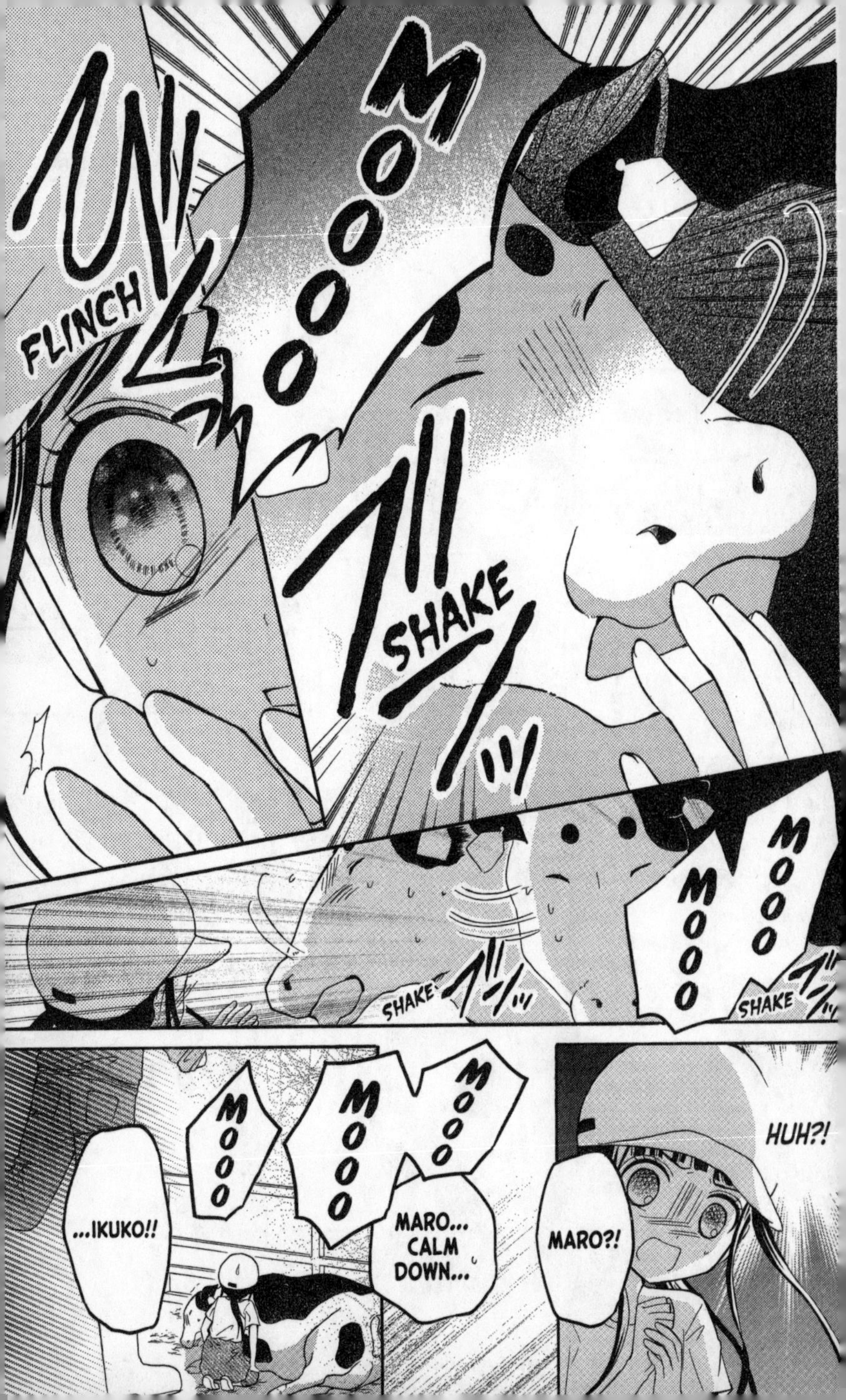
MOOOOOO
FLINCH
SHAKE
MOOOO
SHAKE
MOOOO
SHAKE
HUH?!
MARO?!
MOOOO
MOOOO
MOOOO
MARO... CALM DOWN...
...IKUKO!!

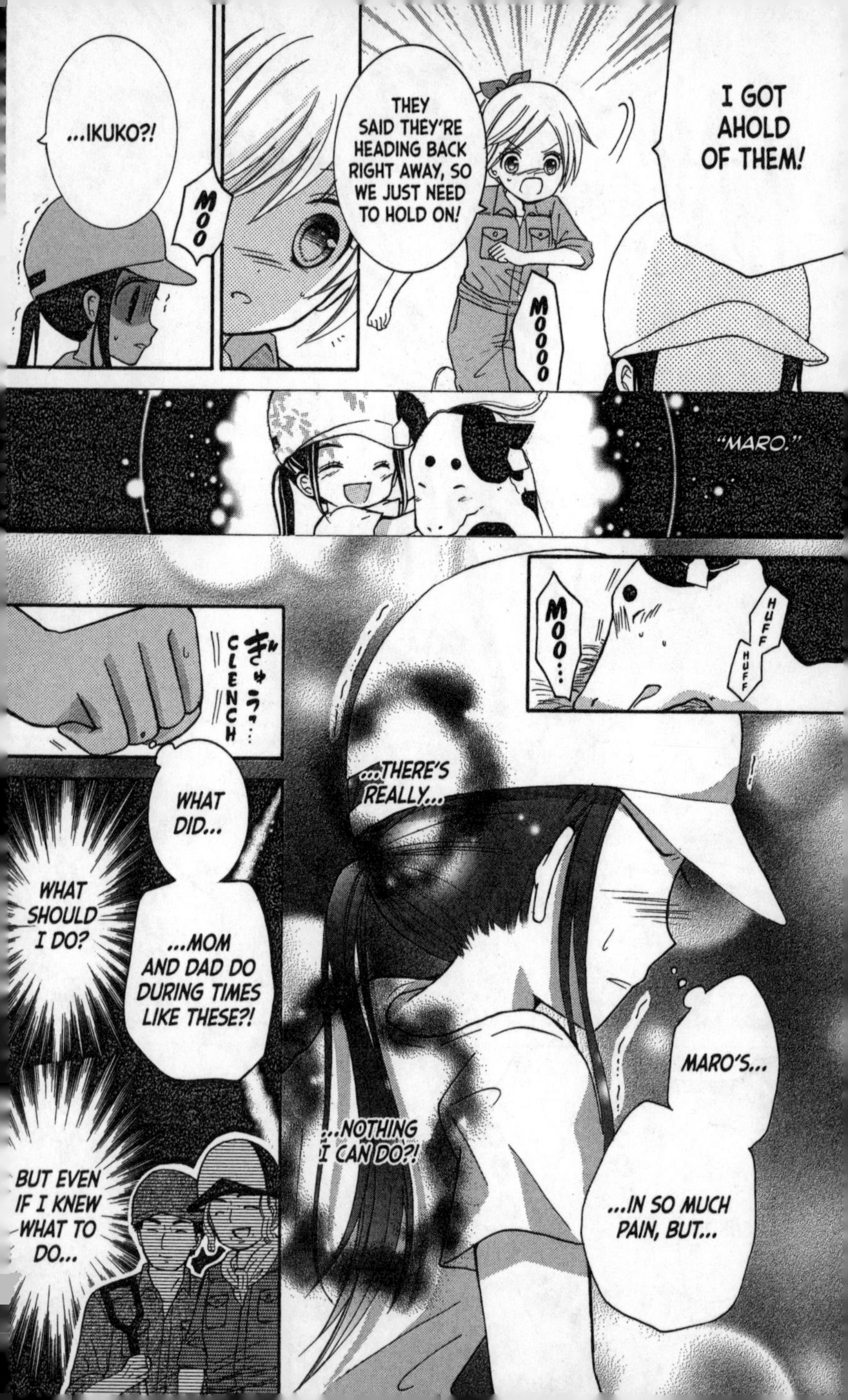
I GOT AHOLD OF THEM!
THEY SAID THEY'RE HEADING BACK RIGHT AWAY, SO WE JUST NEED TO HOLD ON!
MOOOO
MOO
...IKUKO?!
"MARO."
HUFF HUFF
MOO...
MARO'S...
...IN SO MUCH PAIN, BUT...
...THERE'S REALLY...
...NOTHING I CAN DO?!
CLENCH
WHAT DID...
...MOM AND DAD DO DURING TIMES LIKE THESE?!
WHAT SHOULD I DO?
BUT EVEN IF I KNEW WHAT TO DO...

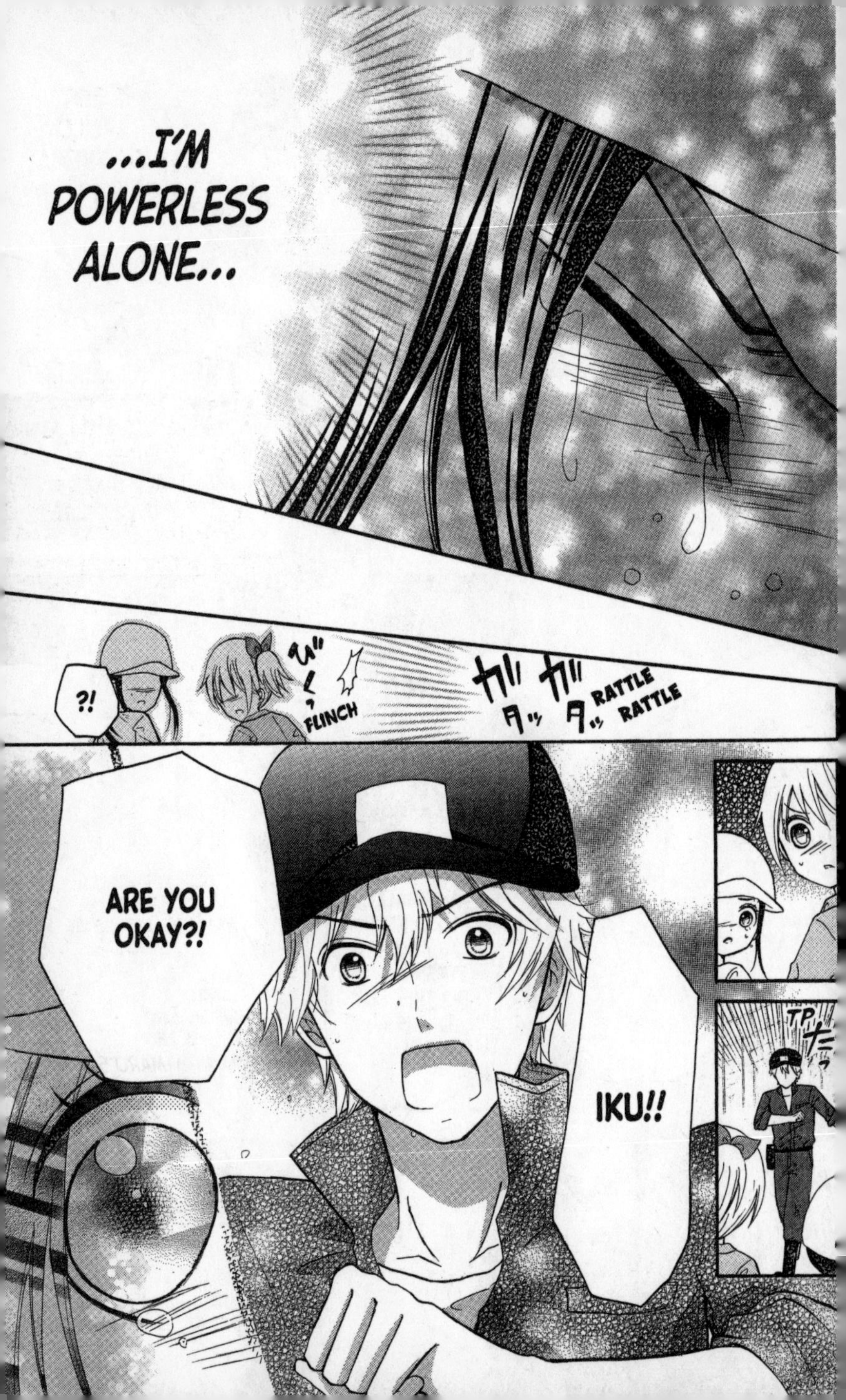
...I'M POWERLESS ALONE...
RATTLE RATTLE
FLINCH
?!
TP
IKU!!
ARE YOU OKAY?!

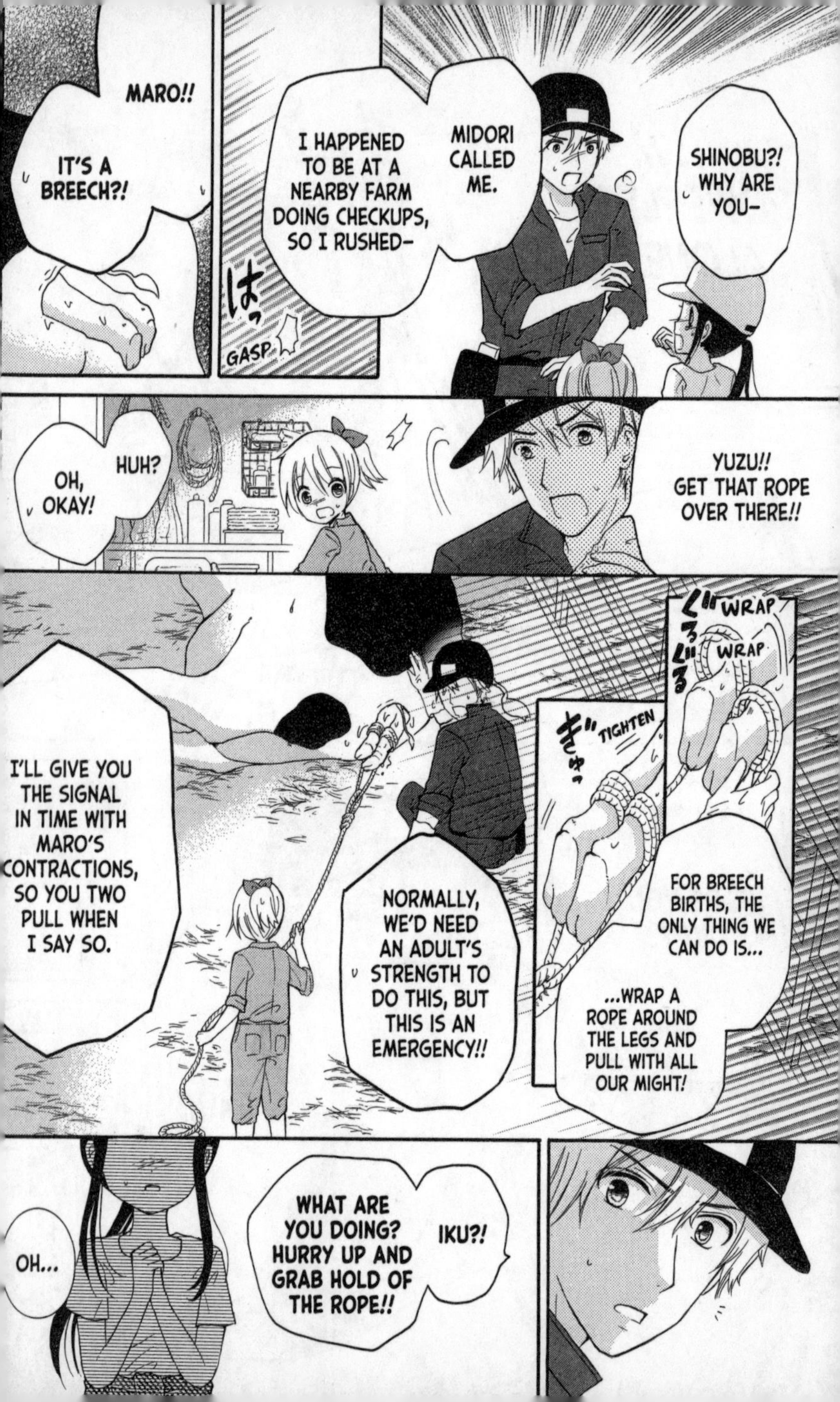
SHINOBU?! WHY ARE YOU–
MIDORI CALLED ME.
I HAPPENED TO BE AT A NEARBY FARM DOING CHECKUPS, SO I RUSHED–
はっ
GASP
MARO!!
IT'S A BREECH?!
YUZU!! GET THAT ROPE OVER THERE!!
HUH?
OH, OKAY!
ぐるぐる
WRAP
WRAP
ぎゅっ
TIGHTEN
FOR BREECH BIRTHS, THE ONLY THING WE CAN DO IS...
...WRAP A ROPE AROUND THE LEGS AND PULL WITH ALL OUR MIGHT!
NORMALLY, WE'D NEED AN ADULT'S STRENGTH TO DO THIS, BUT THIS IS AN EMERGENCY!!
I'LL GIVE YOU THE SIGNAL IN TIME WITH MARO'S CONTRACTIONS, SO YOU TWO PULL WHEN I SAY SO.
IKU?!
WHAT ARE YOU DOING? HURRY UP AND GRAB HOLD OF THE ROPE!!
OH...

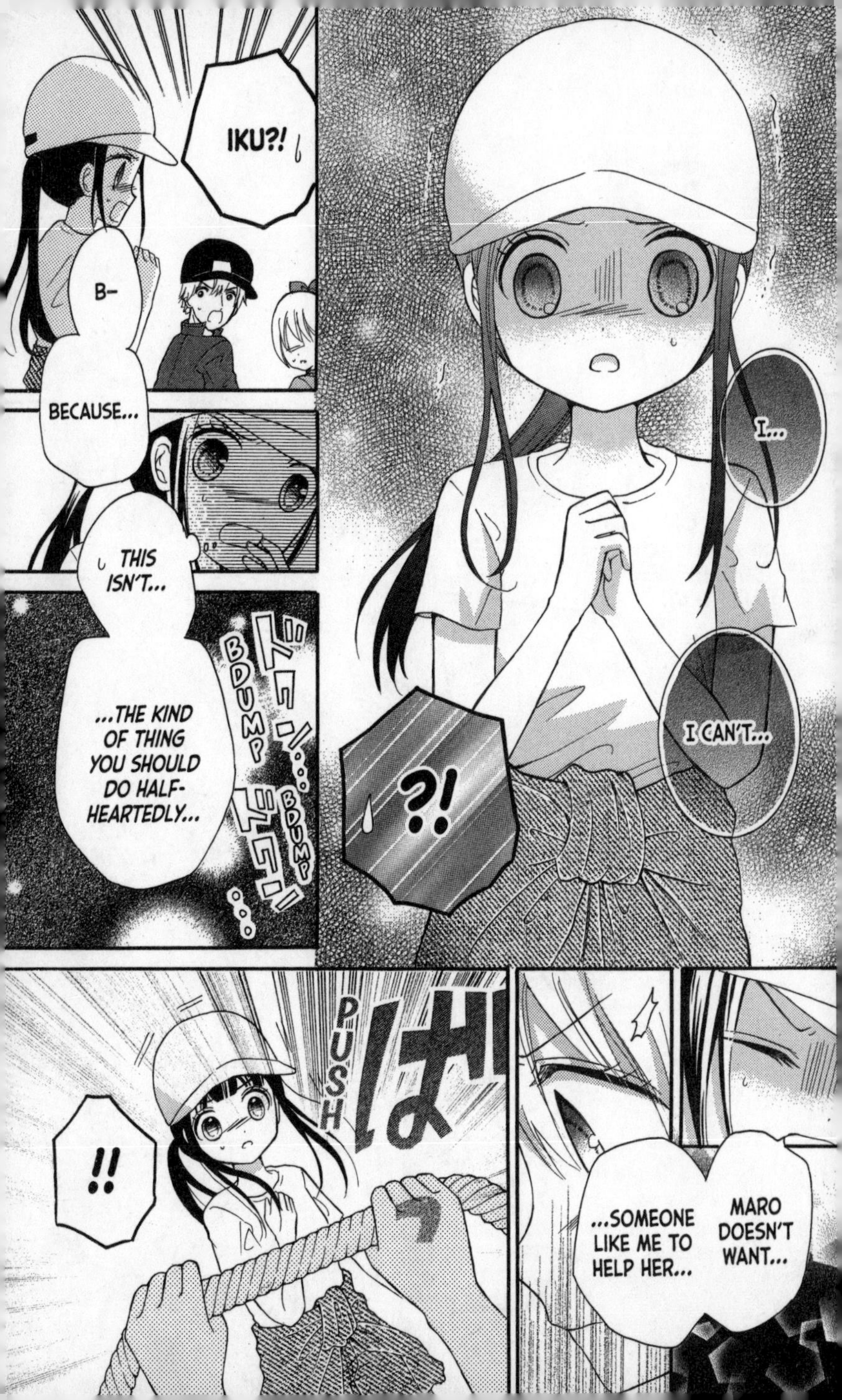
I...
I CAN'T...
?!
IKU?!
B–
BECAUSE...
THIS ISN'T...
...THE KIND OF THING YOU SHOULD DO HALF-HEARTEDLY...
BDUMP
BDUMP
MARO DOESN'T WANT...
...SOMEONE LIKE ME TO HELP HER...
PUSH
!!

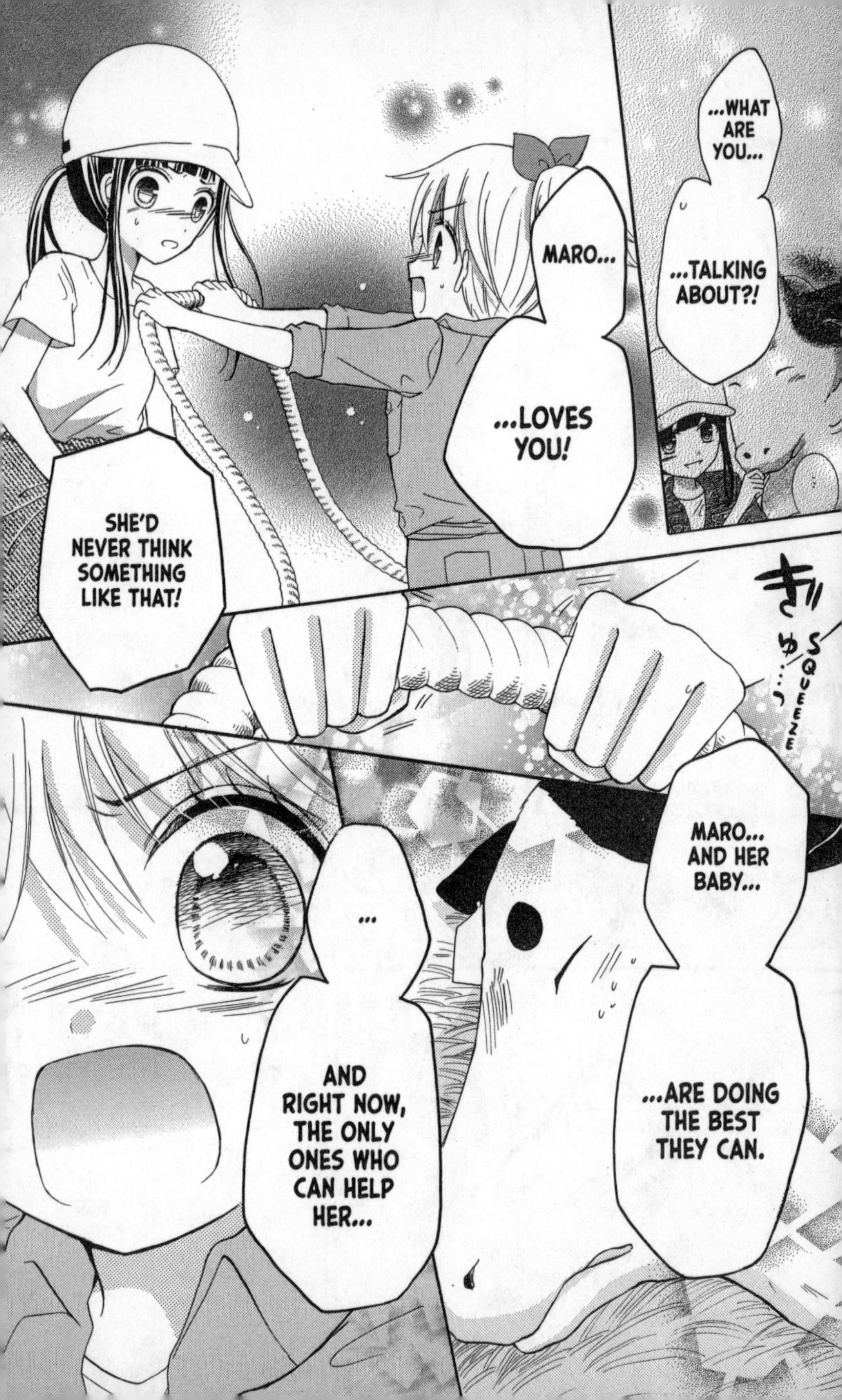
...WHAT ARE YOU...
...TALKING ABOUT?!
MARO...
...LOVES YOU!
SHE'D NEVER THINK SOMETHING LIKE THAT!
ぎゅ...
SQUEEZE
MARO... AND HER BABY...
...ARE DOING THE BEST THEY CAN.
...
AND RIGHT NOW, THE ONLY ONES WHO CAN HELP HER...

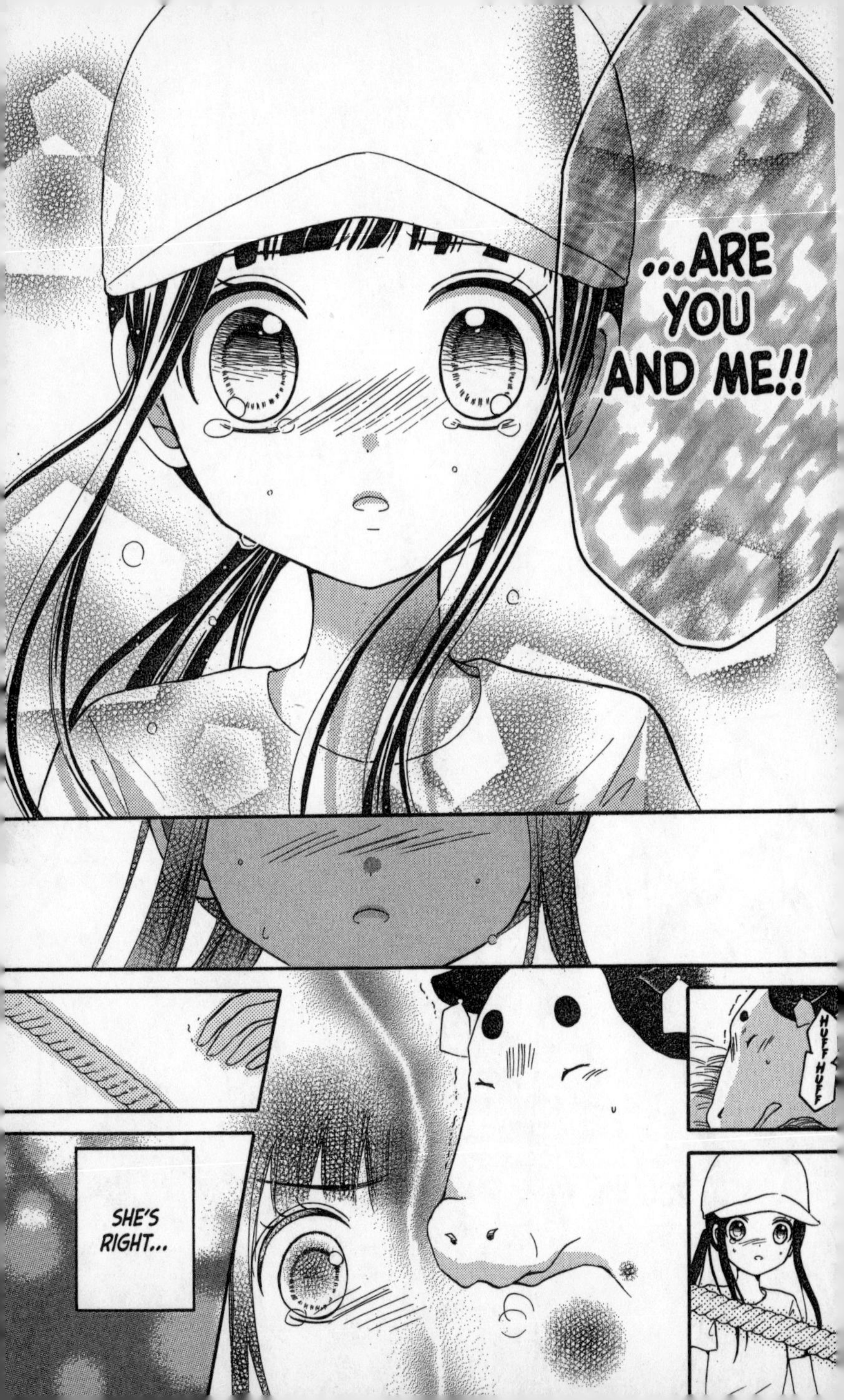
...ARE YOU AND ME!!
HUFF HUFF
SHE'S RIGHT...

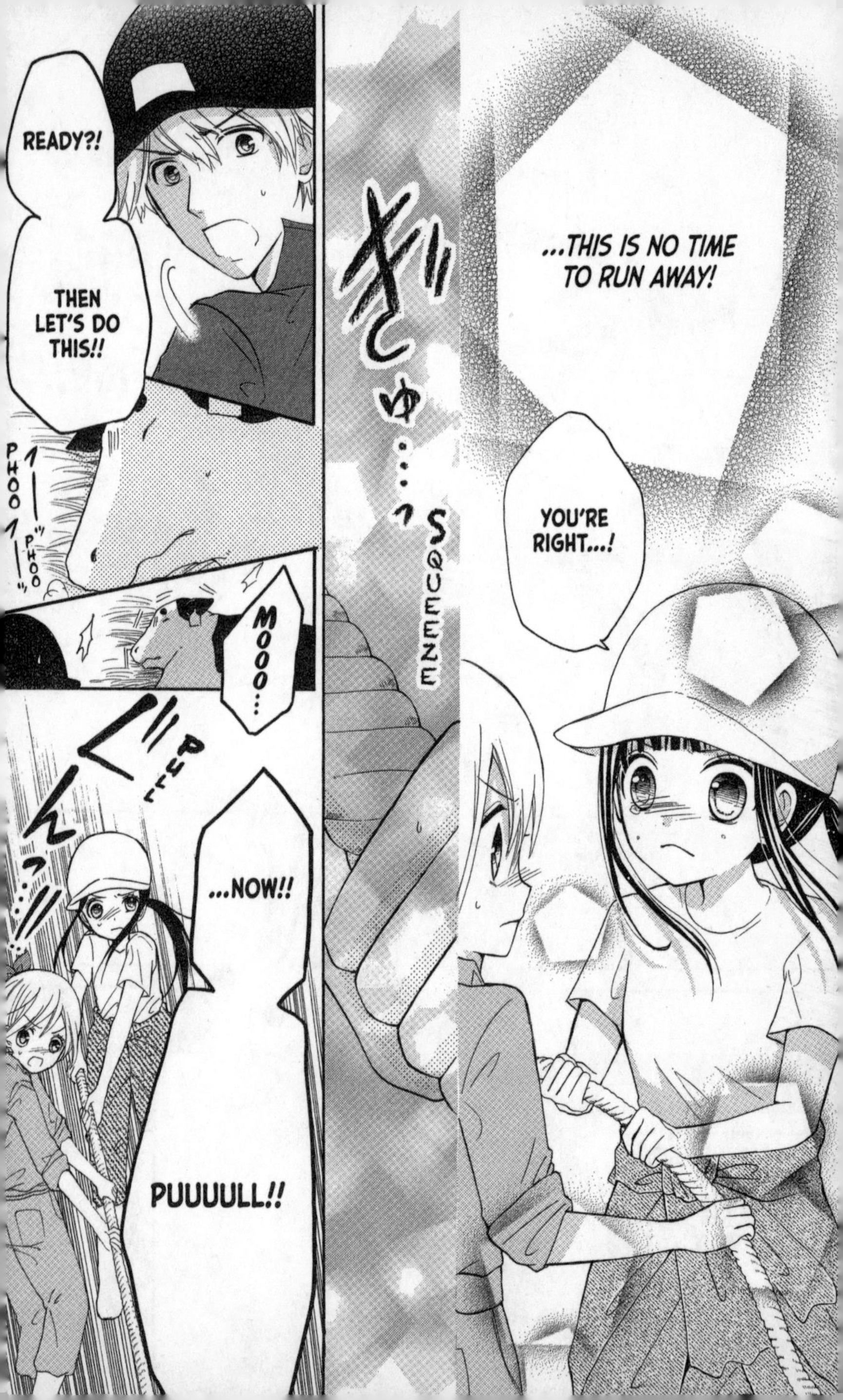
...THIS IS NO TIME TO RUN AWAY!
YOU'RE RIGHT...!
ぎゅ…っ
SQUEEZE
READY?!
THEN LET'S DO THIS!!
PHOO
PHOO
MOOO...
PULL
...NOW!!
PUUUULL!!

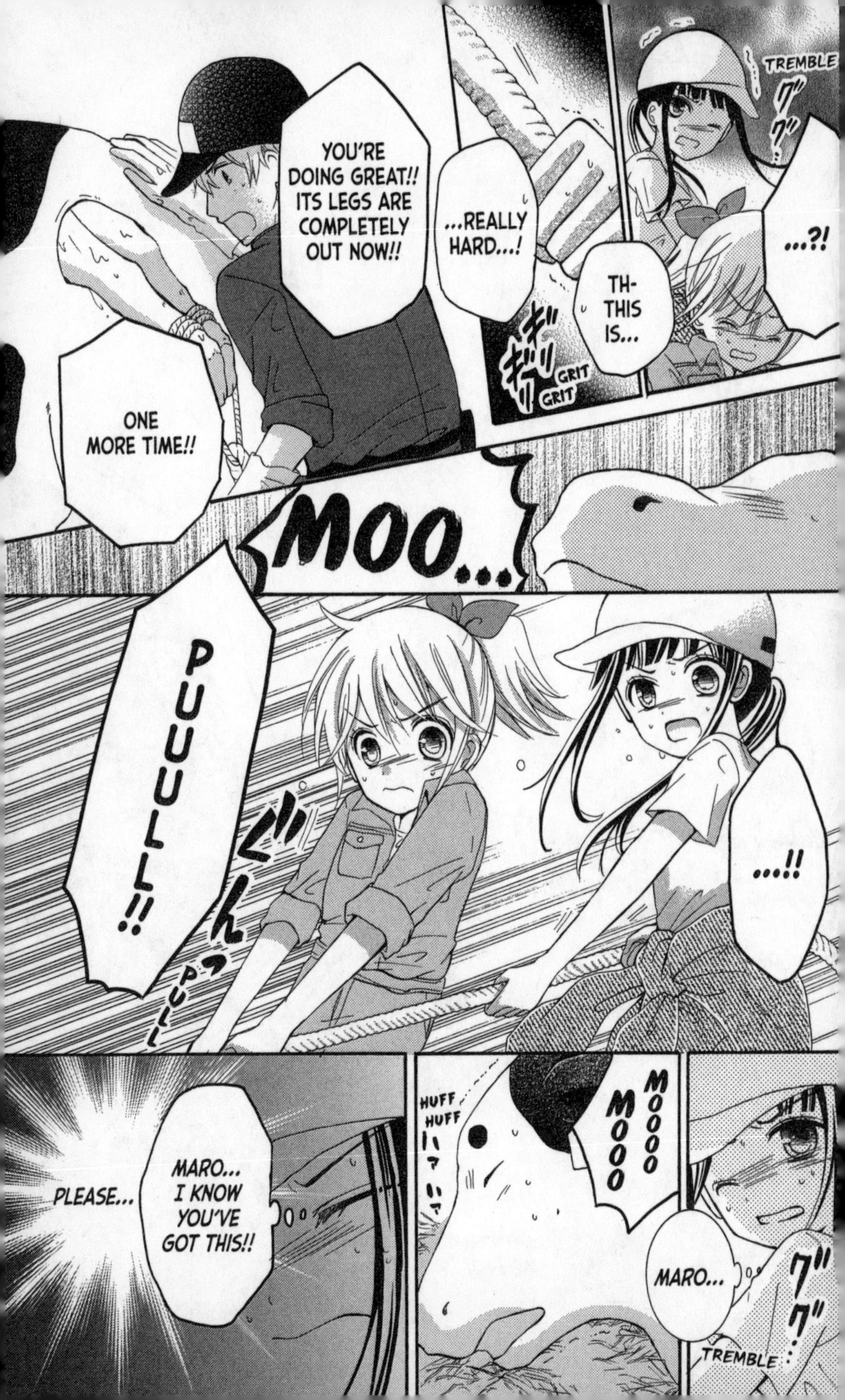
TREMBLE
...?!
TH- THIS IS...
GRIT GRIT
...REALLY HARD...!
YOU'RE DOING GREAT!! ITS LEGS ARE COMPLETELY OUT NOW!!
ONE MORE TIME!!
MOO...
...!!
PUUULLL!!
PULL
TREMBLE
MARO...
MOOOO MOOOO
HUFF HUFF
MARO... I KNOW YOU'VE GOT THIS!!
PLEASE...

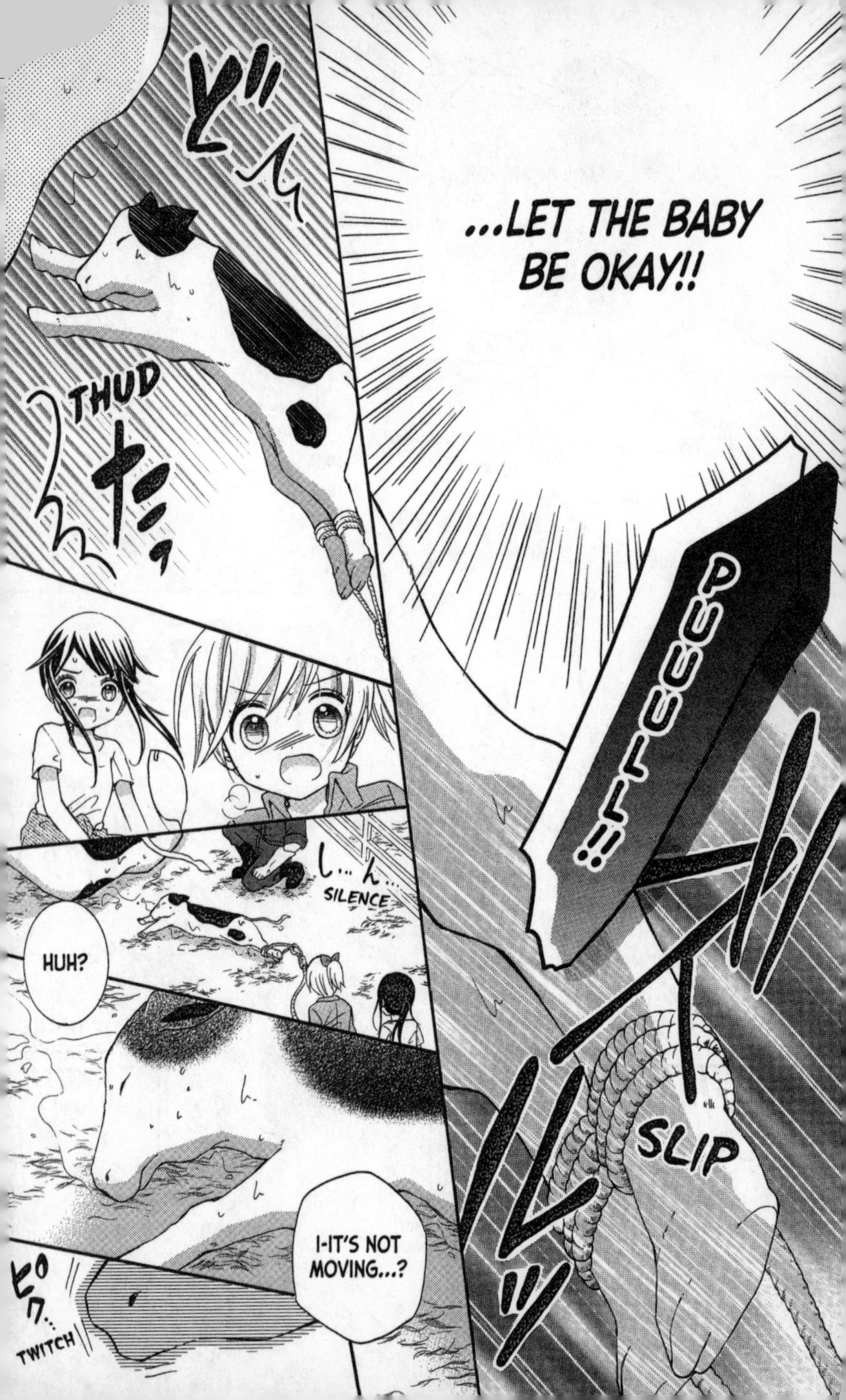
...LET THE BABY BE OKAY!!
PUUUULL!!
SLIP
THUD
SILENCE
HUH?
I-IT'S NOT MOVING...?
TWITCH

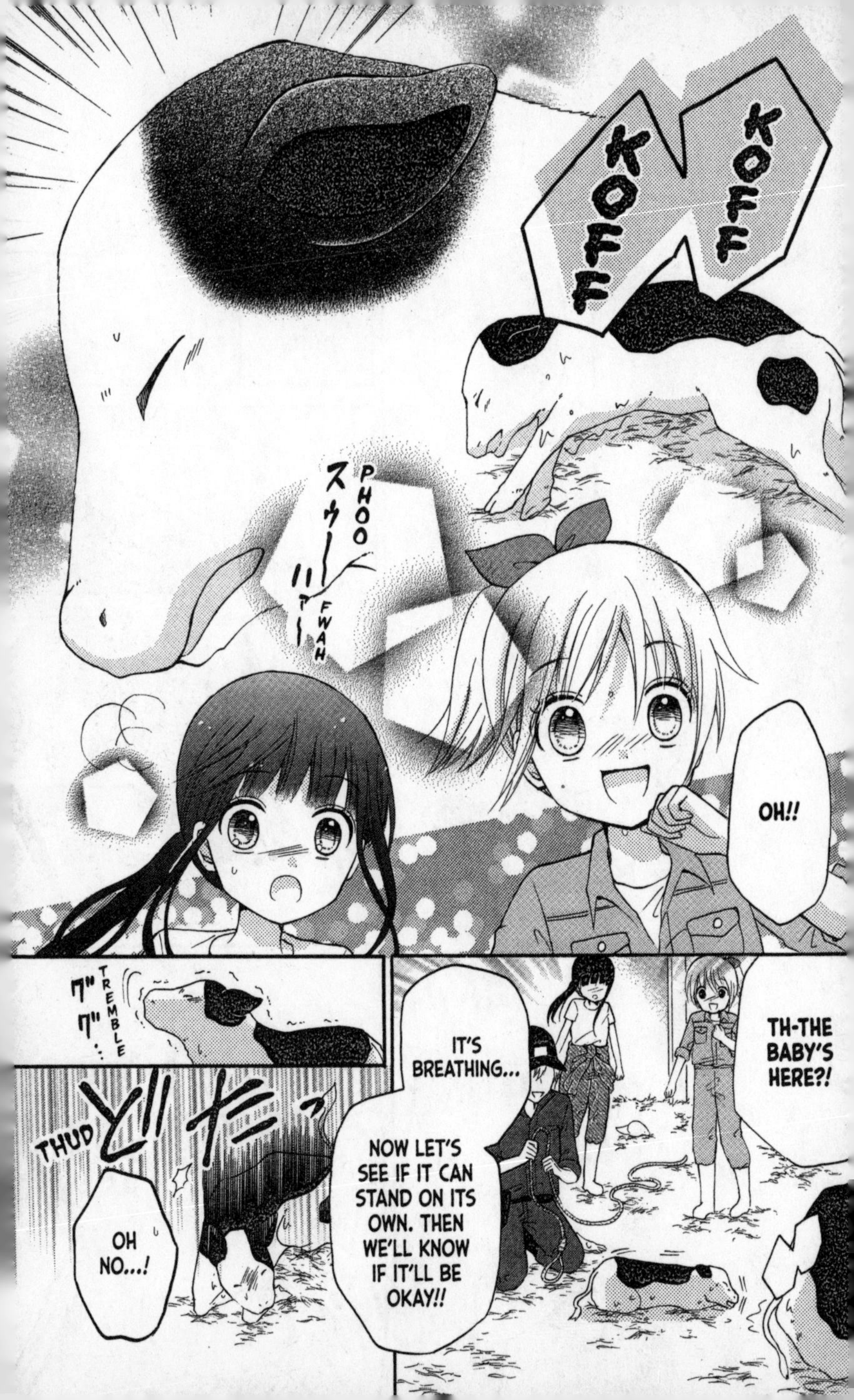
KOFF KOFF
PHOO
スゥー
ハァー
FWAH
OH!!
TH-THE BABY'S HERE?!
IT'S BREATHING...
NOW LET'S SEE IF IT CAN STAND ON ITS OWN. THEN WE'LL KNOW IF IT'LL BE OKAY!!
グ グ
TREMBLE
THUD
OH NO...!

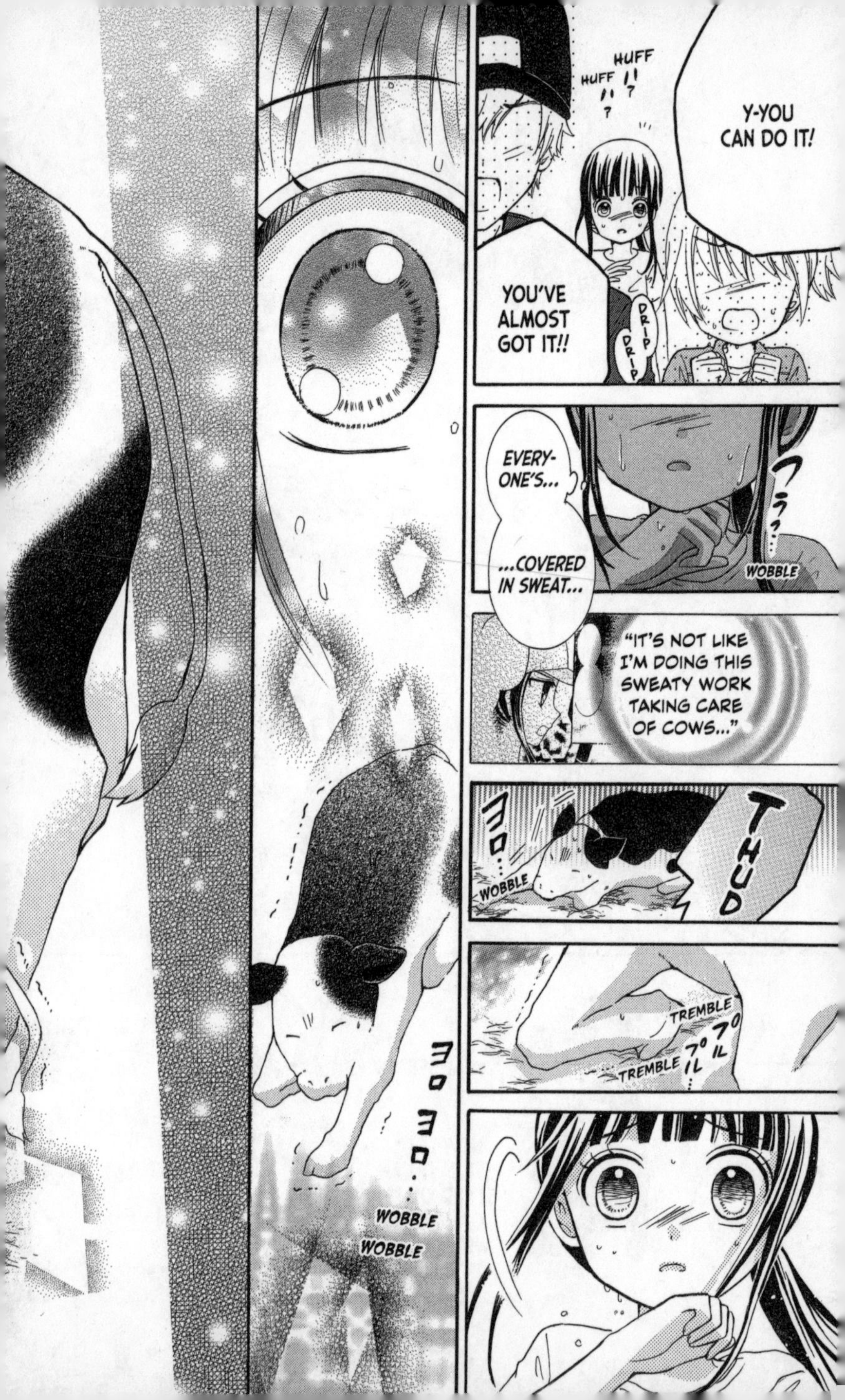
Y-YOU CAN DO IT!
HUFF HUFF
YOU'VE ALMOST GOT IT!!
DRIP DRIP
フラ…
WOBBLE
EVERY-ONE'S...
...COVERED IN SWEAT...
"IT'S NOT LIKE I'M DOING THIS SWEATY WORK TAKING CARE OF COWS..."
THUD
ヨロ…
WOBBLE
プルプル…
TREMBLE TREMBLE
ヨロヨロ…
WOBBLE WOBBLE

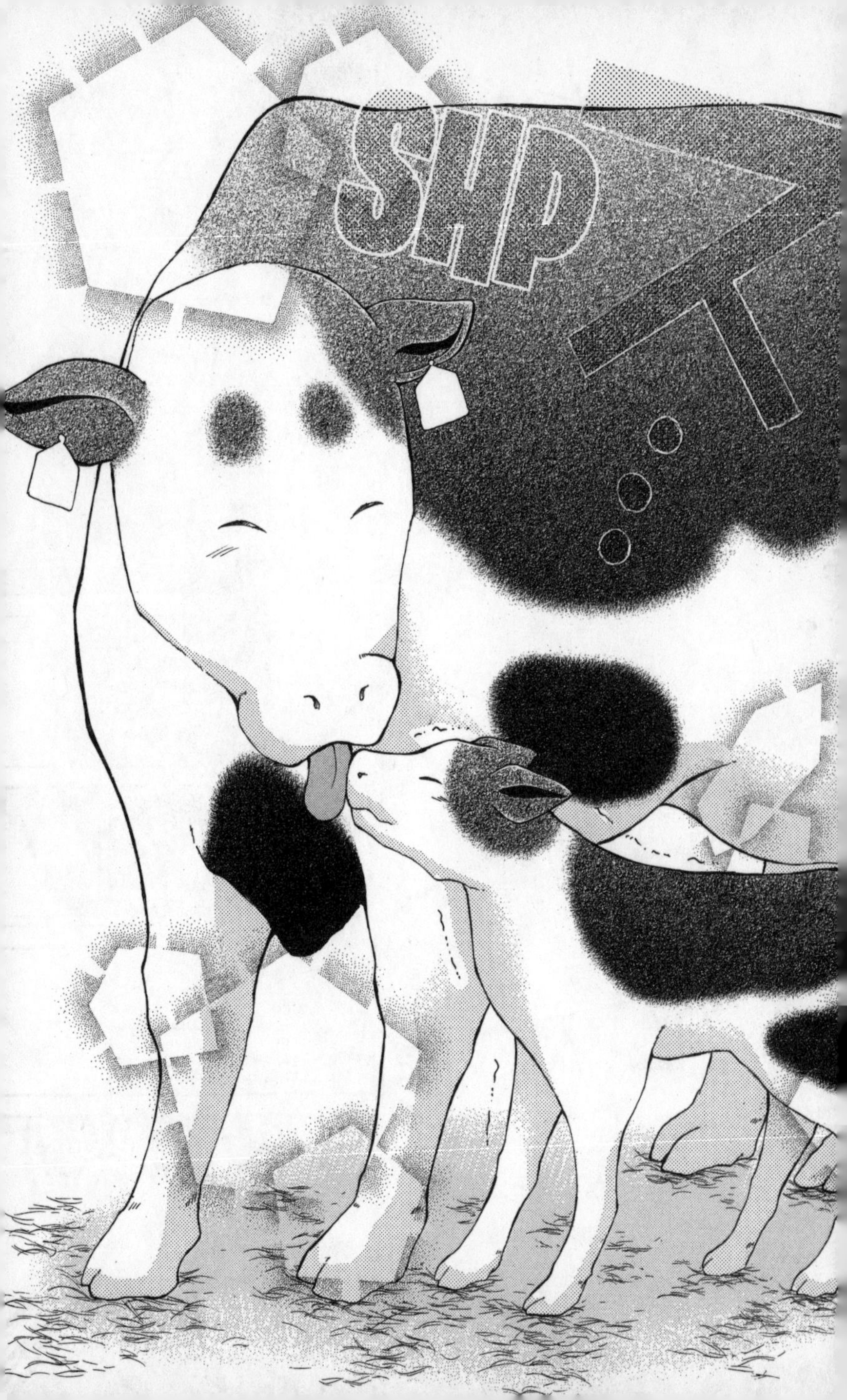
SHP

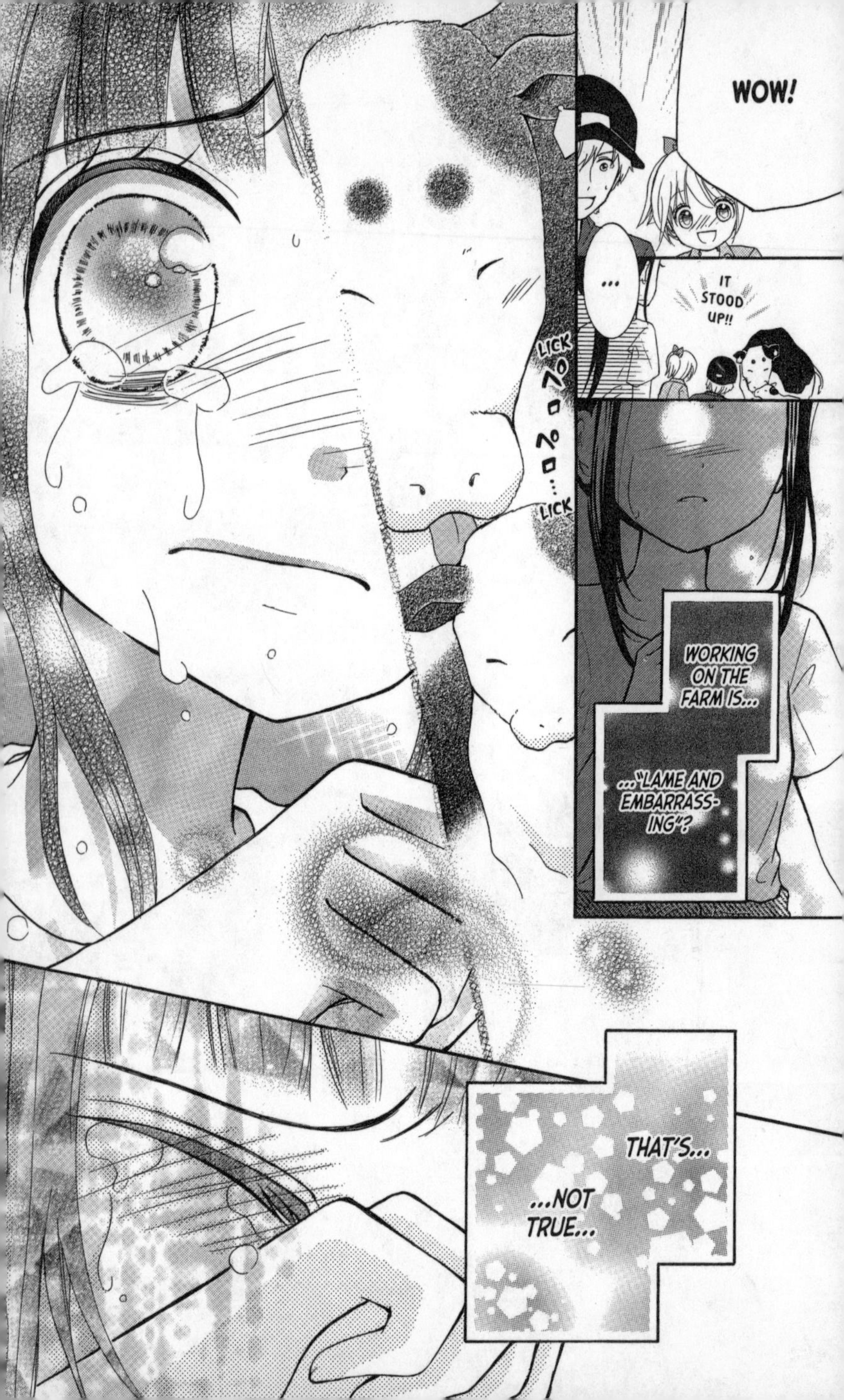
WOW!
...
IT STOOD UP!!
WORKING ON THE FARM IS...
..."LAME AND EMBARRASSING"?
LICK
ペロペロ...
LICK
THAT'S...
...NOT TRUE...

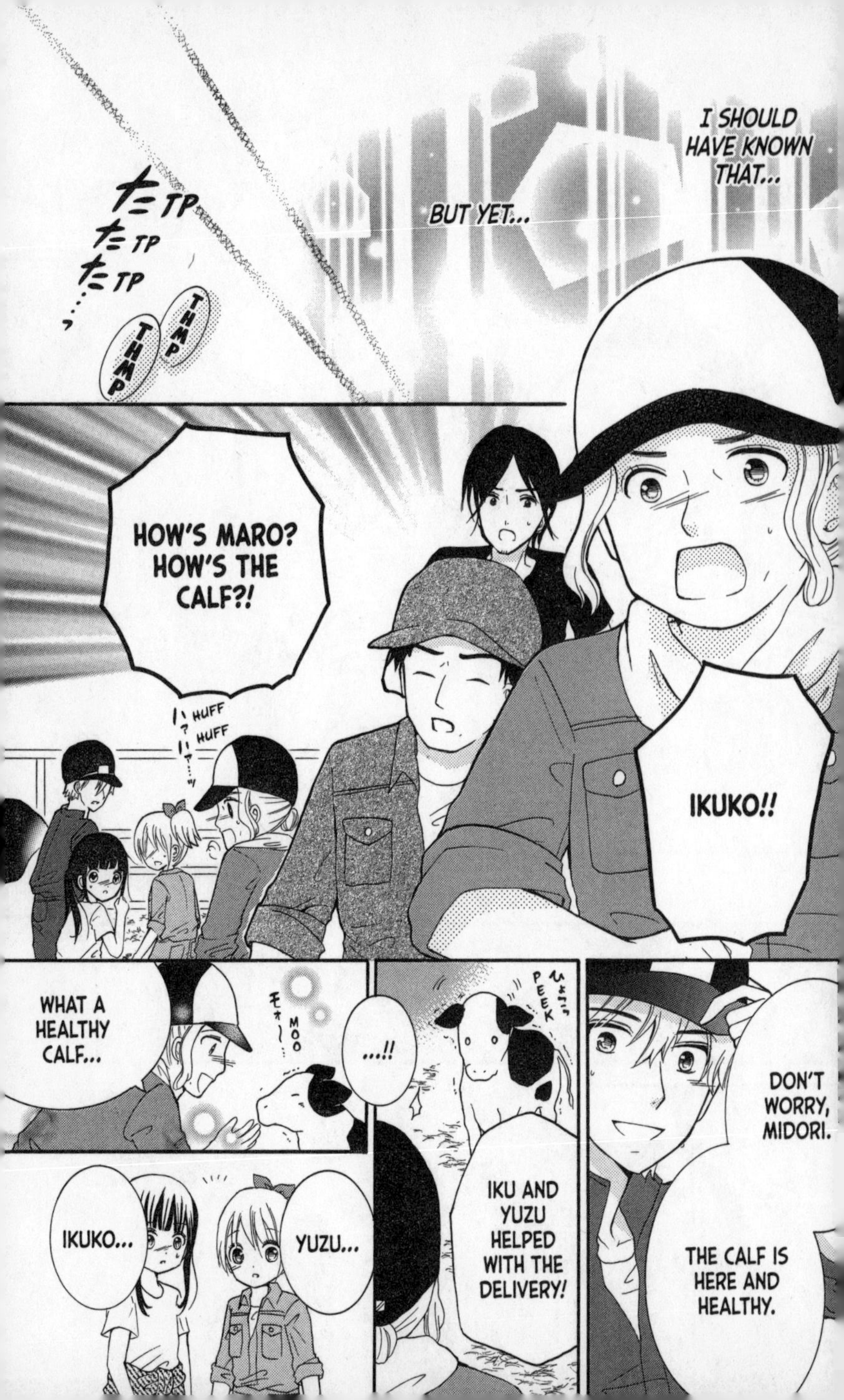
I SHOULD HAVE KNOWN THAT...
BUT YET...
たTP たTP たTP...
THMP THMP
IKUKO!!
HOW'S MARO? HOW'S THE CALF?!
ハァハァ... HUFF HUFF
DON'T WORRY, MIDORI.
THE CALF IS HERE AND HEALTHY.
IKU AND YUZU HELPED WITH THE DELIVERY!
PEEK
...!!
MOO
WHAT A HEALTHY CALF...
YUZU...
IKUKO...

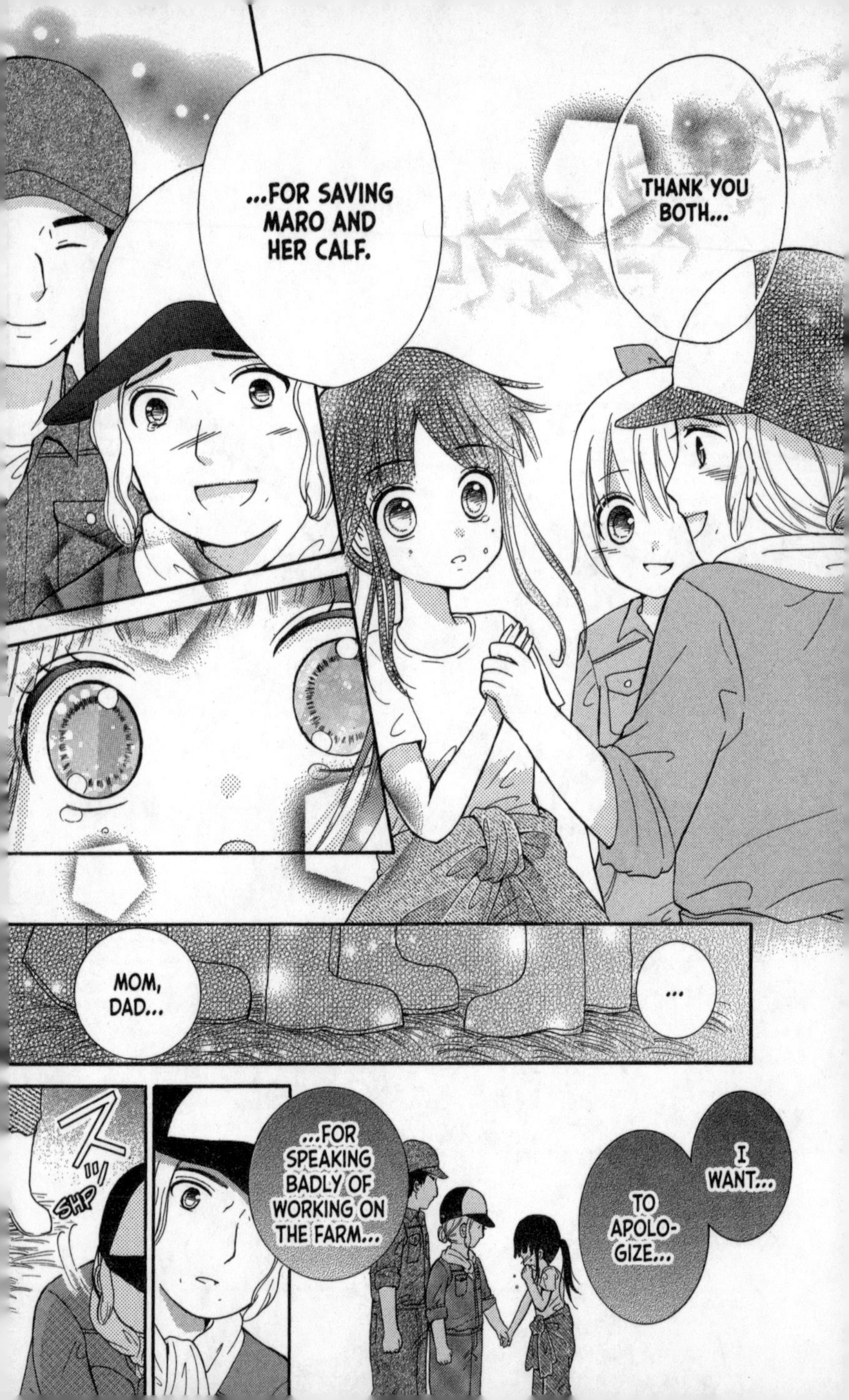
THANK YOU BOTH...
...FOR SAVING MARO AND HER CALF.
...
MOM, DAD...
I WANT...
TO APOLO-GIZE...
...FOR SPEAKING BADLY OF WORKING ON THE FARM...
SHP

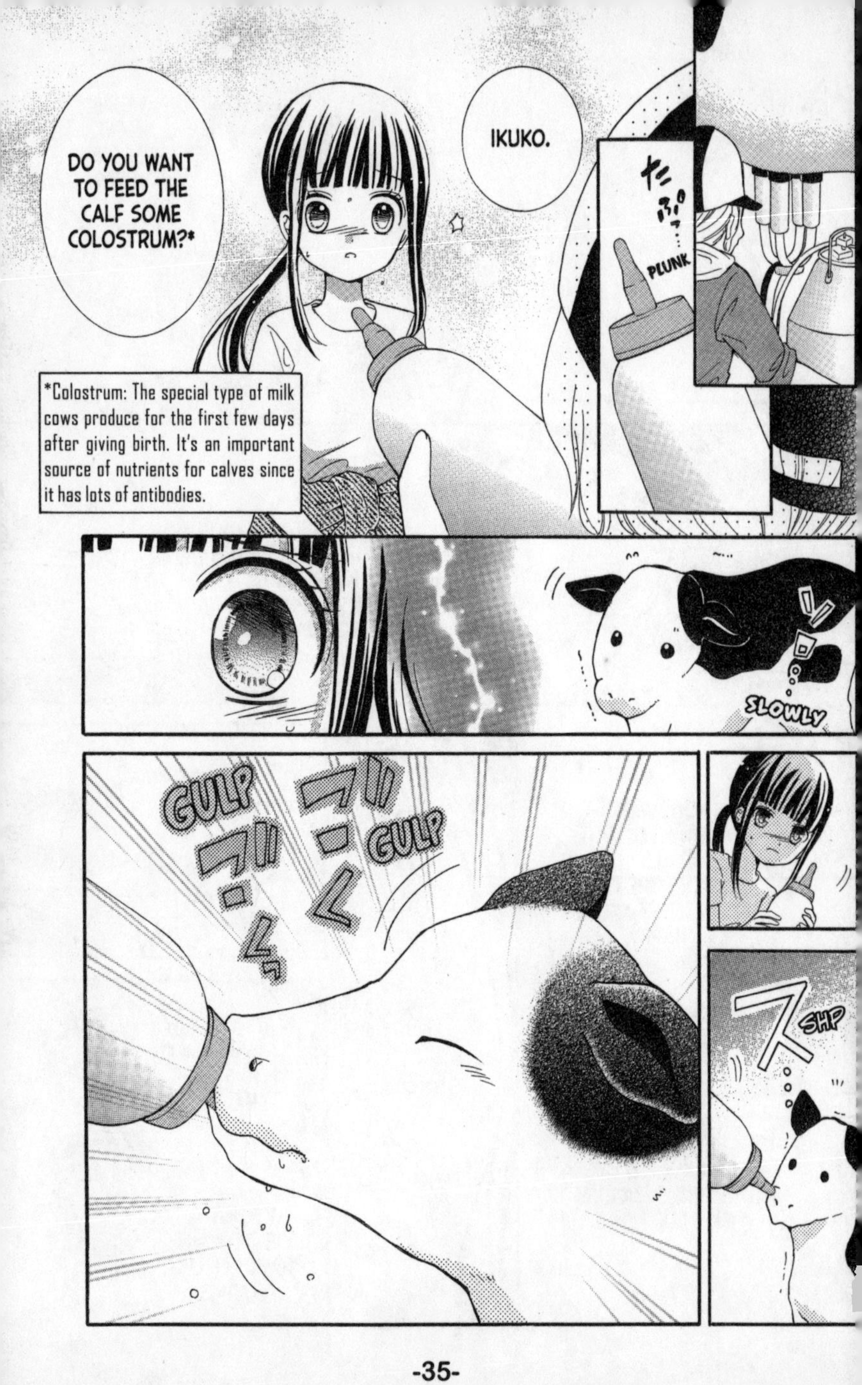
IKUKO.
DO YOU WANT TO FEED THE CALF SOME COLOSTRUM?*
*Colostrum: The special type of milk cows produce for the first few days after giving birth. It's an important source of nutrients for calves since it has lots of antibodies.
PLUNK
SLOWLY
SHP
GULP
GULP

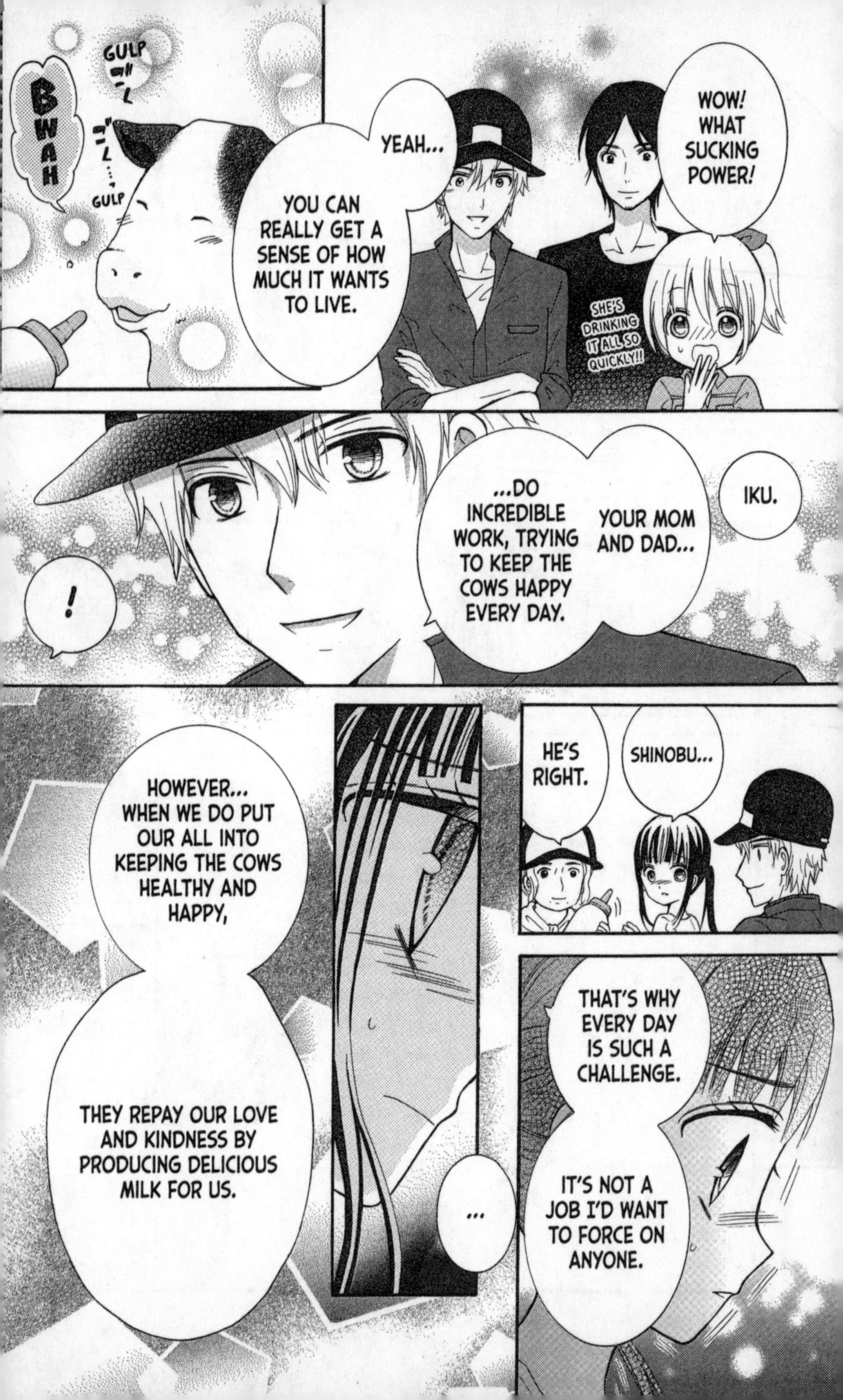
WOW! WHAT SUCKING POWER!
SHE'S DRINKING IT ALL SO QUICKLY!!
YEAH...
YOU CAN REALLY GET A SENSE OF HOW MUCH IT WANTS TO LIVE.
GULP
BWAH
GULP
IKU.
YOUR MOM AND DAD...
...DO INCREDIBLE WORK, TRYING TO KEEP THE COWS HAPPY EVERY DAY.
!
SHINOBU...
HE'S RIGHT.
THAT'S WHY EVERY DAY IS SUCH A CHALLENGE.
IT'S NOT A JOB I'D WANT TO FORCE ON ANYONE.
...
HOWEVER... WHEN WE DO PUT OUR ALL INTO KEEPING THE COWS HEALTHY AND HAPPY,
THEY REPAY OUR LOVE AND KINDNESS BY PRODUCING DELICIOUS MILK FOR US.

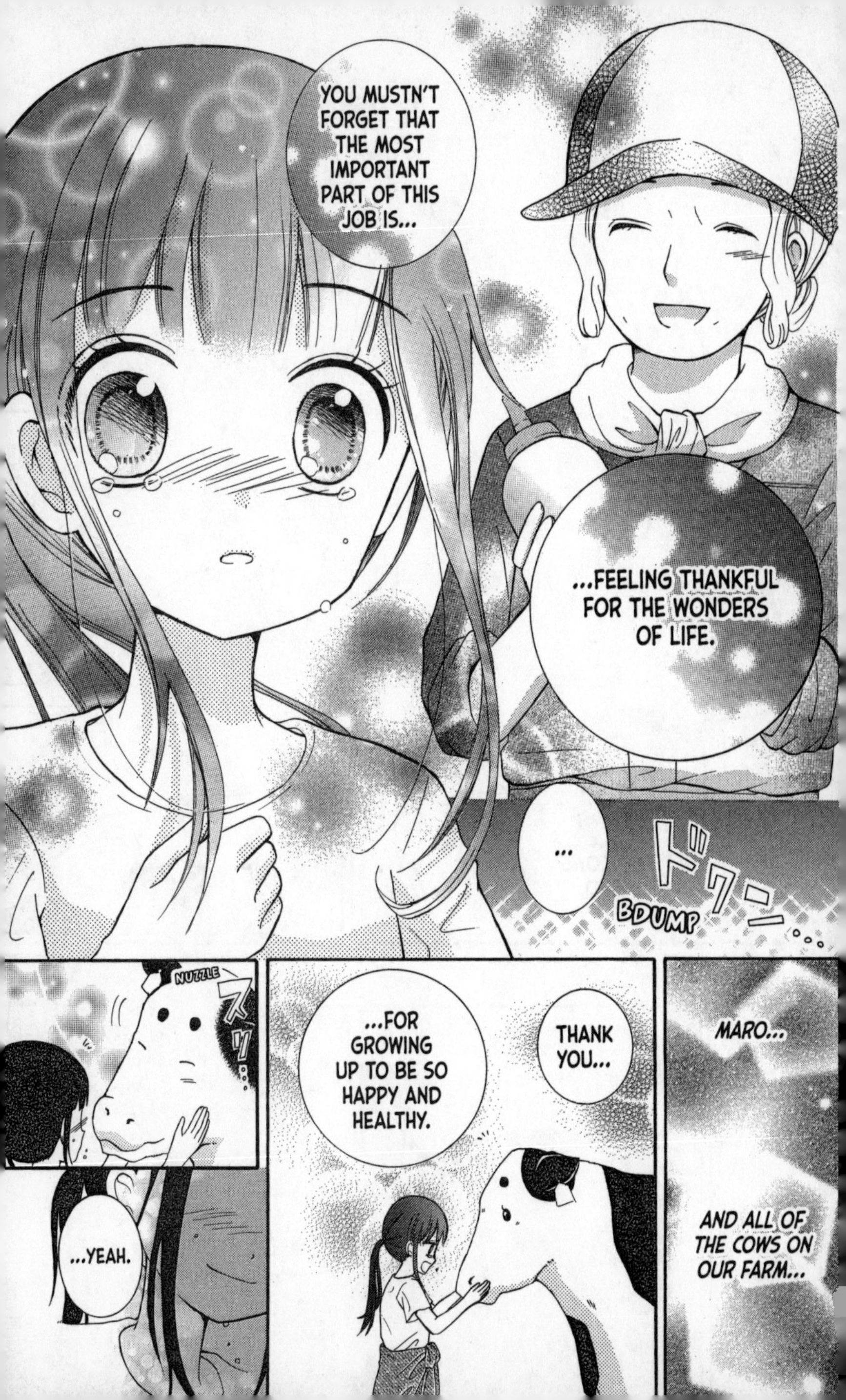
YOU MUSTN'T FORGET THAT THE MOST IMPORTANT PART OF THIS JOB IS...
...FEELING THANKFUL FOR THE WONDERS OF LIFE.
...
BDUMP
MARO...
AND ALL OF THE COWS ON OUR FARM...
THANK YOU...
...FOR GROWING UP TO BE SO HAPPY AND HEALTHY.
NUZZLE
...YEAH.

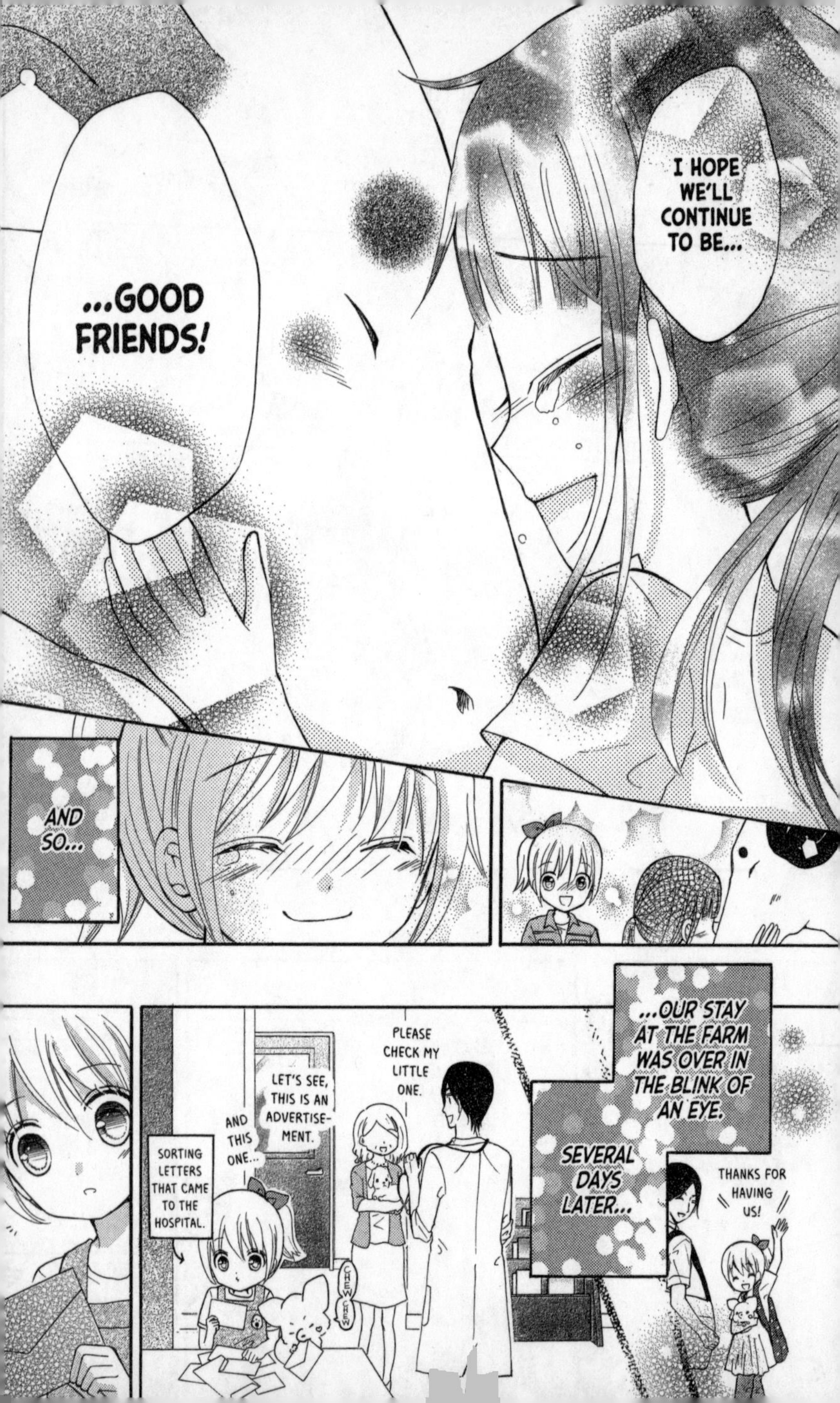
I HOPE WE'LL CONTINUE TO BE...
...GOOD FRIENDS!
AND SO...
...OUR STAY AT THE FARM WAS OVER IN THE BLINK OF AN EYE.
THANKS FOR HAVING US!
SEVERAL DAYS LATER...
PLEASE CHECK MY LITTLE ONE.
LET'S SEE, THIS IS AN ADVERTISE-MENT.
AND THIS ONE...
SORTING LETTERS THAT CAME TO THE HOSPITAL.
CHEW CHEW

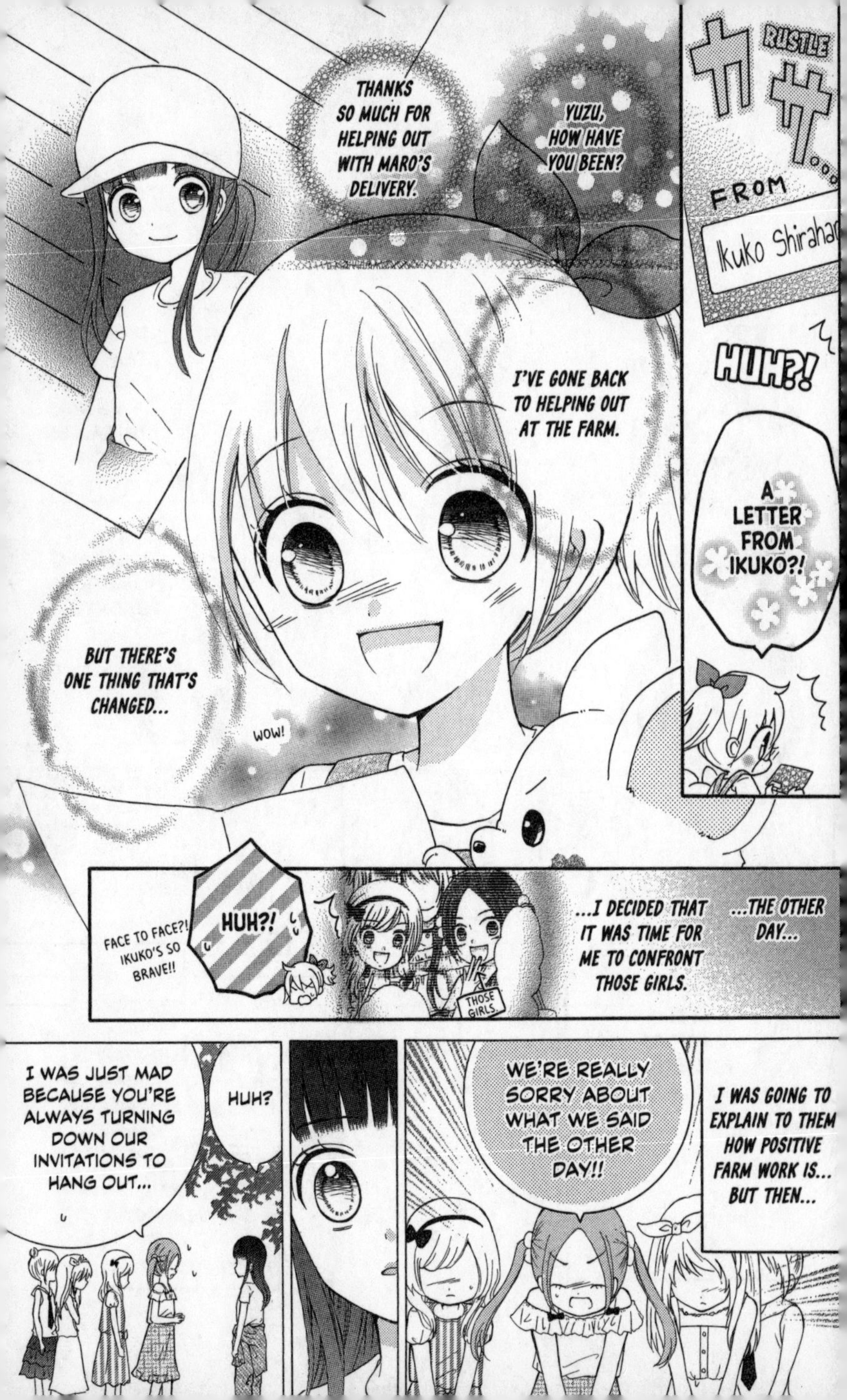
RUSTLE
FROM
Ikuko Shirahar
HUH?!
A LETTER FROM IKUKO?!
YUZU, HOW HAVE YOU BEEN?
THANKS SO MUCH FOR HELPING OUT WITH MARO'S DELIVERY.
I'VE GONE BACK TO HELPING OUT AT THE FARM.
BUT THERE'S ONE THING THAT'S CHANGED...
WOW!
...THE OTHER DAY...
...I DECIDED THAT IT WAS TIME FOR ME TO CONFRONT THOSE GIRLS.
THOSE GIRLS.
HUH?!
FACE TO FACE?! IKUKO'S SO BRAVE!!
I WAS GOING TO EXPLAIN TO THEM HOW POSITIVE FARM WORK IS... BUT THEN...
WE'RE REALLY SORRY ABOUT WHAT WE SAID THE OTHER DAY!!
HUH?
I WAS JUST MAD BECAUSE YOU'RE ALWAYS TURNING DOWN OUR INVITATIONS TO HANG OUT...

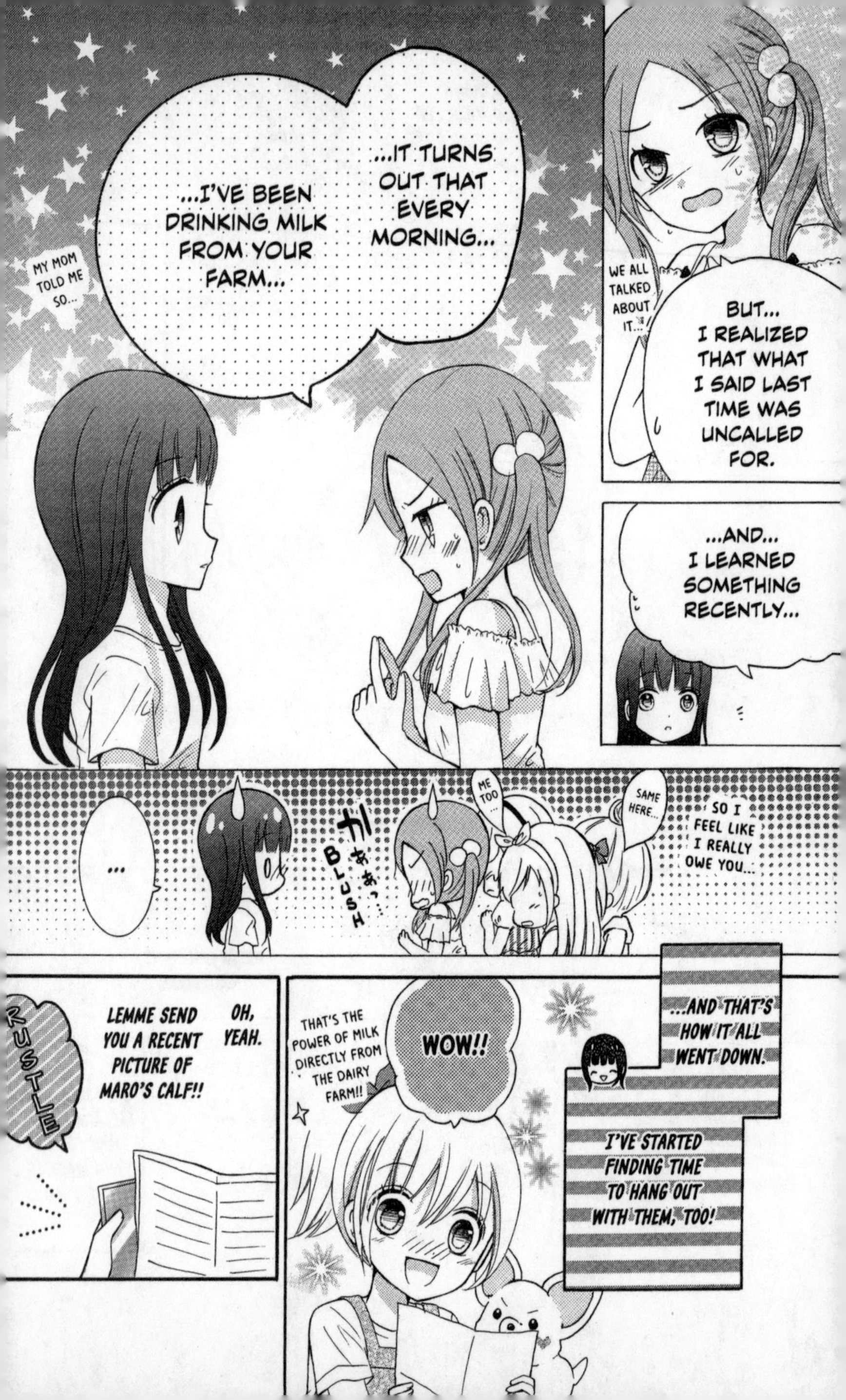
BUT... I REALIZED THAT WHAT I SAID LAST TIME WAS UNCALLED FOR.
WE ALL TALKED ABOUT IT...
...AND... I LEARNED SOMETHING RECENTLY...
...IT TURNS OUT THAT EVERY MORNING...
...I'VE BEEN DRINKING MILK FROM YOUR FARM...
MY MOM TOLD ME SO...
SO I FEEL LIKE I REALLY OWE YOU...
SAME HERE...
ME TOO...
カあぁ…
BLUSH
...
...AND THAT'S HOW IT ALL WENT DOWN.
I'VE STARTED FINDING TIME TO HANG OUT WITH THEM, TOO!
WOW!!
THAT'S THE POWER OF MILK DIRECTLY FROM THE DAIRY FARM!!
OH, YEAH.
LEMME SEND YOU A RECENT PICTURE OF MARO'S CALF!!
RUSTLE

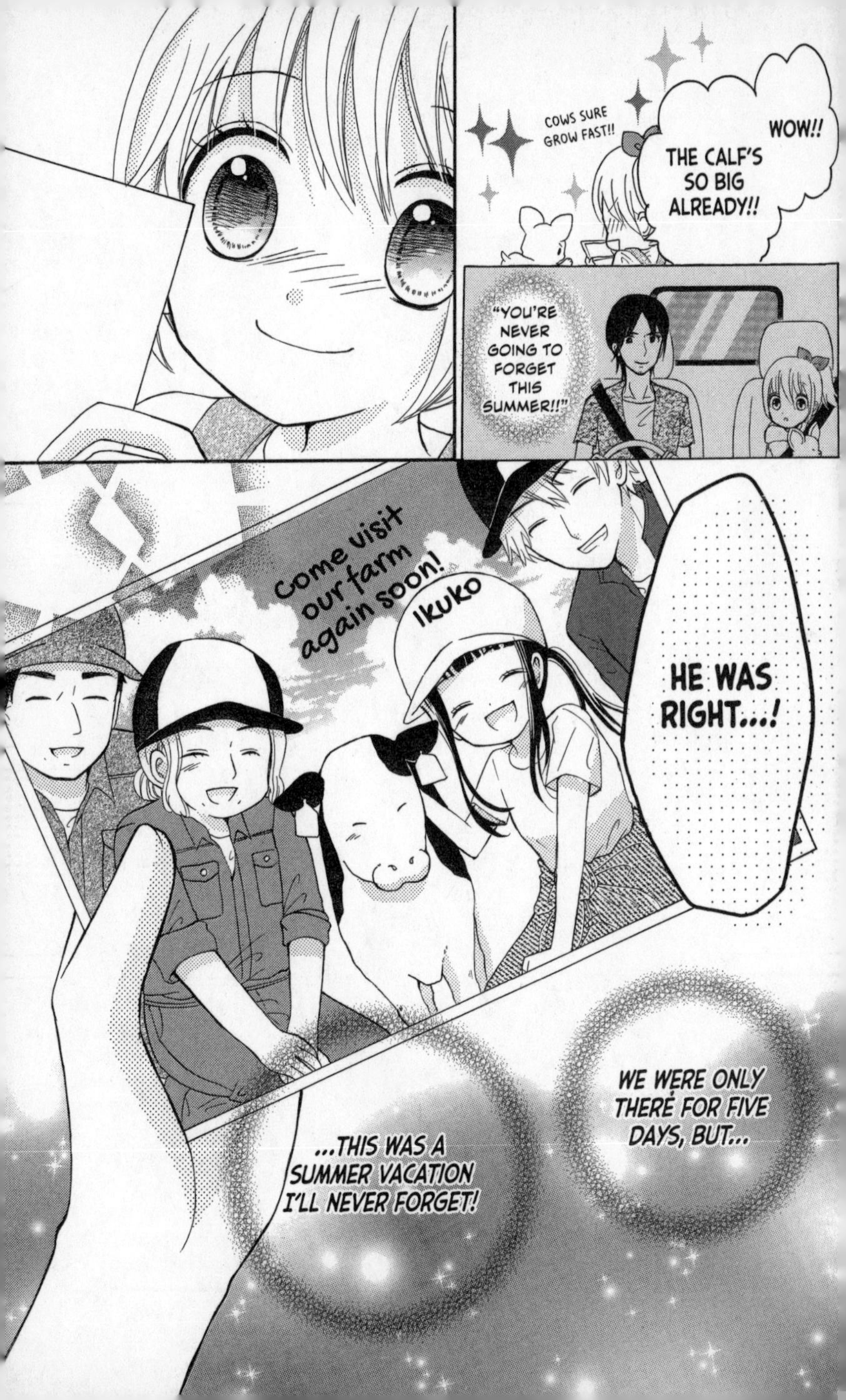
WOW!! THE CALF'S SO BIG ALREADY!!
COWS SURE GROW FAST!!
"YOU'RE NEVER GOING TO FORGET THIS SUMMER!!"
HE WAS RIGHT...!
Come visit our farm again soon!
Ikuko
WE WERE ONLY THERE FOR FIVE DAYS, BUT...
...THIS WAS A SUMMER VACATION I'LL NEVER FORGET!

YUZU THE PET VET

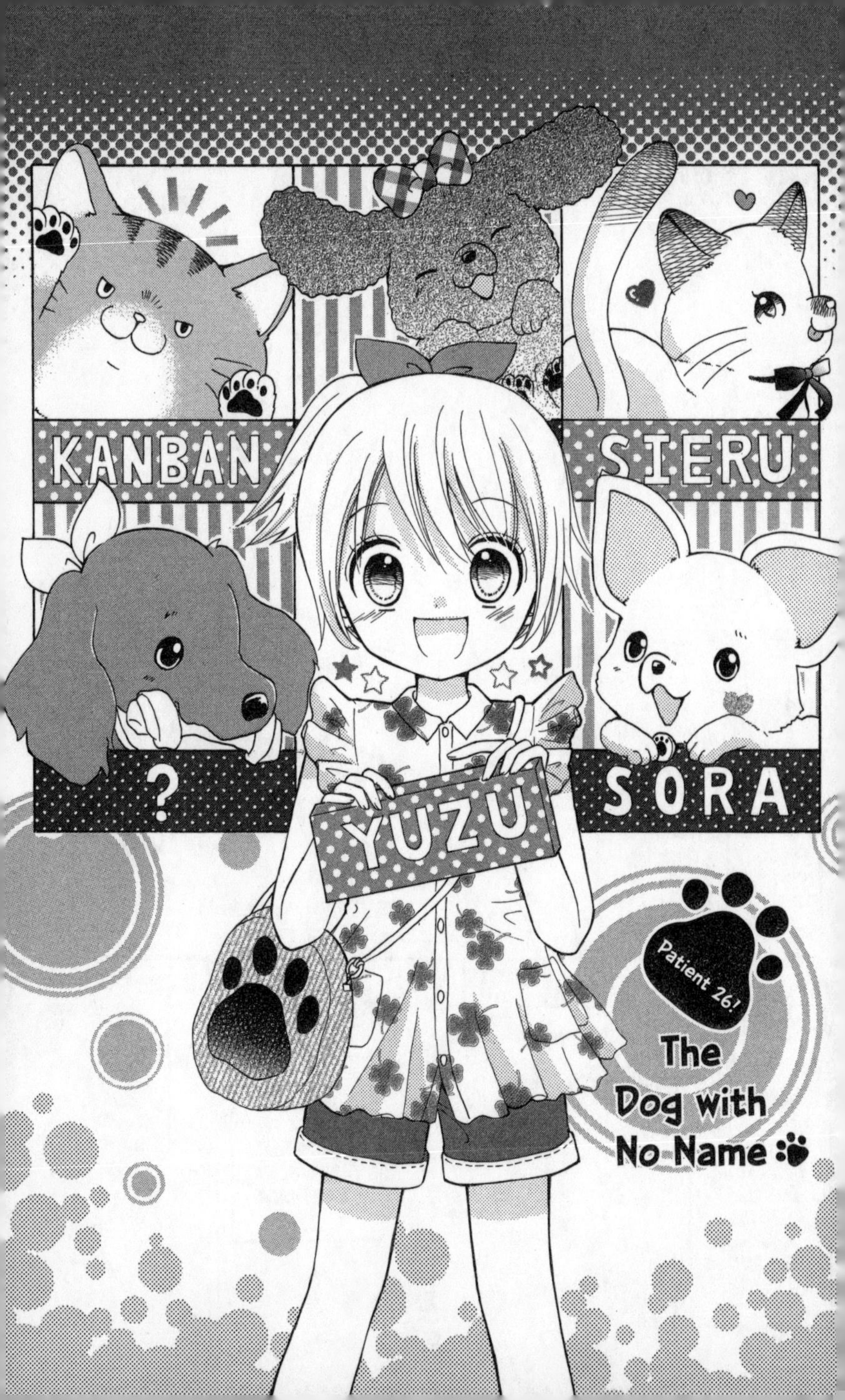
SIERU
KANBAN
SORA
?
YUZU
Patient 26!
The Dog with No Name

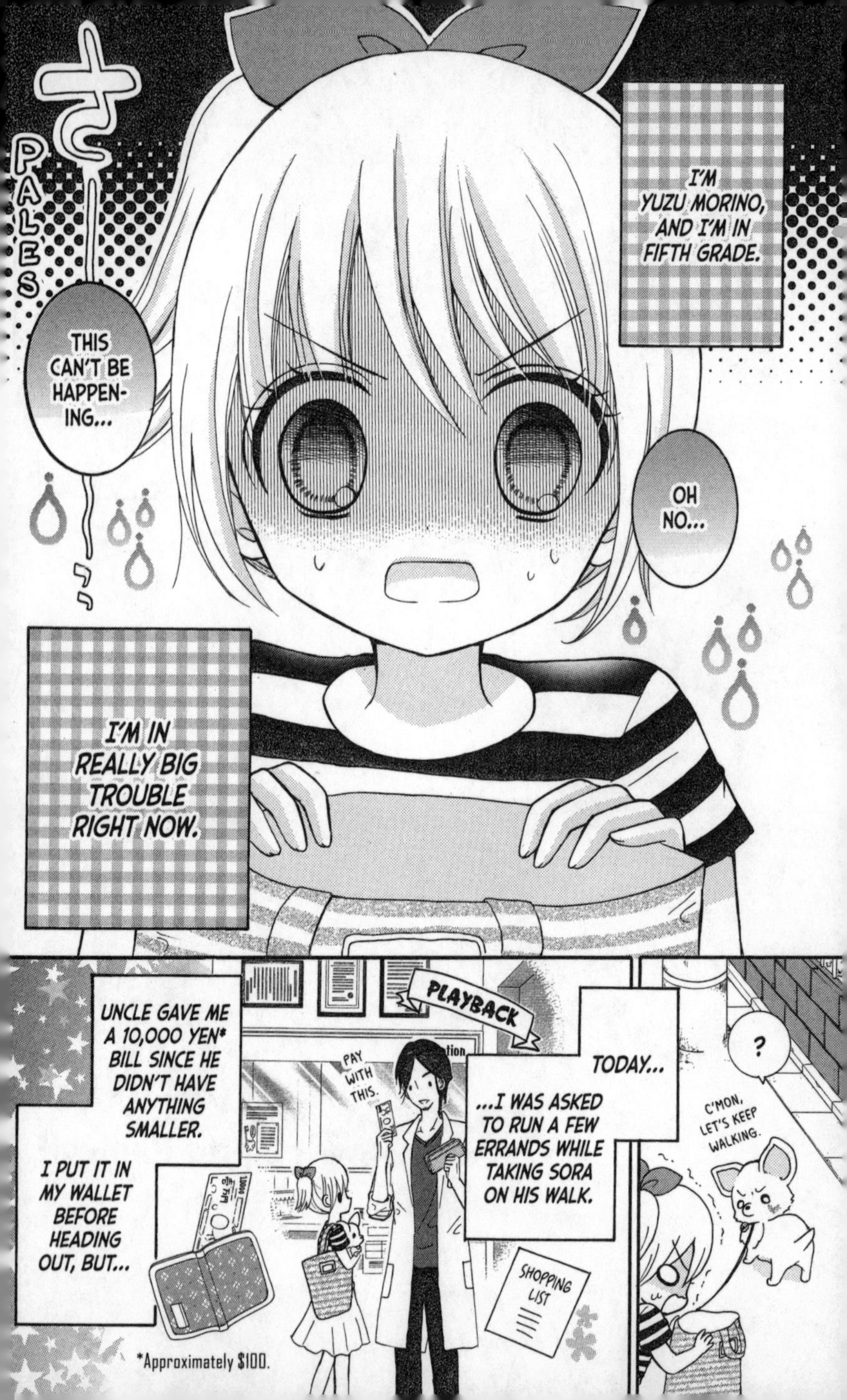
I'M YUZU MORINO, AND I'M IN FIFTH GRADE.
OH NO...
PALES
THIS CAN'T BE HAPPEN-ING...
I'M IN REALLY BIG TROUBLE RIGHT NOW.
?
C'MON, LET'S KEEP WALKING.
PLAYBACK
TODAY...
...I WAS ASKED TO RUN A FEW ERRANDS WHILE TAKING SORA ON HIS WALK.
SHOPPING LIST
PAY WITH THIS.
UNCLE GAVE ME A 10,000 YEN* BILL SINCE HE DIDN'T HAVE ANYTHING SMALLER.
I PUT IT IN MY WALLET BEFORE HEADING OUT, BUT...

*Approximately $100.

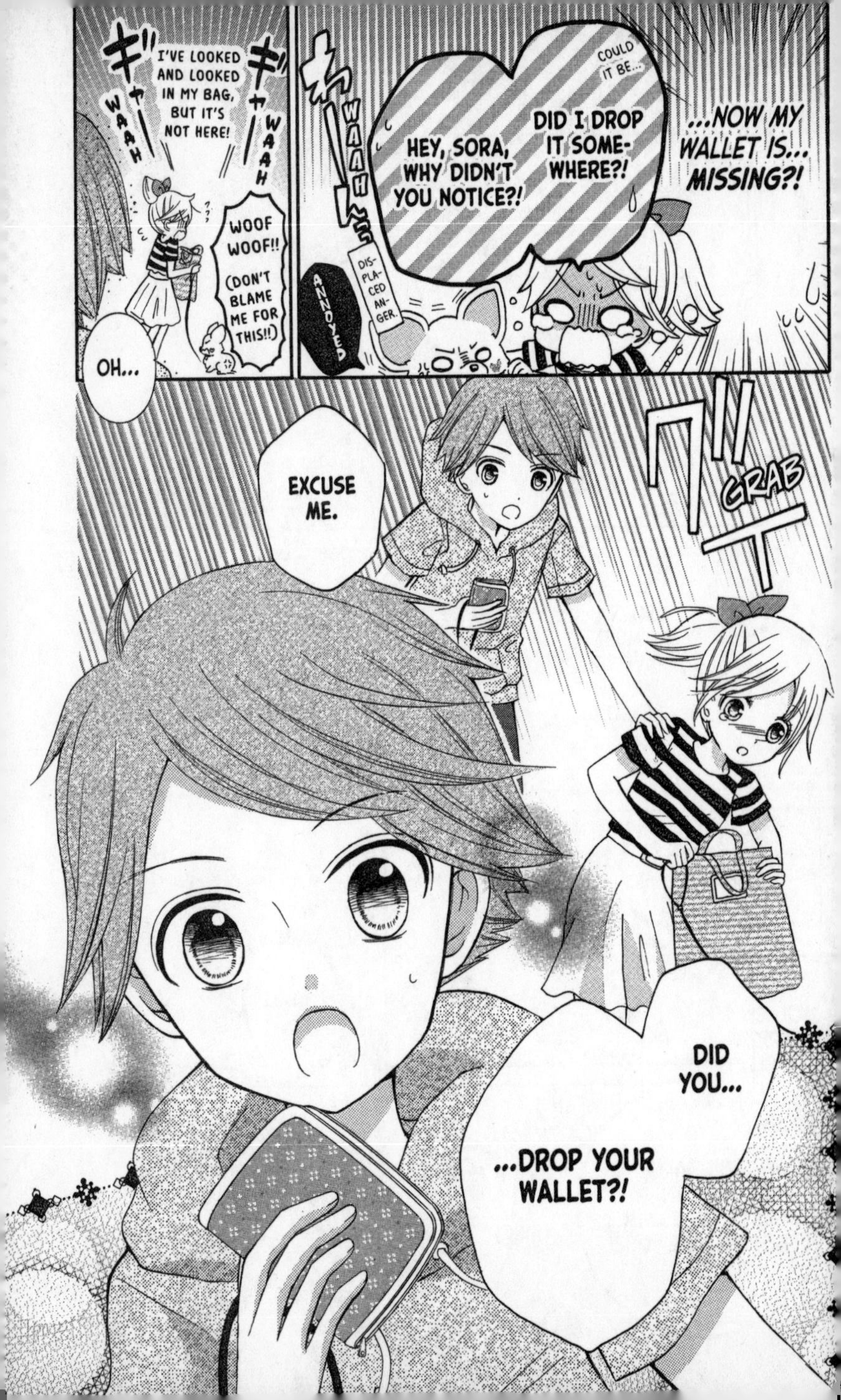
...NOW MY WALLET IS... MISSING?!
COULD IT BE...
DID I DROP IT SOMEWHERE?!
HEY, SORA, WHY DIDN'T YOU NOTICE?!
WAAAH
DISPLACED ANGER.
ANNOYED
WAAAH
I'VE LOOKED AND LOOKED IN MY BAG, BUT IT'S NOT HERE!
WAAAH
WOOF WOOF!! (DON'T BLAME ME FOR THIS!!)
OH...
GRAB
EXCUSE ME.
DID YOU...
...DROP YOUR WALLET?!

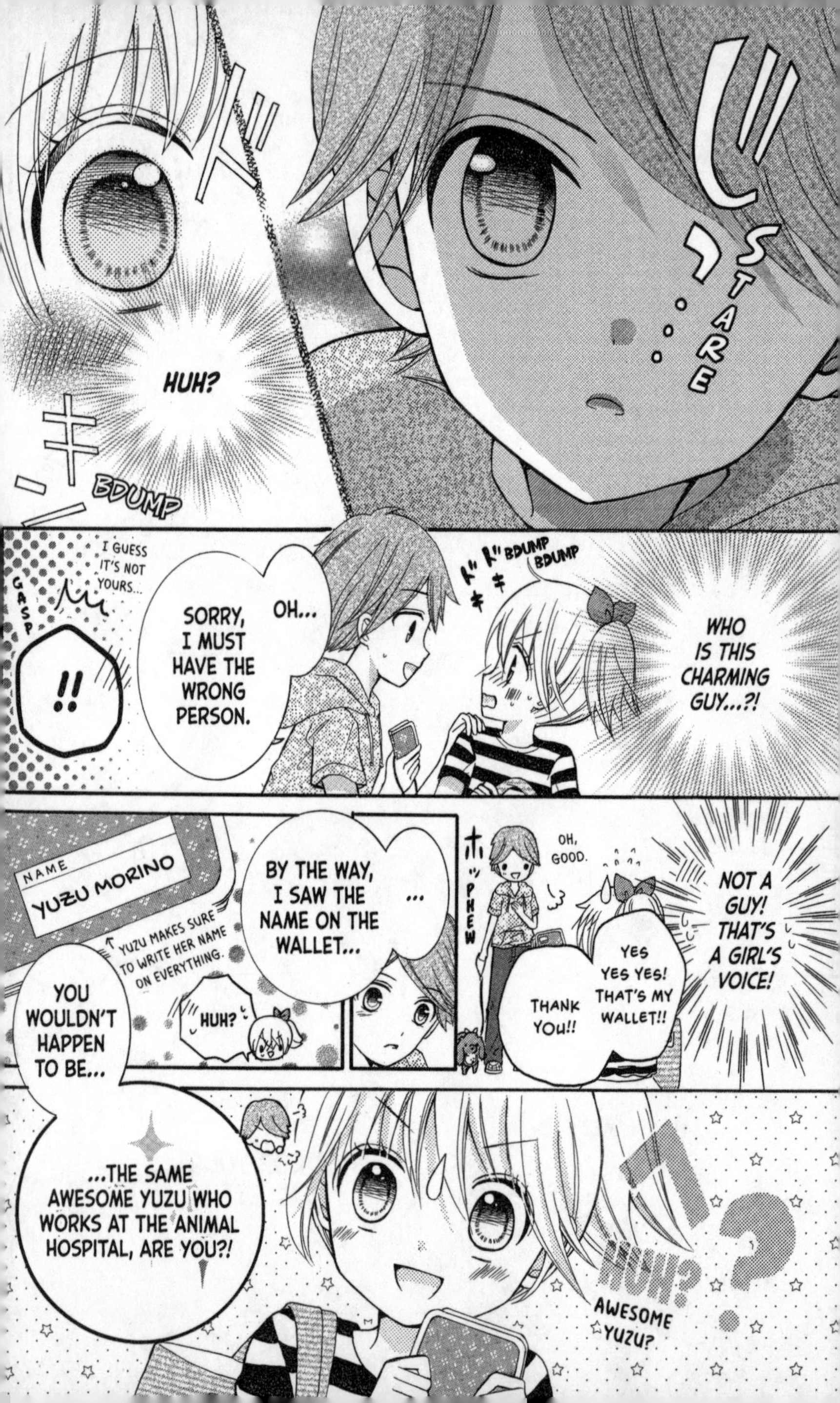
STARE
HUH?
BDUMP
WHO IS THIS CHARMING GUY...?!
BDUMP BDUMP
OH...
SORRY, I MUST HAVE THE WRONG PERSON.
!!
GASP
I GUESS IT'S NOT YOURS...
NOT A GUY! THAT'S A GIRL'S VOICE!
YES YES YES! THAT'S MY WALLET!!
THANK YOU!!
OH, GOOD.
PHEW
...
BY THE WAY, I SAW THE NAME ON THE WALLET...
NAME
YUZU MORINO
YUZU MAKES SURE TO WRITE HER NAME ON EVERYTHING.
HUH?
YOU WOULDN'T HAPPEN TO BE...
HUH?
AWESOME YUZU?
...THE SAME AWESOME YUZU WHO WORKS AT THE ANIMAL HOSPITAL, ARE YOU?!

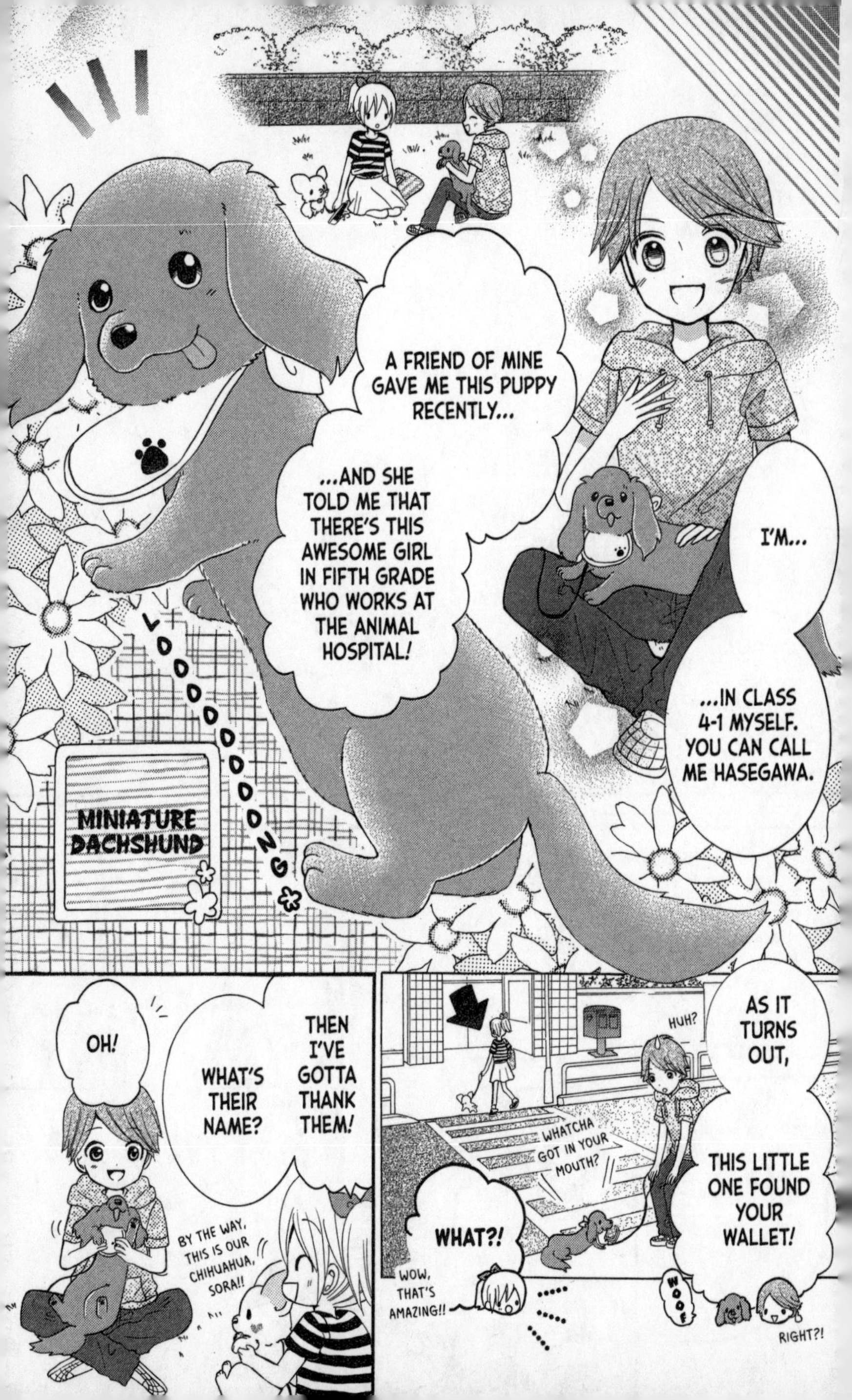
I'M...
...IN CLASS 4-1 MYSELF. YOU CAN CALL ME HASEGAWA.
A FRIEND OF MINE GAVE ME THIS PUPPY RECENTLY...
...AND SHE TOLD ME THAT THERE'S THIS AWESOME GIRL IN FIFTH GRADE WHO WORKS AT THE ANIMAL HOSPITAL!
LOOOOOOOONG
MINIATURE DACHSHUND
AS IT TURNS OUT,
HUH?
THIS LITTLE ONE FOUND YOUR WALLET!
WHATCHA GOT IN YOUR MOUTH?
WHAT?!
WOOF
RIGHT?!
WOW, THAT'S AMAZING!!
THEN I'VE GOTTA THANK THEM!
WHAT'S THEIR NAME?
OH!
BY THE WAY, THIS IS OUR CHIHUAHUA, SORA!!

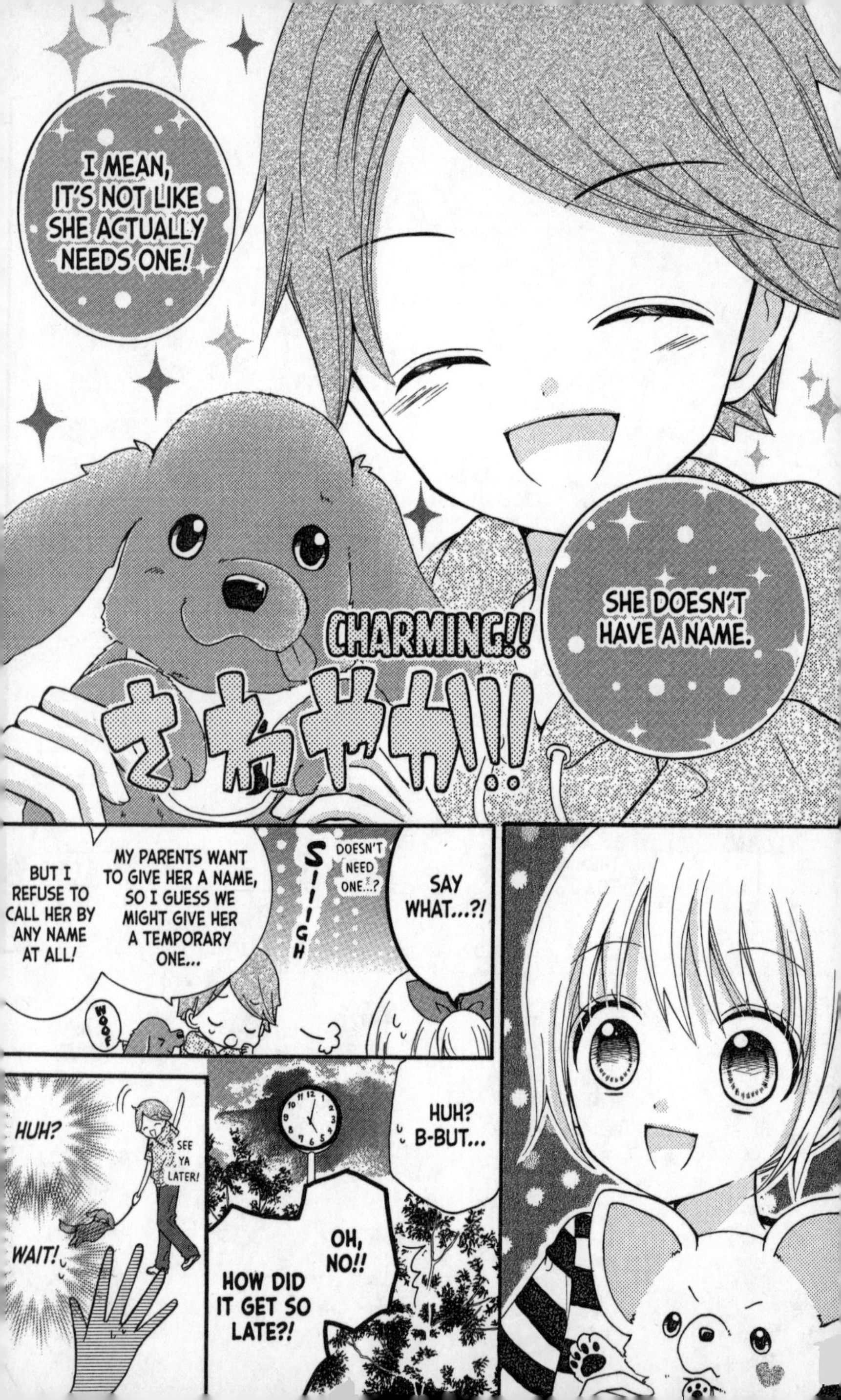
SHE DOESN'T HAVE A NAME.
CHARMING!!
I MEAN, IT'S NOT LIKE SHE ACTUALLY NEEDS ONE!
SAY WHAT...?!
DOESN'T NEED ONE...?
SIIIIGH
MY PARENTS WANT TO GIVE HER A NAME, SO I GUESS WE MIGHT GIVE HER A TEMPORARY ONE...
BUT I REFUSE TO CALL HER BY ANY NAME AT ALL!
WOOF
HUH? B-BUT...
OH, NO!!
HOW DID IT GET SO LATE?!
SEE YA LATER!
HUH?
WAIT!

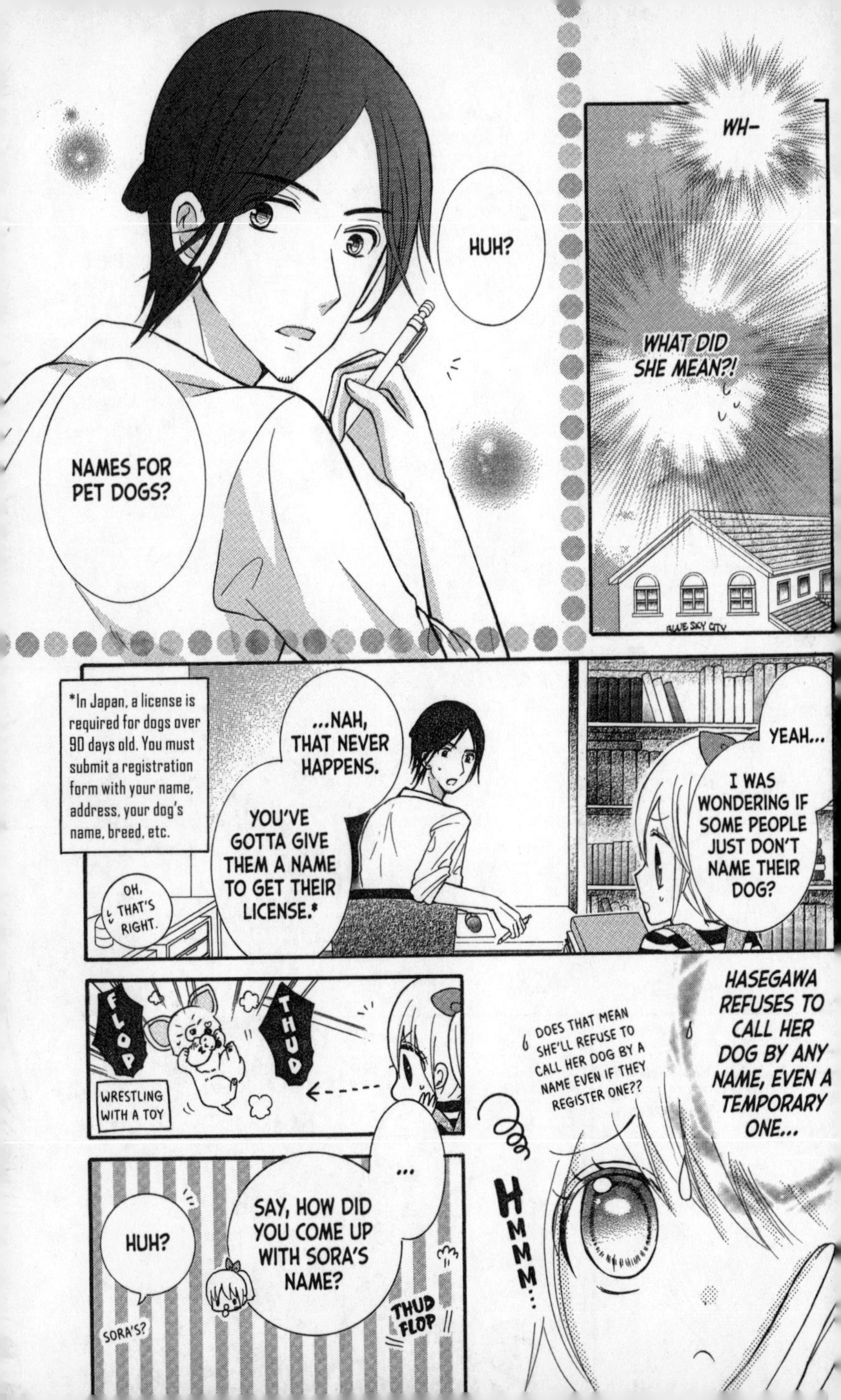

WH–
WHAT DID SHE MEAN?!
BLUE SKY CITY
HUH?
NAMES FOR PET DOGS?
YEAH...
I WAS WONDERING IF SOME PEOPLE JUST DON'T NAME THEIR DOG?
...NAH, THAT NEVER HAPPENS.
YOU'VE GOTTA GIVE THEM A NAME TO GET THEIR LICENSE.*
OH, THAT'S RIGHT.
*In Japan, a license is required for dogs over 90 days old. You must submit a registration form with your name, address, your dog's name, breed, etc.
HASEGAWA REFUSES TO CALL HER DOG BY ANY NAME, EVEN A TEMPORARY ONE...
DOES THAT MEAN SHE'LL REFUSE TO CALL HER DOG BY A NAME EVEN IF THEY REGISTER ONE??
HMMM...
THUD
FLOP
WRESTLING WITH A TOY
...
SAY, HOW DID YOU COME UP WITH SORA'S NAME?
HUH?
SORA'S?
THUD FLOP

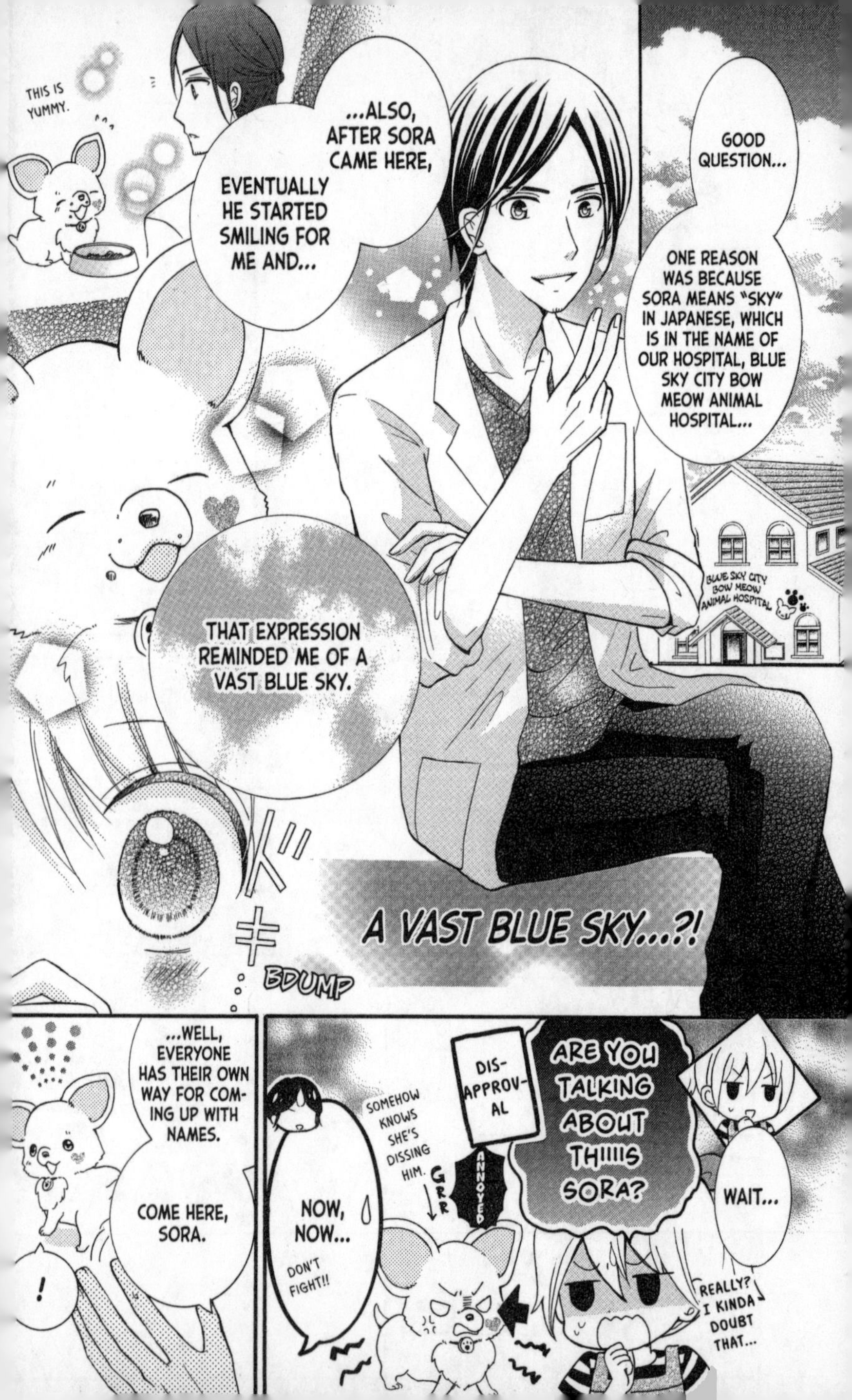
GOOD QUESTION...
ONE REASON WAS BECAUSE SORA MEANS "SKY" IN JAPANESE, WHICH IS IN THE NAME OF OUR HOSPITAL, BLUE SKY CITY BOW MEOW ANIMAL HOSPITAL...
BLUE SKY CITY BOW MEOW ANIMAL HOSPITAL
...ALSO, AFTER SORA CAME HERE,
EVENTUALLY HE STARTED SMILING FOR ME AND...
THIS IS YUMMY.
THAT EXPRESSION REMINDED ME OF A VAST BLUE SKY.
A VAST BLUE SKY...?!
BDUMP
ARE YOU TALKING ABOUT THIIIIS SORA?
WAIT...
REALLY? I KINDA DOUBT THAT...
DIS-APPROV-AL
ANNOYED
GRR
SOMEHOW KNOWS SHE'S DISSING HIM.
NOW, NOW...
DON'T FIGHT!!
...WELL, EVERYONE HAS THEIR OWN WAY FOR COM-ING UP WITH NAMES.
COME HERE, SORA.
!

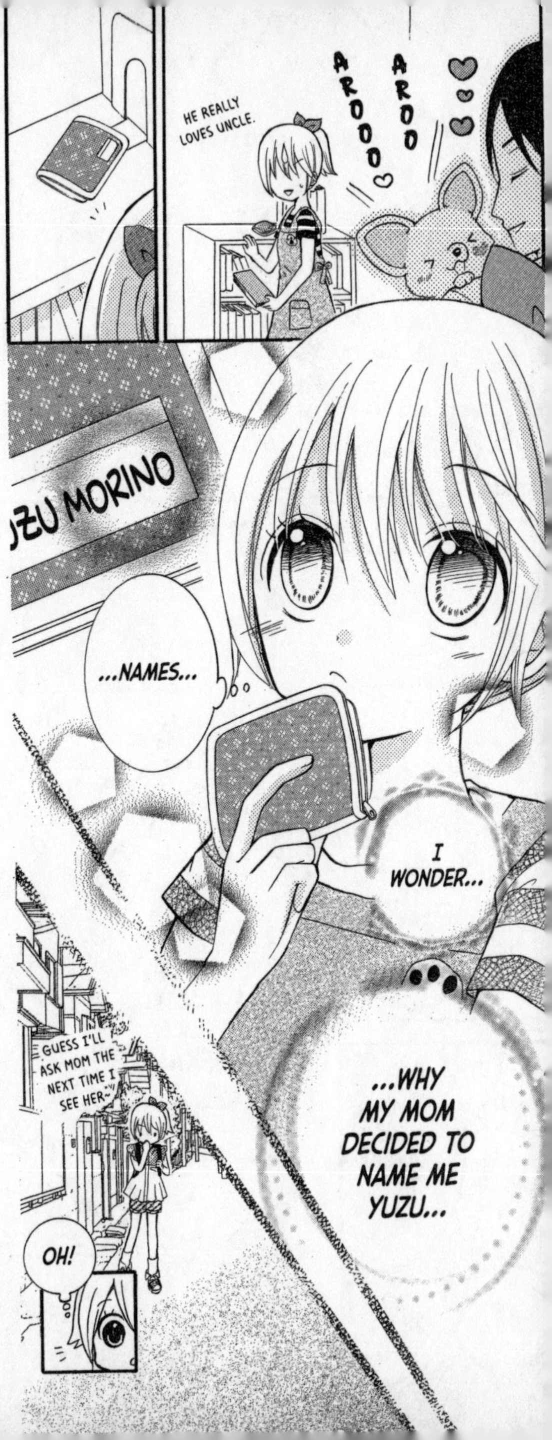
AROOO
AROO
HE REALLY LOVES UNCLE.
YUZU MORINO
...NAMES...
I WONDER...
...WHY MY MOM DECIDED TO NAME ME YUZU...
GUESS I'LL ASK MOM THE NEXT TIME I SEE HER~
OH!

## FARMS

FOR THE FINAL CHAPTER IN VOLUME SIX AND THE FIRST CHAPTER IN THIS VOLUME, I GOT TO VISIT A REAL FARM TO INTERVIEW THE PEOPLE THERE. ✧ I HADN'T SEEN A COW IN PERSON SINCE I WAS A KID, AND THE FIRST THING I THOUGHT WAS...

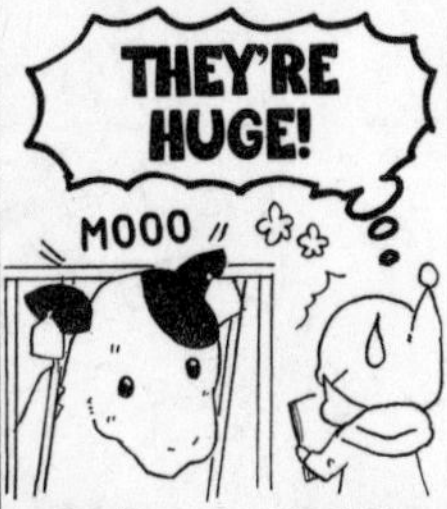
THEY'RE HUGE!
MOOO

(LOL). I WAS SHOCKED SINCE I'D TOTALLY FORGOTTEN HOW BIG THEY COULD BE—SO MUCH BIGGER THAN HUMANS! BUT THEIR EYES ARE SO ROUND AND CUTE, DON'T YOU AGREE? ♡ ♡♡

I LEARNED ALL KINDS OF AMAZING THINGS FROM THE PEOPLE I TALKED TO! THANK YOU SO MUCH FOR ANSWERING ALL MY QUESTIONS DESPITE BEING SO BUSY! ✧

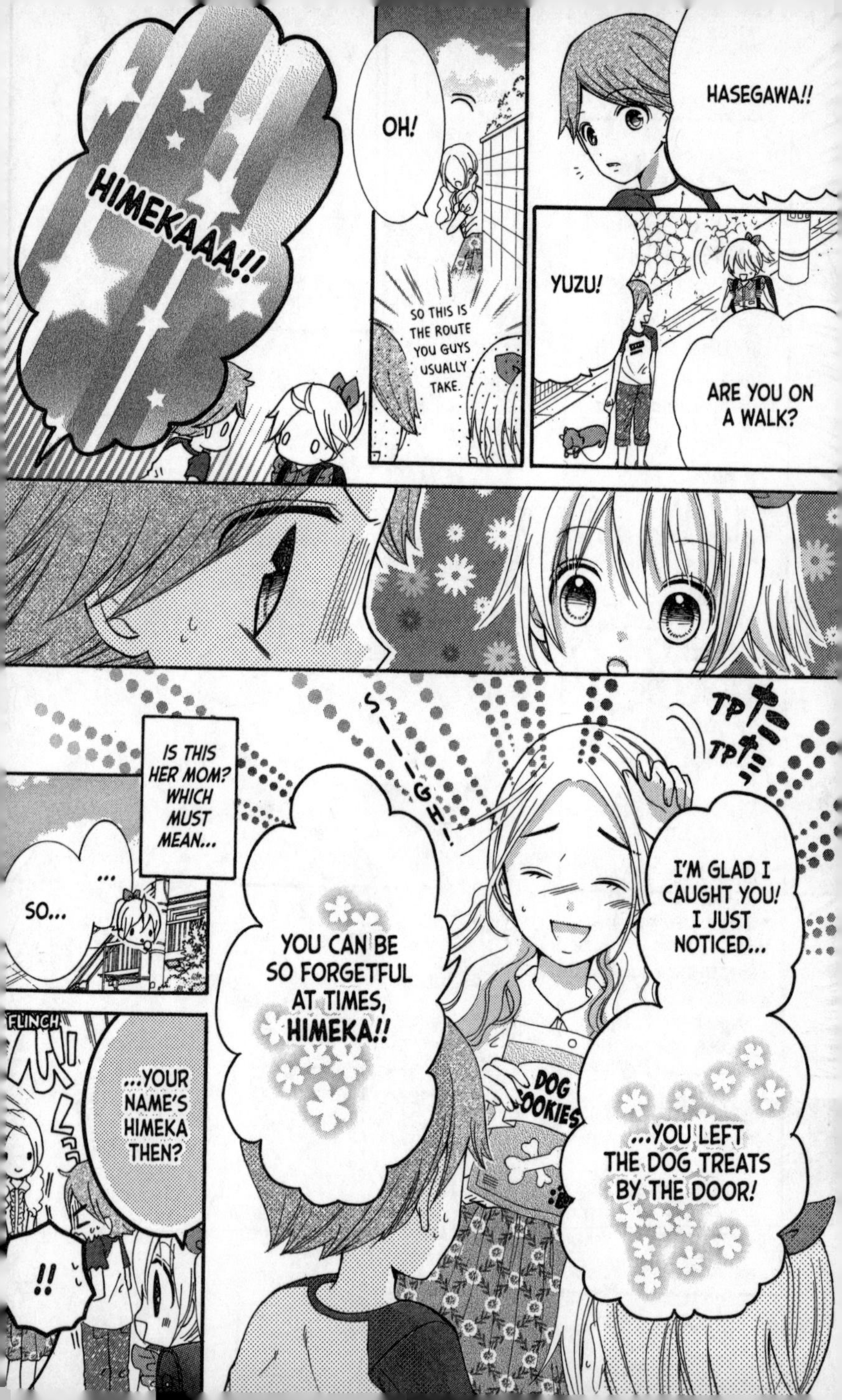

HASEGAWA!!
YUZU!
ARE YOU ON A WALK?
OH!
SO THIS IS THE ROUTE YOU GUYS USUALLY TAKE.
HIMEKAAA!!
TP TP
I'M GLAD I CAUGHT YOU! I JUST NOTICED...
...YOU LEFT THE DOG TREATS BY THE DOOR!
S-I-G-H!
YOU CAN BE SO FORGETFUL AT TIMES, HIMEKA!!
DOG COOKIES
IS THIS HER MOM? WHICH MUST MEAN...
...
SO...
FLINCH
...YOUR NAME'S HIMEKA THEN?
!!

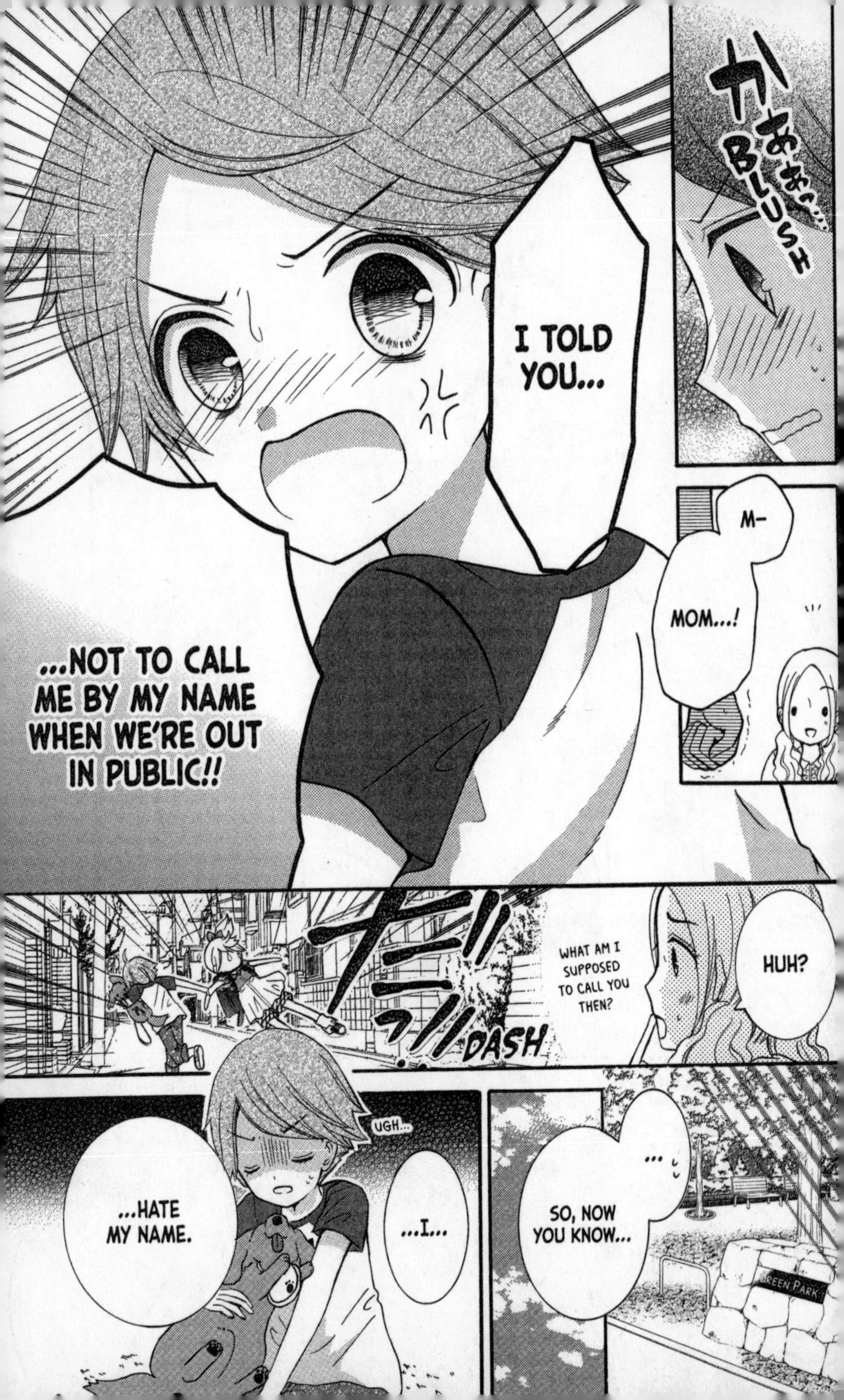
BLUSH
M-
MOM...!
I TOLD YOU...
...NOT TO CALL ME BY MY NAME WHEN WE'RE OUT IN PUBLIC!!
HUH?
WHAT AM I SUPPOSED TO CALL YOU THEN?
DASH
...
SO, NOW YOU KNOW...
GREEN PARK
UGH...
...I...
...HATE MY NAME.

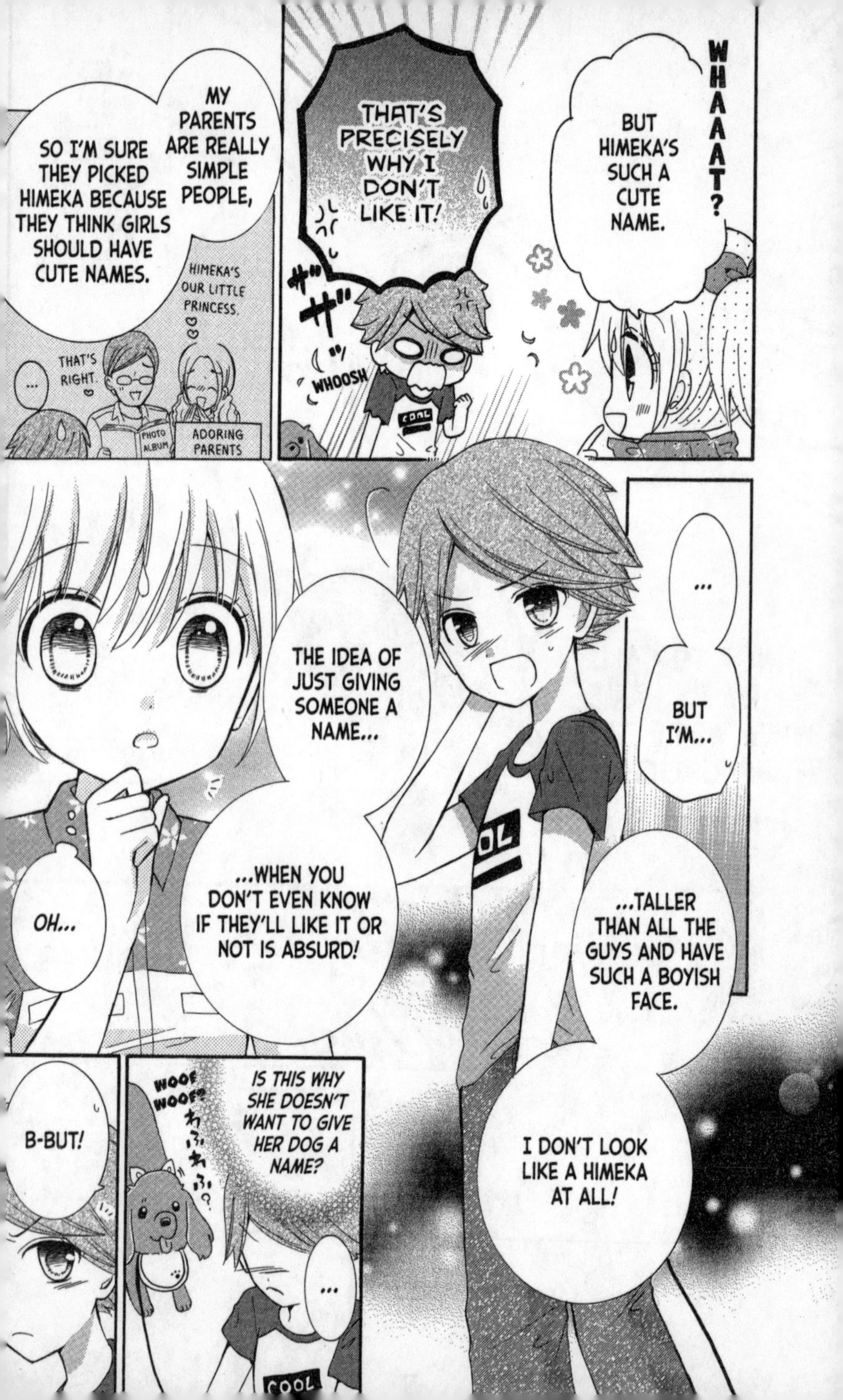
WHAAAT?
BUT HIMEKA'S SUCH A CUTE NAME.
THAT'S PRECISELY WHY I DON'T LIKE IT!
WHOOSH
COOL
MY PARENTS ARE REALLY SIMPLE PEOPLE,
SO I'M SURE THEY PICKED HIMEKA BECAUSE THEY THINK GIRLS SHOULD HAVE CUTE NAMES.
HIMEKA'S OUR LITTLE PRINCESS.
THAT'S RIGHT.
...
PHOTO ALBUM
ADORING PARENTS
...
BUT I'M...
...TALLER THAN ALL THE GUYS AND HAVE SUCH A BOYISH FACE.
I DON'T LOOK LIKE A HIMEKA AT ALL!
THE IDEA OF JUST GIVING SOMEONE A NAME...
...WHEN YOU DON'T EVEN KNOW IF THEY'LL LIKE IT OR NOT IS ABSURD!
OH...
IS THIS WHY SHE DOESN'T WANT TO GIVE HER DOG A NAME?
WOOF WOOF?
...
COOL
B-BUT!

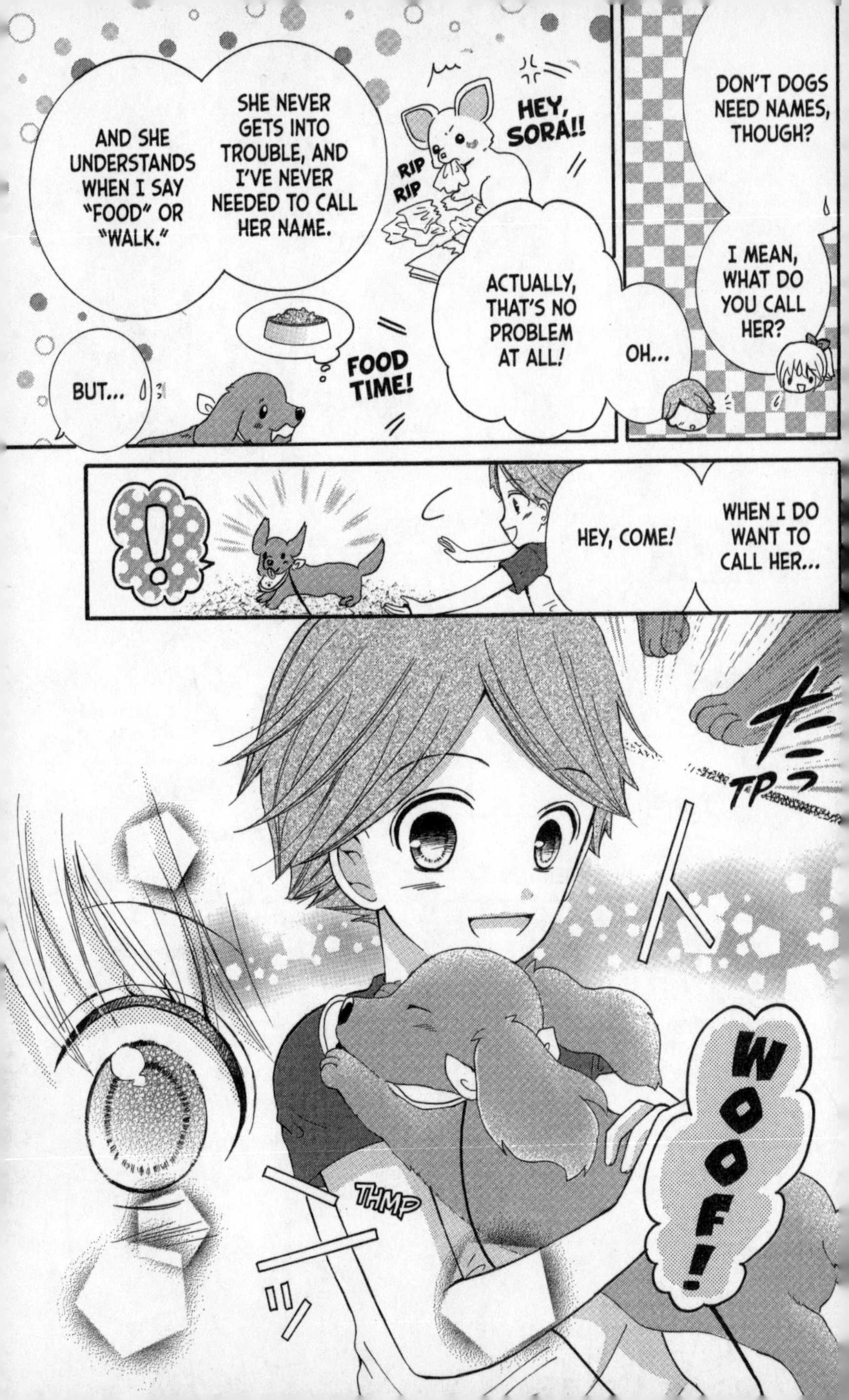
DON'T DOGS NEED NAMES, THOUGH?
I MEAN, WHAT DO YOU CALL HER?
OH...
ACTUALLY, THAT'S NO PROBLEM AT ALL!
HEY, SORA!!
RIP RIP
SHE NEVER GETS INTO TROUBLE, AND I'VE NEVER NEEDED TO CALL HER NAME.
AND SHE UNDERSTANDS WHEN I SAY "FOOD" OR "WALK."
FOOD TIME!
BUT...
WHEN I DO WANT TO CALL HER...
HEY, COME!
!
TP
WOOF!
THMP

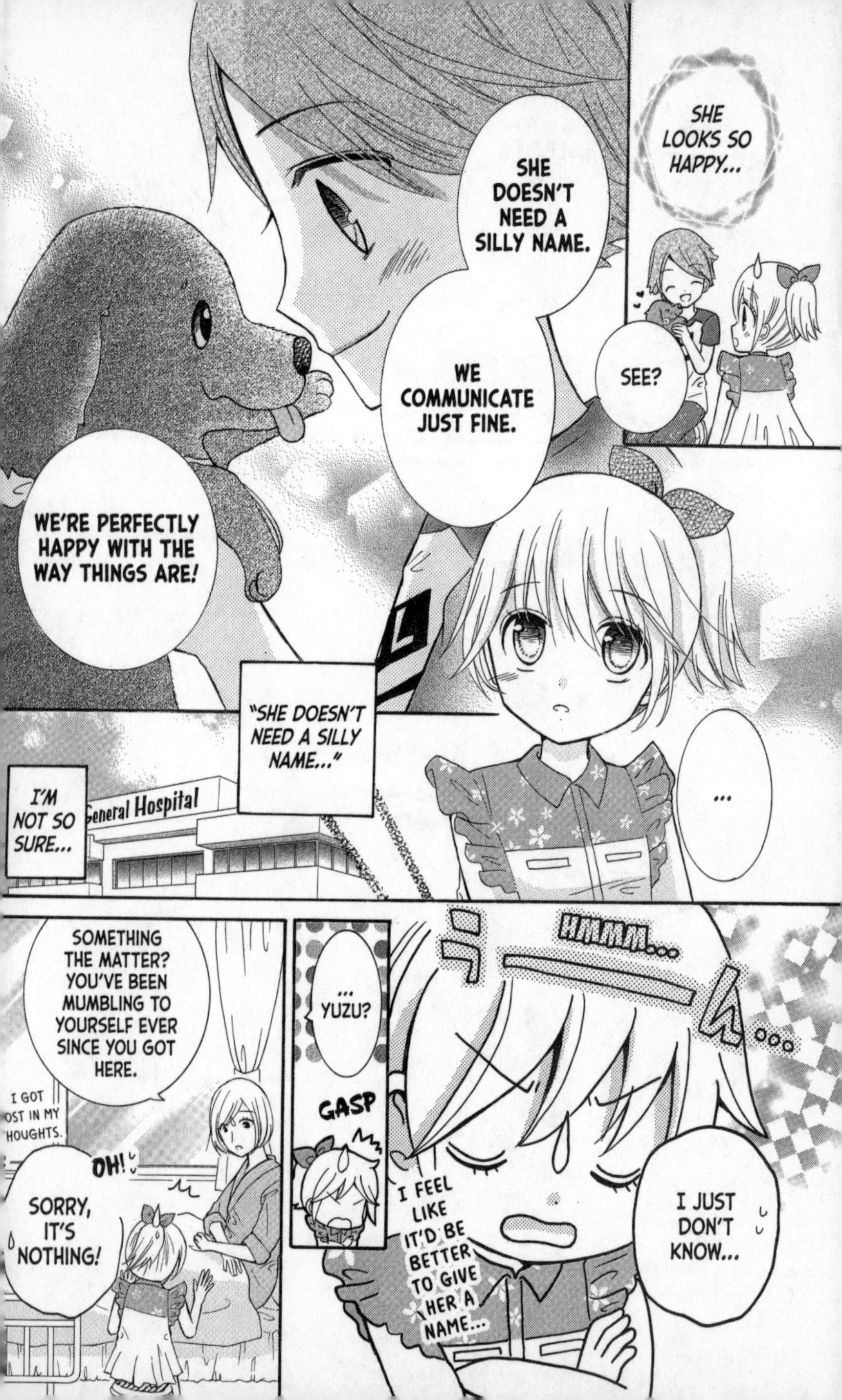

SHE LOOKS SO HAPPY...
SEE?
SHE DOESN'T NEED A SILLY NAME.
WE COMMUNICATE JUST FINE.
WE'RE PERFECTLY HAPPY WITH THE WAY THINGS ARE!
...
"SHE DOESN'T NEED A SILLY NAME..."
I'M NOT SO SURE...
General Hospital
HMMM...
I JUST DON'T KNOW...
I FEEL LIKE IT'D BE BETTER TO GIVE HER A NAME...
... YUZU?
GASP
SOMETHING THE MATTER? YOU'VE BEEN MUMBLING TO YOURSELF EVER SINCE YOU GOT HERE.
OH!
SORRY, IT'S NOTHING!
I GOT OST IN MY HOUGHTS.

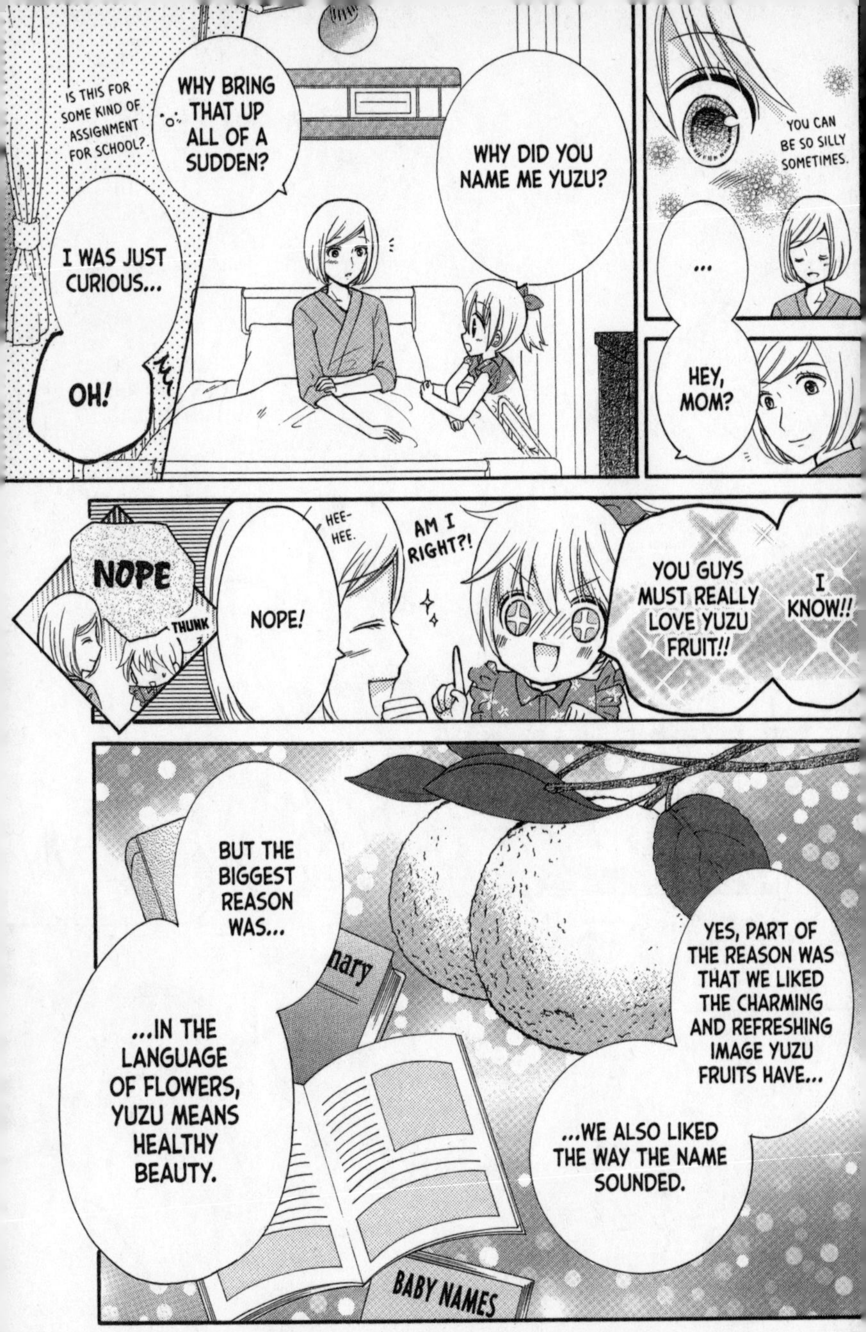
YOU CAN BE SO SILLY SOMETIMES.
...
HEY, MOM?
WHY DID YOU NAME ME YUZU?
WHY BRING THAT UP ALL OF A SUDDEN?
IS THIS FOR SOME KIND OF ASSIGNMENT FOR SCHOOL?
I WAS JUST CURIOUS...
OH!
I KNOW!!
YOU GUYS MUST REALLY LOVE YUZU FRUIT!!
AM I RIGHT?!
HEE-HEE.
NOPE!
NOPE
THUNK
YES, PART OF THE REASON WAS THAT WE LIKED THE CHARMING AND REFRESHING IMAGE YUZU FRUITS HAVE...
...WE ALSO LIKED THE WAY THE NAME SOUNDED.
BUT THE BIGGEST REASON WAS...
...IN THE LANGUAGE OF FLOWERS, YUZU MEANS HEALTHY BEAUTY.
BABY NAMES

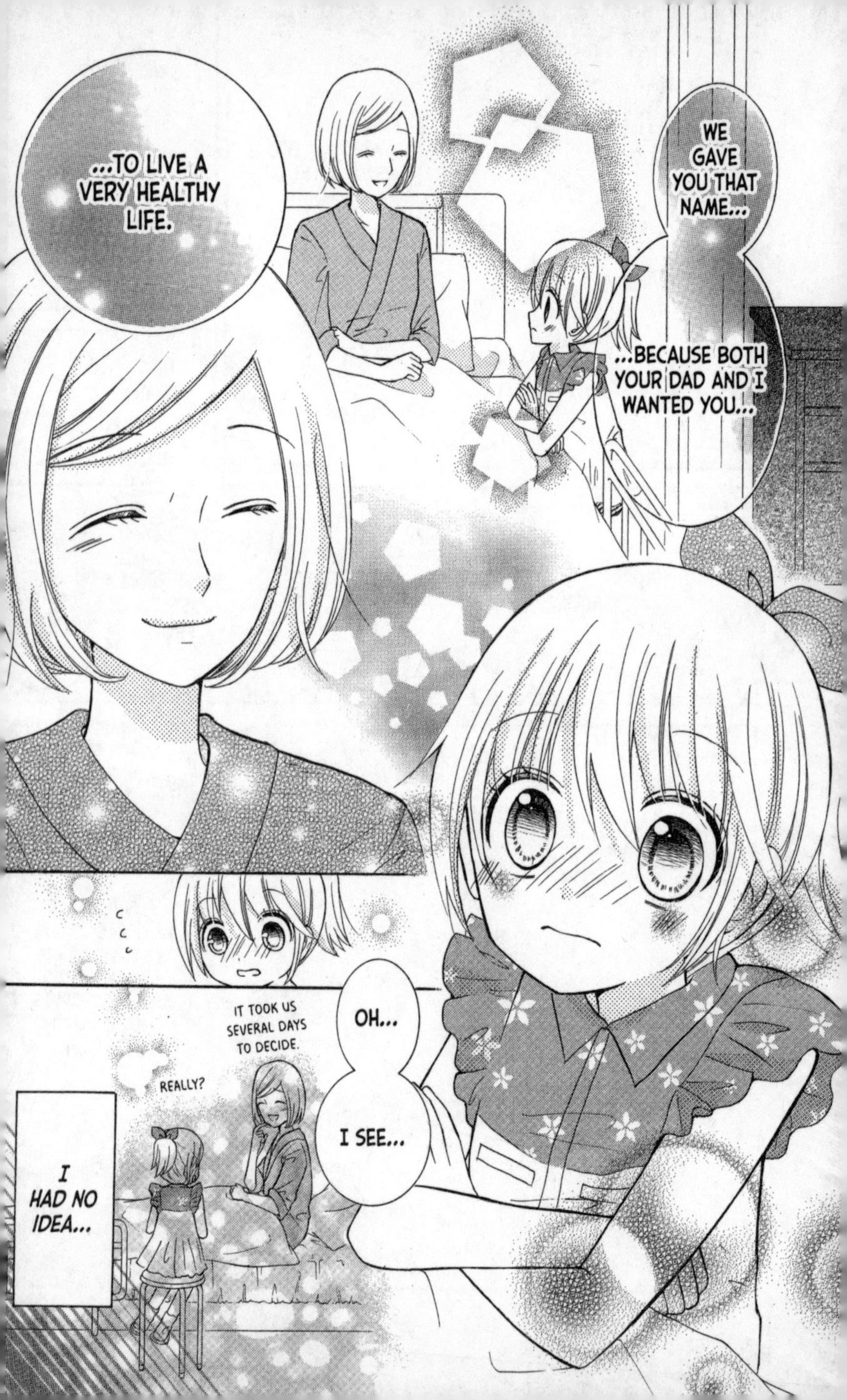
WE GAVE YOU THAT NAME...
...BECAUSE BOTH YOUR DAD AND I WANTED YOU...
...TO LIVE A VERY HEALTHY LIFE.
OH...
I SEE...
IT TOOK US SEVERAL DAYS TO DECIDE.
REALLY?
I HAD NO IDEA...

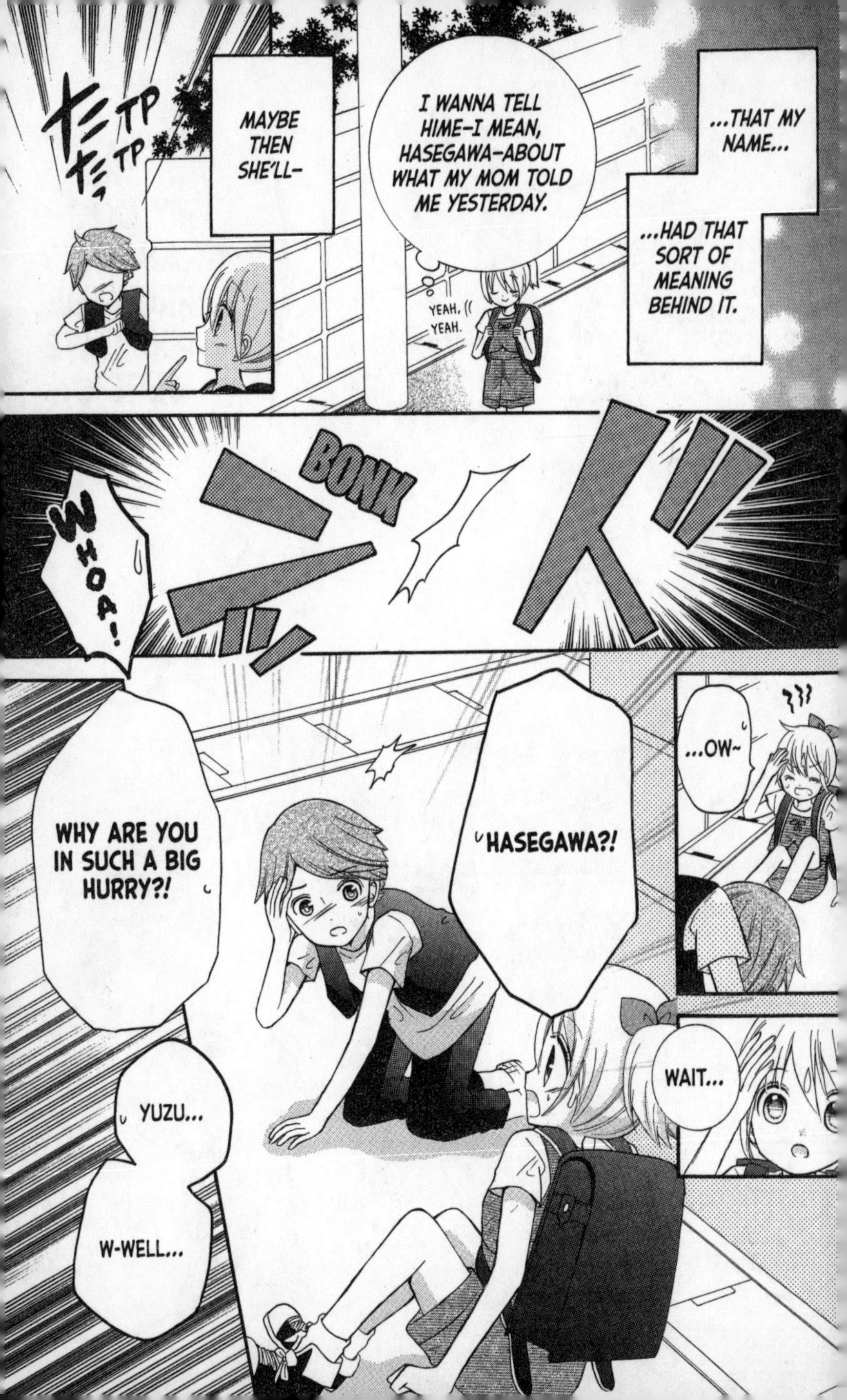
...THAT MY NAME...
...HAD THAT SORT OF MEANING BEHIND IT.
I WANNA TELL HIME—I MEAN, HASEGAWA—ABOUT WHAT MY MOM TOLD ME YESTERDAY.
YEAH, YEAH.
MAYBE THEN SHE'LL-
TP TP
BONK
WHOA!
...OW~
WAIT...
HASEGAWA?!
WHY ARE YOU IN SUCH A BIG HURRY?!
YUZU...
W-WELL...

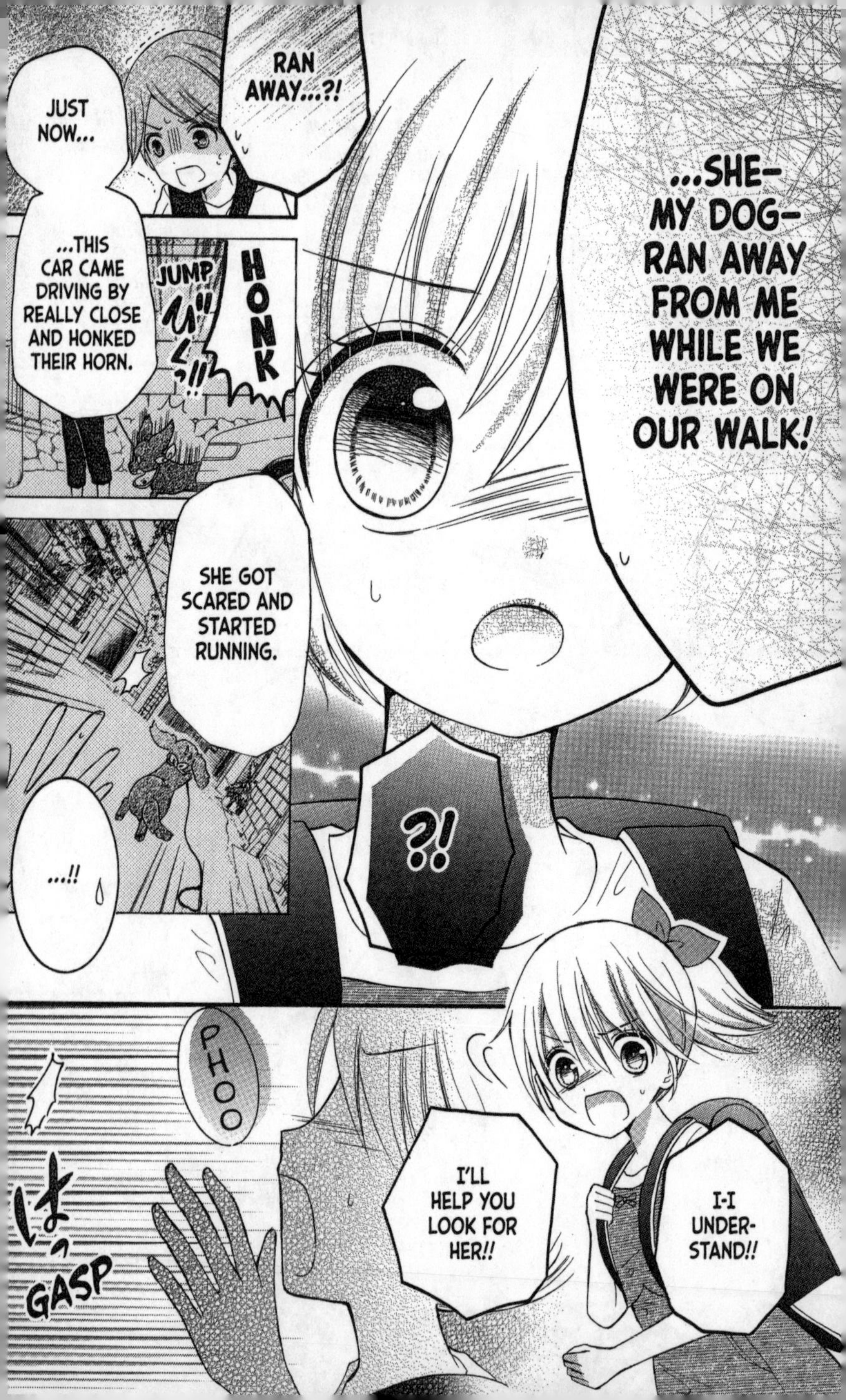
...SHE- MY DOG- RAN AWAY FROM ME WHILE WE WERE ON OUR WALK!
RAN AWAY...?!
JUST NOW...
...THIS CAR CAME DRIVING BY REALLY CLOSE AND HONKED THEIR HORN.
HONK
JUMP
SHE GOT SCARED AND STARTED RUNNING.
...!!
?!
I-I UNDER-STAND!!
I'LL HELP YOU LOOK FOR HER!!
PHOO
GASP

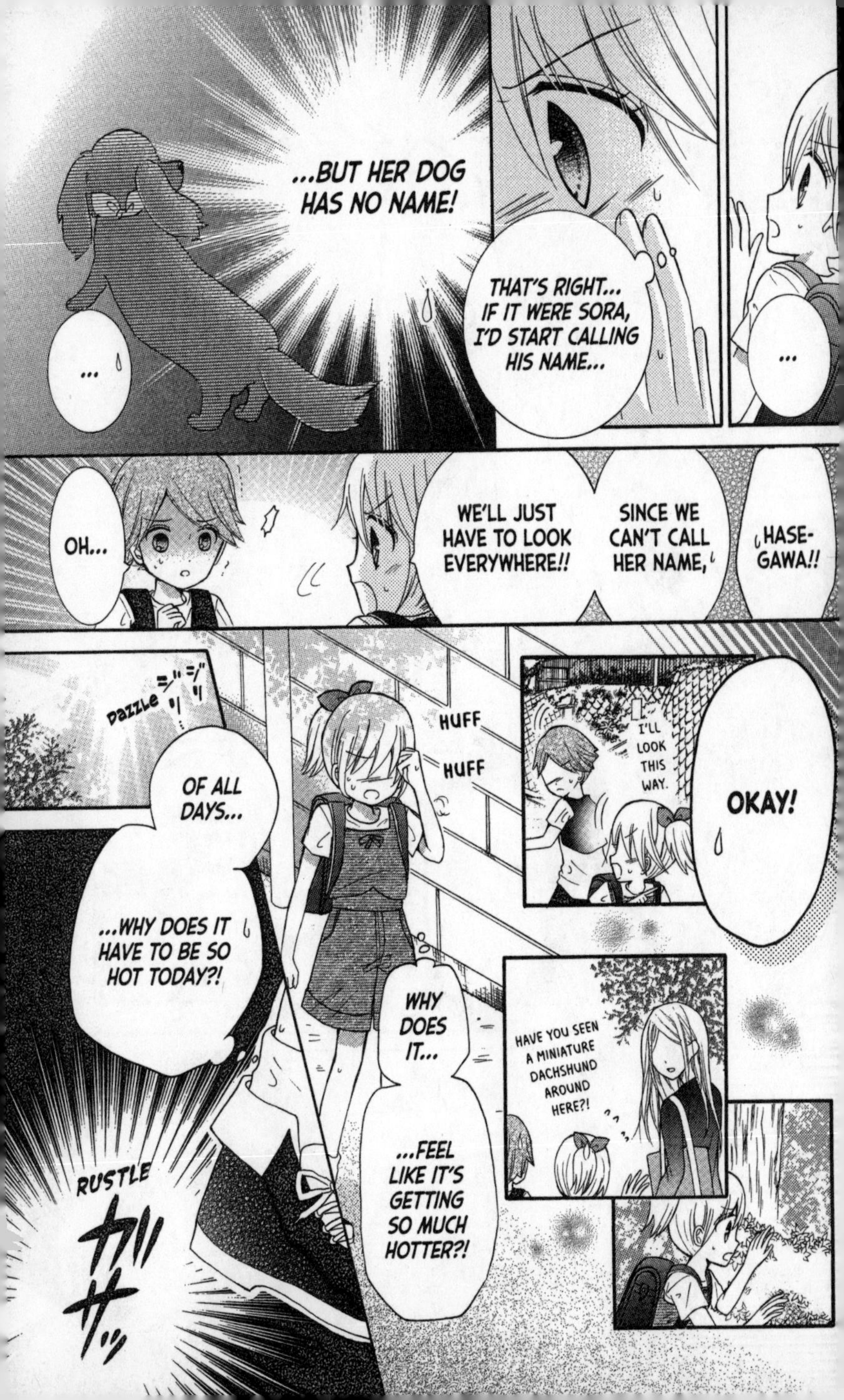
...
THAT'S RIGHT... IF IT WERE SORA, I'D START CALLING HIS NAME...
...BUT HER DOG HAS NO NAME!
...
HASE-GAWA!!
SINCE WE CAN'T CALL HER NAME,
WE'LL JUST HAVE TO LOOK EVERYWHERE!!
OH...
I'LL LOOK THIS WAY.
OKAY!
HAVE YOU SEEN A MINIATURE DACHSHUND AROUND HERE?!
HUFF
HUFF
Dazzle
OF ALL DAYS...
...WHY DOES IT HAVE TO BE SO HOT TODAY?!
WHY DOES IT...
...FEEL LIKE IT'S GETTING SO MUCH HOTTER?!
RUSTLE

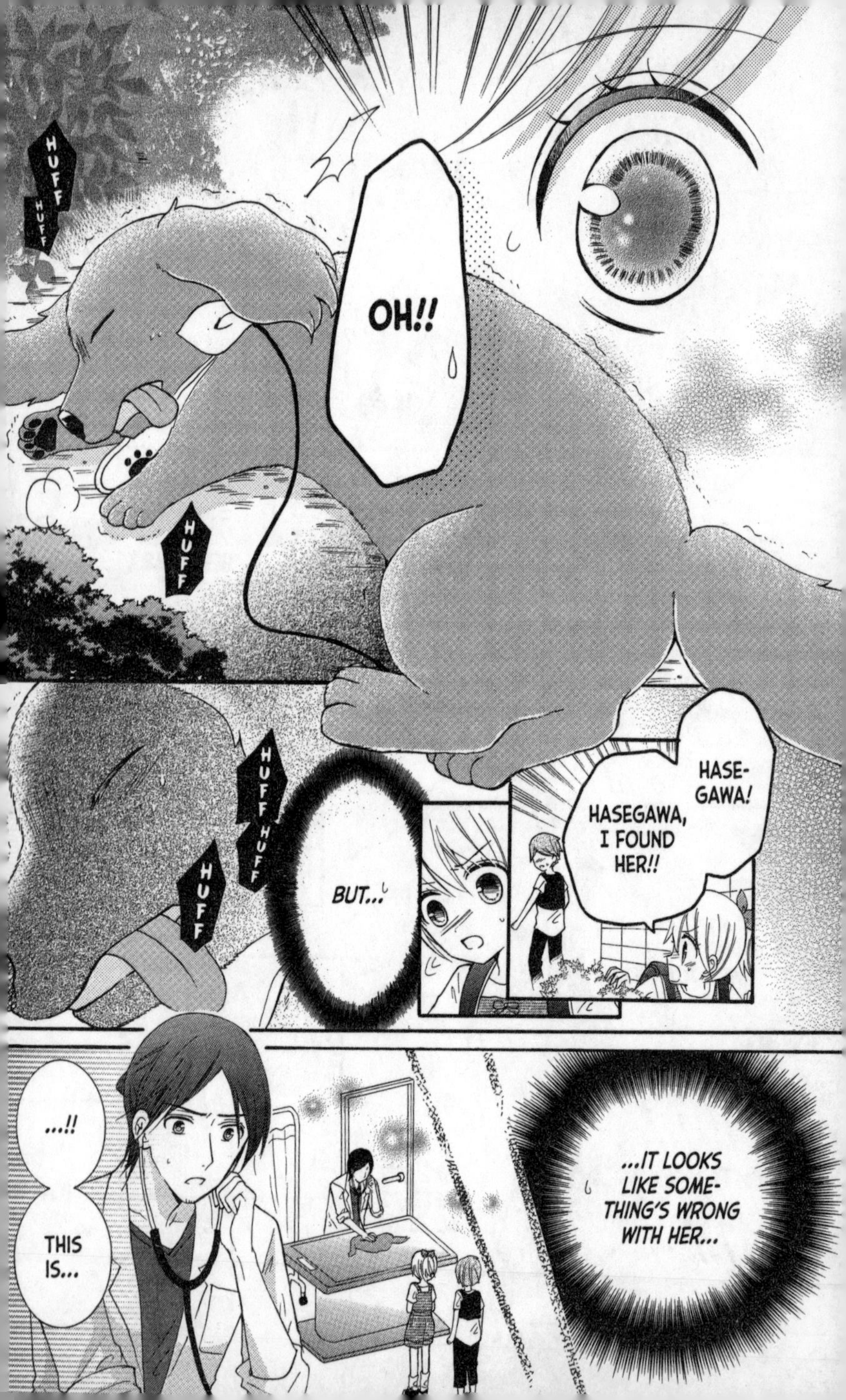
OH!!
HUFF
HUFF
HUFF
HUFF
HASE-
GAWA!
HASEGAWA, I FOUND HER!!
BUT...
HUFF
HUFF
HUFF
...IT LOOKS LIKE SOME-THING'S WRONG WITH HER...
...!!
THIS IS...

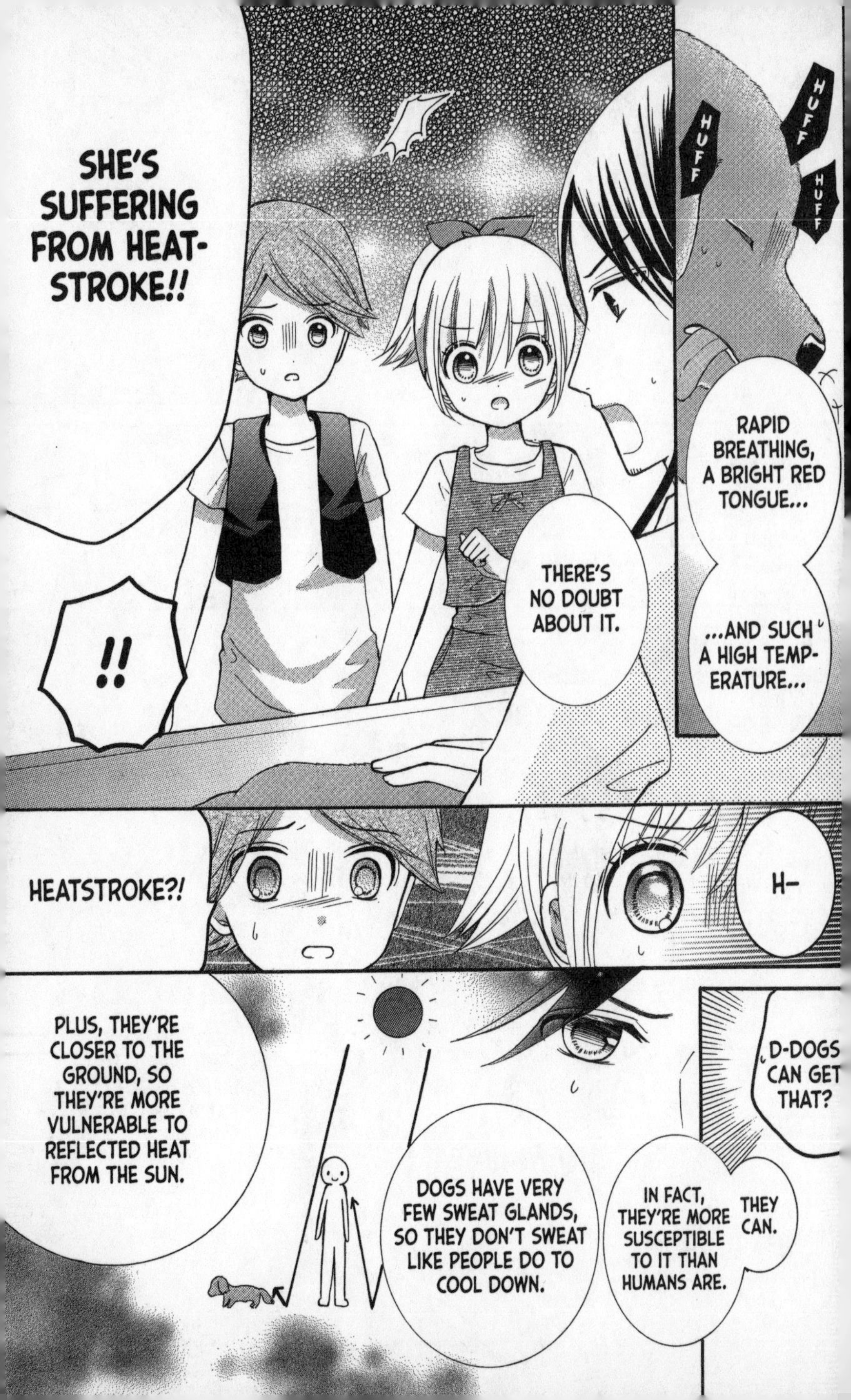
HUFF
HUFF
HUFF
RAPID BREATHING, A BRIGHT RED TONGUE...
...AND SUCH A HIGH TEMPERATURE...
THERE'S NO DOUBT ABOUT IT.
SHE'S SUFFERING FROM HEATSTROKE!!
!!
H-
HEATSTROKE?!
D-DOGS CAN GET THAT?
THEY CAN.
IN FACT, THEY'RE MORE SUSCEPTIBLE TO IT THAN HUMANS ARE.
DOGS HAVE VERY FEW SWEAT GLANDS, SO THEY DON'T SWEAT LIKE PEOPLE DO TO COOL DOWN.
PLUS, THEY'RE CLOSER TO THE GROUND, SO THEY'RE MORE VULNERABLE TO REFLECTED HEAT FROM THE SUN.

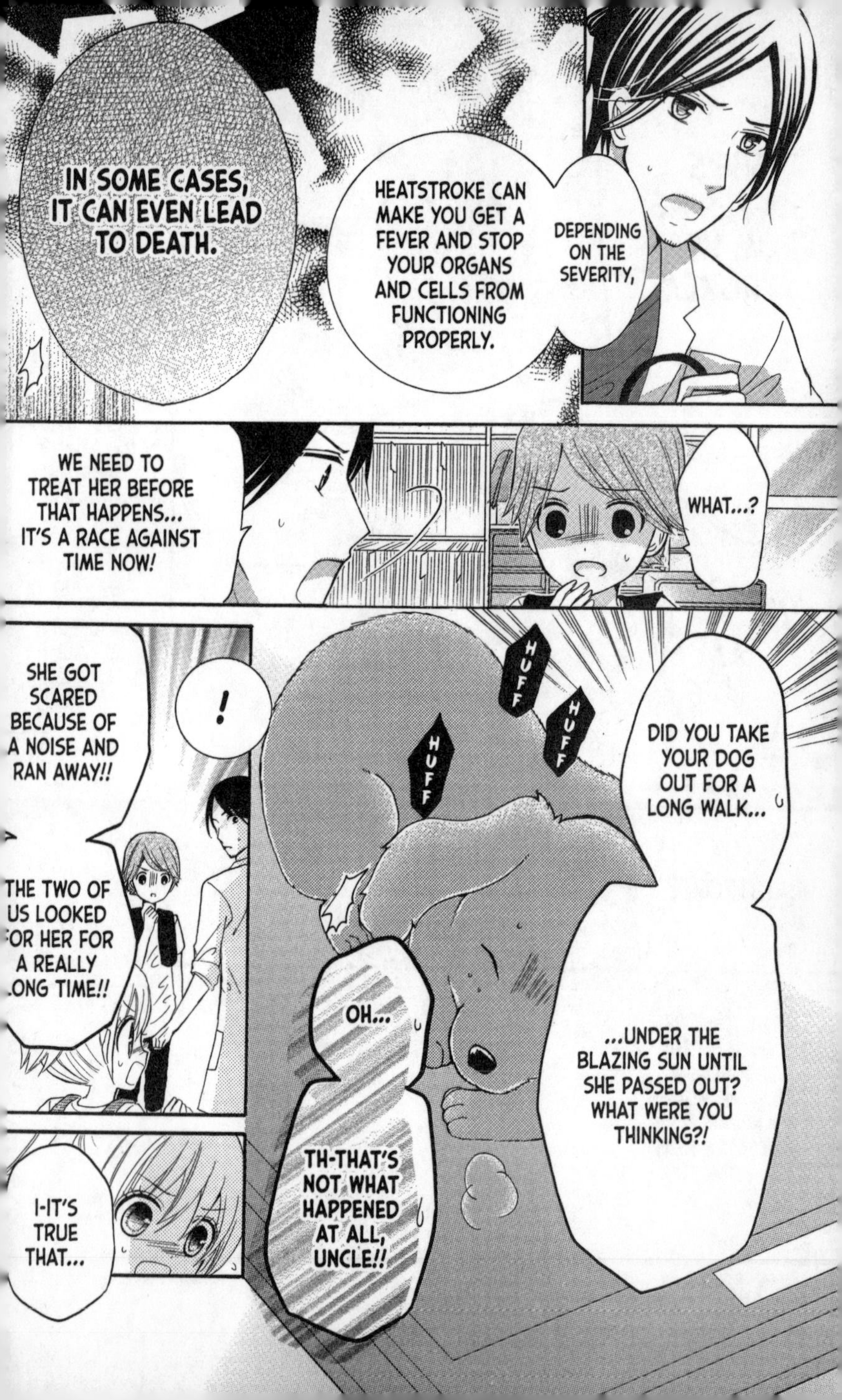
DEPENDING ON THE SEVERITY,
HEATSTROKE CAN MAKE YOU GET A FEVER AND STOP YOUR ORGANS AND CELLS FROM FUNCTIONING PROPERLY.
IN SOME CASES, IT CAN EVEN LEAD TO DEATH.
WHAT...?
WE NEED TO TREAT HER BEFORE THAT HAPPENS... IT'S A RACE AGAINST TIME NOW!
HUFF
HUFF
HUFF
DID YOU TAKE YOUR DOG OUT FOR A LONG WALK...
...UNDER THE BLAZING SUN UNTIL SHE PASSED OUT? WHAT WERE YOU THINKING?!
OH...
TH-THAT'S NOT WHAT HAPPENED AT ALL, UNCLE!!
!
SHE GOT SCARED BECAUSE OF A NOISE AND RAN AWAY!!
THE TWO OF US LOOKED FOR HER FOR A REALLY LONG TIME!!
I-IT'S TRUE THAT...

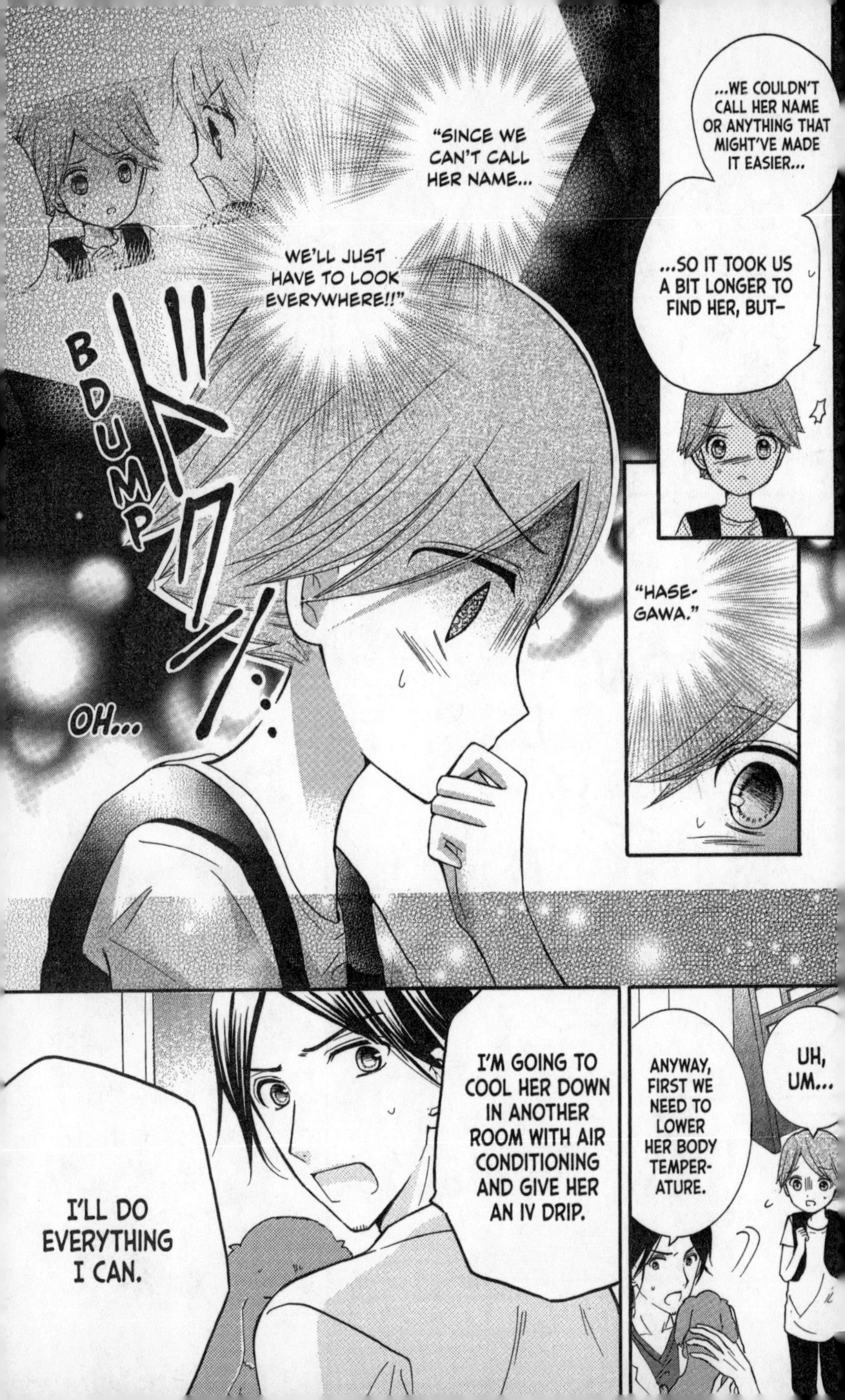
...WE COULDN'T CALL HER NAME OR ANYTHING THAT MIGHT'VE MADE IT EASIER...
...SO IT TOOK US A BIT LONGER TO FIND HER, BUT–
"HASE-GAWA."
"SINCE WE CAN'T CALL HER NAME...
WE'LL JUST HAVE TO LOOK EVERYWHERE!!"
BDUMP
OH...
UH, UM...
ANYWAY, FIRST WE NEED TO LOWER HER BODY TEMPER-ATURE.
I'M GOING TO COOL HER DOWN IN ANOTHER ROOM WITH AIR CONDITIONING AND GIVE HER AN IV DRIP.
I'LL DO EVERYTHING I CAN.

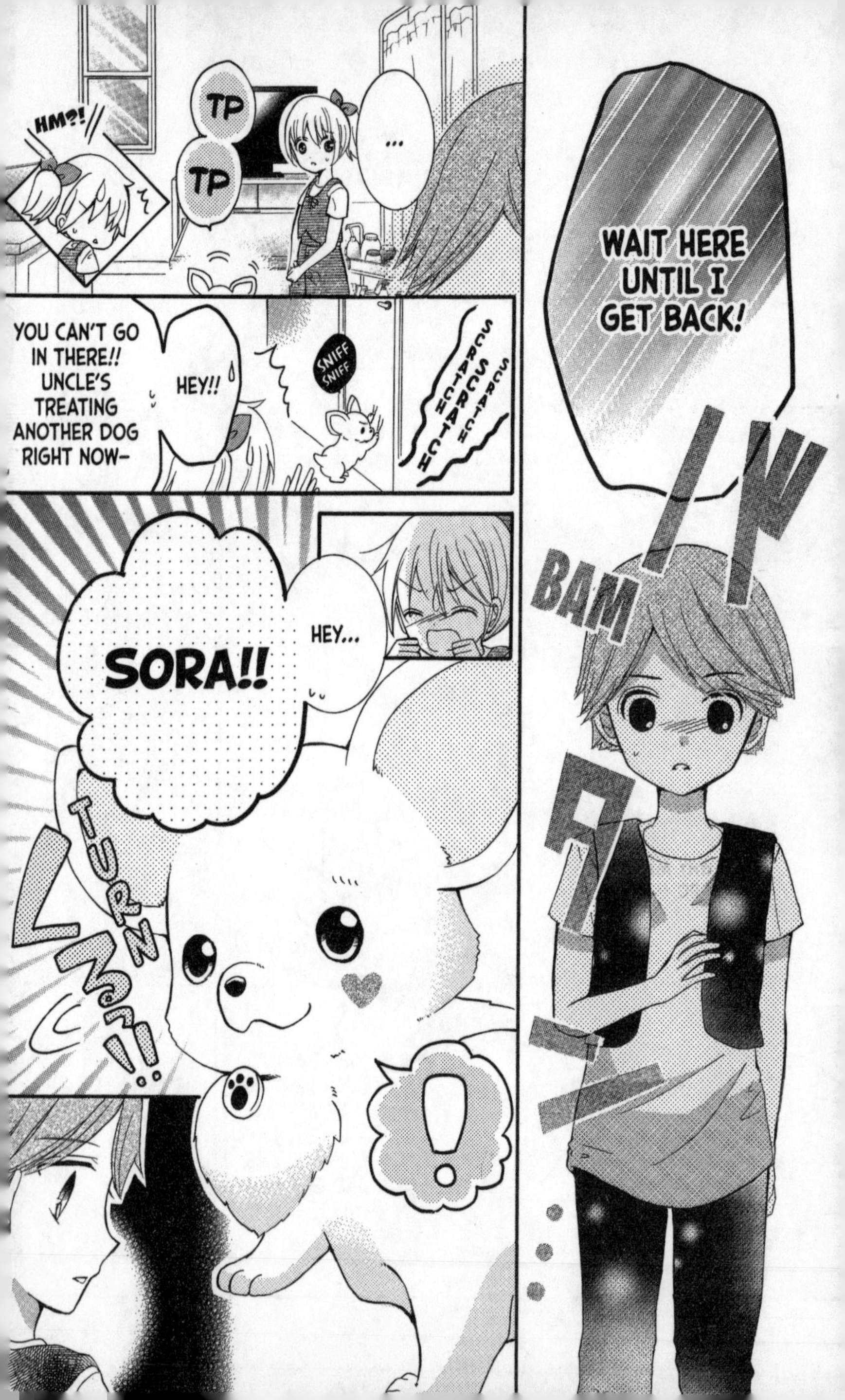
WAIT HERE UNTIL I GET BACK!
BAM
...
TP
TP
HM?!
SCRATCH SCRATCH SCRATCH
SNIFF SNIFF
HEY!!
YOU CAN'T GO IN THERE!! UNCLE'S TREATING ANOTHER DOG RIGHT NOW–
HEY...
SORA!!
TURN!!
!

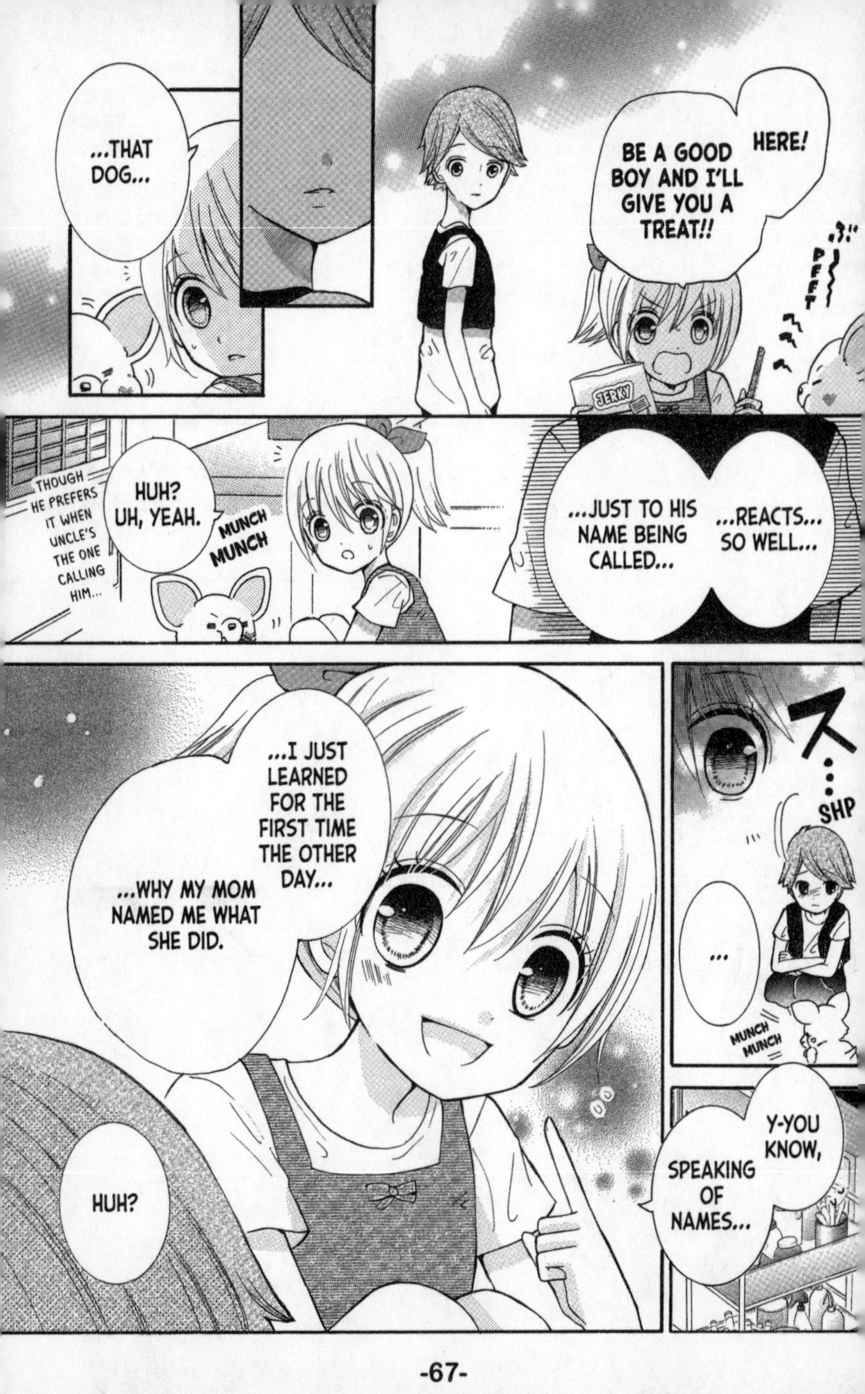
HERE!
BE A GOOD BOY AND I'LL GIVE YOU A TREAT!!
PFFT
JERKY
...THAT DOG...
...REACTS... SO WELL...
...JUST TO HIS NAME BEING CALLED...
HUH? UH, YEAH.
MUNCH MUNCH
THOUGH HE PREFERS IT WHEN UNCLE'S THE ONE CALLING HIM...
ス... SHP
...
MUNCH MUNCH
Y-YOU KNOW,
SPEAKING OF NAMES...
...I JUST LEARNED FOR THE FIRST TIME THE OTHER DAY...
...WHY MY MOM NAMED ME WHAT SHE DID.
HUH?

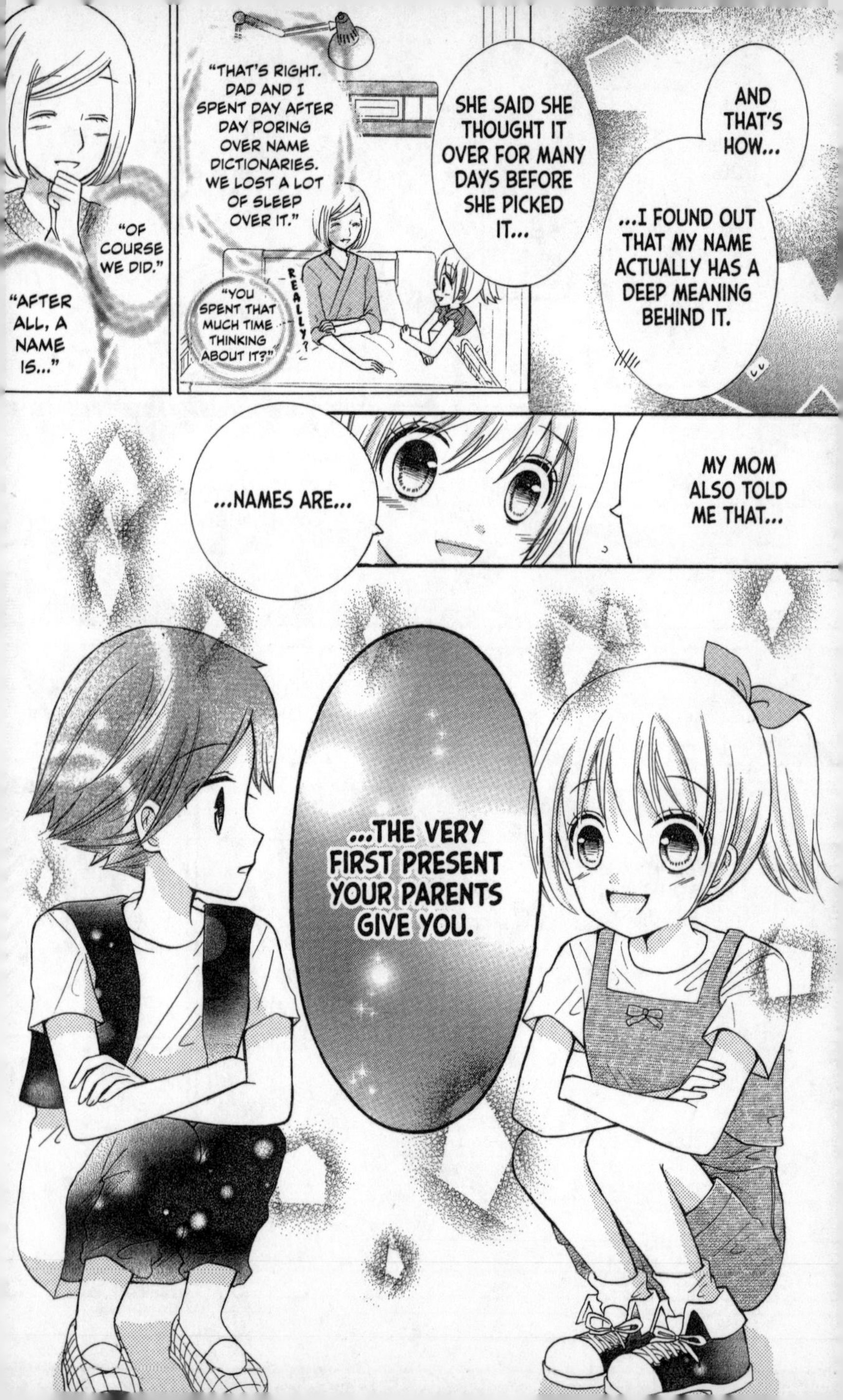
AND THAT'S HOW...
...I FOUND OUT THAT MY NAME ACTUALLY HAS A DEEP MEANING BEHIND IT.
SHE SAID SHE THOUGHT IT OVER FOR MANY DAYS BEFORE SHE PICKED IT...
"THAT'S RIGHT. DAD AND I SPENT DAY AFTER DAY PORING OVER NAME DICTIONARIES. WE LOST A LOT OF SLEEP OVER IT."
REALLY?
"YOU SPENT THAT MUCH TIME THINKING ABOUT IT?"
"OF COURSE WE DID."
"AFTER ALL, A NAME IS..."
MY MOM ALSO TOLD ME THAT...
...NAMES ARE...
...THE VERY FIRST PRESENT YOUR PARENTS GIVE YOU.

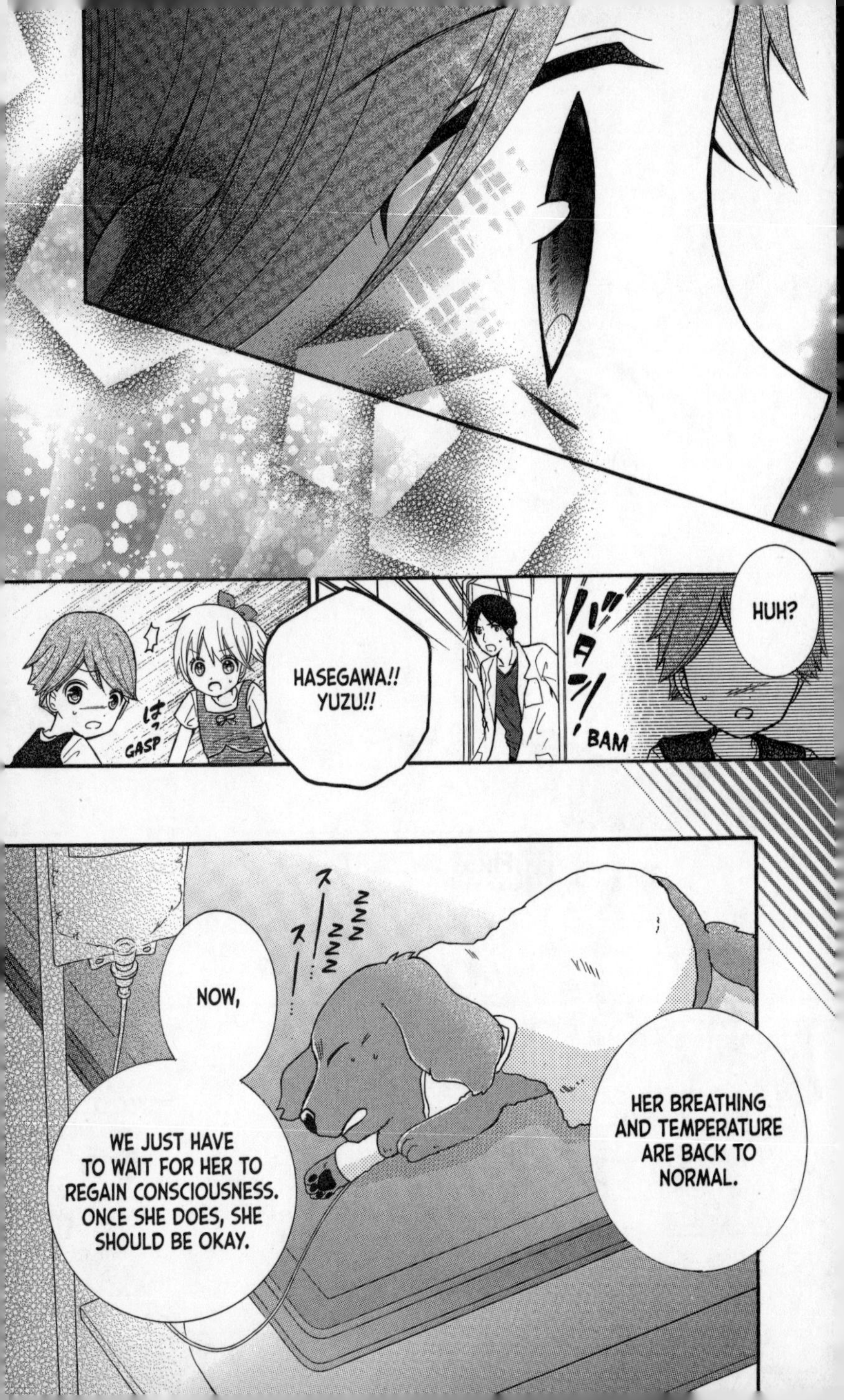
HUH?
バタン!
BAM
HASEGAWA!! YUZU!!
はっ
GASP
HER BREATHING AND TEMPERATURE ARE BACK TO NORMAL.
ZZZ ZZZ ZZZ
NOW,
WE JUST HAVE TO WAIT FOR HER TO REGAIN CONSCIOUSNESS. ONCE SHE DOES, SHE SHOULD BE OKAY.

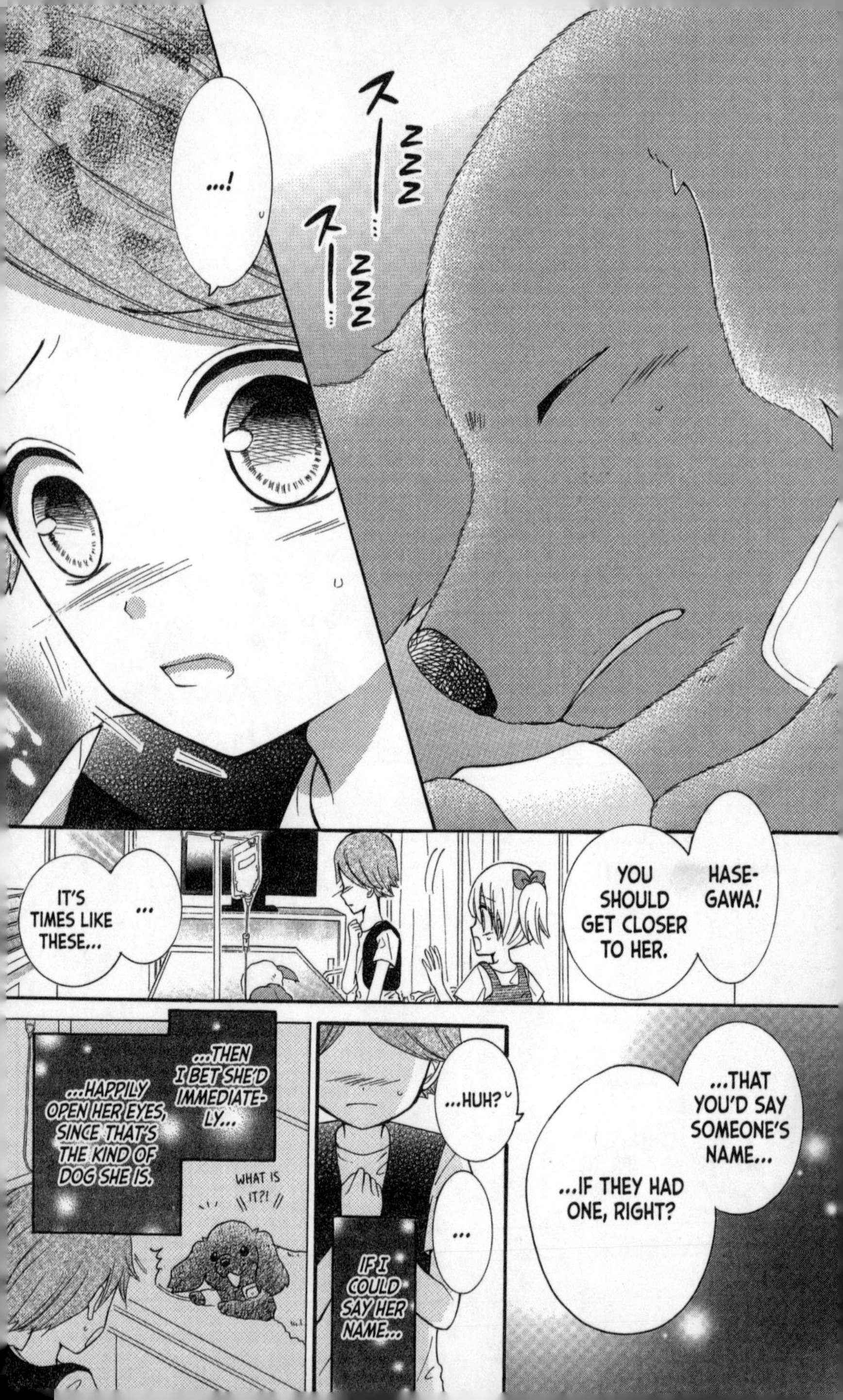
スー…スー…
ZZZ ZZZ
...!
HASE-GAWA!
YOU SHOULD GET CLOSER TO HER.
...
IT'S TIMES LIKE THESE...
...THAT YOU'D SAY SOMEONE'S NAME...
...IF THEY HAD ONE, RIGHT?
...HUH?
...
IF I COULD SAY HER NAME...
...THEN I BET SHE'D IMMEDIATE-LY...
...HAPPILY OPEN HER EYES, SINCE THAT'S THE KIND OF DOG SHE IS.
WHAT IS IT?!

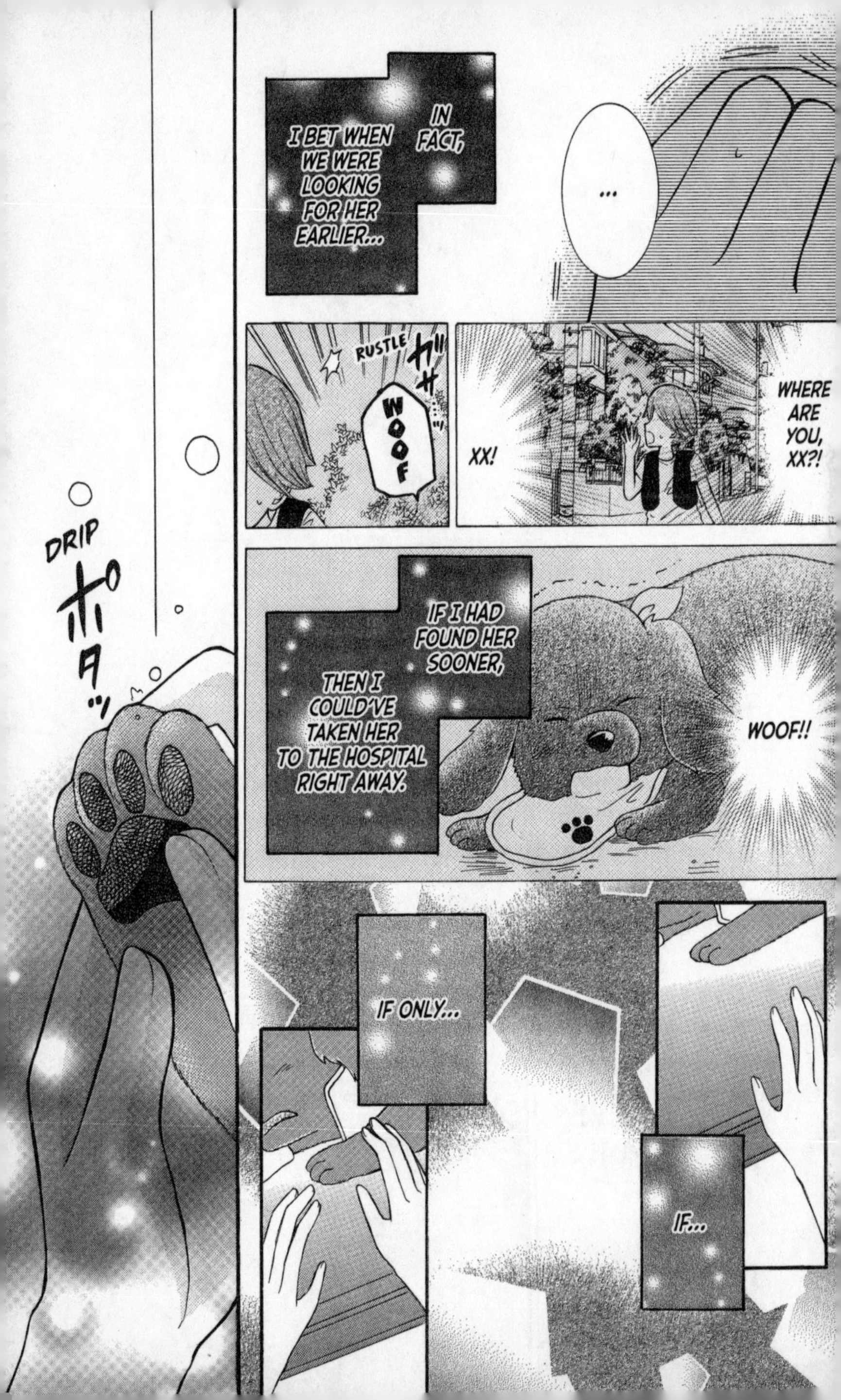
...
IN FACT,
I BET WHEN WE WERE LOOKING FOR HER EARLIER...
WHERE ARE YOU, XX?!
XX!
RUSTLE
WOOF
WOOF!!
IF I HAD FOUND HER SOONER,
THEN I COULD'VE TAKEN HER TO THE HOSPITAL RIGHT AWAY.
IF...
IF ONLY...
DRIP
ポタッ

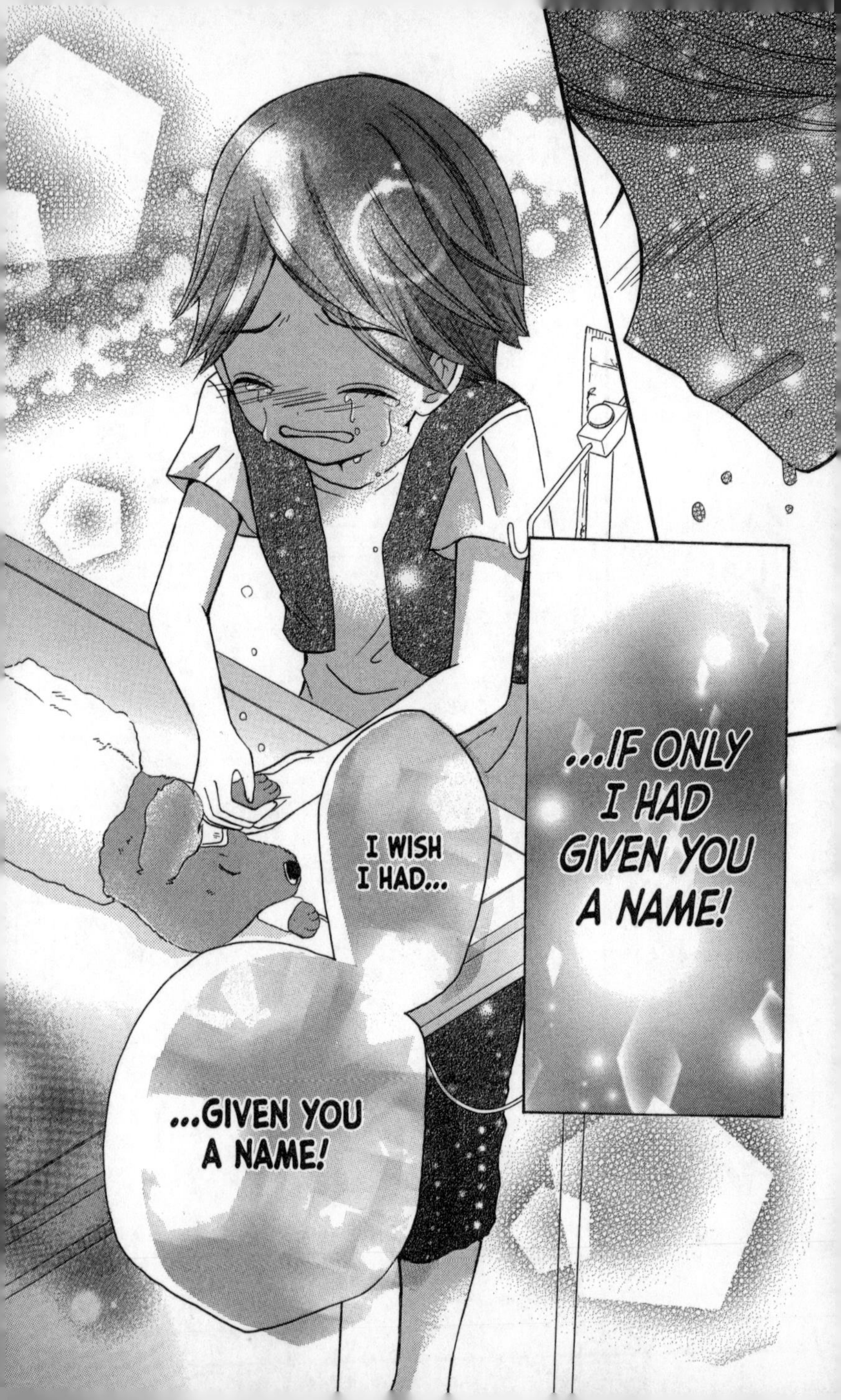
...IF ONLY I HAD GIVEN YOU A NAME!
I WISH I HAD...
...GIVEN YOU A NAME!

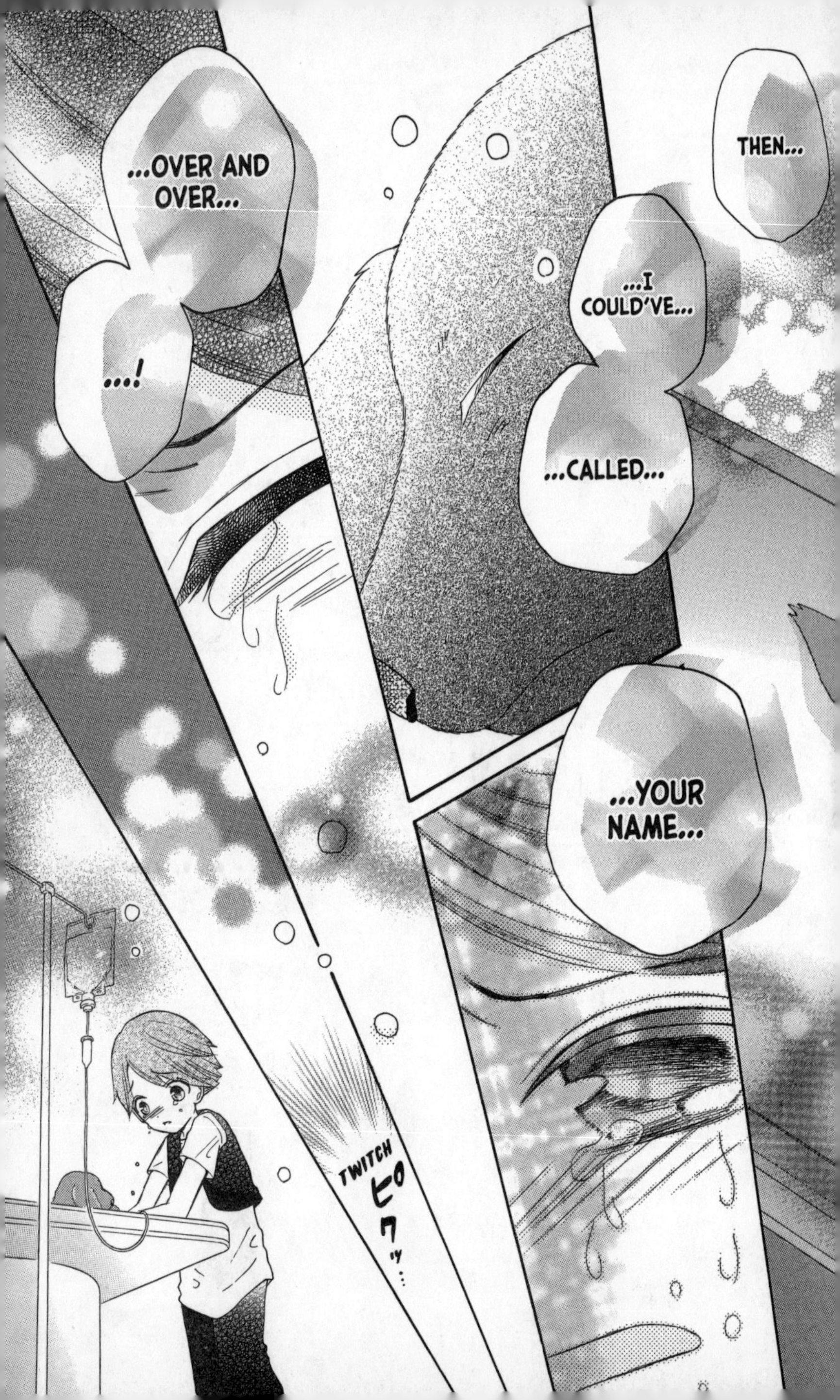
THEN...
...I COULD'VE...
...CALLED...
...YOUR NAME...
...OVER AND OVER...
...!
TWITCH
ピクッ...

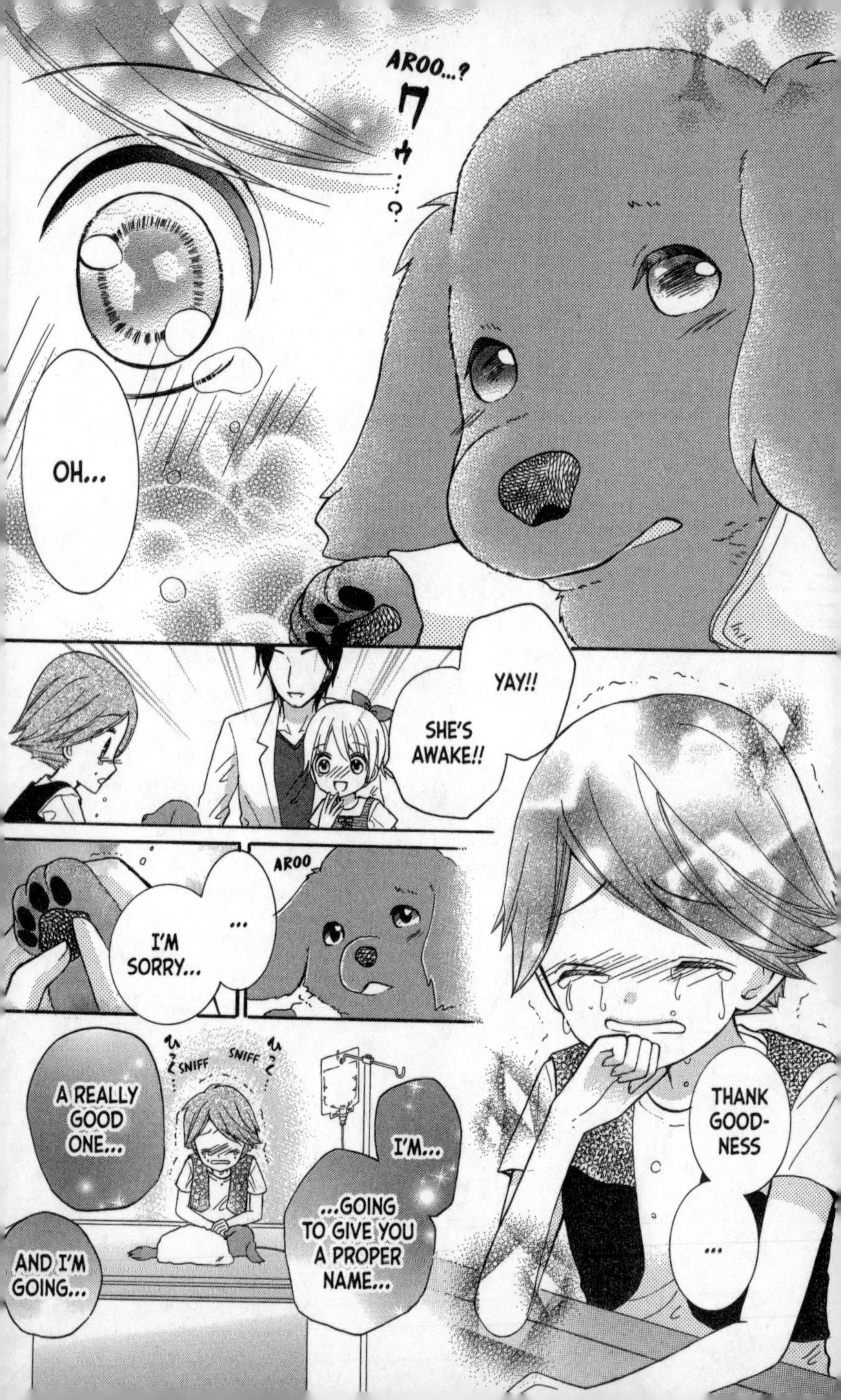
AROO...?
ワゥ…？
OH...
YAY!!
SHE'S AWAKE!!
THANK GOODNESS
...
...
I'M SORRY...
AROO
SNIFF
SNIFF
I'M...
...GOING TO GIVE YOU A PROPER NAME...
A REALLY GOOD ONE...
AND I'M GOING...

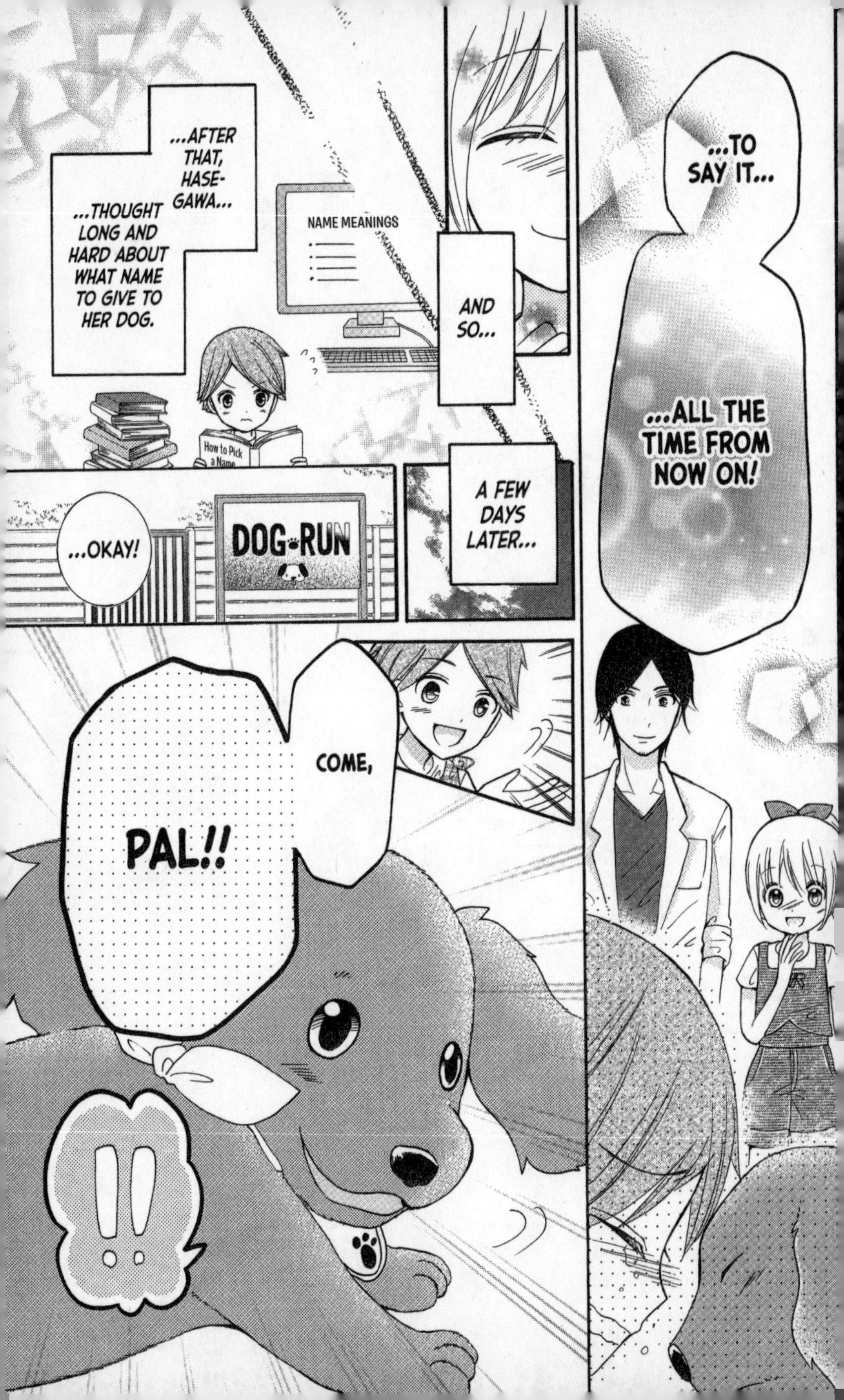
...TO SAY IT...
...ALL THE TIME FROM NOW ON!
AND SO...
...AFTER THAT, HASE-GAWA...
...THOUGHT LONG AND HARD ABOUT WHAT NAME TO GIVE TO HER DOG.
NAME MEANINGS
How to Pick a Name
A FEW DAYS LATER...
DOG·RUN
...OKAY!
COME,
PAL!!
!!

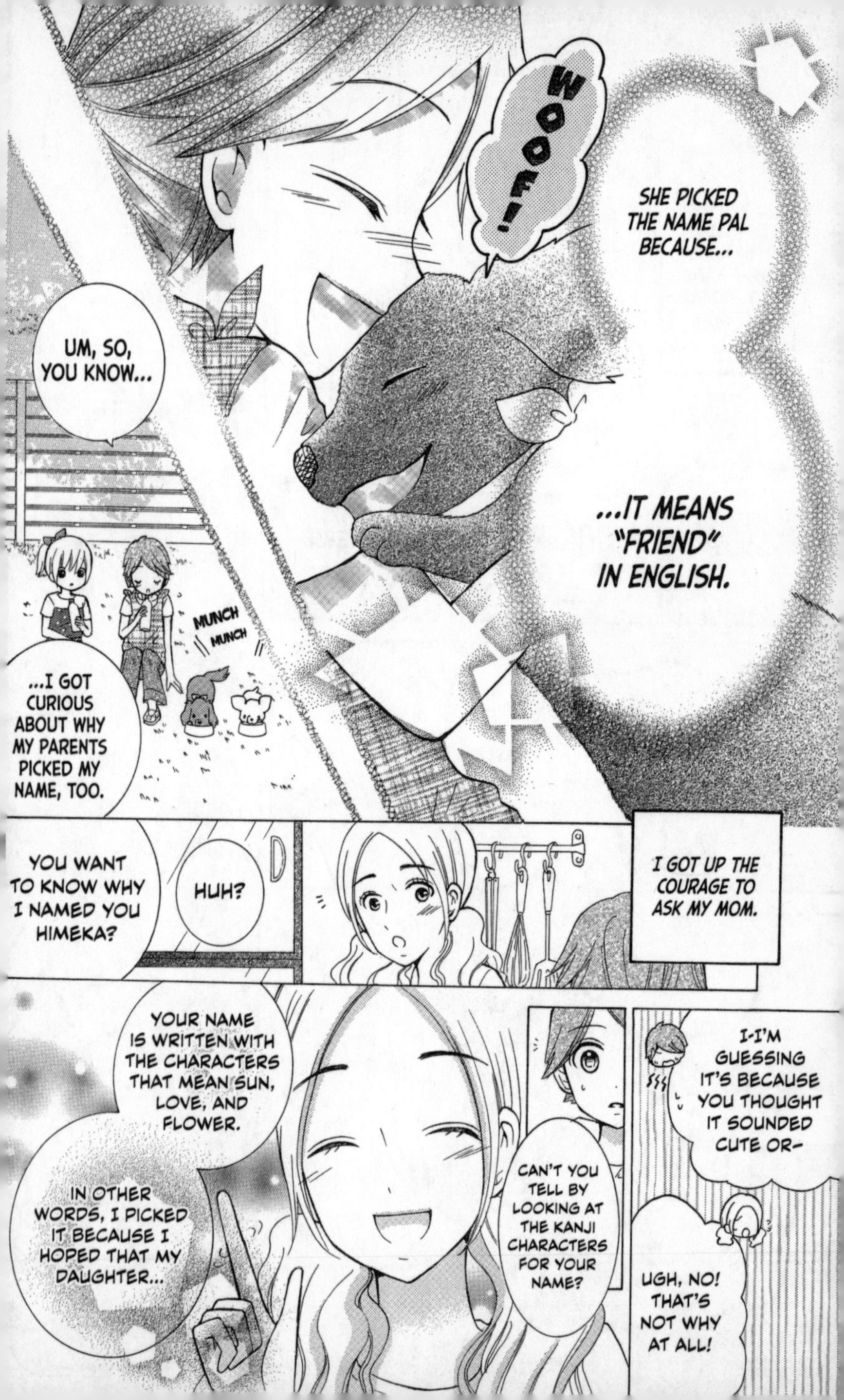

SHE PICKED THE NAME PAL BECAUSE...
WOOF!
...IT MEANS "FRIEND" IN ENGLISH.
UM, SO, YOU KNOW...
MUNCH MUNCH
...I GOT CURIOUS ABOUT WHY MY PARENTS PICKED MY NAME, TOO.
I GOT UP THE COURAGE TO ASK MY MOM.
HUH?
YOU WANT TO KNOW WHY I NAMED YOU HIMEKA?
I-I'M GUESSING IT'S BECAUSE YOU THOUGHT IT SOUNDED CUTE OR-
UGH, NO! THAT'S NOT WHY AT ALL!
CAN'T YOU TELL BY LOOKING AT THE KANJI CHARACTERS FOR YOUR NAME?
YOUR NAME IS WRITTEN WITH THE CHARACTERS THAT MEAN SUN, LOVE, AND FLOWER.
IN OTHER WORDS, I PICKED IT BECAUSE I HOPED THAT MY DAUGHTER...

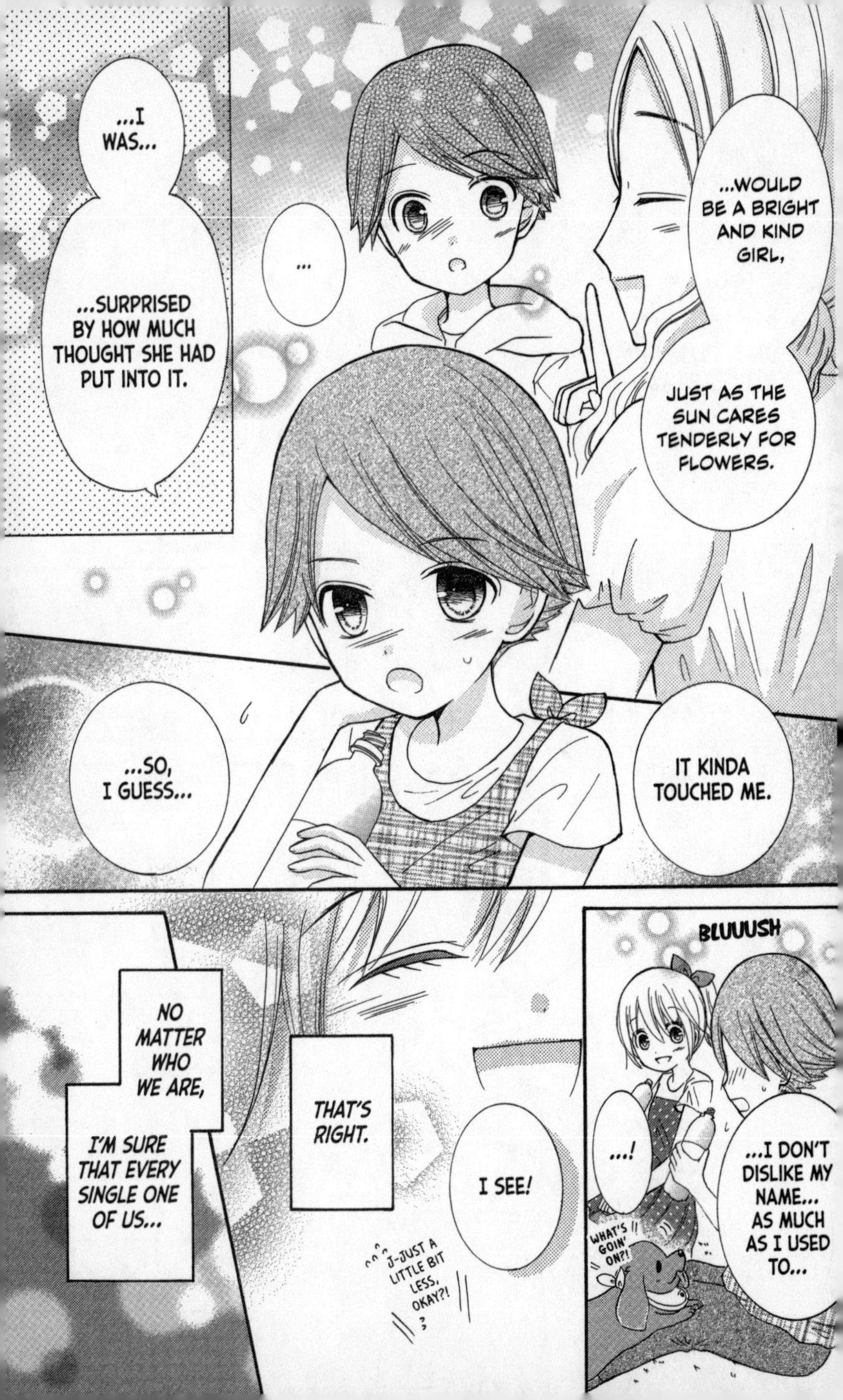
...WOULD BE A BRIGHT AND KIND GIRL,
JUST AS THE SUN CARES TENDERLY FOR FLOWERS.
...
...I WAS...
...SURPRISED BY HOW MUCH THOUGHT SHE HAD PUT INTO IT.
IT KINDA TOUCHED ME.
...SO, I GUESS...
BLUUUSH
...I DON'T DISLIKE MY NAME... AS MUCH AS I USED TO...
...!
WHAT'S GOIN' ON?!
I SEE!
J-JUST A LITTLE BIT LESS, OKAY?!
THAT'S RIGHT.
NO MATTER WHO WE ARE,
I'M SURE THAT EVERY SINGLE ONE OF US...

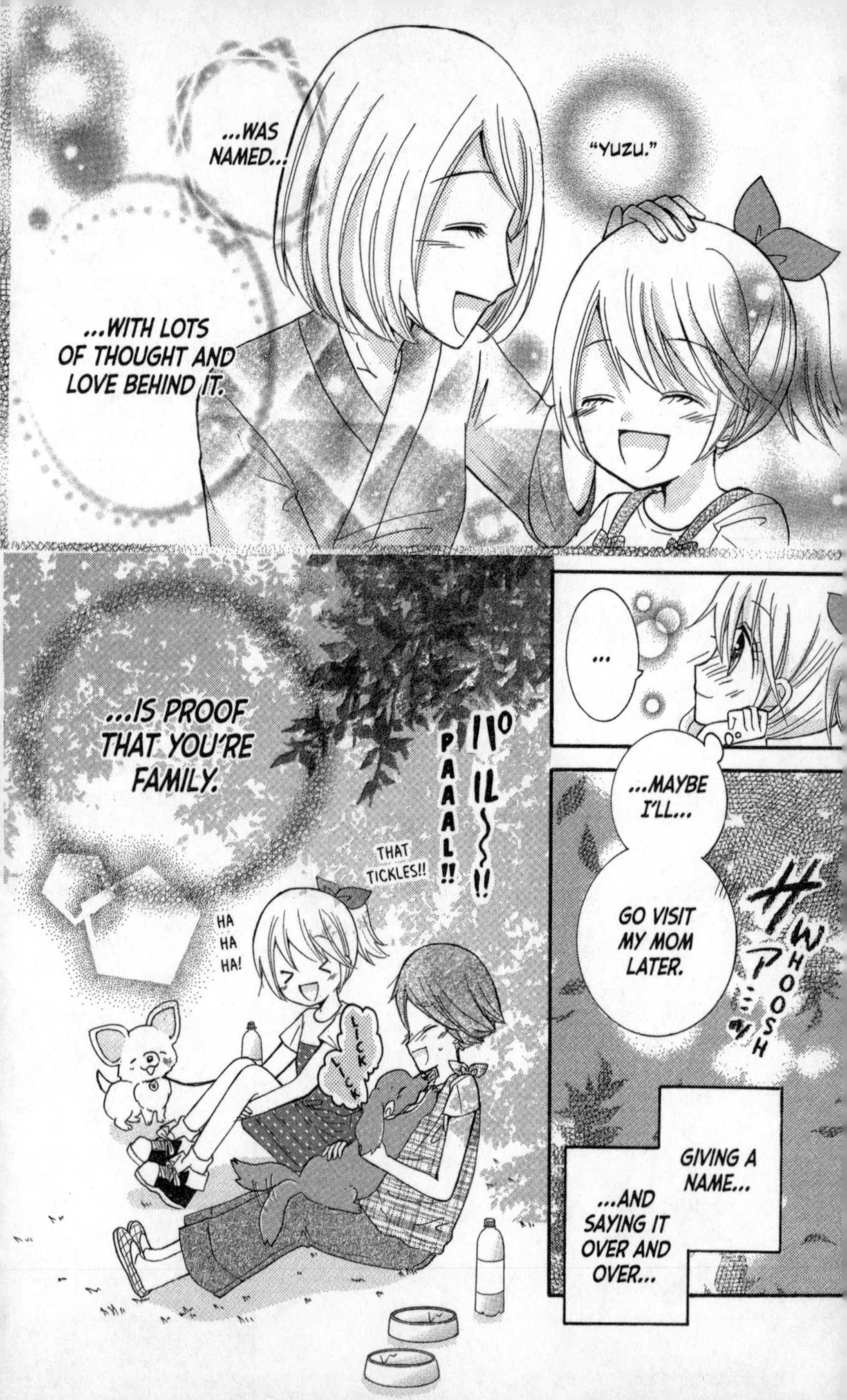
"YUZU."
...WAS NAMED...
...WITH LOTS OF THOUGHT AND LOVE BEHIND IT.
...
...MAYBE I'LL...
GO VISIT MY MOM LATER.
HWP
WHOOSH
GIVING A NAME...
...AND SAYING IT OVER AND OVER...
...IS PROOF THAT YOU'RE FAMILY.
IL~~!!
PAAAL!!
THAT TICKLES!!
HA HA HA!
LICK LICK

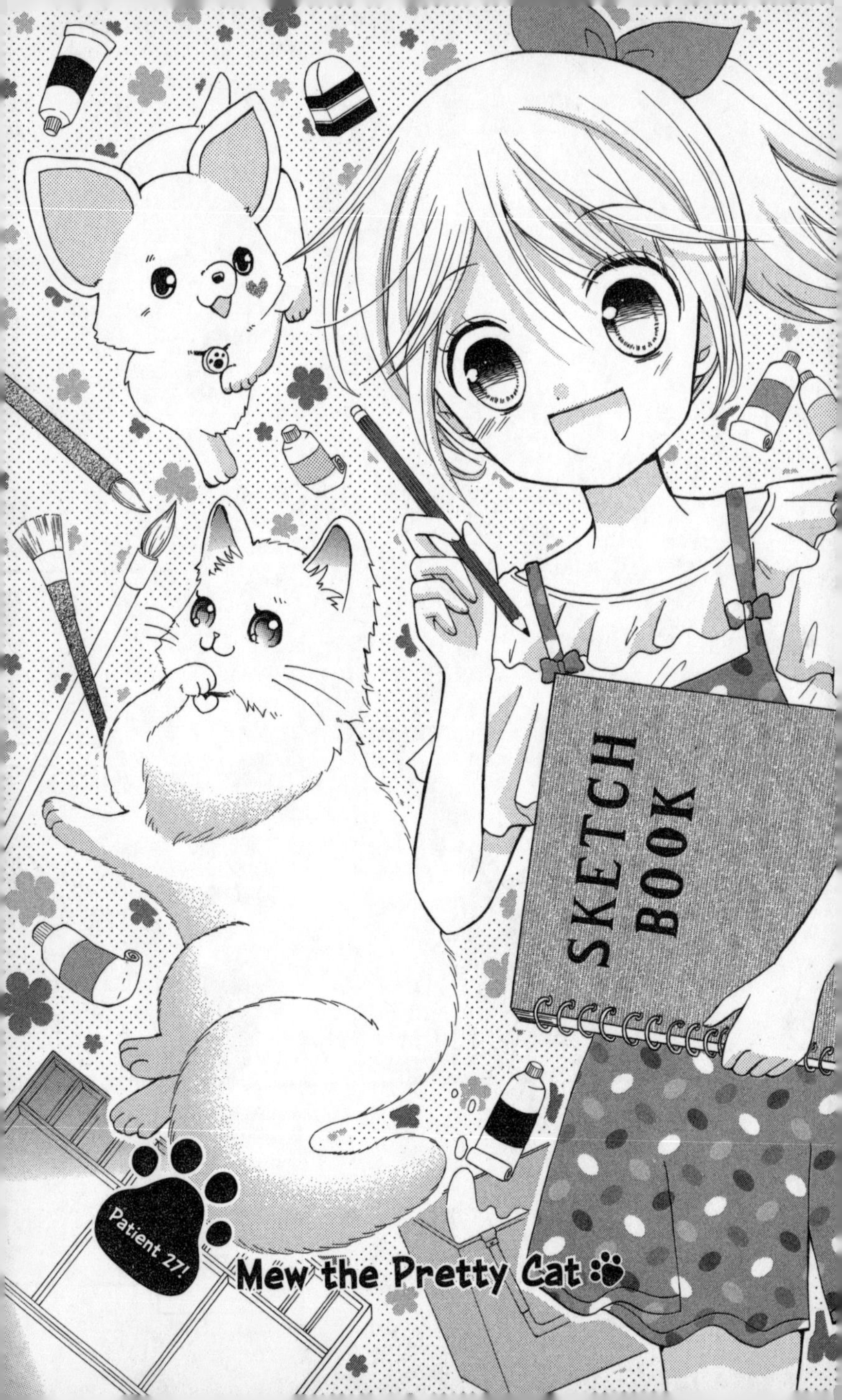
SKETCH BOOK
Patient 27!
Mew the Pretty Cat

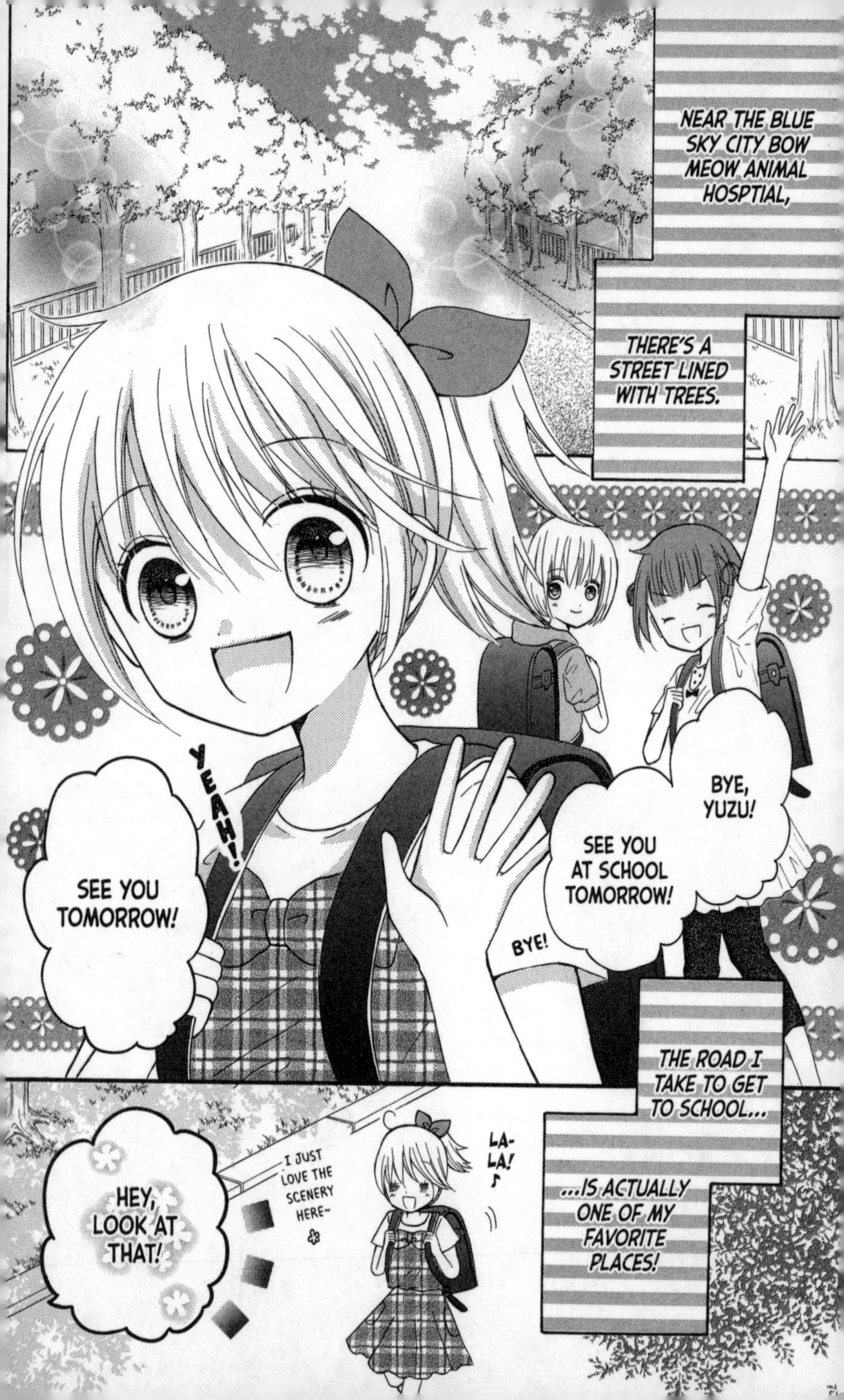
NEAR THE BLUE SKY CITY BOW MEOW ANIMAL HOSPTIAL,
THERE'S A STREET LINED WITH TREES.
BYE, YUZU!
SEE YOU AT SCHOOL TOMORROW!
BYE!
YEAH!
SEE YOU TOMORROW!
THE ROAD I TAKE TO GET TO SCHOOL...
...IS ACTUALLY ONE OF MY FAVORITE PLACES!
LA-LA! ♪
I JUST LOVE THE SCENERY HERE~
HEY, LOOK AT THAT!

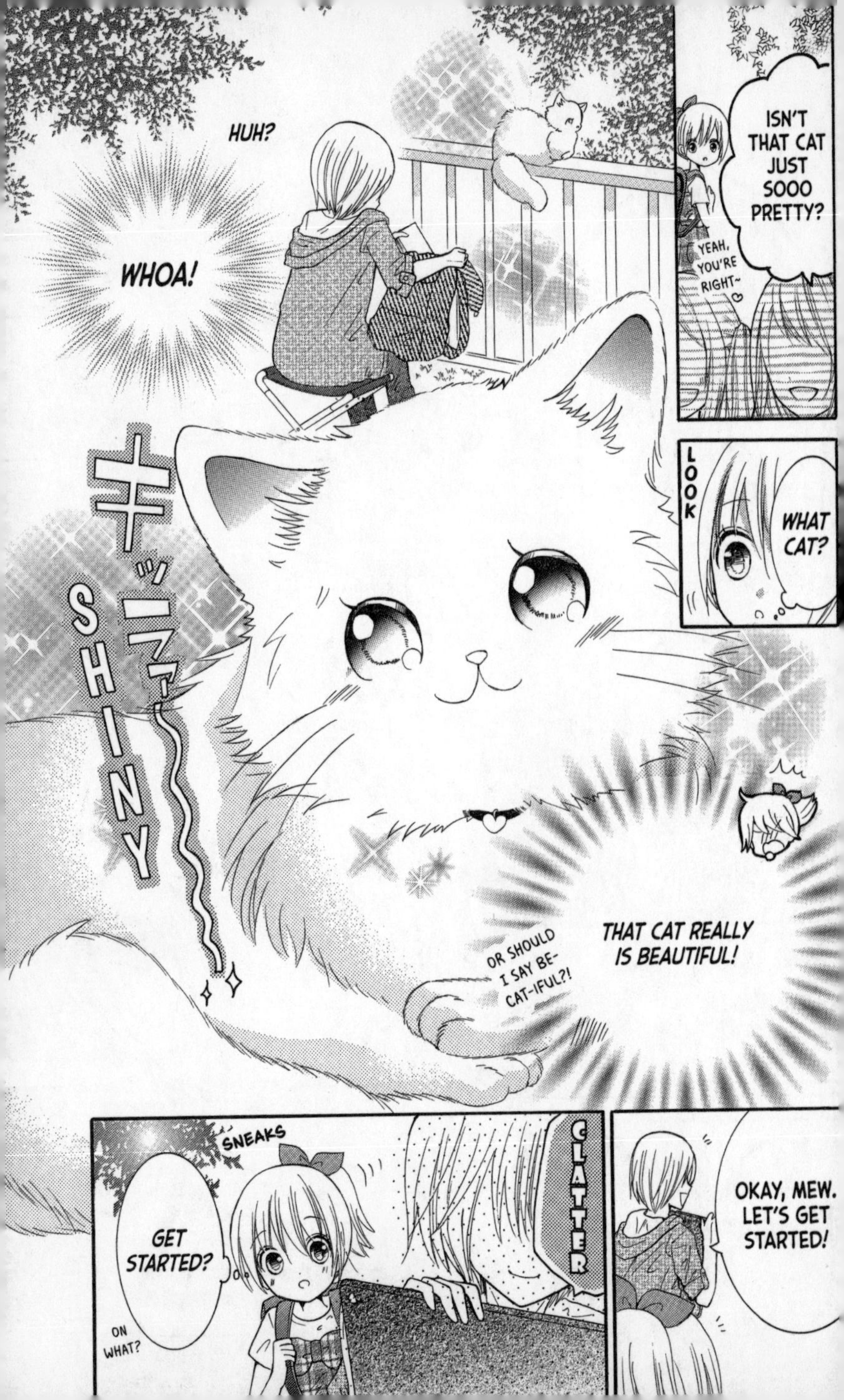

ISN'T THAT CAT JUST SOOO PRETTY?
YEAH, YOU'RE RIGHT~
LOOK
WHAT CAT?
HUH?
WHOA!
SHINY
THAT CAT REALLY IS BEAUTIFUL!
OR SHOULD I SAY BE-CAT-IFUL?!
OKAY, MEW. LET'S GET STARTED!
CLATTER
SNEAKS
GET STARTED?
ON WHAT?

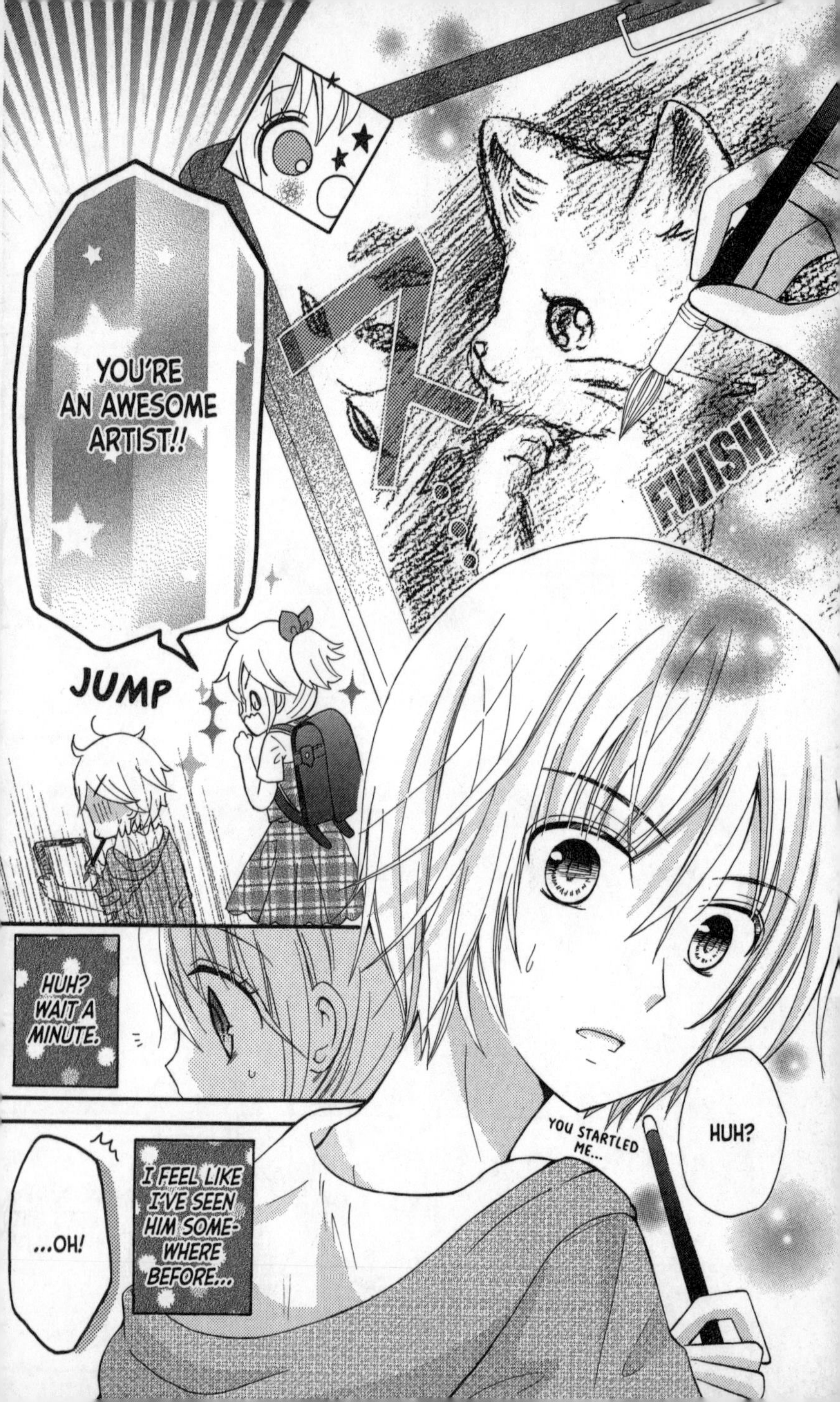
FINISH
YOU'RE AN AWESOME ARTIST!!
JUMP
HUH?
YOU STARTLED ME...
HUH? WAIT A MINUTE.
I FEEL LIKE I'VE SEEN HIM SOME-WHERE BEFORE...
...OH!

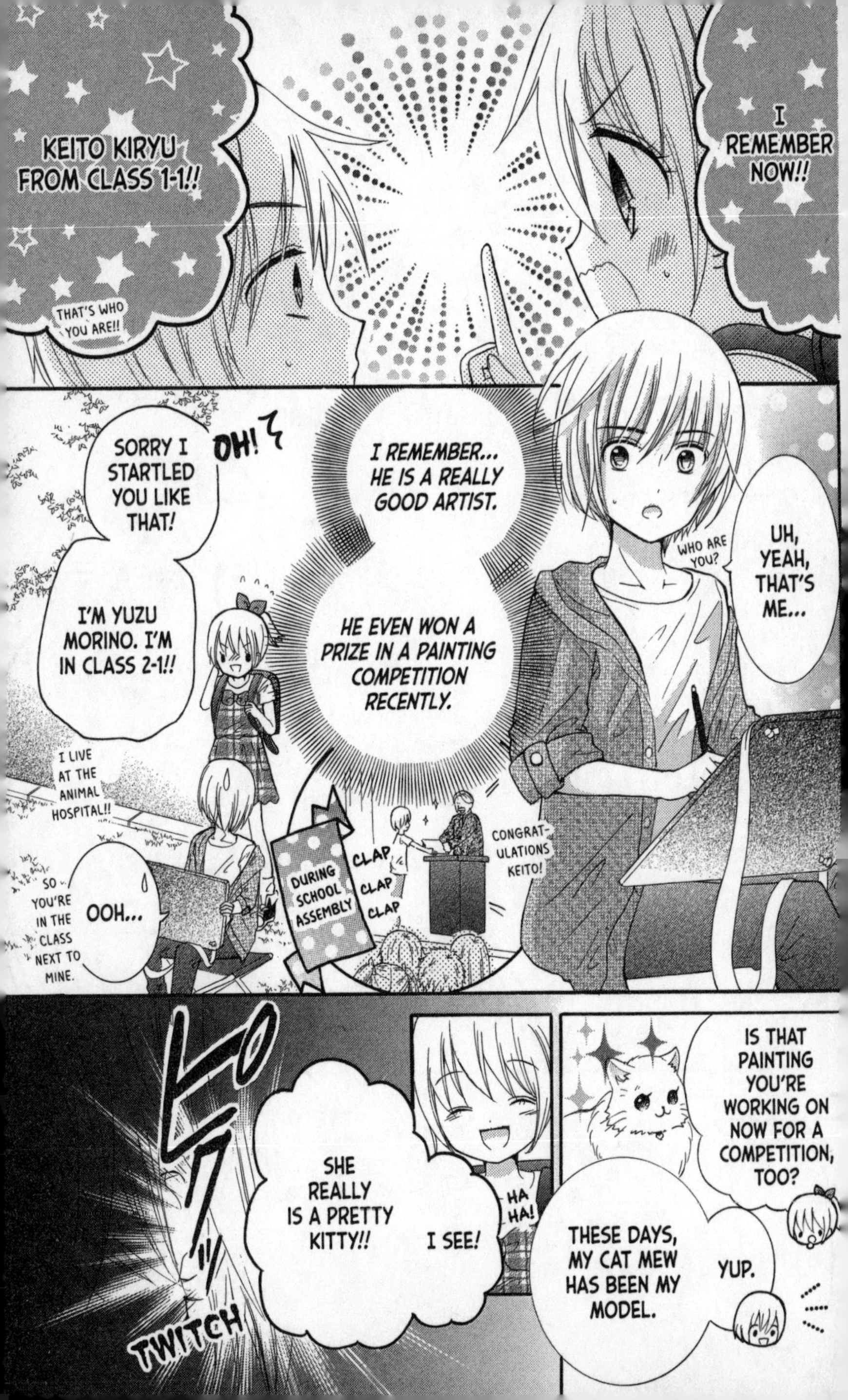
I REMEMBER NOW!!
KEITO KIRYU FROM CLASS 1-1!!
THAT'S WHO YOU ARE!!
UH, YEAH, THAT'S ME...
WHO ARE YOU?
I REMEMBER... HE IS A REALLY GOOD ARTIST.
HE EVEN WON A PRIZE IN A PAINTING COMPETITION RECENTLY.
CONGRAT-ULATIONS KEITO!
CLAP
CLAP
CLAP
DURING SCHOOL ASSEMBLY
OH!
SORRY I STARTLED YOU LIKE THAT!
I'M YUZU MORINO. I'M IN CLASS 2-1!!
I LIVE AT THE ANIMAL HOSPITAL!!
OOH...
SO YOU'RE IN THE CLASS NEXT TO MINE.
IS THAT PAINTING YOU'RE WORKING ON NOW FOR A COMPETITION, TOO?
YUP.
THESE DAYS, MY CAT MEW HAS BEEN MY MODEL.
HA HA!
I SEE!
SHE REALLY IS A PRETTY KITTY!!
TWITCH

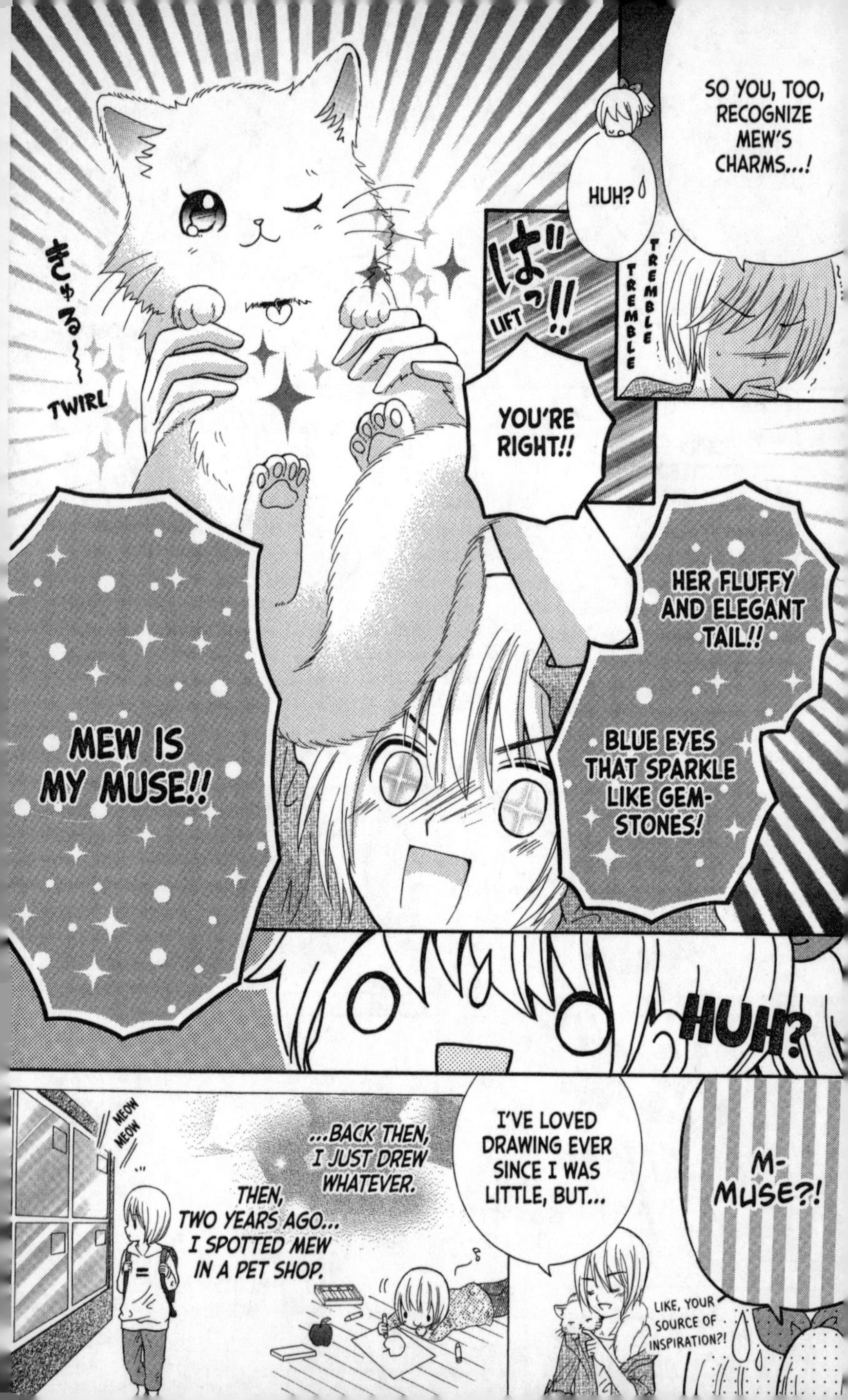
SO YOU, TOO, RECOGNIZE MEW'S CHARMS...!
HUH?
TREMBLE TREMBLE
ばっ!!
LIFT
YOU'RE RIGHT!!
HER FLUFFY AND ELEGANT TAIL!!
BLUE EYES THAT SPARKLE LIKE GEM-STONES!
MEW IS MY MUSE!!
きゅる~
TWIRL
HUH?
M-MUSE?!
LIKE, YOUR SOURCE OF INSPIRATION?!
I'VE LOVED DRAWING EVER SINCE I WAS LITTLE, BUT...
...BACK THEN, I JUST DREW WHATEVER.
THEN, TWO YEARS AGO... I SPOTTED MEW IN A PET SHOP.
MEOW MEOW

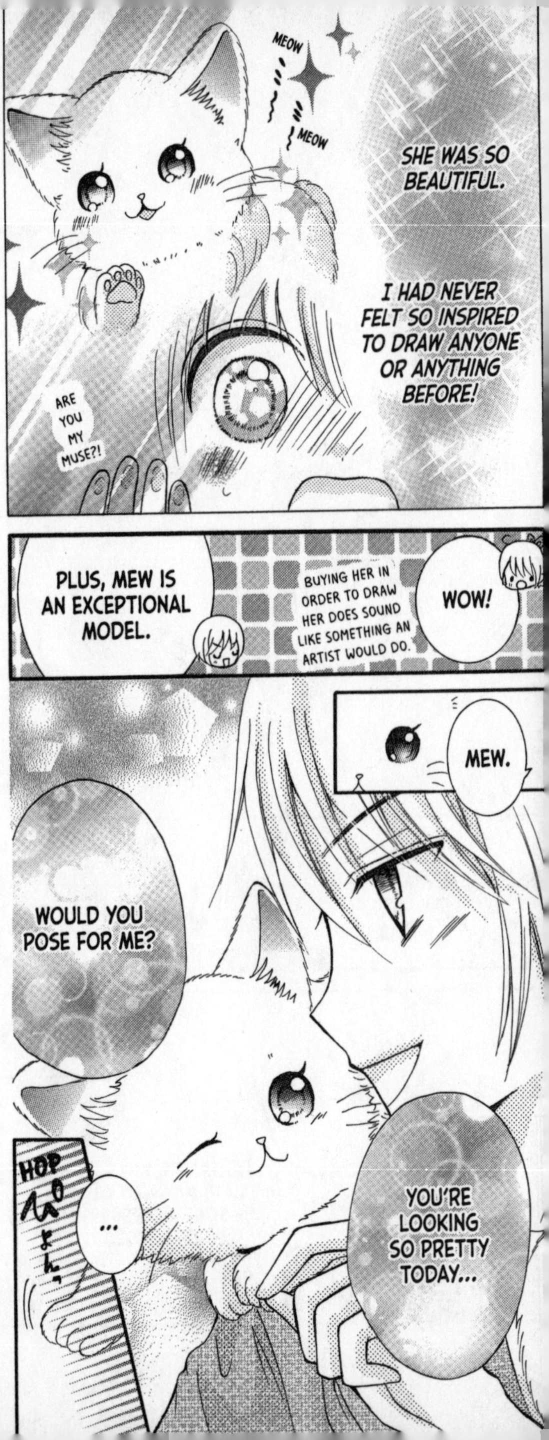
SHE WAS SO BEAUTIFUL.
I HAD NEVER FELT SO INSPIRED TO DRAW ANYONE OR ANYTHING BEFORE!
MEOW
MEOW
ARE YOU MY MUSE?!
WOW!
BUYING HER IN ORDER TO DRAW HER DOES SOUND LIKE SOMETHING AN ARTIST WOULD DO.
PLUS, MEW IS AN EXCEPTIONAL MODEL.
MEW.
YOU'RE LOOKING SO PRETTY TODAY...
WOULD YOU POSE FOR ME?
...
HOP

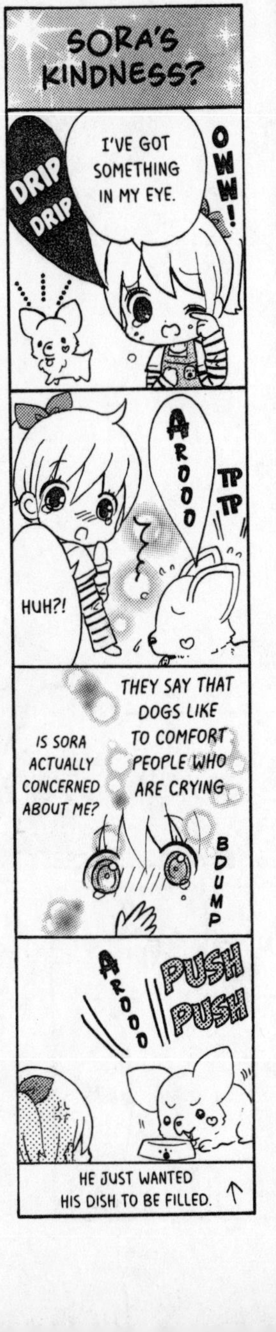
SORA'S KINDNESS?
OWW!
I'VE GOT SOMETHING IN MY EYE.
DRIP DRIP
AROOO
TP TP
HUH?!
THEY SAY THAT DOGS LIKE TO COMFORT PEOPLE WHO ARE CRYING.
IS SORA ACTUALLY CONCERNED ABOUT ME?
BDUMP
PUSH PUSH
AROOO
HE JUST WANTED HIS DISH TO BE FILLED.

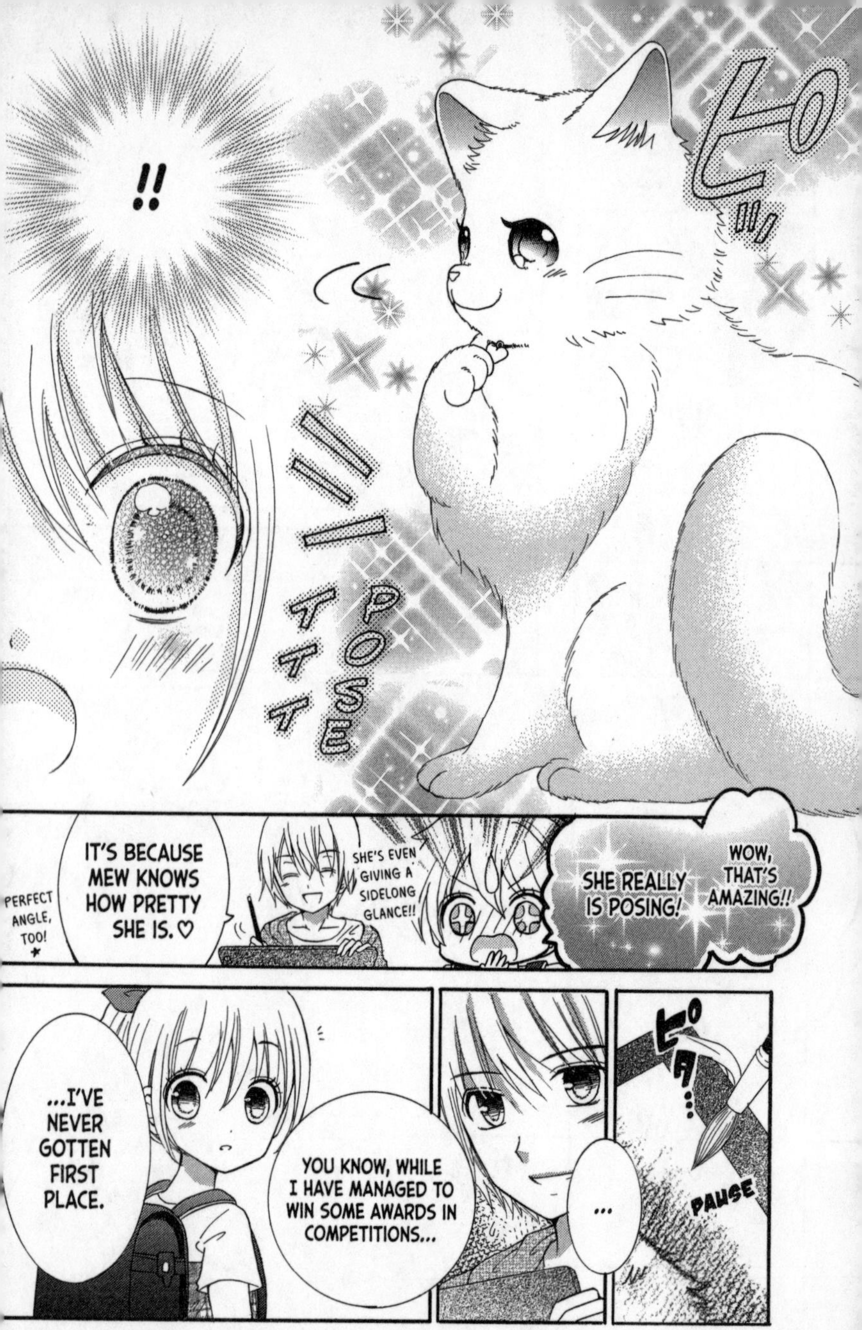
!!
POSE
WOW, THAT'S AMAZING!!
SHE REALLY IS POSING!
SHE'S EVEN GIVING A SIDELONG GLANCE!!
IT'S BECAUSE MEW KNOWS HOW PRETTY SHE IS. ♡
PERFECT ANGLE, TOO! ★
PAUSE
...
YOU KNOW, WHILE I HAVE MANAGED TO WIN SOME AWARDS IN COMPETITIONS...
...I'VE NEVER GOTTEN FIRST PLACE.

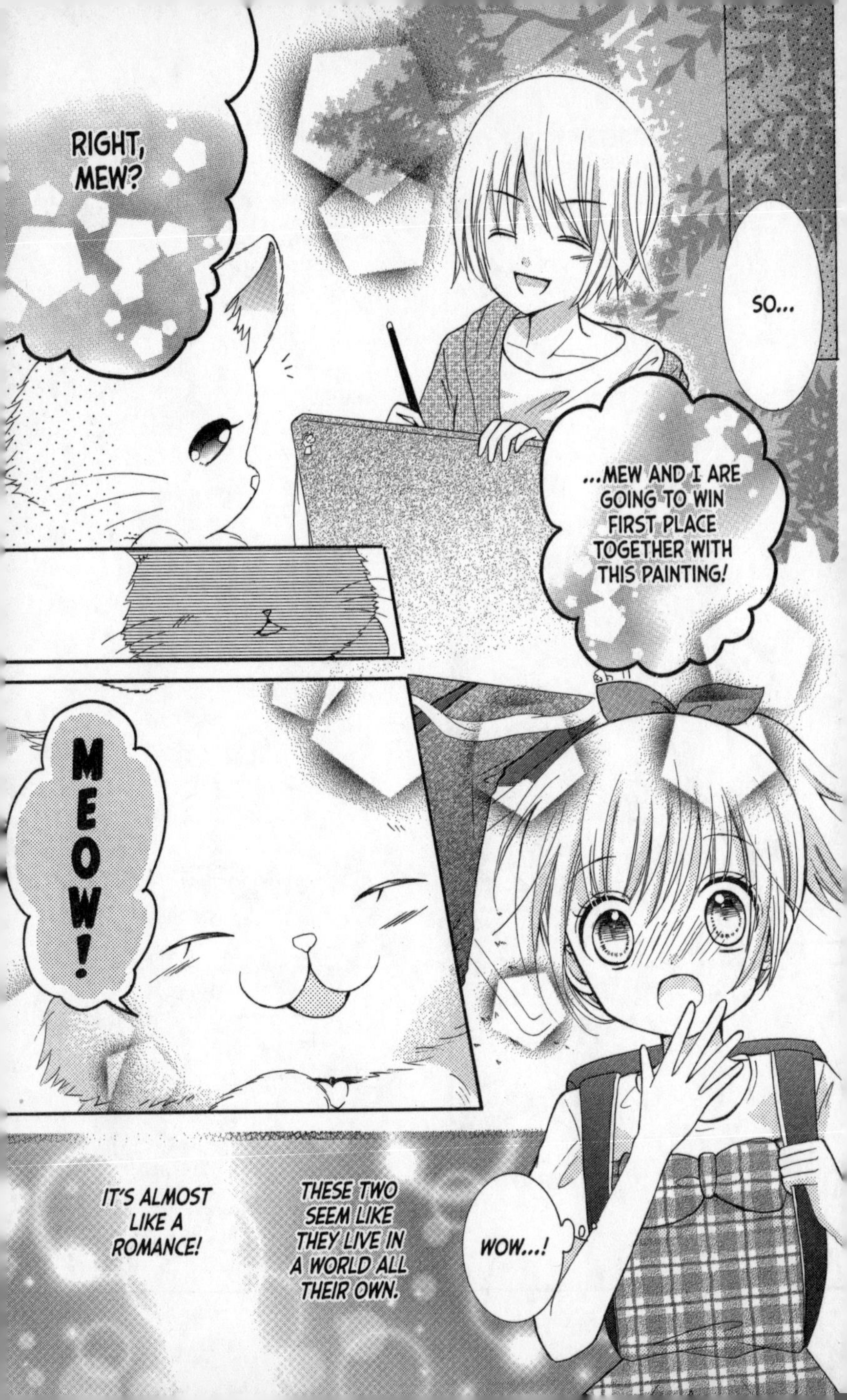
SO...
...MEW AND I ARE GOING TO WIN FIRST PLACE TOGETHER WITH THIS PAINTING!
RIGHT, MEW?
MEOW!
WOW...!
THESE TWO SEEM LIKE THEY LIVE IN A WORLD ALL THEIR OWN.
IT'S ALMOST LIKE A ROMANCE!

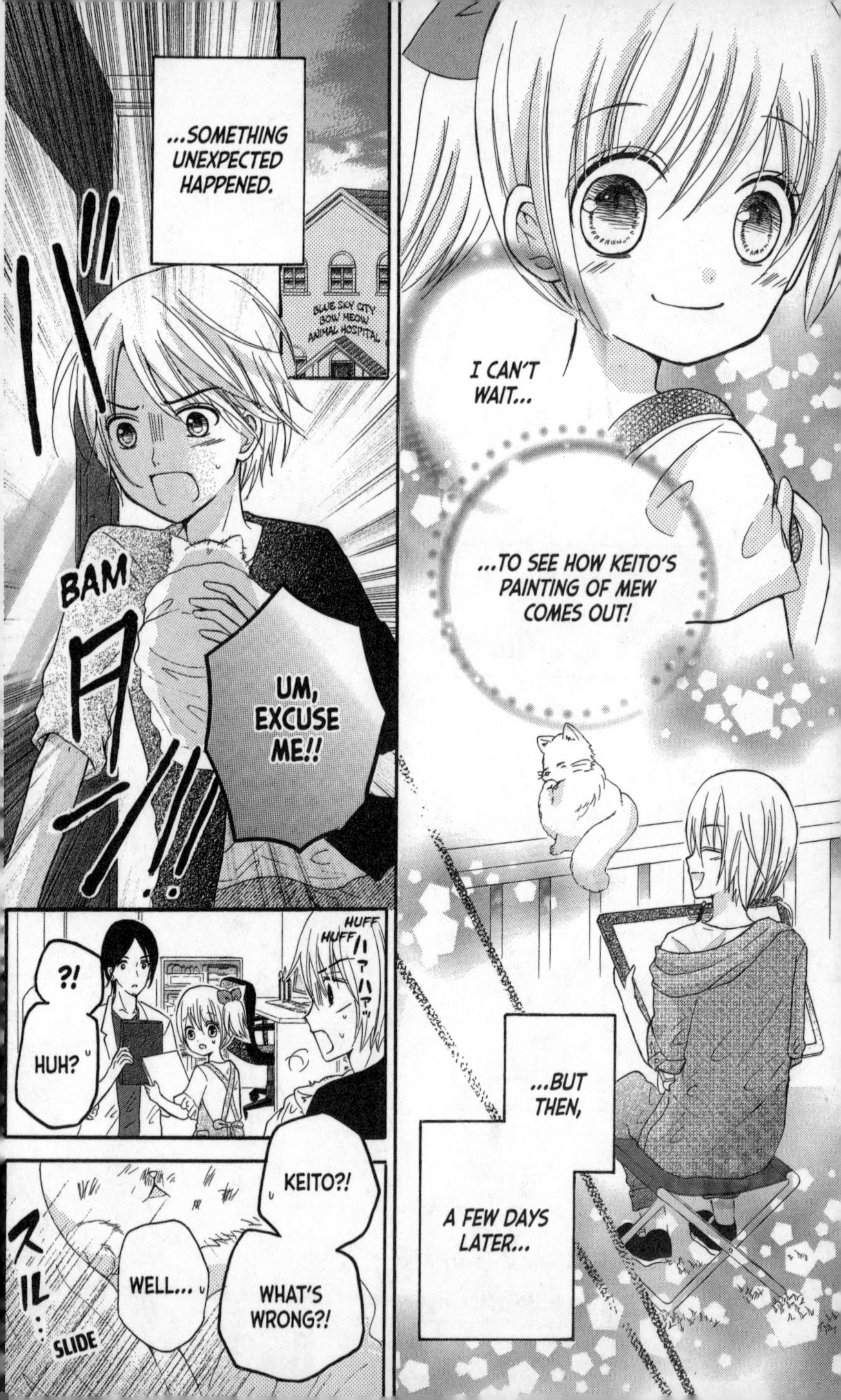
I CAN'T WAIT...
...TO SEE HOW KEITO'S PAINTING OF MEW COMES OUT!
...BUT THEN,
A FEW DAYS LATER...
...SOMETHING UNEXPECTED HAPPENED.
BLUE SKY CITY BOW MEOW ANIMAL HOSPITAL
BAM
UM, EXCUSE ME!!
HUFF HUFF
?!
HUH?
KEITO?!
WHAT'S WRONG?!
WELL...
SLIDE

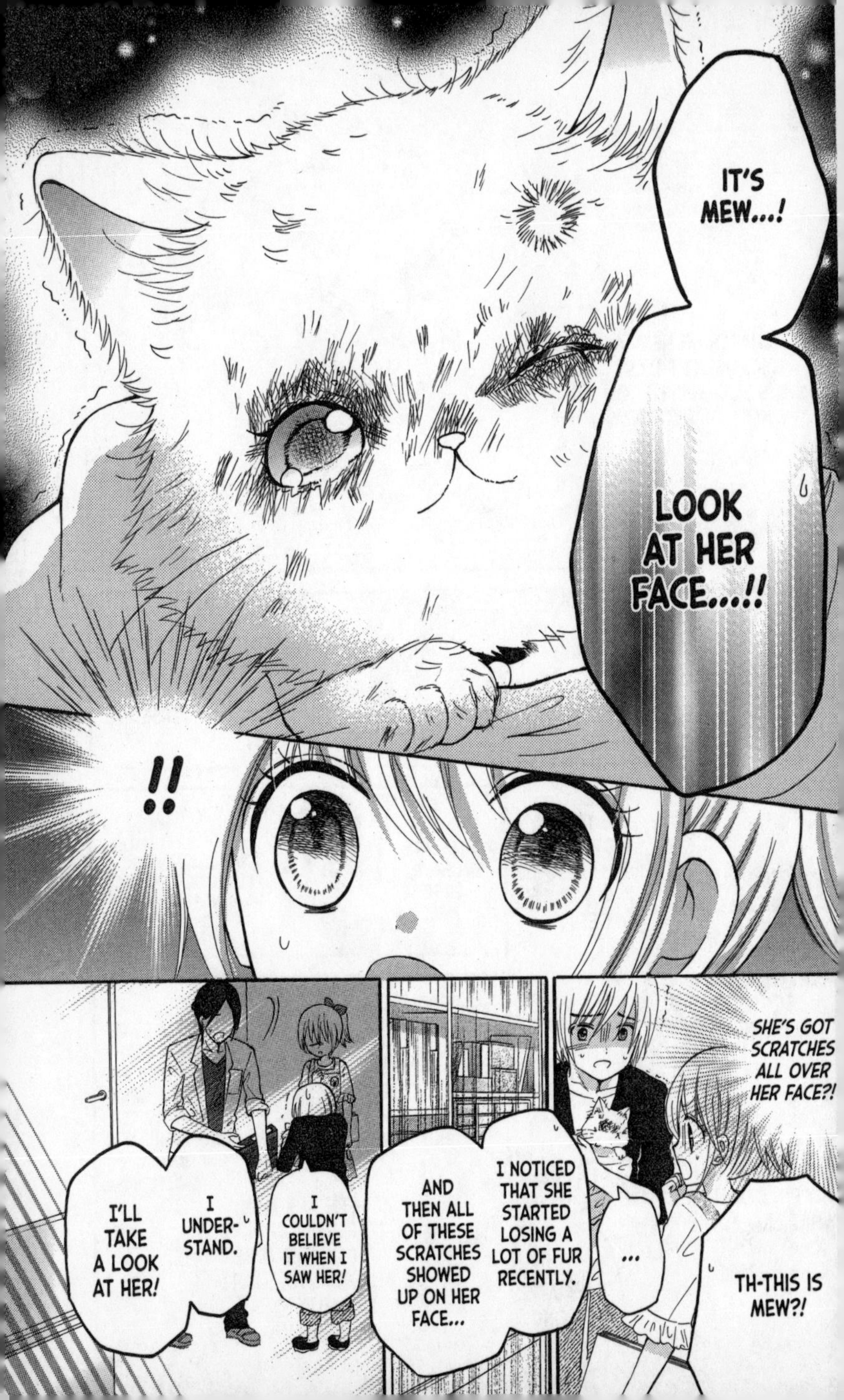
IT'S MEW...!
LOOK AT HER FACE...!!
!!
SHE'S GOT SCRATCHES ALL OVER HER FACE?!
TH-THIS IS MEW?!
...
I NOTICED THAT SHE STARTED LOSING A LOT OF FUR RECENTLY.
AND THEN ALL OF THESE SCRATCHES SHOWED UP ON HER FACE...
I COULDN'T BELIEVE IT WHEN I SAW HER!
I UNDERSTAND.
I'LL TAKE A LOOK AT HER!

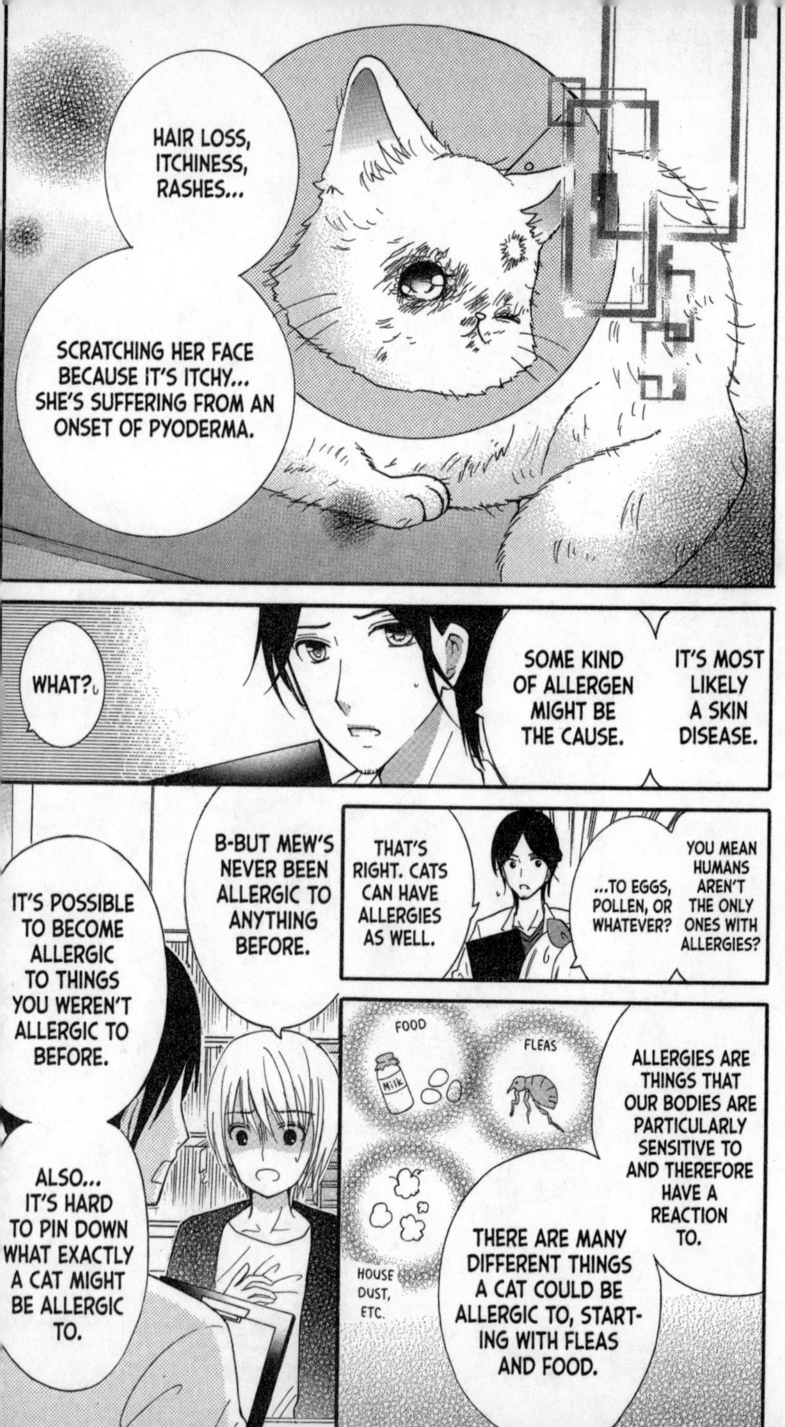
HAIR LOSS, ITCHINESS, RASHES...
SCRATCHING HER FACE BECAUSE IT'S ITCHY... SHE'S SUFFERING FROM AN ONSET OF PYODERMA.
IT'S MOST LIKELY A SKIN DISEASE.
SOME KIND OF ALLERGEN MIGHT BE THE CAUSE.
WHAT?
YOU MEAN HUMANS AREN'T THE ONLY ONES WITH ALLERGIES?
...TO EGGS, POLLEN, OR WHATEVER?
THAT'S RIGHT. CATS CAN HAVE ALLERGIES AS WELL.
ALLERGIES ARE THINGS THAT OUR BODIES ARE PARTICULARLY SENSITIVE TO AND THEREFORE HAVE A REACTION TO.
FLEAS
FOOD
Milk
HOUSE DUST, ETC.
THERE ARE MANY DIFFERENT THINGS A CAT COULD BE ALLERGIC TO, STARTING WITH FLEAS AND FOOD.
B-BUT MEW'S NEVER BEEN ALLERGIC TO ANYTHING BEFORE.
IT'S POSSIBLE TO BECOME ALLERGIC TO THINGS YOU WEREN'T ALLERGIC TO BEFORE.
ALSO... IT'S HARD TO PIN DOWN WHAT EXACTLY A CAT MIGHT BE ALLERGIC TO.

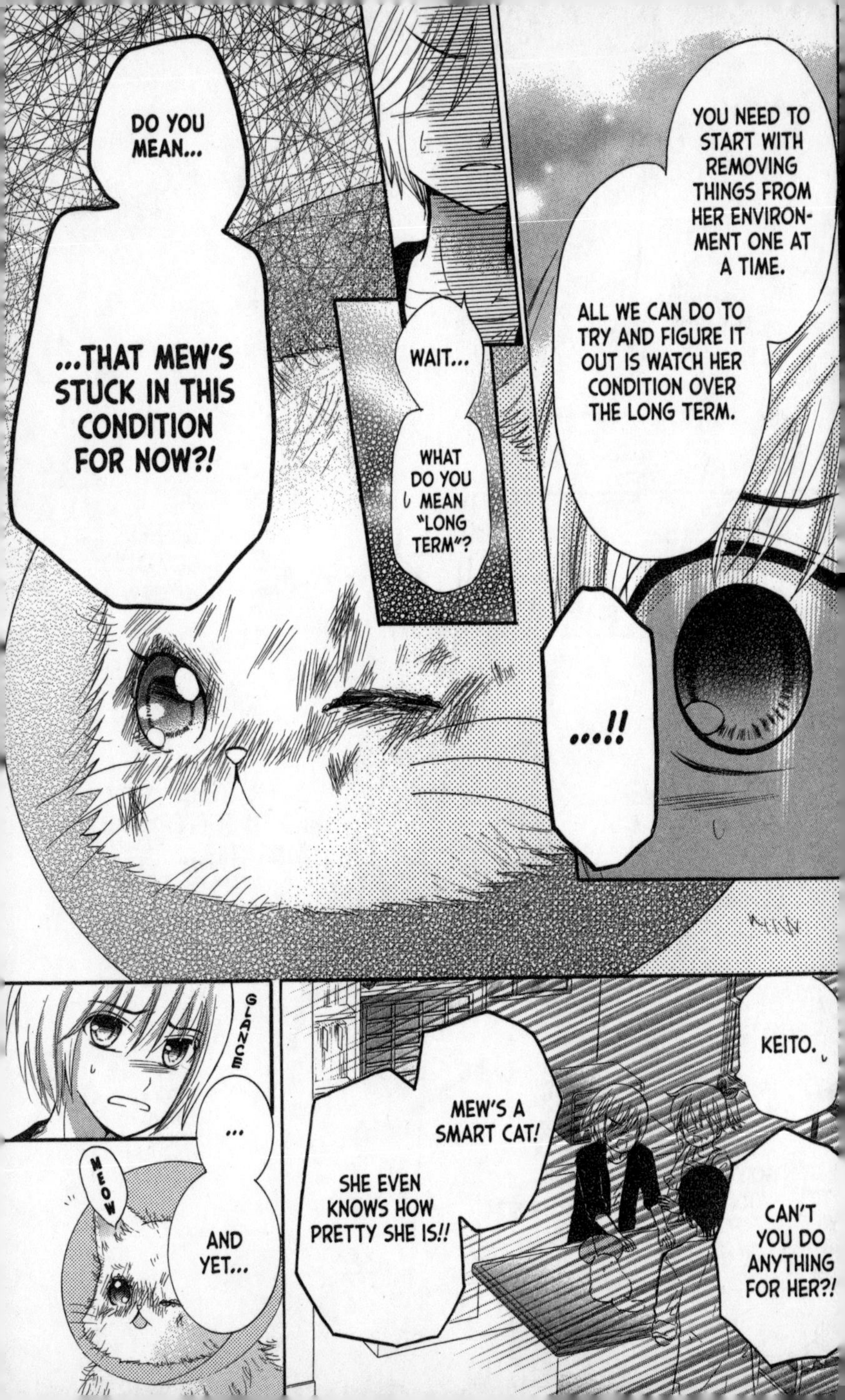
YOU NEED TO START WITH REMOVING THINGS FROM HER ENVIRON-MENT ONE AT A TIME.
ALL WE CAN DO TO TRY AND FIGURE IT OUT IS WATCH HER CONDITION OVER THE LONG TERM.
WAIT...
WHAT DO YOU MEAN "LONG TERM"?
...!!
DO YOU MEAN...
...THAT MEW'S STUCK IN THIS CONDITION FOR NOW?!
KEITO.
CAN'T YOU DO ANYTHING FOR HER?!
MEW'S A SMART CAT!
SHE EVEN KNOWS HOW PRETTY SHE IS!!
GLANCE
...
MEOW
AND YET...

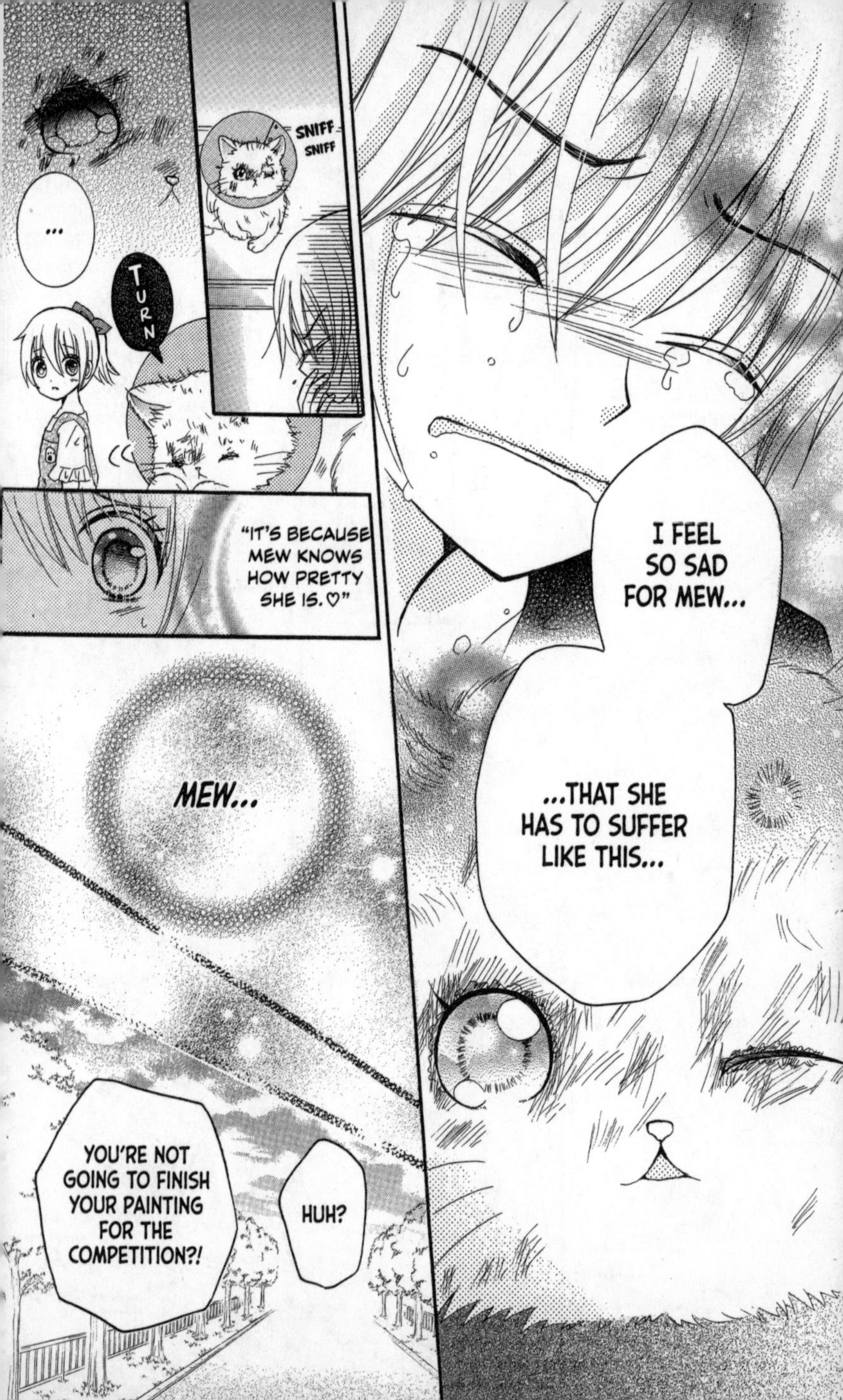
I FEEL SO SAD FOR MEW...
...THAT SHE HAS TO SUFFER LIKE THIS...
SNIFF SNIFF
...
TURN
"IT'S BECAUSE MEW KNOWS HOW PRETTY SHE IS.♡"
MEW...
HUH?
YOU'RE NOT GOING TO FINISH YOUR PAINTING FOR THE COMPETITION?!

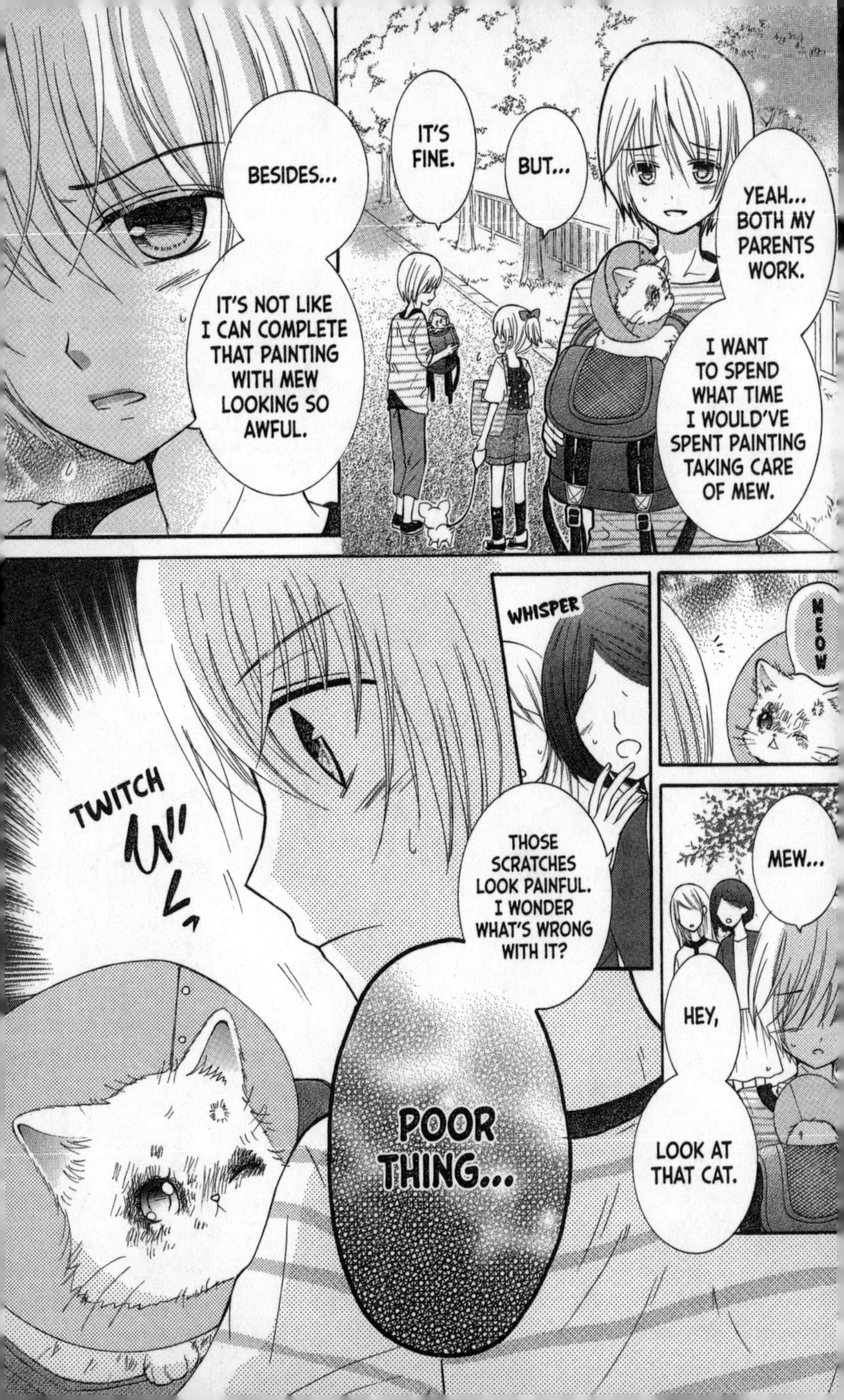
YEAH... BOTH MY PARENTS WORK.
I WANT TO SPEND WHAT TIME I WOULD'VE SPENT PAINTING TAKING CARE OF MEW.
BUT...
IT'S FINE.
BESIDES...
IT'S NOT LIKE I CAN COMPLETE THAT PAINTING WITH MEW LOOKING SO AWFUL.
MEOW
MEW...
HEY,
LOOK AT THAT CAT.
WHISPER
THOSE SCRATCHES LOOK PAINFUL. I WONDER WHAT'S WRONG WITH IT?
TWITCH
POOR THING...

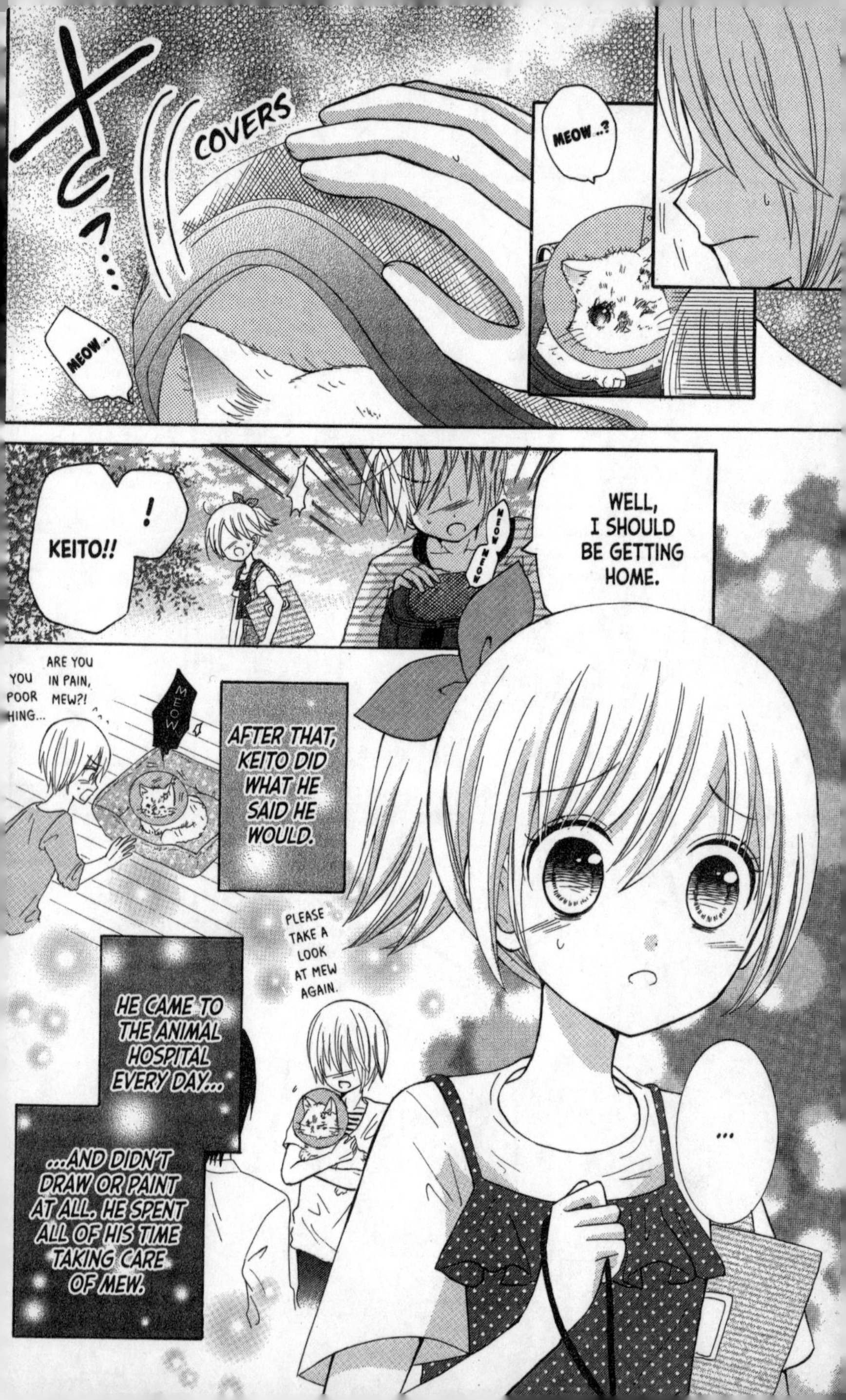
MEOW..?
COVERS
MEOW...
WELL, I SHOULD BE GETTING HOME.
MEOW MEOW
!
KEITO!!
...
AFTER THAT, KEITO DID WHAT HE SAID HE WOULD.
ARE YOU IN PAIN, MEW?!
YOU POOR HING...
MEOW
PLEASE TAKE A LOOK AT MEW AGAIN.
HE CAME TO THE ANIMAL HOSPITAL EVERY DAY...
...AND DIDN'T DRAW OR PAINT AT ALL. HE SPENT ALL OF HIS TIME TAKING CARE OF MEW.

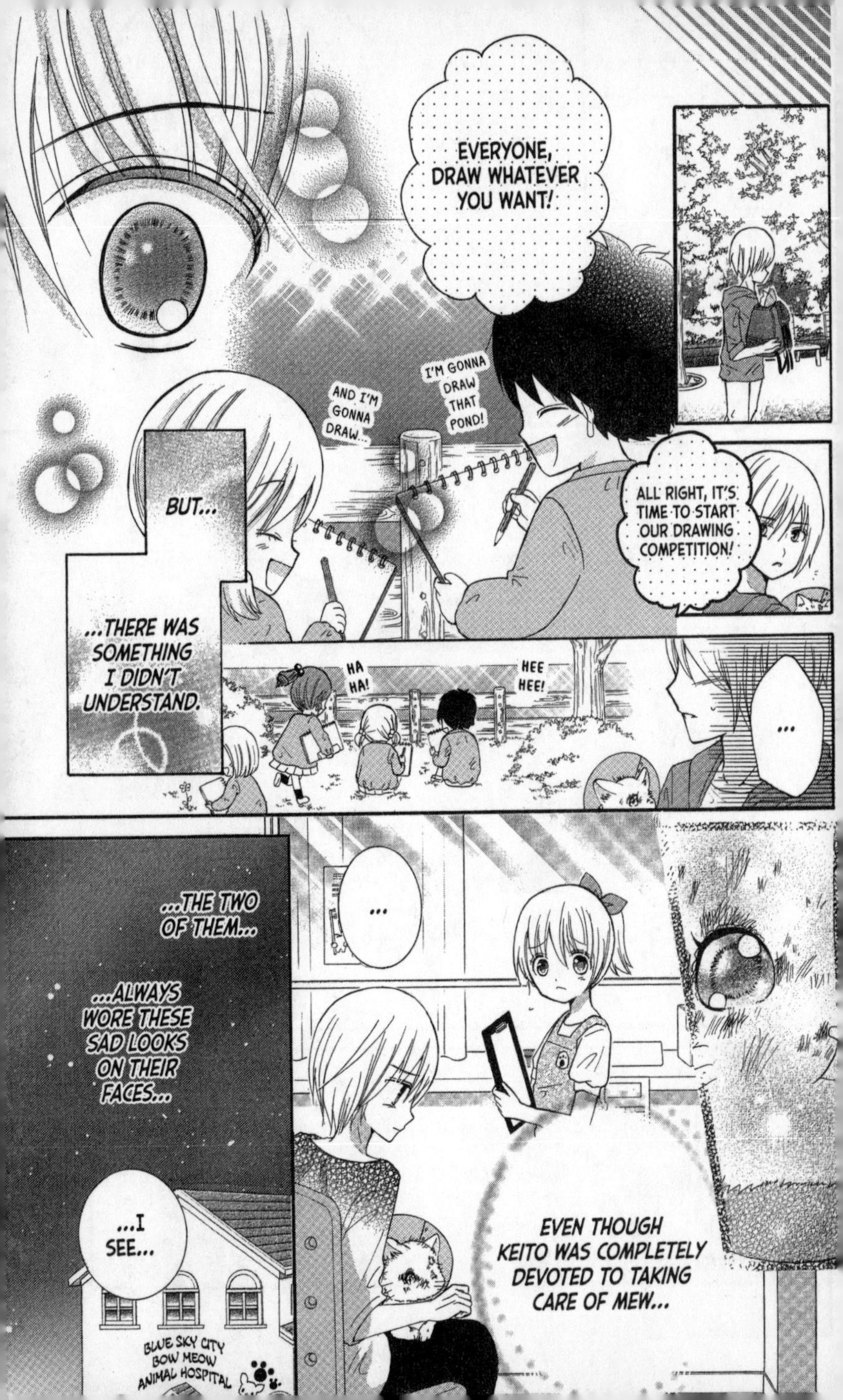
ALL RIGHT, IT'S TIME TO START OUR DRAWING COMPETITION!
EVERYONE, DRAW WHATEVER YOU WANT!
I'M GONNA DRAW THAT POND!
AND I'M GONNA DRAW...
BUT...
...THERE WAS SOMETHING I DIDN'T UNDERSTAND.
...
HEE HEE!
HA HA!
EVEN THOUGH KEITO WAS COMPLETELY DEVOTED TO TAKING CARE OF MEW...
...
...THE TWO OF THEM...
...ALWAYS WORE THESE SAD LOOKS ON THEIR FACES...
...I SEE...
BLUE SKY CITY BOW MEOW ANIMAL HOSPITAL

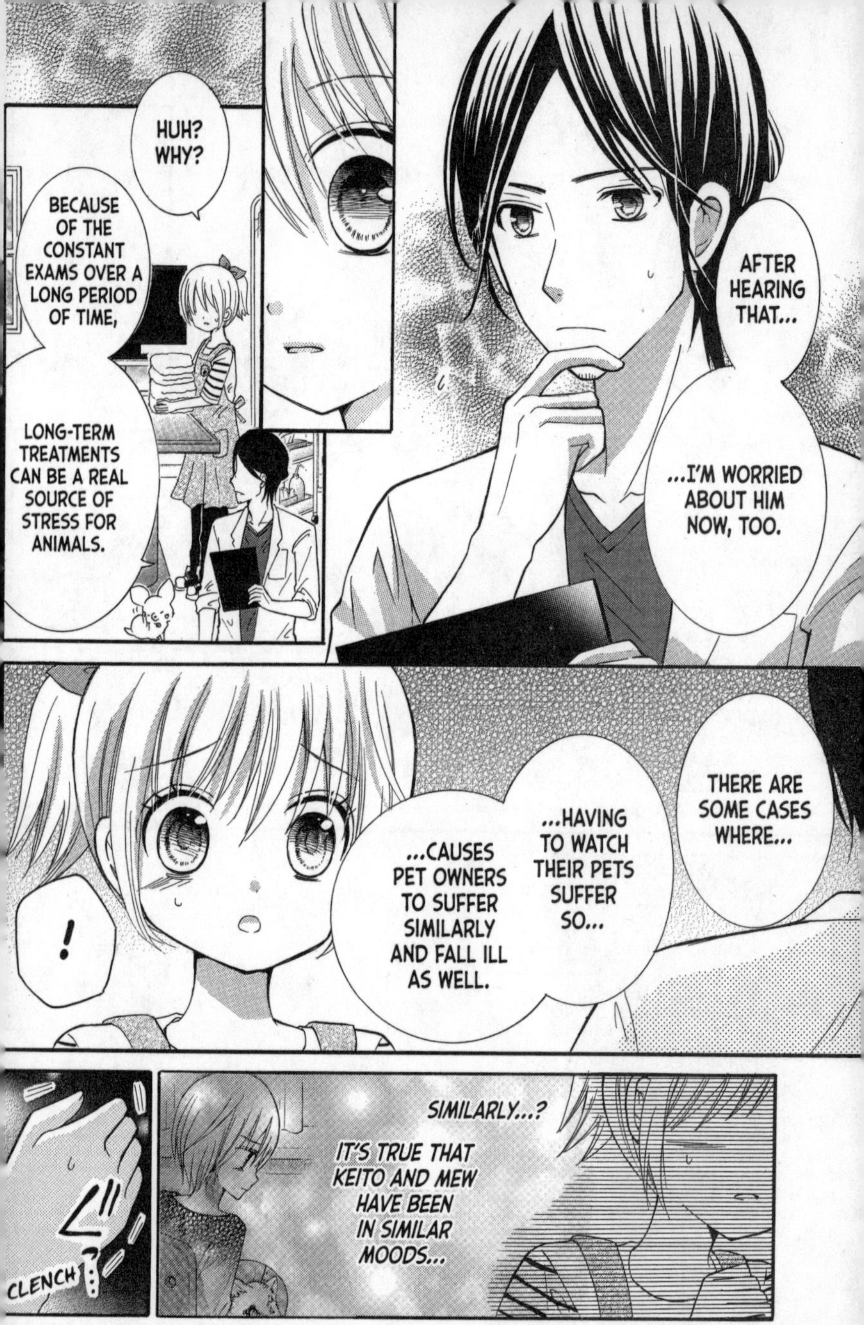
AFTER HEARING THAT...
...I'M WORRIED ABOUT HIM NOW, TOO.
HUH? WHY?
BECAUSE OF THE CONSTANT EXAMS OVER A LONG PERIOD OF TIME,
LONG-TERM TREATMENTS CAN BE A REAL SOURCE OF STRESS FOR ANIMALS.
THERE ARE SOME CASES WHERE...
...HAVING TO WATCH THEIR PETS SUFFER SO...
...CAUSES PET OWNERS TO SUFFER SIMILARLY AND FALL ILL AS WELL.
!
SIMILARLY...?
IT'S TRUE THAT KEITO AND MEW HAVE BEEN IN SIMILAR MOODS...
CLENCH

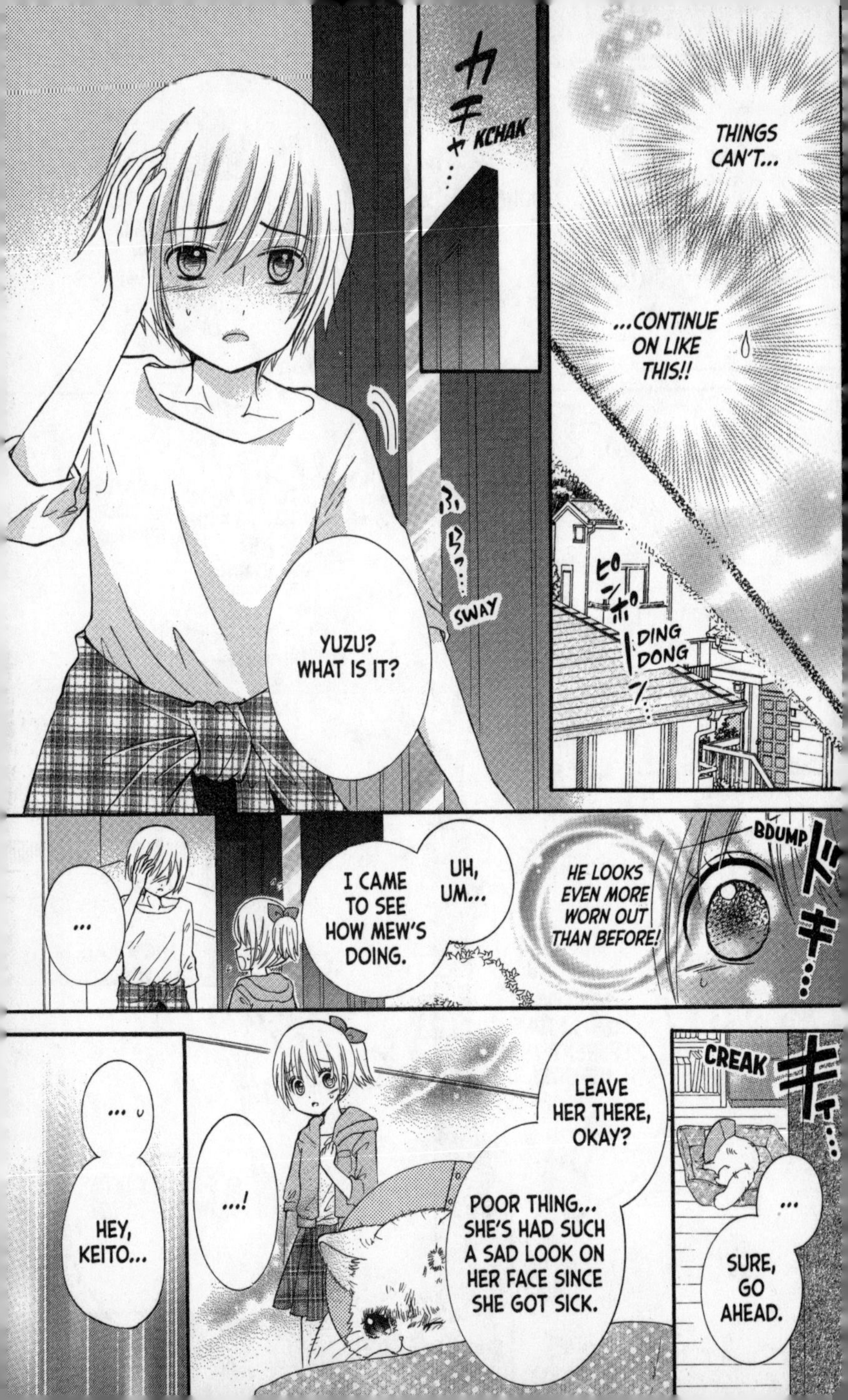
THINGS CAN'T...
...CONTINUE ON LIKE THIS!!
ピンポーン…
DING DONG
カチャ…
KCHAK
ふらっ…
SWAY
YUZU? WHAT IS IT?
ドキ…
BDUMP
HE LOOKS EVEN MORE WORN OUT THAN BEFORE!
UH, UM...
I CAME TO SEE HOW MEW'S DOING.
...
キィ…
CREAK
...
SURE, GO AHEAD.
LEAVE HER THERE, OKAY?
POOR THING... SHE'S HAD SUCH A SAD LOOK ON HER FACE SINCE SHE GOT SICK.
...!
...
HEY, KEITO...

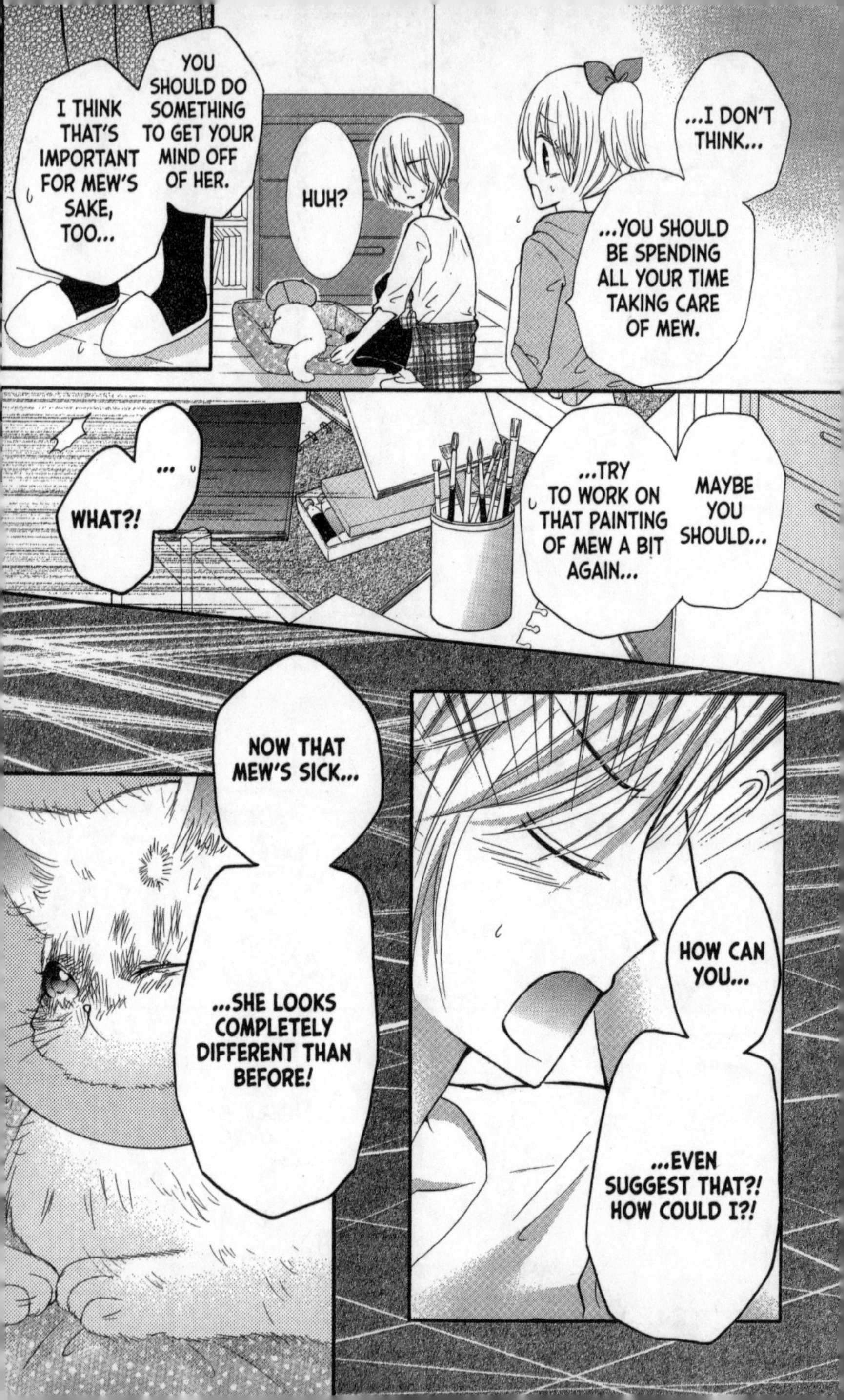
...I DON'T THINK...
...YOU SHOULD BE SPENDING ALL YOUR TIME TAKING CARE OF MEW.
HUH?
YOU SHOULD DO SOMETHING TO GET YOUR MIND OFF OF HER.
I THINK THAT'S IMPORTANT FOR MEW'S SAKE, TOO...
MAYBE YOU SHOULD...
...TRY TO WORK ON THAT PAINTING OF MEW A BIT AGAIN...
...
WHAT?!
HOW CAN YOU...
...EVEN SUGGEST THAT?! HOW COULD I?!
NOW THAT MEW'S SICK...
...SHE LOOKS COMPLETELY DIFFERENT THAN BEFORE!

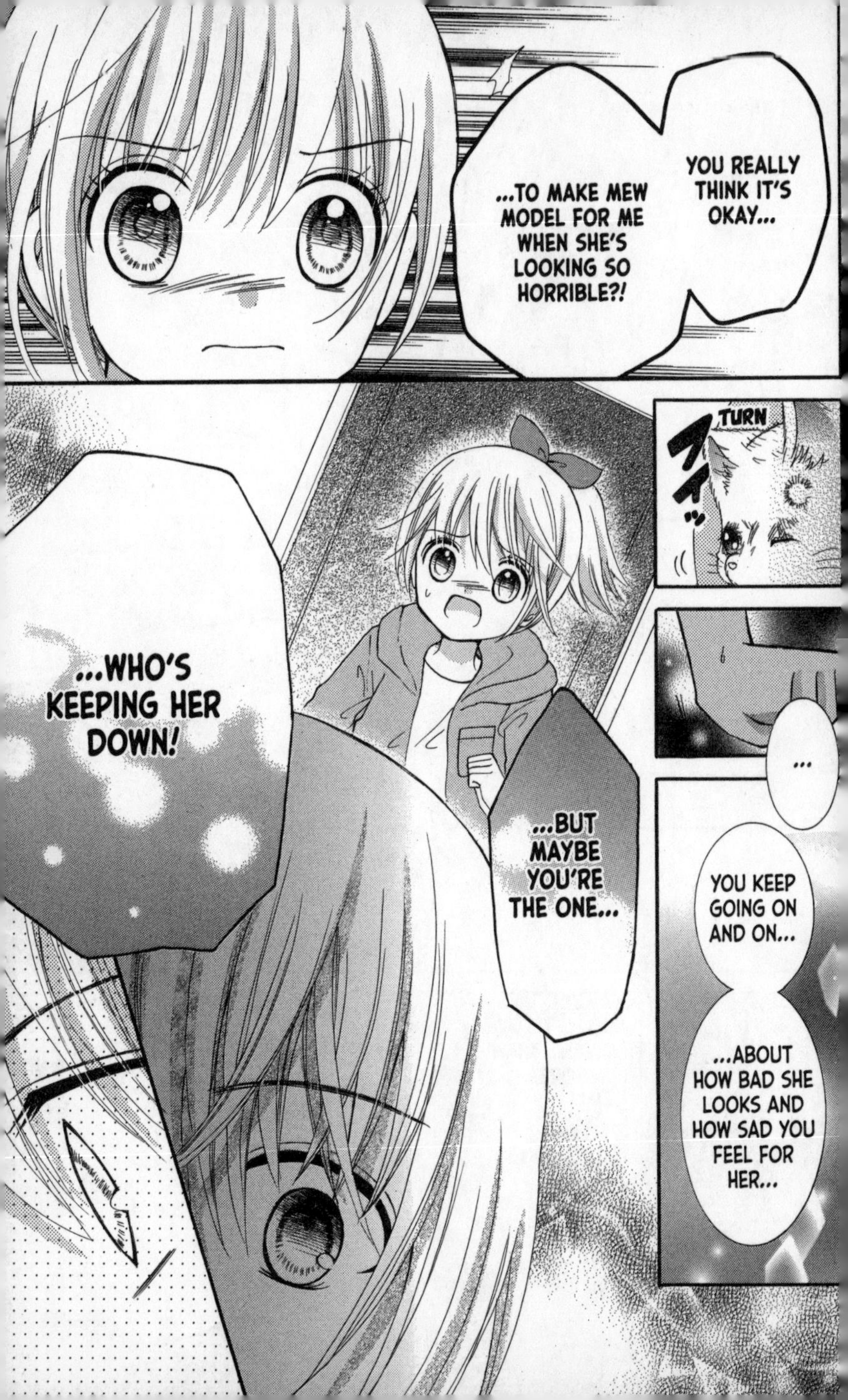

YOU REALLY THINK IT'S OKAY...
...TO MAKE MEW MODEL FOR ME WHEN SHE'S LOOKING SO HORRIBLE?!
TURN
...
YOU KEEP GOING ON AND ON...
...ABOUT HOW BAD SHE LOOKS AND HOW SAD YOU FEEL FOR HER...
...BUT MAYBE YOU'RE THE ONE...
...WHO'S KEEPING HER DOWN!

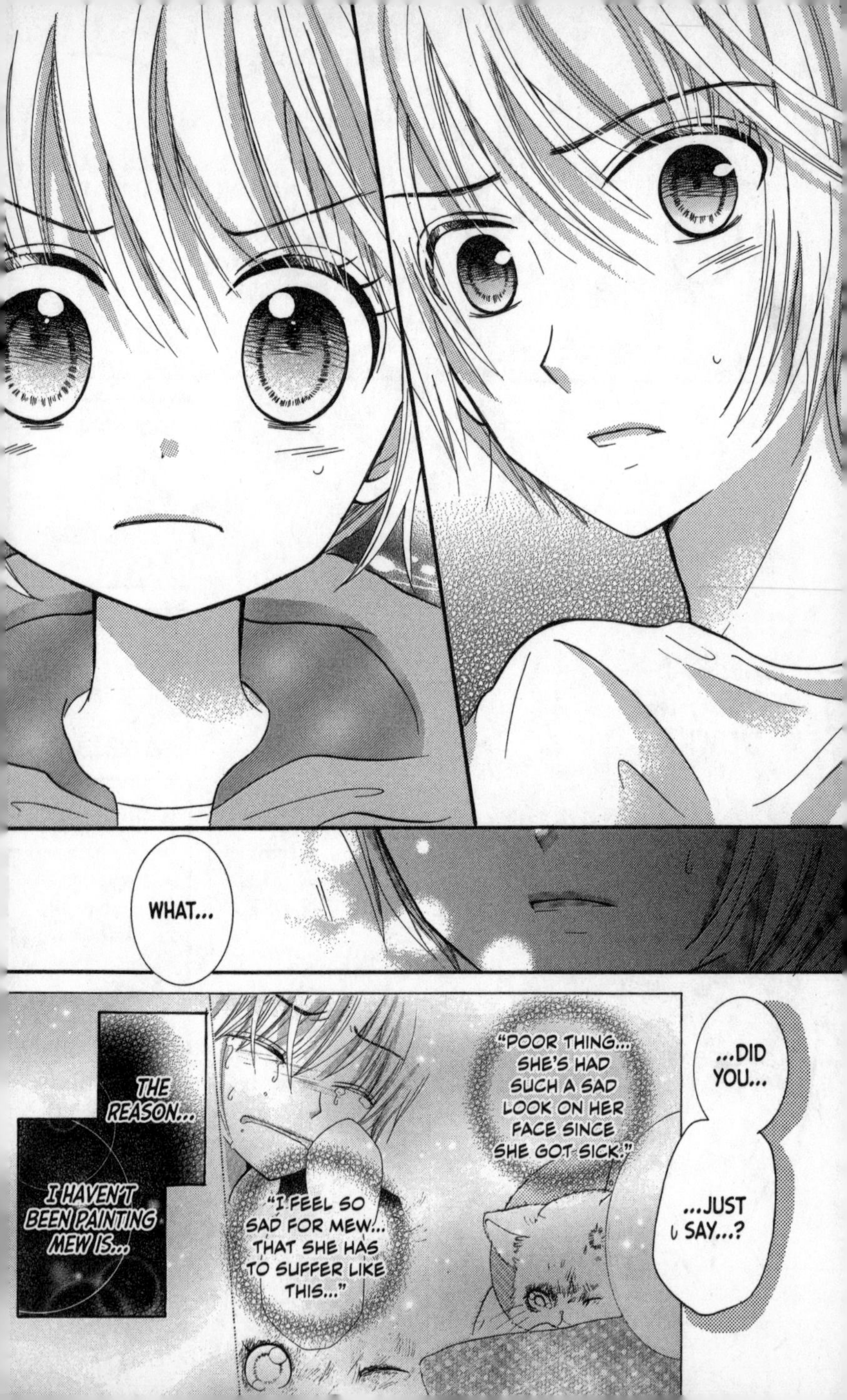
WHAT...
...DID YOU...
...JUST SAY...?
"POOR THING... SHE'S HAD SUCH A SAD LOOK ON HER FACE SINCE SHE GOT SICK."
"I FEEL SO SAD FOR MEW... THAT SHE HAS TO SUFFER LIKE THIS..."
THE REASON...
I HAVEN'T BEEN PAINTING MEW IS...

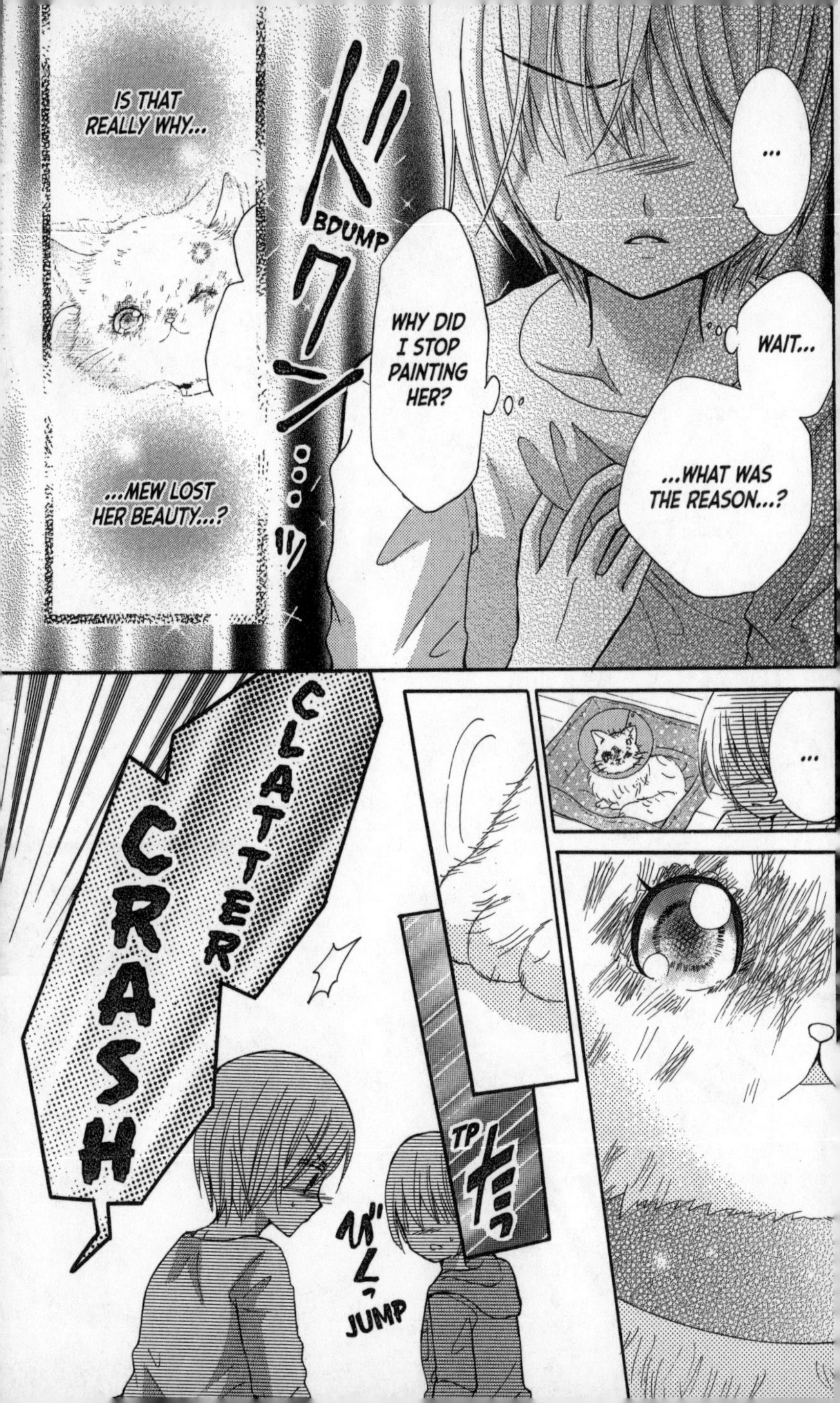
...
WAIT...
...WHAT WAS THE REASON...?
WHY DID I STOP PAINTING HER?
BDUMP
IS THAT REALLY WHY...
...MEW LOST HER BEAUTY...?
...
TP
CLATTER
CRASH
JUMP

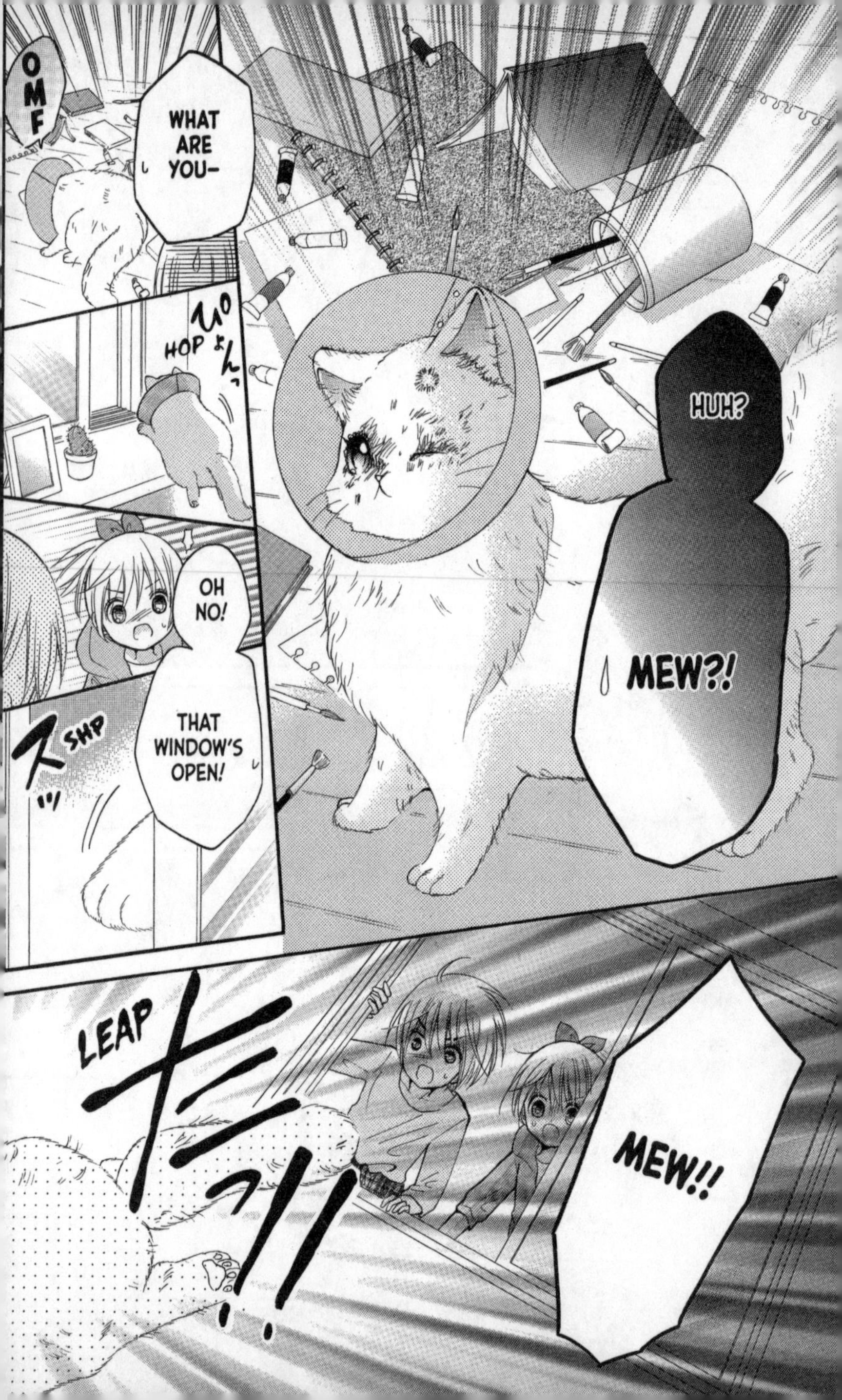
HUH?
MEW?!
OMF
WHAT ARE YOU–
HOP
OH NO!
THAT WINDOW'S OPEN!
SHP
MEW!!
LEAP

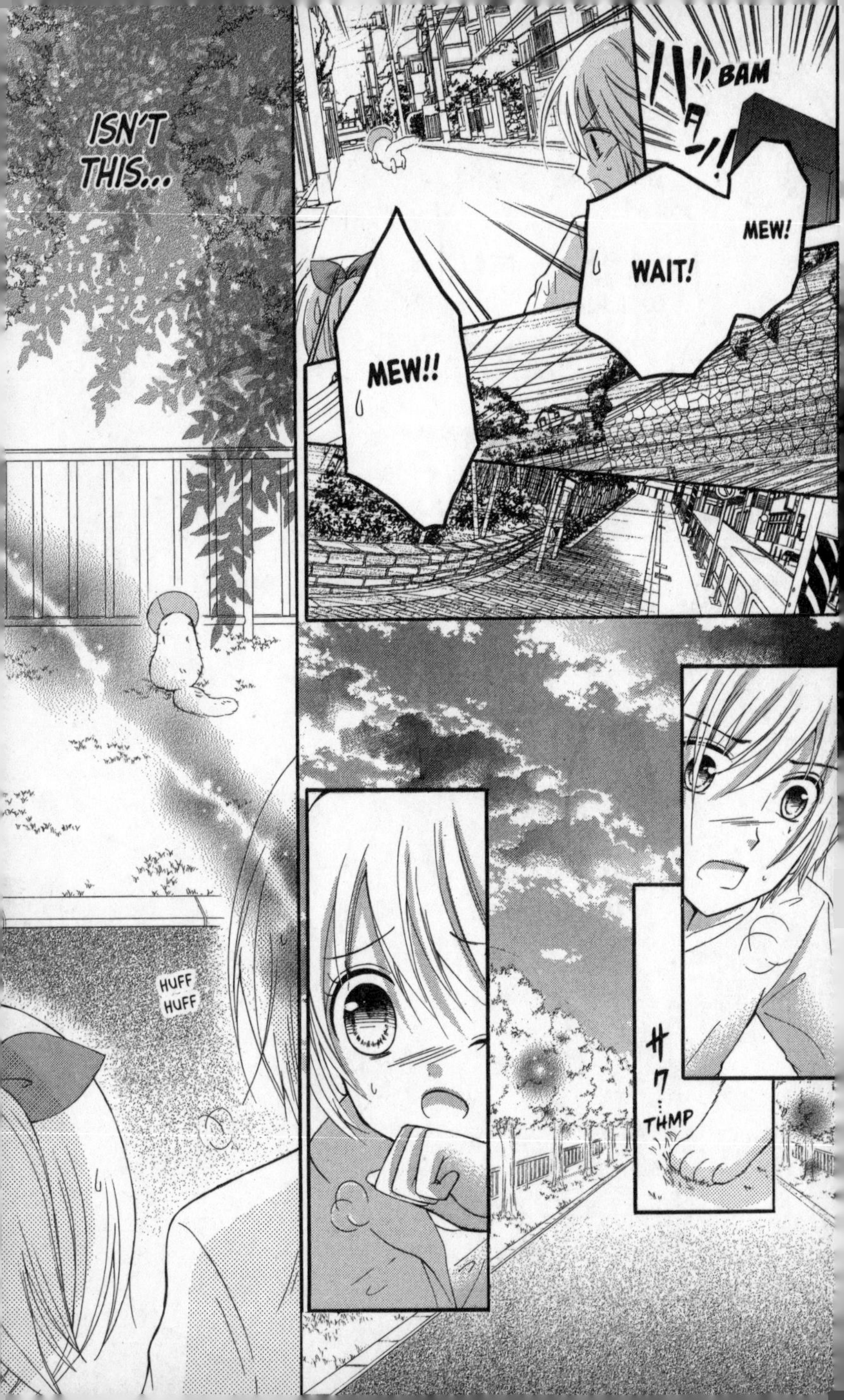
バタン!!
BAM
MEW!
WAIT!
MEW!!
サク…
THMP
ISN'T THIS...
HUFF HUFF

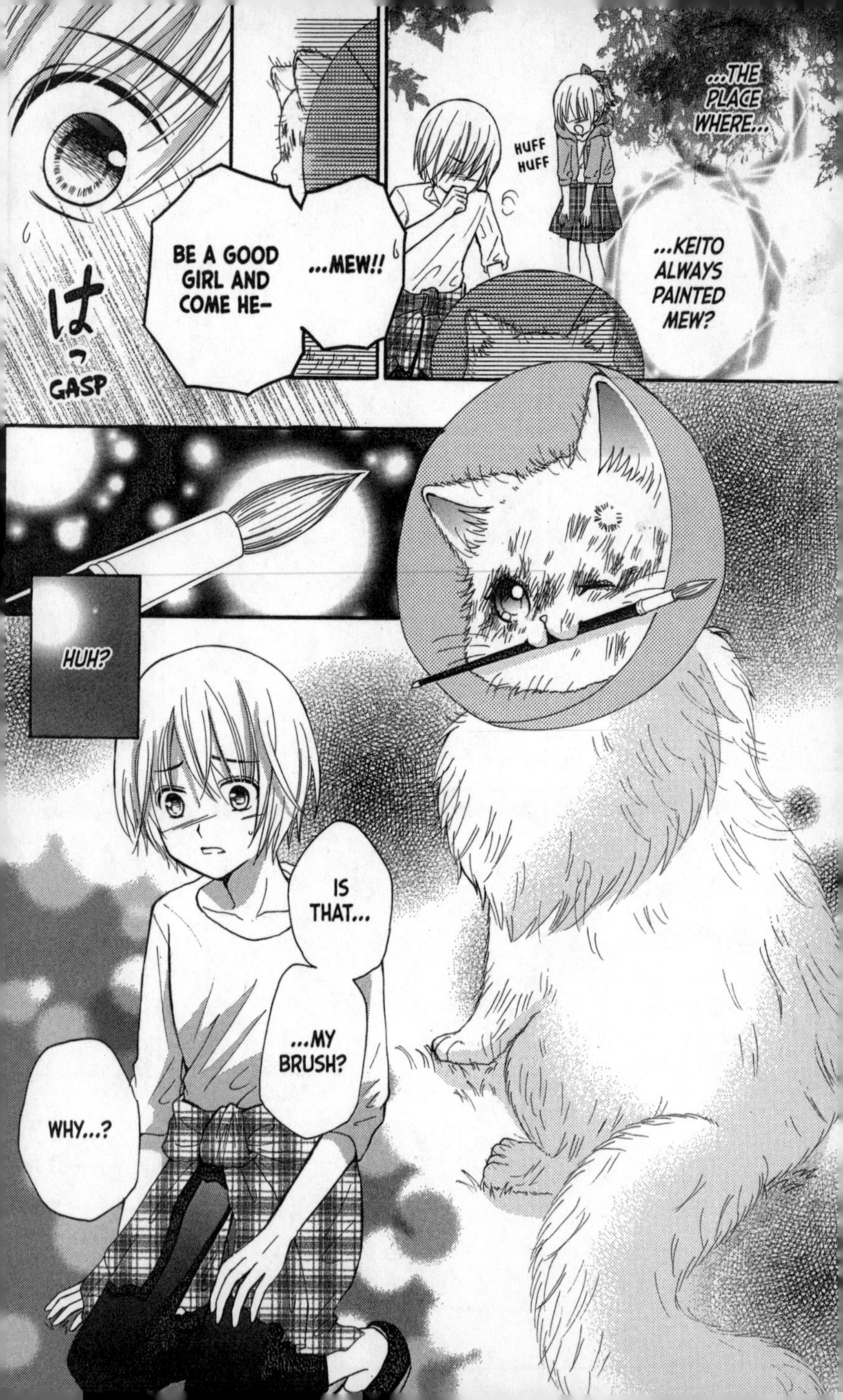
...THE PLACE WHERE...
HUFF HUFF
...KEITO ALWAYS PAINTED MEW?
BE A GOOD GIRL AND COME HE-
...MEW!!
は っ
GASP
HUH?
IS THAT...
...MY BRUSH?
WHY...?

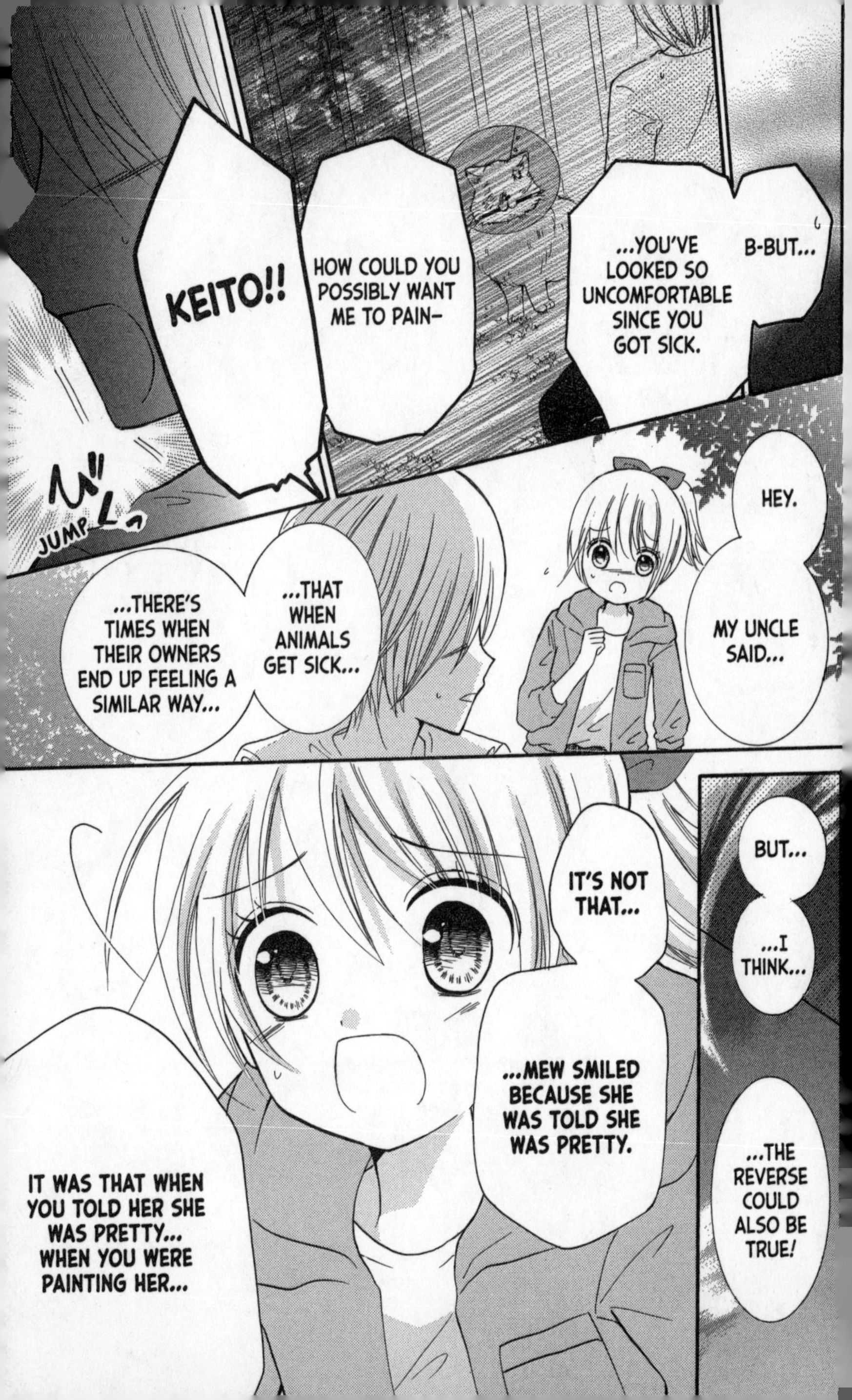
B-BUT...
...YOU'VE LOOKED SO UNCOMFORTABLE SINCE YOU GOT SICK.
HOW COULD YOU POSSIBLY WANT ME TO PAIN–
KEITO!!
JUMP
HEY.
MY UNCLE SAID...
...THAT WHEN ANIMALS GET SICK...
...THERE'S TIMES WHEN THEIR OWNERS END UP FEELING A SIMILAR WAY...
BUT...
...I THINK...
...THE REVERSE COULD ALSO BE TRUE!
IT'S NOT THAT...
...MEW SMILED BECAUSE SHE WAS TOLD SHE WAS PRETTY.
IT WAS THAT WHEN YOU TOLD HER SHE WAS PRETTY... WHEN YOU WERE PAINTING HER...

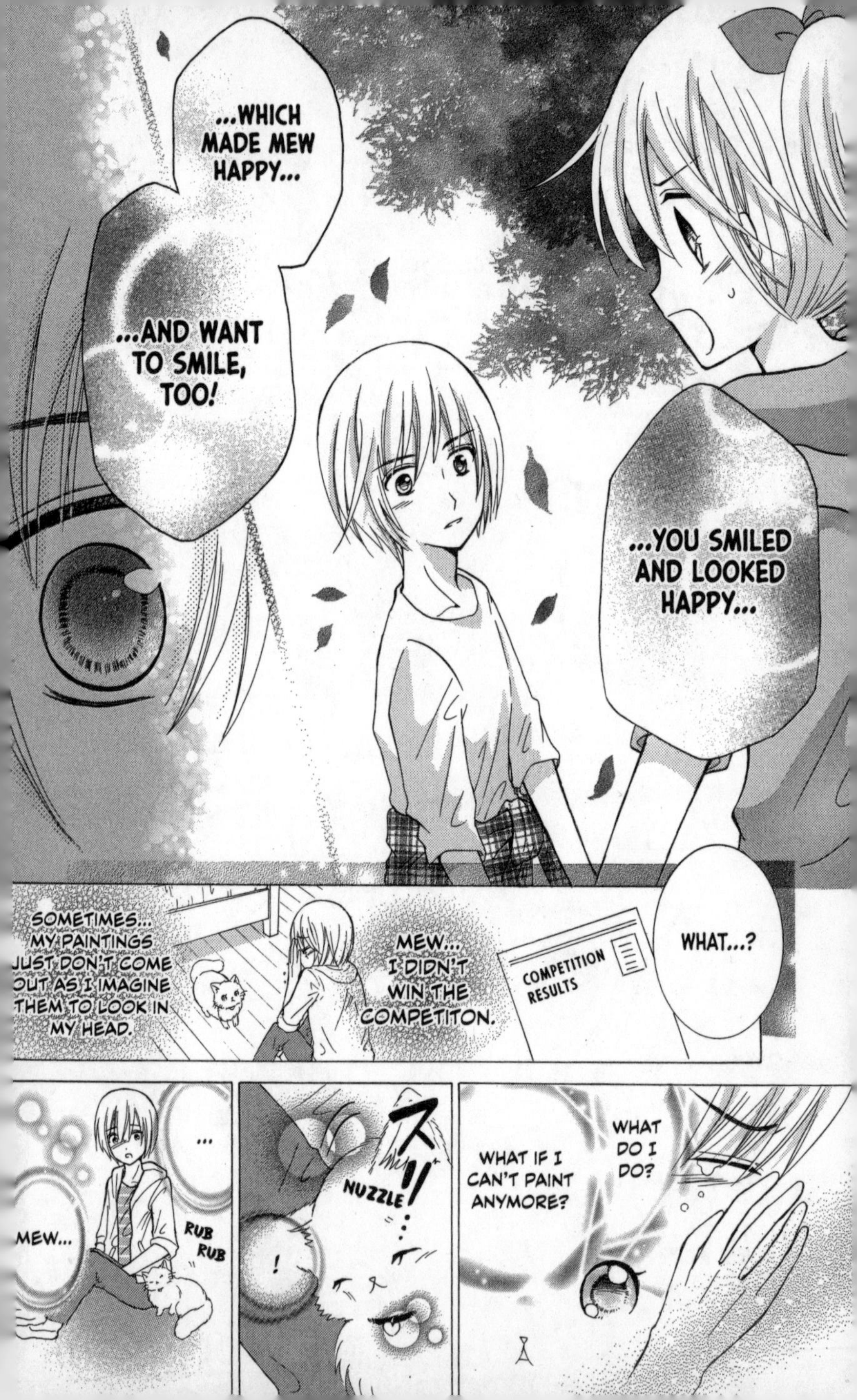
...YOU SMILED AND LOOKED HAPPY...
...WHICH MADE MEW HAPPY...
...AND WANT TO SMILE, TOO!
WHAT...?
COMPETITION RESULTS
MEW... I DIDN'T WIN THE COMPETITON.
SOMETIMES... MY PAINTINGS JUST DON'T COME OUT AS I IMAGINE THEM TO LOOK IN MY HEAD.
WHAT DO I DO?
WHAT IF I CAN'T PAINT ANYMORE?
スリ
NUZZLE
!
...
MEW...
RUB RUB

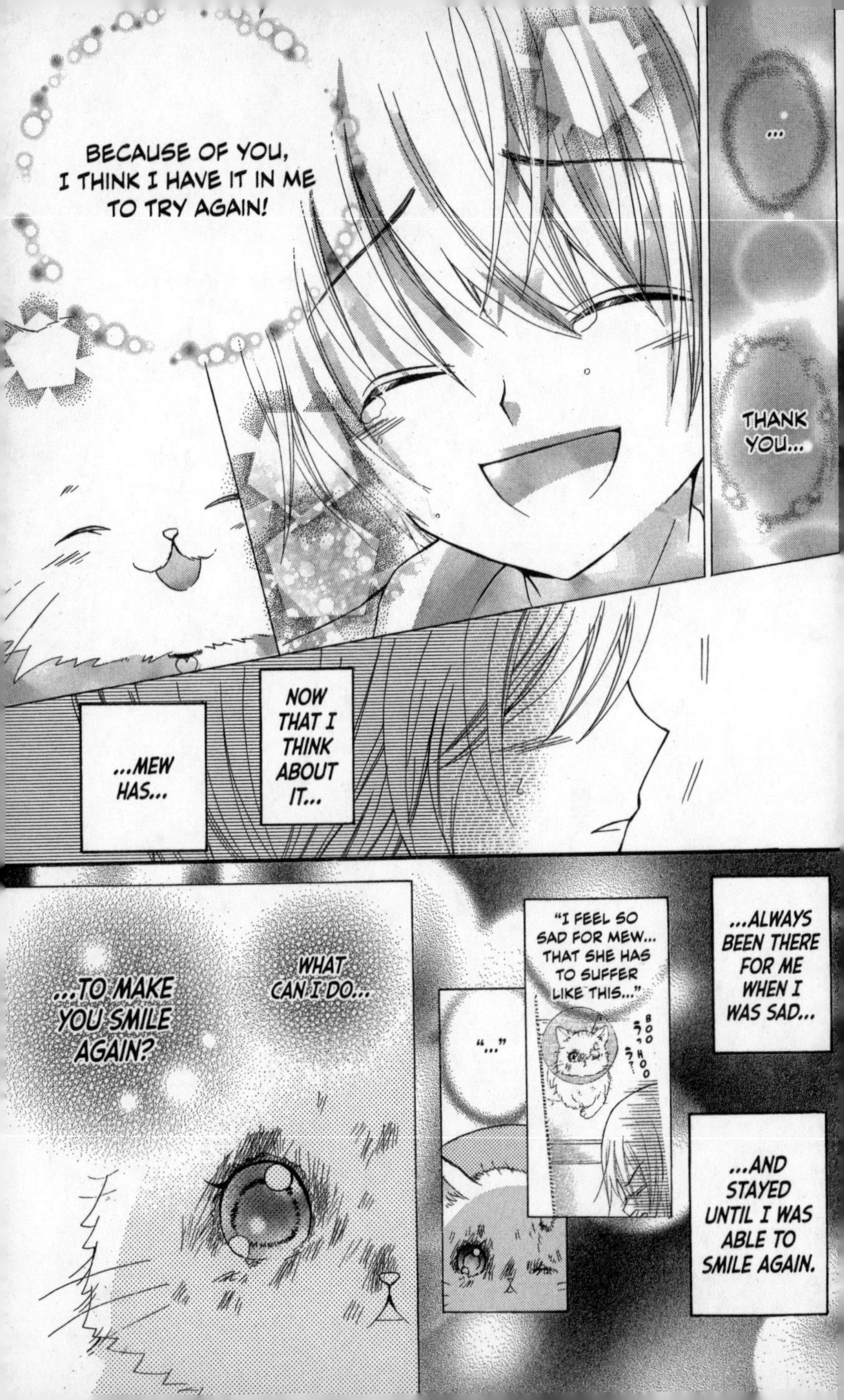
...
THANK YOU...
BECAUSE OF YOU, I THINK I HAVE IT IN ME TO TRY AGAIN!
NOW THAT I THINK ABOUT IT...
...MEW HAS...
...ALWAYS BEEN THERE FOR ME WHEN I WAS SAD...
"I FEEL SO SAD FOR MEW... THAT SHE HAS TO SUFFER LIKE THIS..."
BOO HOO
"..."
...AND STAYED UNTIL I WAS ABLE TO SMILE AGAIN.
WHAT CAN I DO...
...TO MAKE YOU SMILE AGAIN?

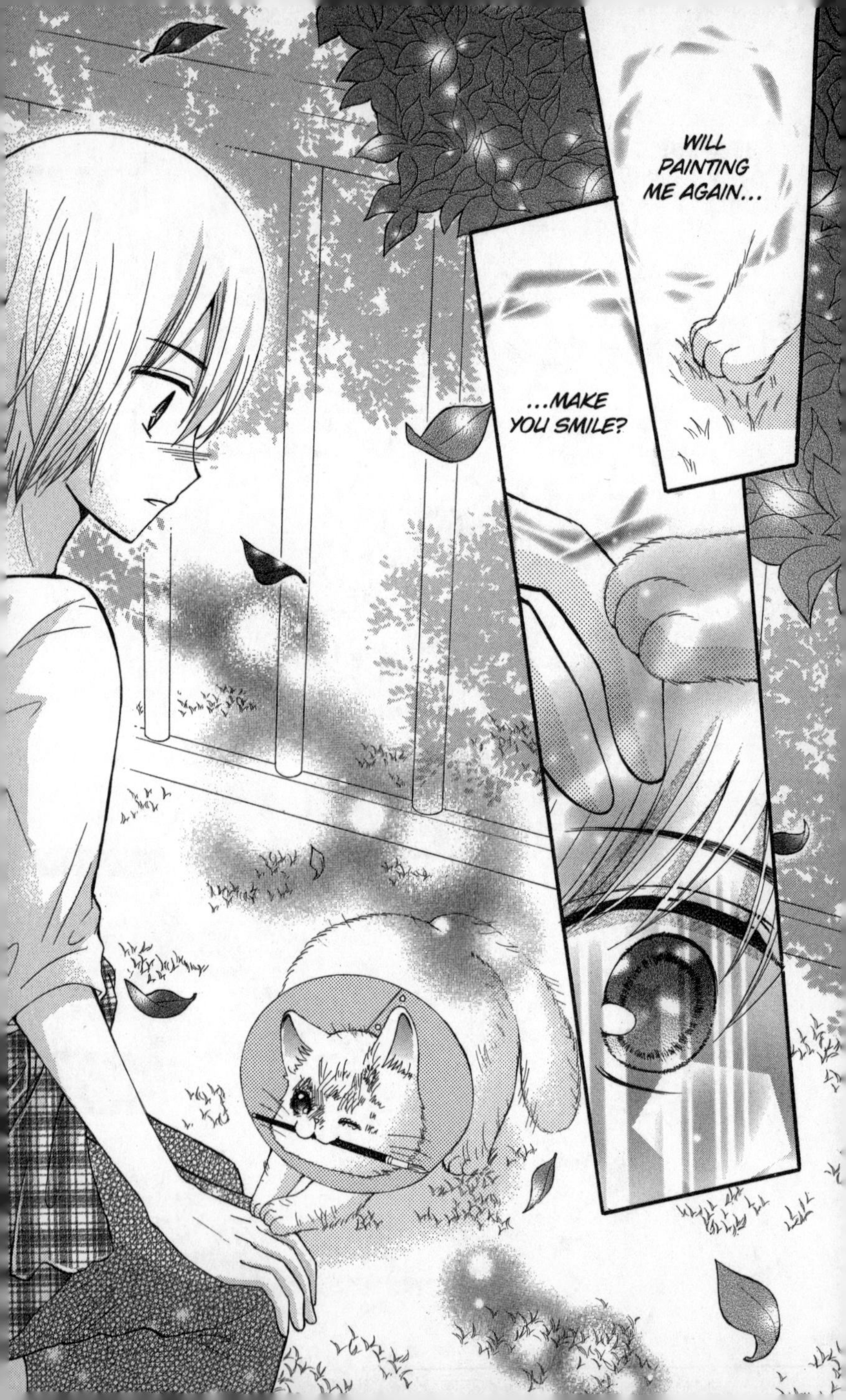
WILL PAINTING ME AGAIN...
...MAKE YOU SMILE?

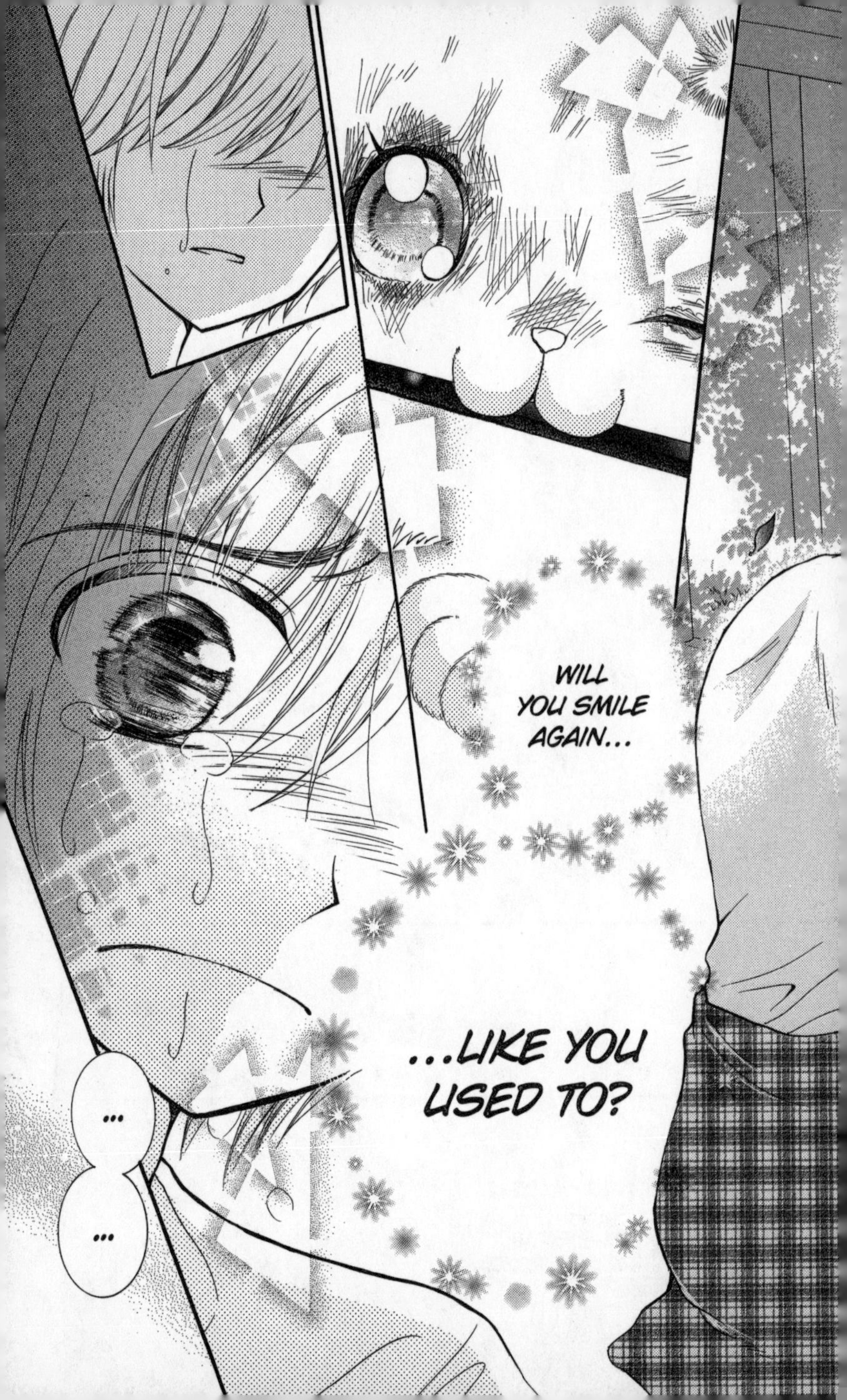
WILL YOU SMILE AGAIN...
...LIKE YOU USED TO?
...
...

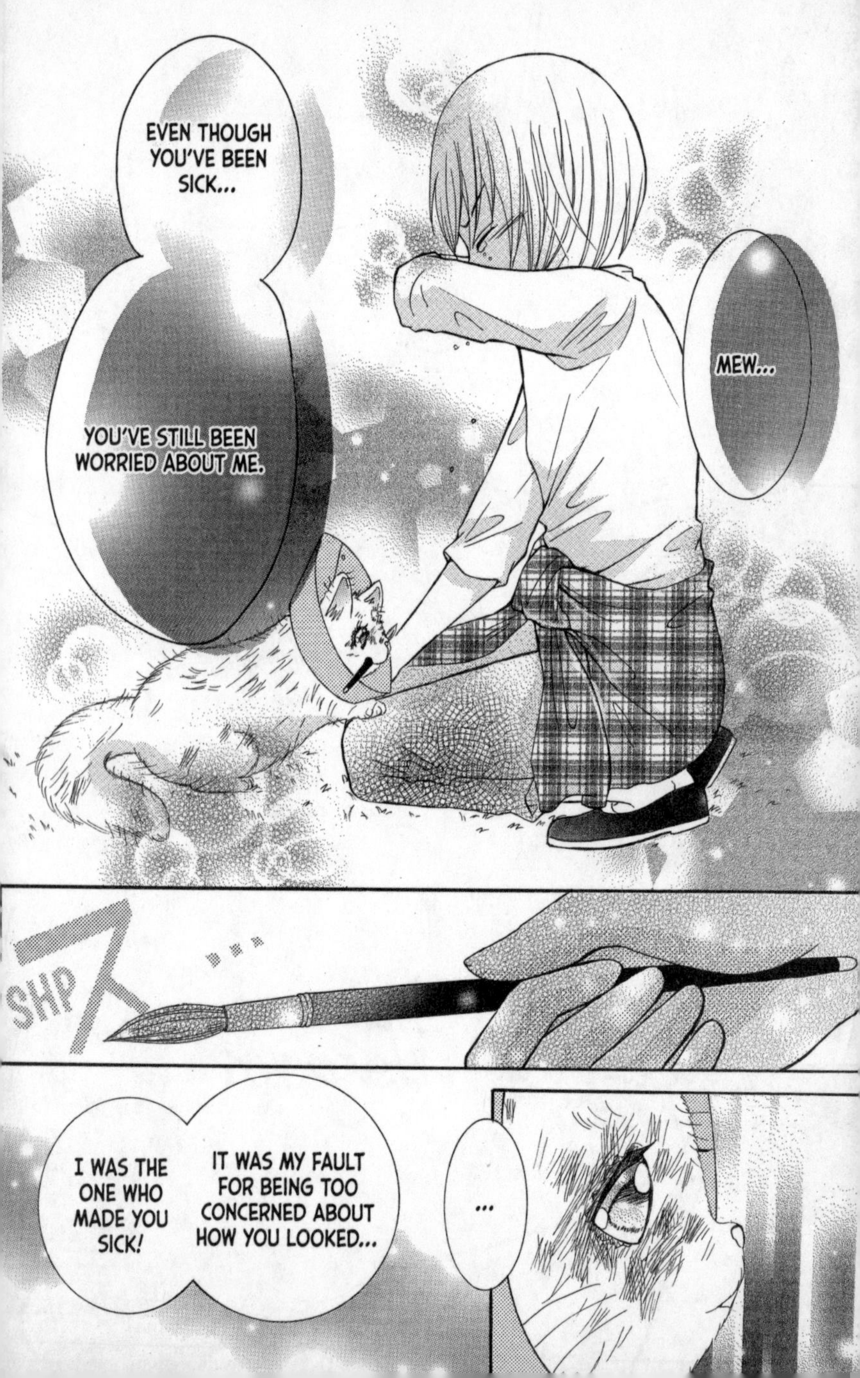
EVEN THOUGH YOU'VE BEEN SICK...
YOU'VE STILL BEEN WORRIED ABOUT ME.
MEW...
SHP
...
...
IT WAS MY FAULT FOR BEING TOO CONCERNED ABOUT HOW YOU LOOKED...
I WAS THE ONE WHO MADE YOU SICK!

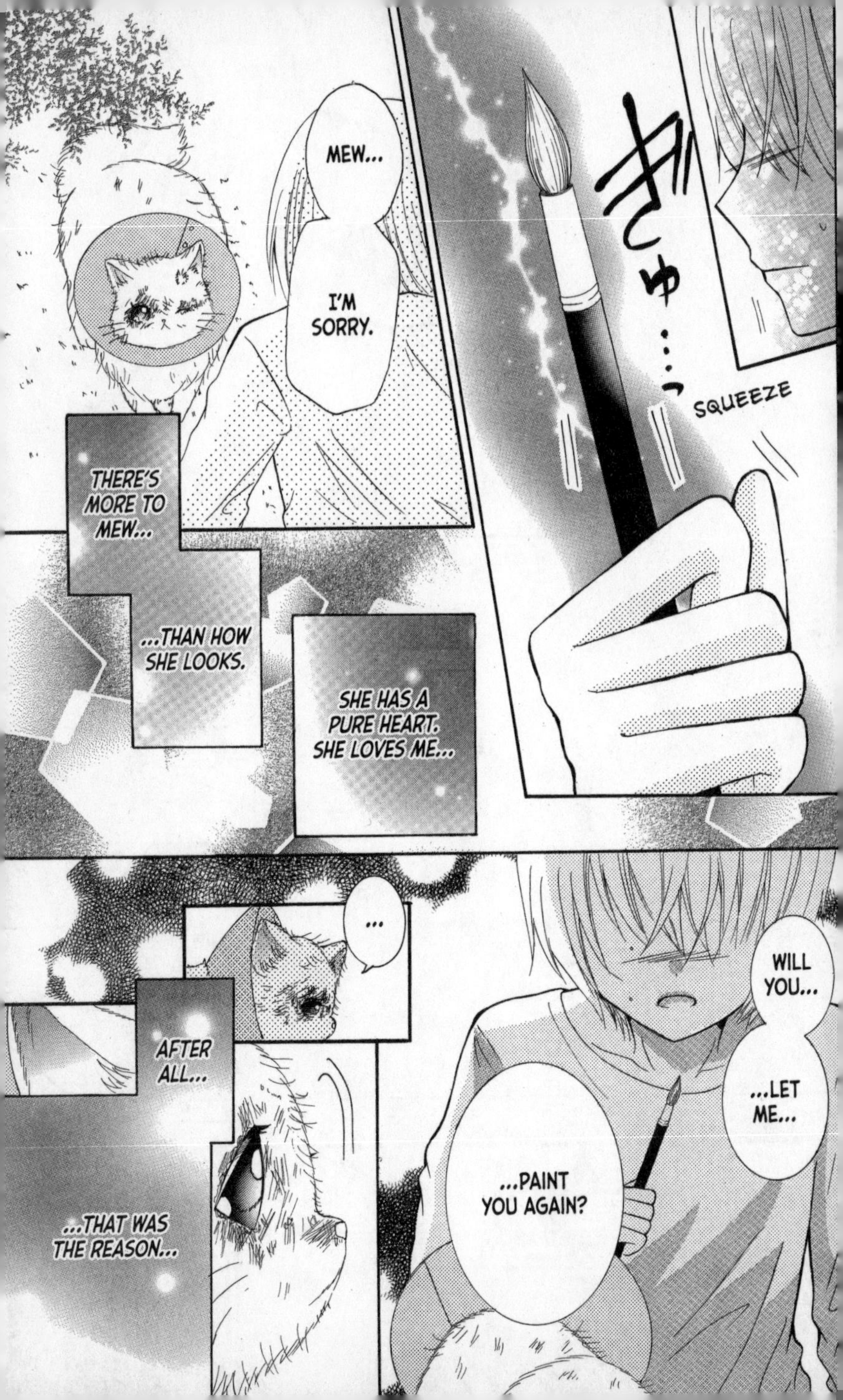
ぎゅ…っ
SQUEEZE
MEW...
I'M SORRY.
THERE'S MORE TO MEW...
...THAN HOW SHE LOOKS.
SHE HAS A PURE HEART. SHE LOVES ME...
WILL YOU...
...LET ME...
...PAINT YOU AGAIN?
...
AFTER ALL...
...THAT WAS THE REASON...

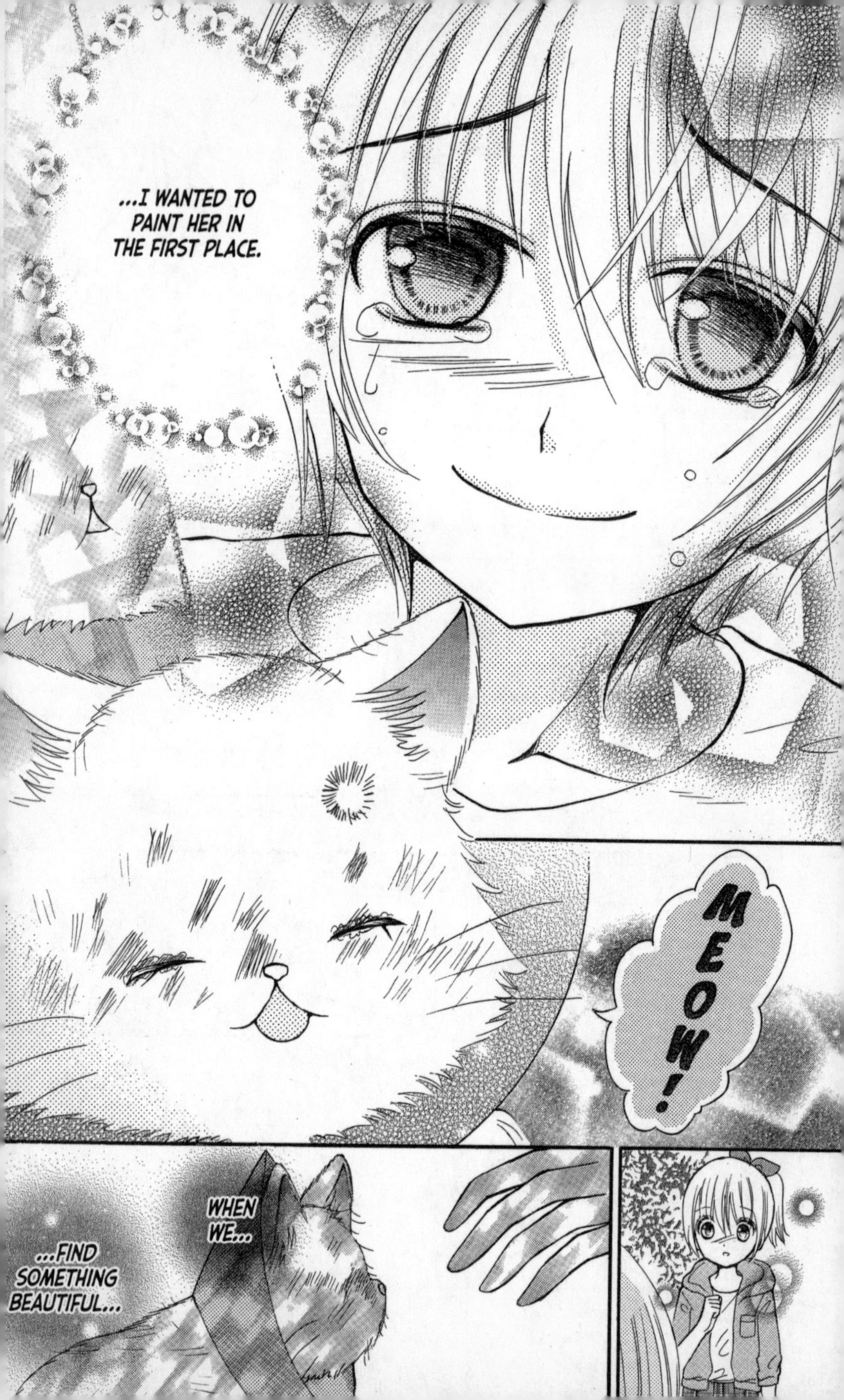
...I WANTED TO PAINT HER IN THE FIRST PLACE.
MEOW!
WHEN WE...
...FIND SOMETHING BEAUTIFUL...

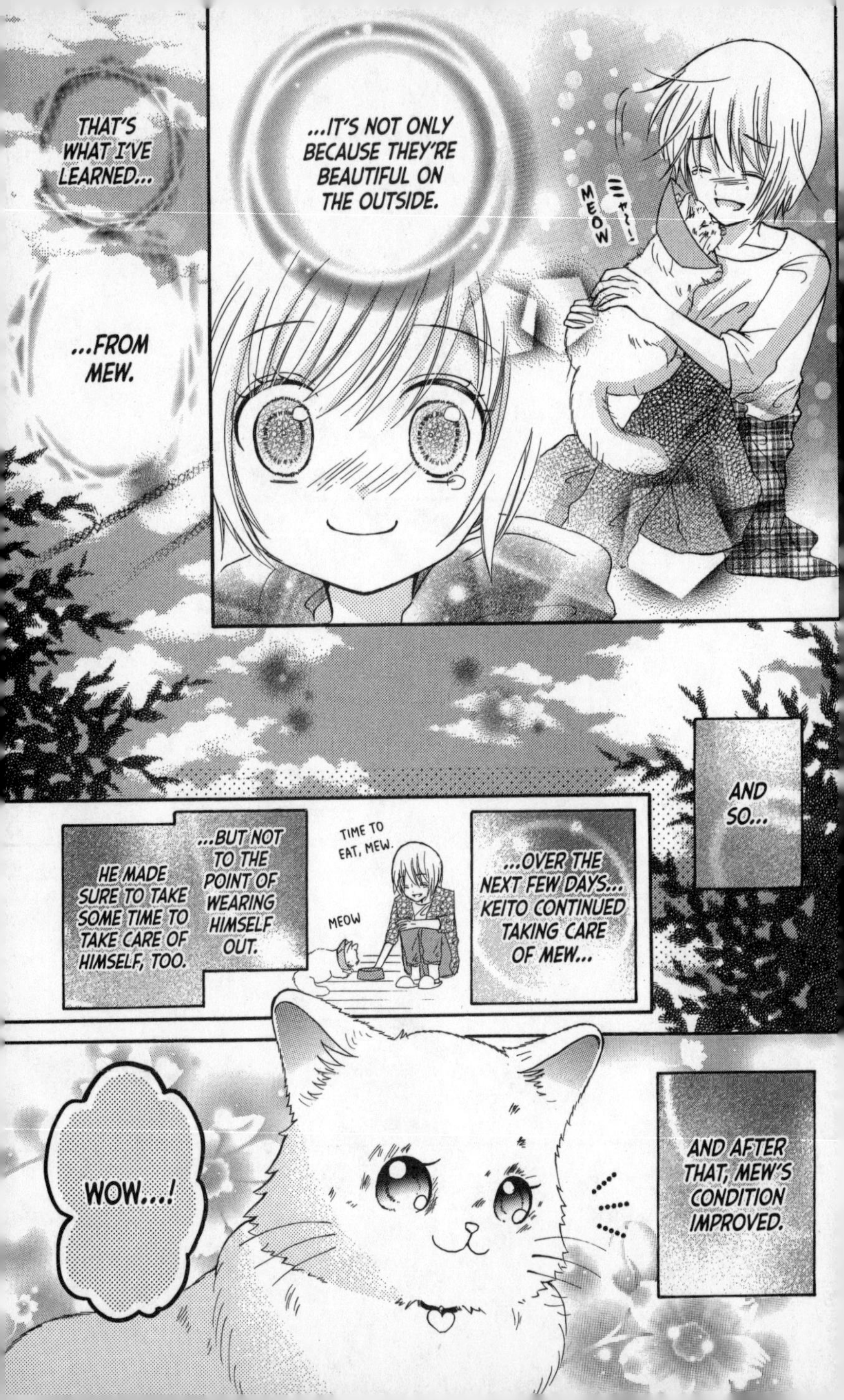

...IT'S NOT ONLY BECAUSE THEY'RE BEAUTIFUL ON THE OUTSIDE.
MEOW
THAT'S WHAT I'VE LEARNED...
...FROM MEW.
AND SO...
...OVER THE NEXT FEW DAYS... KEITO CONTINUED TAKING CARE OF MEW...
TIME TO EAT, MEW.
MEOW
HE MADE SURE TO TAKE SOME TIME TO TAKE CARE OF HIMSELF, TOO.
...BUT NOT TO THE POINT OF WEARING HIMSELF OUT.
AND AFTER THAT, MEW'S CONDITION IMPROVED.
......
WOW...!

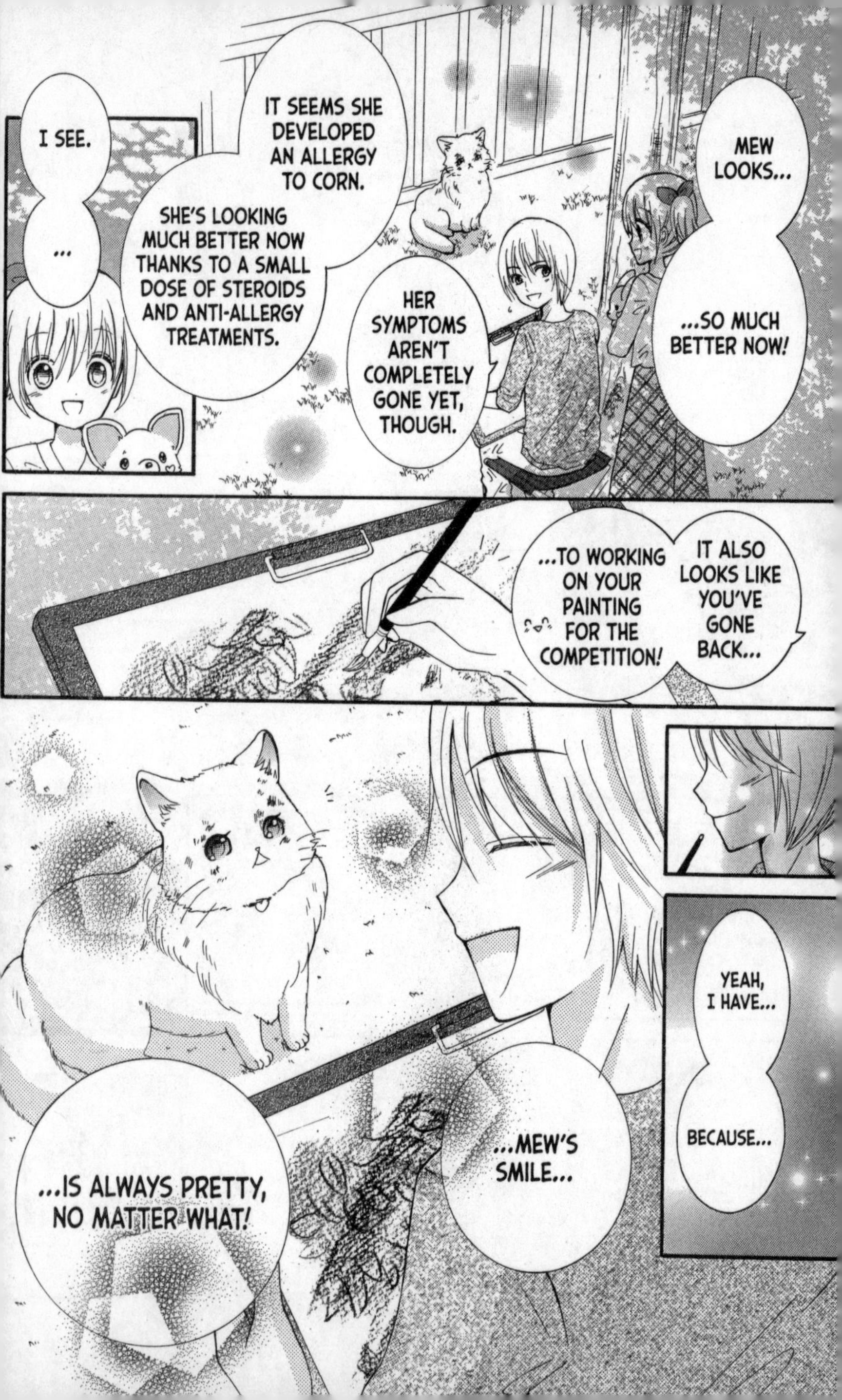
MEW LOOKS...
...SO MUCH BETTER NOW!
IT SEEMS SHE DEVELOPED AN ALLERGY TO CORN.
SHE'S LOOKING MUCH BETTER NOW THANKS TO A SMALL DOSE OF STEROIDS AND ANTI-ALLERGY TREATMENTS.
HER SYMPTOMS AREN'T COMPLETELY GONE YET, THOUGH.
I SEE.
...
IT ALSO LOOKS LIKE YOU'VE GONE BACK...
...TO WORKING ON YOUR PAINTING FOR THE COMPETITION!
YEAH, I HAVE...
BECAUSE...
...MEW'S SMILE...
...IS ALWAYS PRETTY, NO MATTER WHAT!

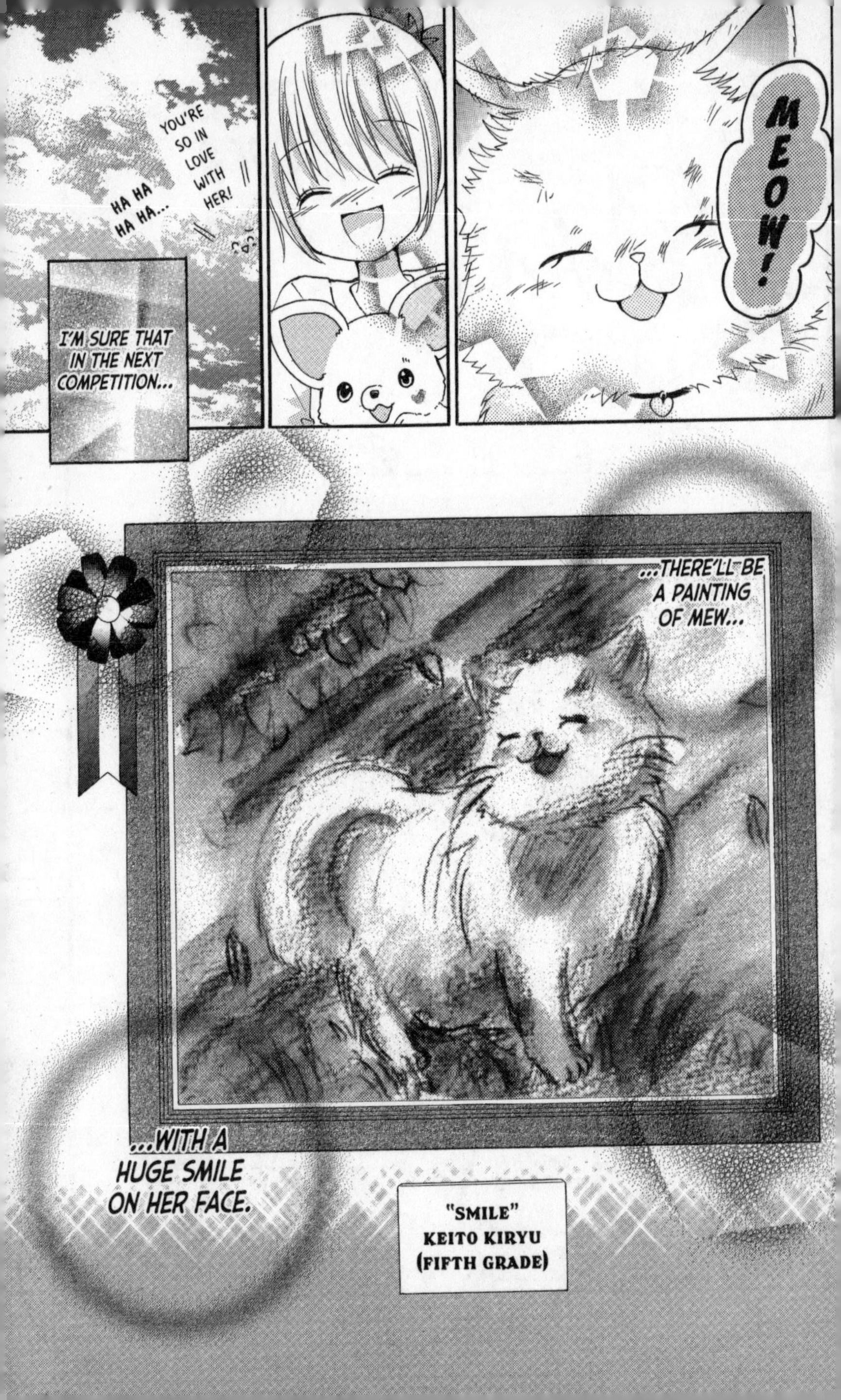
MEOW!
YOU'RE SO IN LOVE WITH HER!
HA HA HA HA...
I'M SURE THAT IN THE NEXT COMPETITION...
...THERE'LL BE A PAINTING OF MEW...
...WITH A HUGE SMILE ON HER FACE.
"SMILE"
KEITO KIRYU
(FIFTH GRADE)

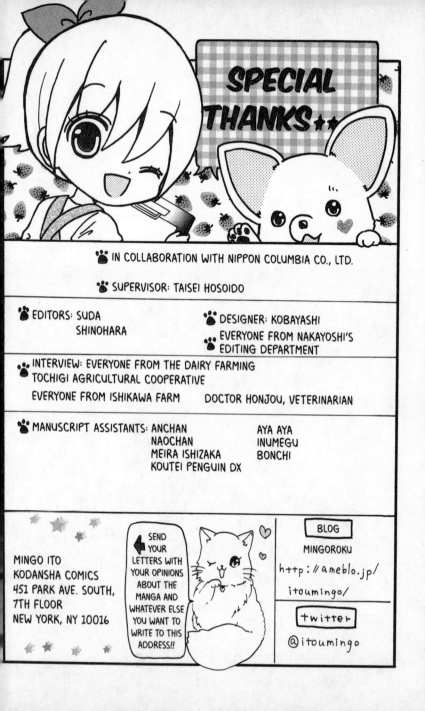

# SPECIAL THANKS‥

🐾 IN COLLABORATION WITH NIPPON COLUMBIA CO., LTD.

🐾 SUPERVISOR: TAISEI HOSOIDO

🐾 EDITORS: SUDA
SHINOHARA

🐾 DESIGNER: KOBAYASHI

🐾 EVERYONE FROM NAKAYOSHI'S EDITING DEPARTMENT

🐾 INTERVIEW: EVERYONE FROM THE DAIRY FARMING TOCHIGI AGRICULTURAL COOPERATIVE

EVERYONE FROM ISHIKAWA FARM          DOCTOR HONJOU, VETERINARIAN

🐾 MANUSCRIPT ASSISTANTS: ANCHAN          AYA AYA
NAOCHAN          INUMEGU
MEIRA ISHIZAKA          BONCHI
KOUTEI PENGUIN DX

MINGO ITO
KODANSHA COMICS
451 PARK AVE. SOUTH,
7TH FLOOR
NEW YORK, NY 10016

SEND YOUR LETTERS WITH YOUR OPINIONS ABOUT THE MANGA AND WHATEVER ELSE YOU WANT TO WRITE TO THIS ADDRESS!!

BLOG
MINGOROKU
http://ameblo.jp/
itoumingo/

twitter
@itoumingo

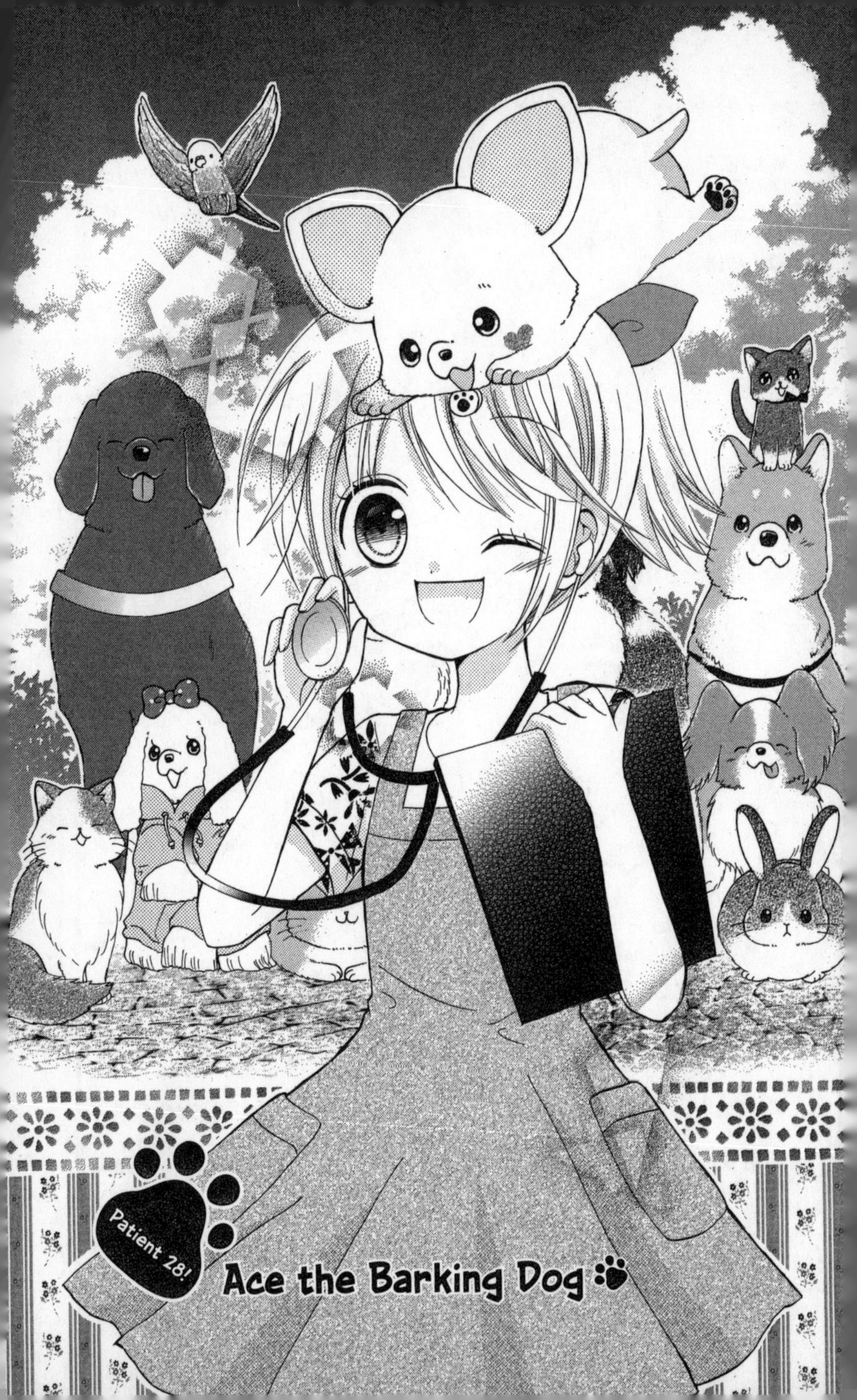
Patient 28!
Ace the Barking Dog

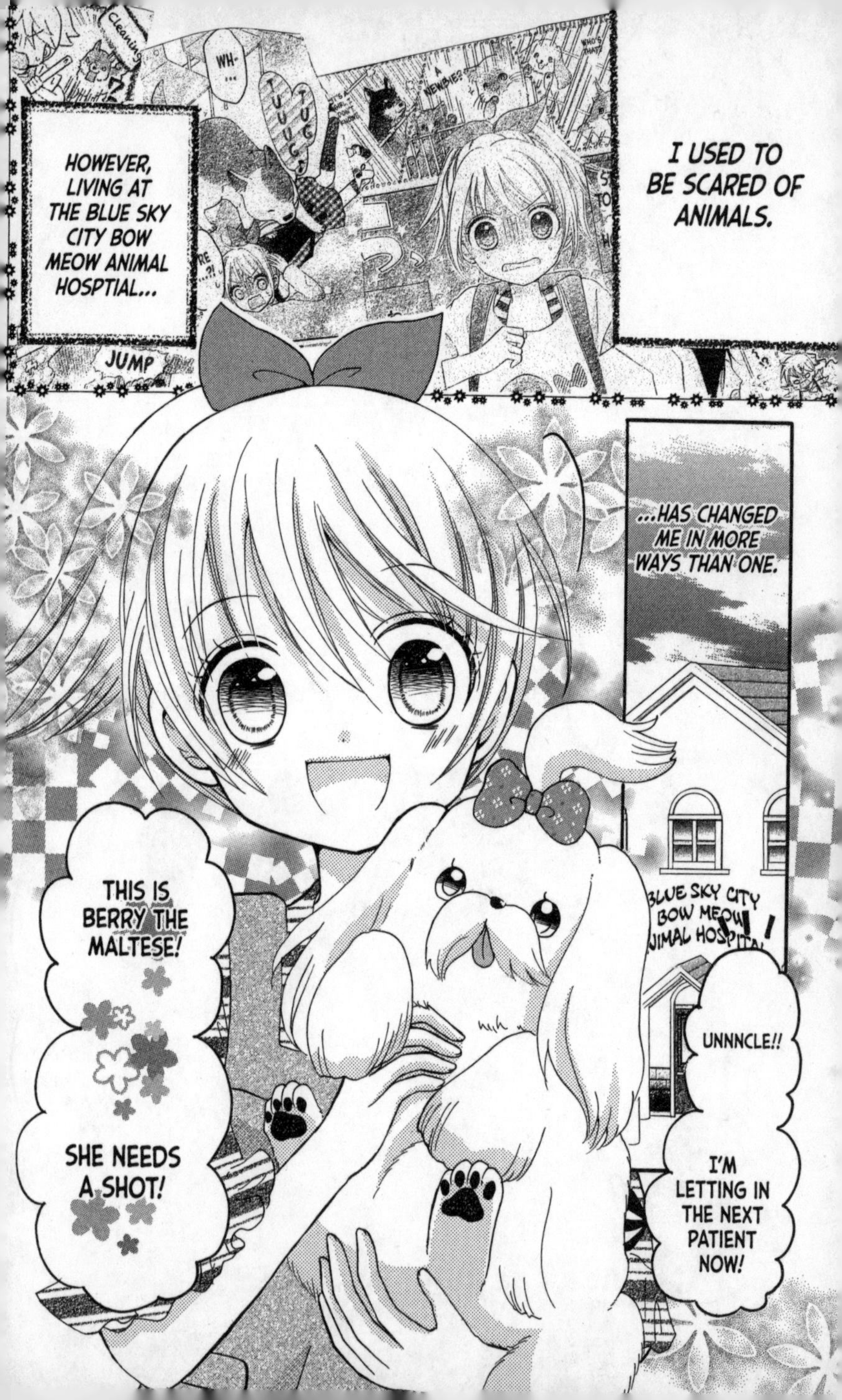
I USED TO BE SCARED OF ANIMALS.
WHO'S THAT?
A NEWBIE?
IT'S A GIRL. I DON'T KNOW!
TUUUG
TUG
WH-...
Cleaning
HOWEVER, LIVING AT THE BLUE SKY CITY BOW MEOW ANIMAL HOSPTIAL...
JUMP
...HAS CHANGED ME IN MORE WAYS THAN ONE.
BLUE SKY CITY BOW MEOW ANIMAL HOSPITAL
THIS IS BERRY THE MALTESE!
SHE NEEDS A SHOT!
UNNNCLE!!
I'M LETTING IN THE NEXT PATIENT NOW!

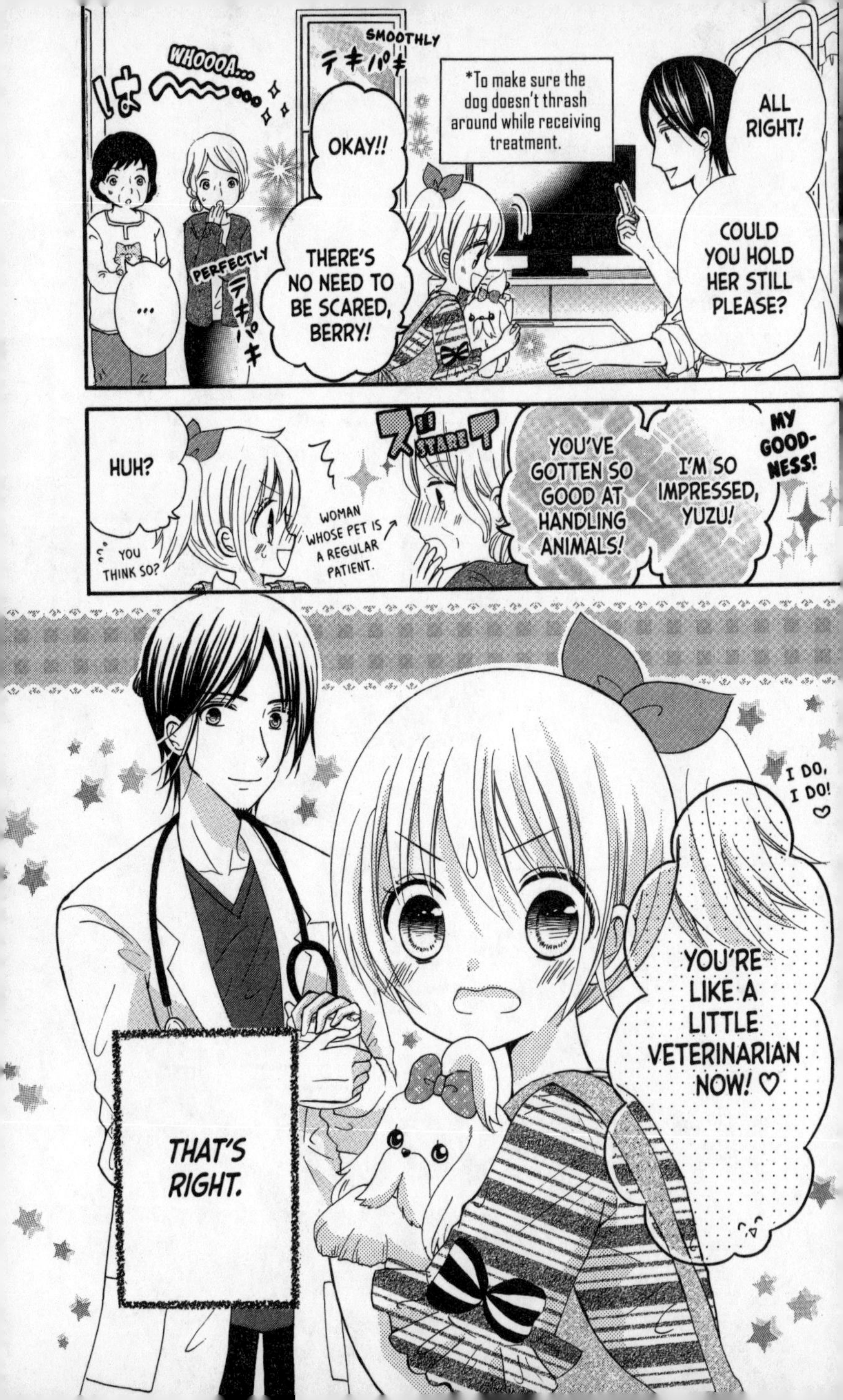
ALL RIGHT!
COULD YOU HOLD HER STILL PLEASE?
*To make sure the dog doesn't thrash around while receiving treatment.
SMOOTHLY
テキパキ
OKAY!!
THERE'S NO NEED TO BE SCARED, BERRY!
PERFECTLY
テキパキ
WHOOOA...
はへ〜〜
...
MY GOODNESS!
I'M SO IMPRESSED, YUZU!
YOU'VE GOTTEN SO GOOD AT HANDLING ANIMALS!
STARE
WOMAN WHOSE PET IS A REGULAR PATIENT.
HUH?
YOU THINK SO?
I DO, I DO! ♡
YOU'RE LIKE A LITTLE VETERINARIAN NOW! ♡
THAT'S RIGHT.

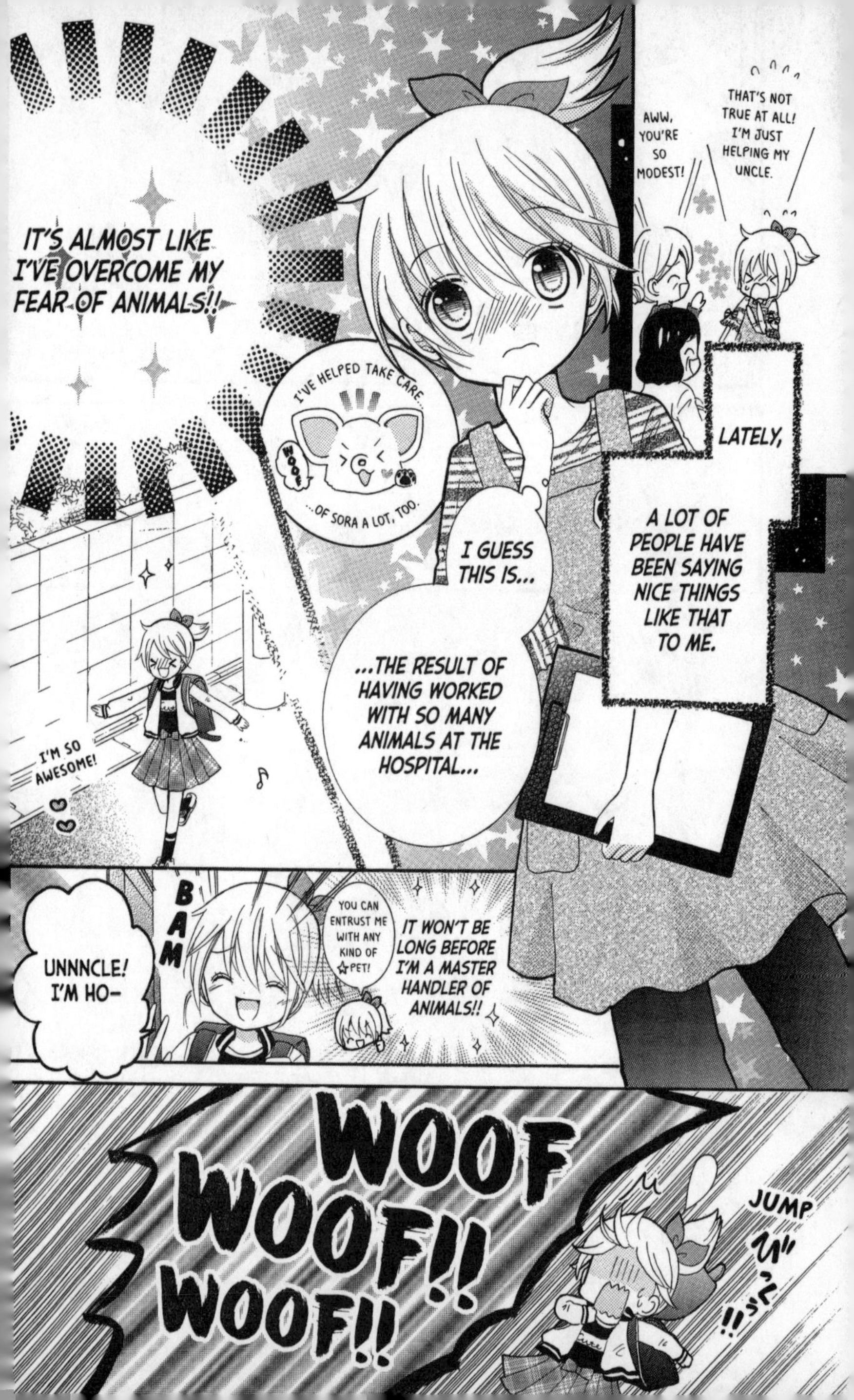

THAT'S NOT TRUE AT ALL! I'M JUST HELPING MY UNCLE.
AWW, YOU'RE SO MODEST!
LATELY,
A LOT OF PEOPLE HAVE BEEN SAYING NICE THINGS LIKE THAT TO ME.
I GUESS THIS IS...
...THE RESULT OF HAVING WORKED WITH SO MANY ANIMALS AT THE HOSPITAL...
I'VE HELPED TAKE CARE...
WOOF
...OF SORA A LOT, TOO.
IT'S ALMOST LIKE I'VE OVERCOME MY FEAR OF ANIMALS!!
I'M SO AWESOME!
IT WON'T BE LONG BEFORE I'M A MASTER HANDLER OF ANIMALS!!
YOU CAN ENTRUST ME WITH ANY KIND OF PET!
BAM
UNNNCLE! I'M HO-
WOOF
WOOF!!
WOOF!!
JUMP
!!

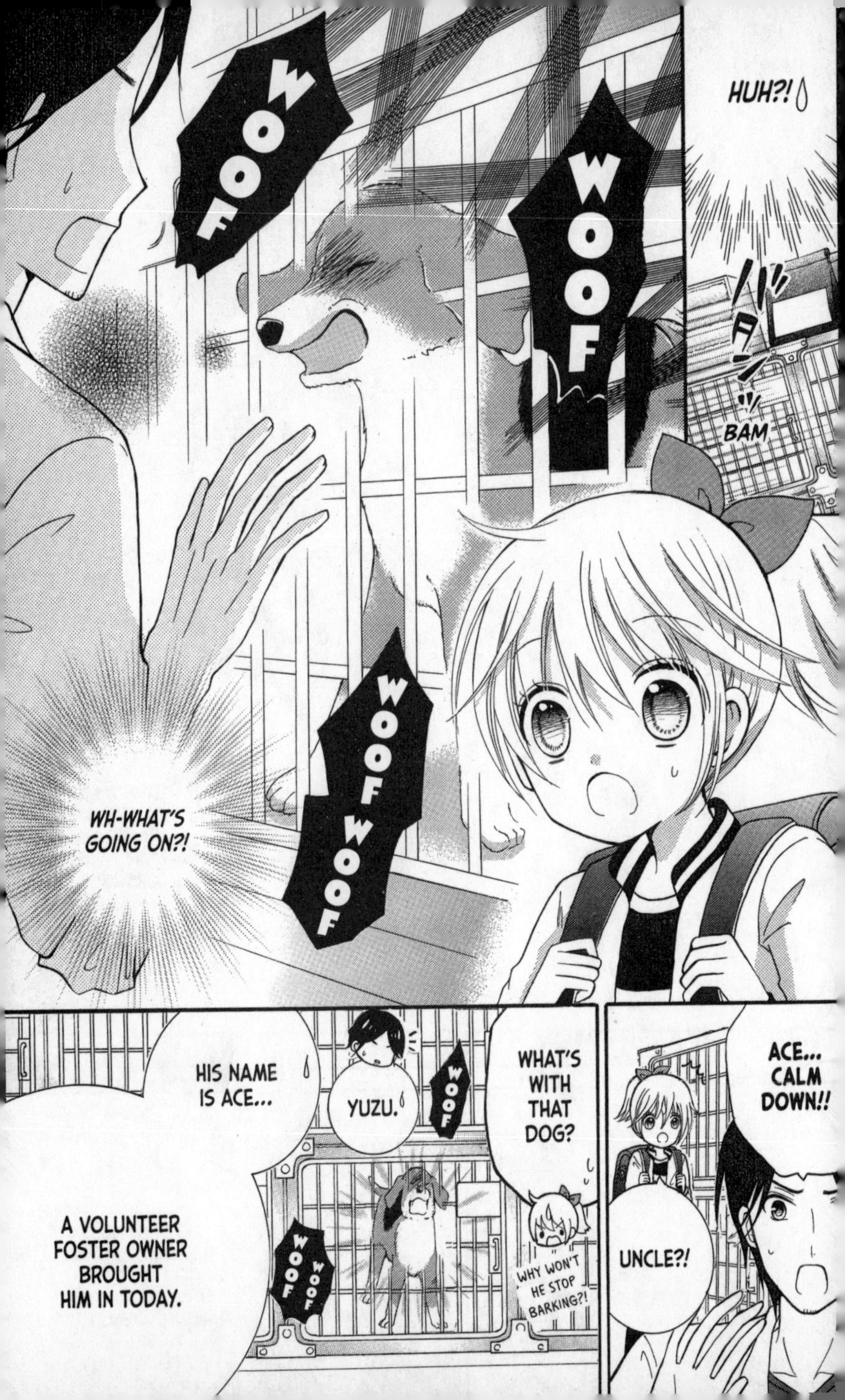
HUH?!
BAM
WOOF
WOOF
WOOF WOOF WOOF
WH-WHAT'S GOING ON?!
ACE... CALM DOWN!!
UNCLE?!
WHAT'S WITH THAT DOG?
WHY WON'T HE STOP BARKING?!
WOOF
YUZU.
HIS NAME IS ACE...
WOOF WOOF
A VOLUNTEER FOSTER OWNER BROUGHT HIM IN TODAY.

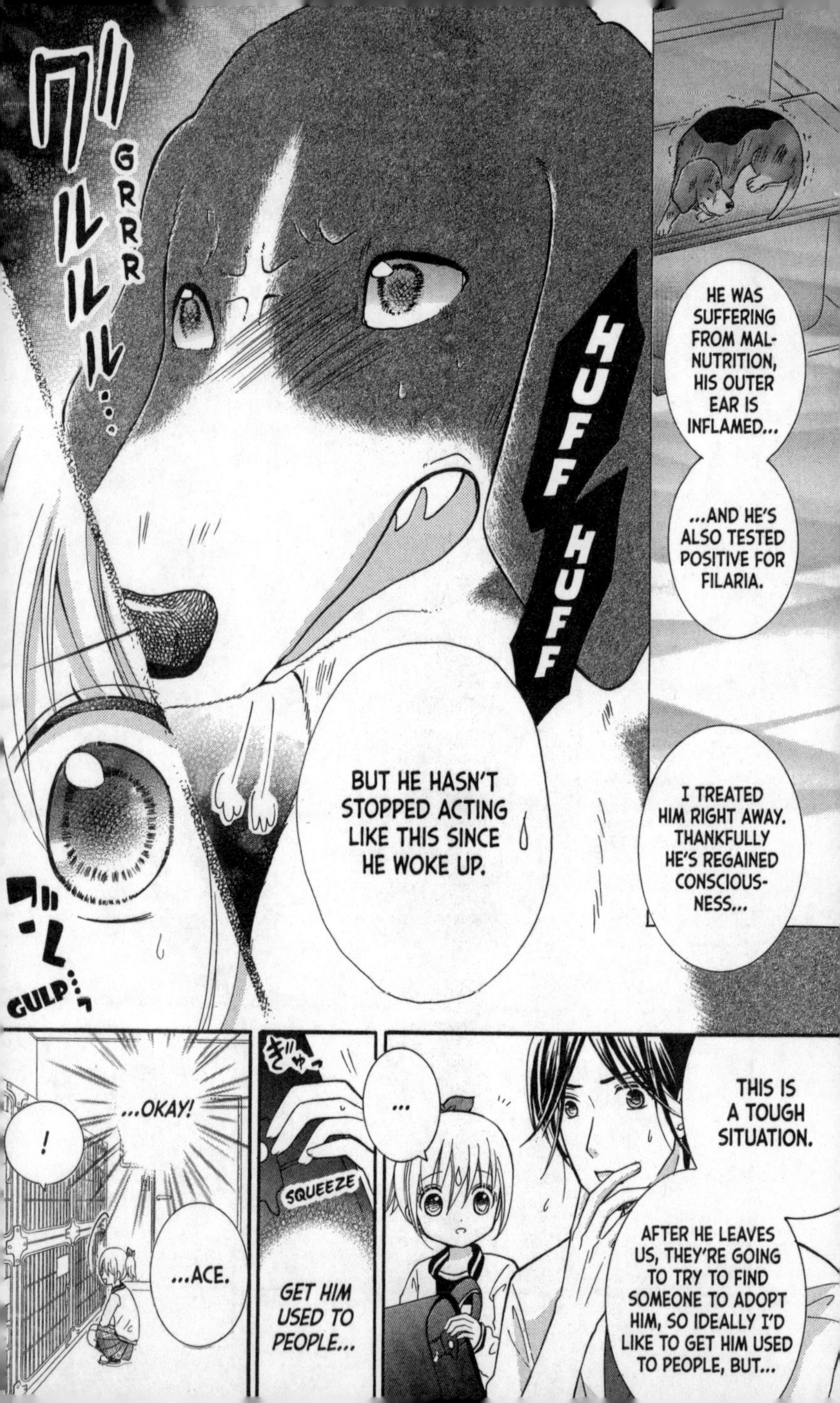
HE WAS SUFFERING FROM MAL-NUTRITION, HIS OUTER EAR IS INFLAMED...
...AND HE'S ALSO TESTED POSITIVE FOR FILARIA.
I TREATED HIM RIGHT AWAY. THANKFULLY HE'S REGAINED CONSCIOUS-NESS...
GRRR
HUFF HUFF
BUT HE HASN'T STOPPED ACTING LIKE THIS SINCE HE WOKE UP.
GULP...
THIS IS A TOUGH SITUATION.
AFTER HE LEAVES US, THEY'RE GOING TO TRY TO FIND SOMEONE TO ADOPT HIM, SO IDEALLY I'D LIKE TO GET HIM USED TO PEOPLE, BUT...
...
SQUEEZE
GET HIM USED TO PEOPLE...
...OKAY!
!
...ACE.

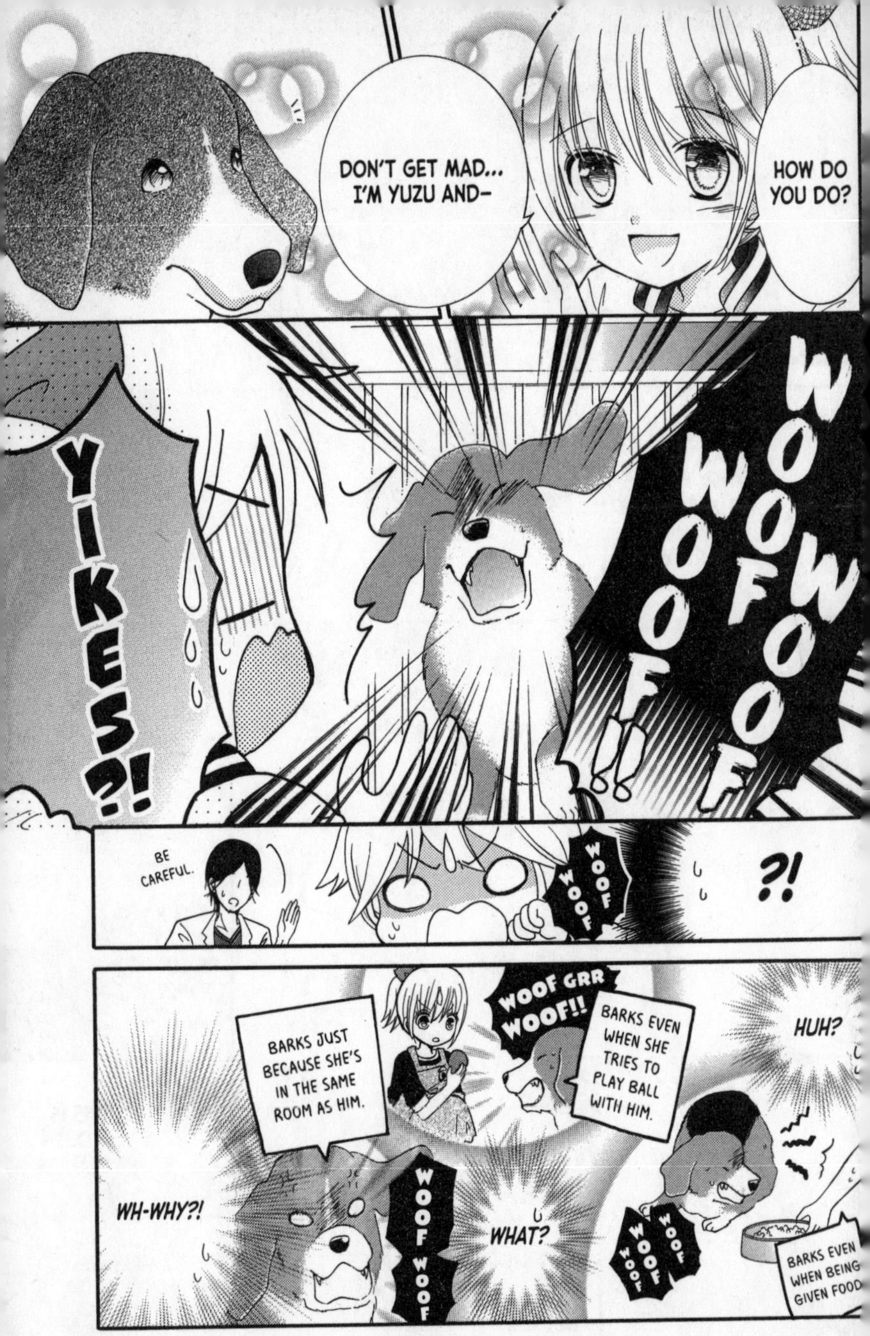
HOW DO YOU DO?
DON'T GET MAD... I'M YUZU AND-
WOOF WOOF WOOF
YIKES?!
?!
WOOF WOOF
BE CAREFUL.
HUH?
BARKS EVEN WHEN SHE TRIES TO PLAY BALL WITH HIM.
WOOF GRR WOOF!!
BARKS JUST BECAUSE SHE'S IN THE SAME ROOM AS HIM.
BARKS EVEN WHEN BEING GIVEN FOOD
WOOF WOOF WOOF
WHAT?
WOOF WOOF
WH-WHY?!

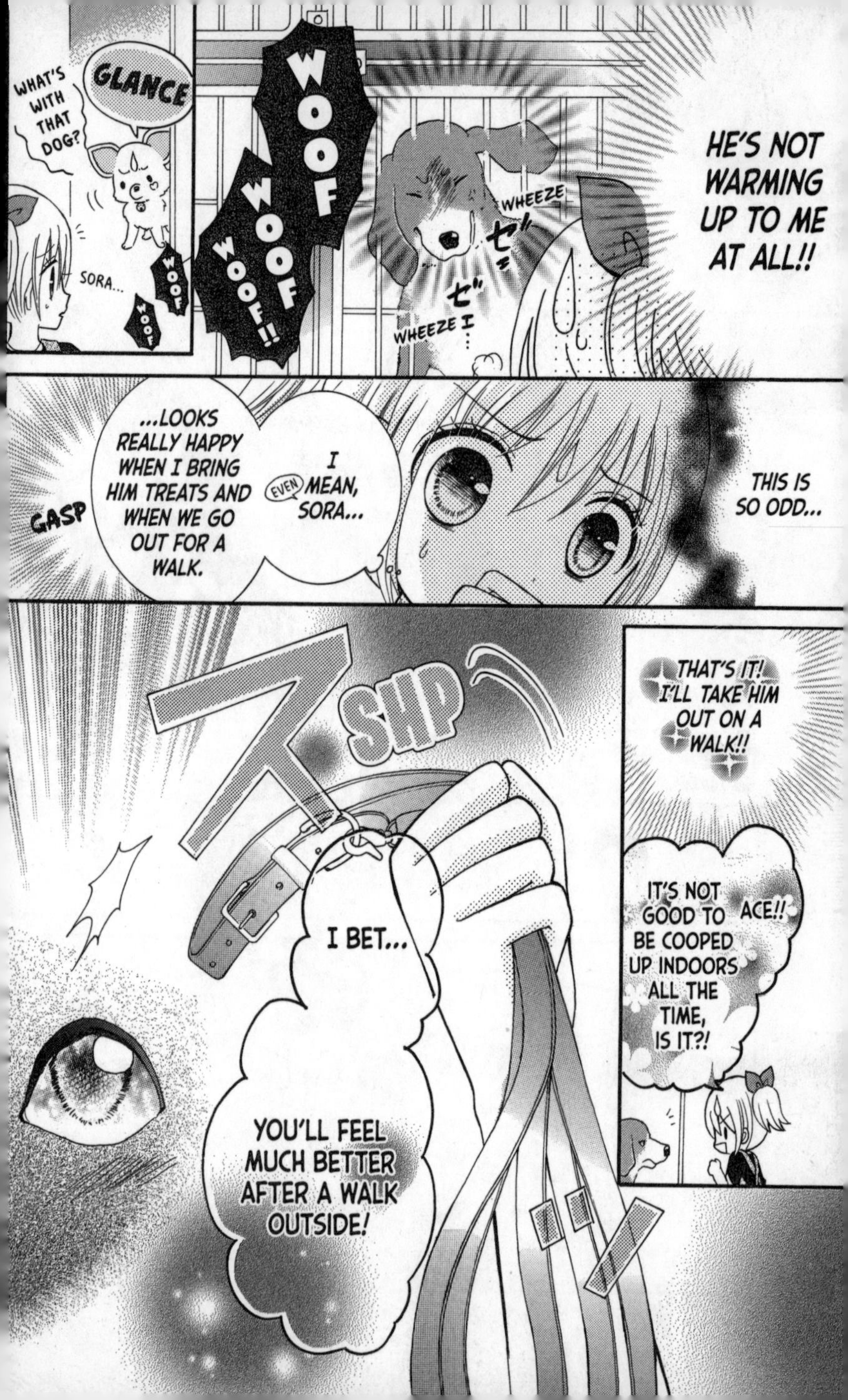
HE'S NOT WARMING UP TO ME AT ALL!!
WOOF WOOF WOOF!!
WHEEZE
ゼー
WHEEZE
ゼー...
GLANCE
WHAT'S WITH THAT DOG?
SORA...
WOOF
WOOF
THIS IS SO ODD...
I MEAN, SORA...
EVEN
...LOOKS REALLY HAPPY WHEN I BRING HIM TREATS AND WHEN WE GO OUT FOR A WALK.
GASP
THAT'S IT! I'LL TAKE HIM OUT ON A WALK!!
ACE!!
IT'S NOT GOOD TO BE COOPED UP INDOORS ALL THE TIME, IS IT?!
SHP
I BET...
YOU'LL FEEL MUCH BETTER AFTER A WALK OUTSIDE!

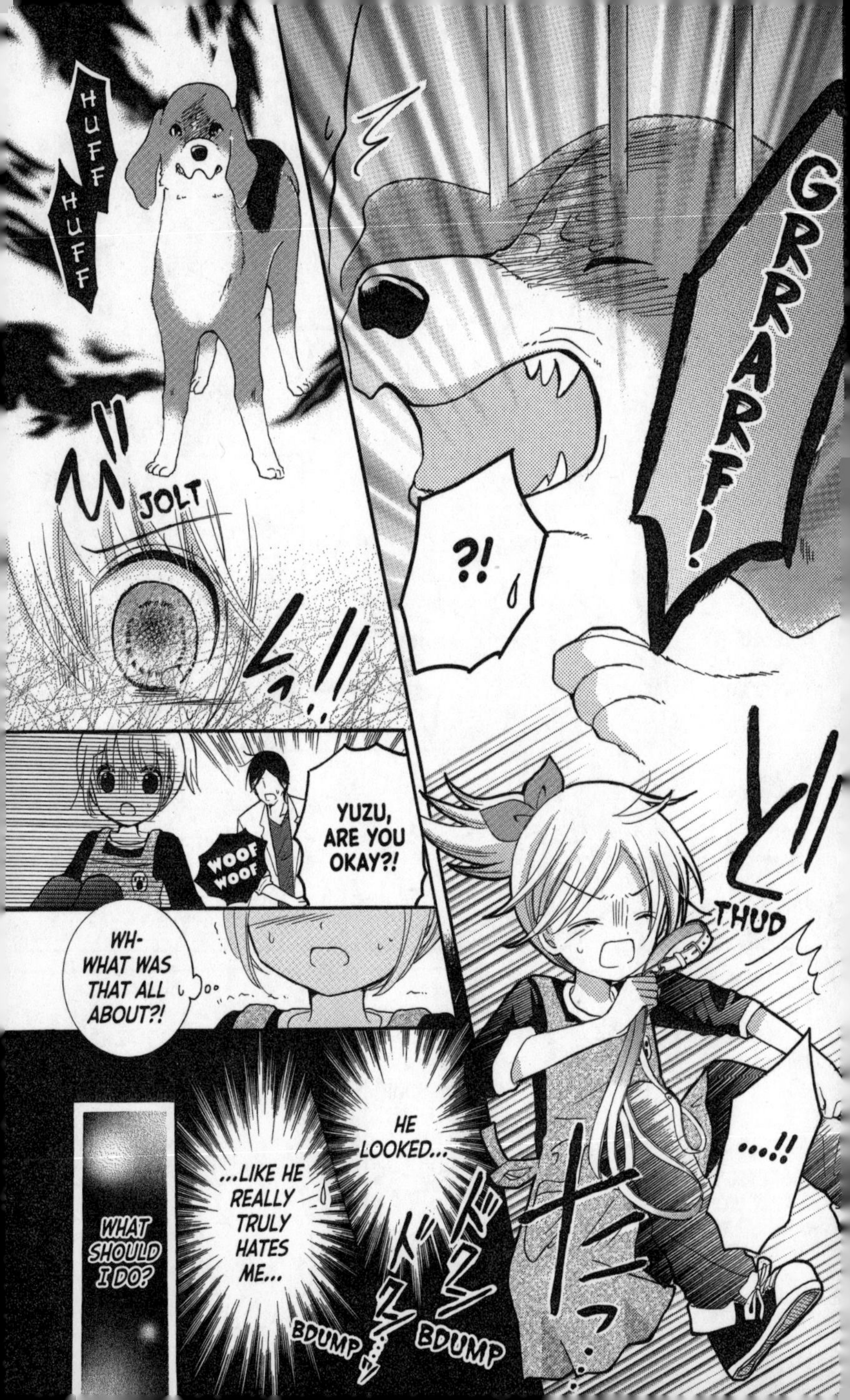
GRRARF!
?!
THUD
...!!
HUFF HUFF
JOLT
YUZU, ARE YOU OKAY?!
WOOF WOOF
WH-WHAT WAS THAT ALL ABOUT?!
HE LOOKED...
...LIKE HE REALLY TRULY HATES ME...
BDUMP BDUMP
WHAT SHOULD I DO?

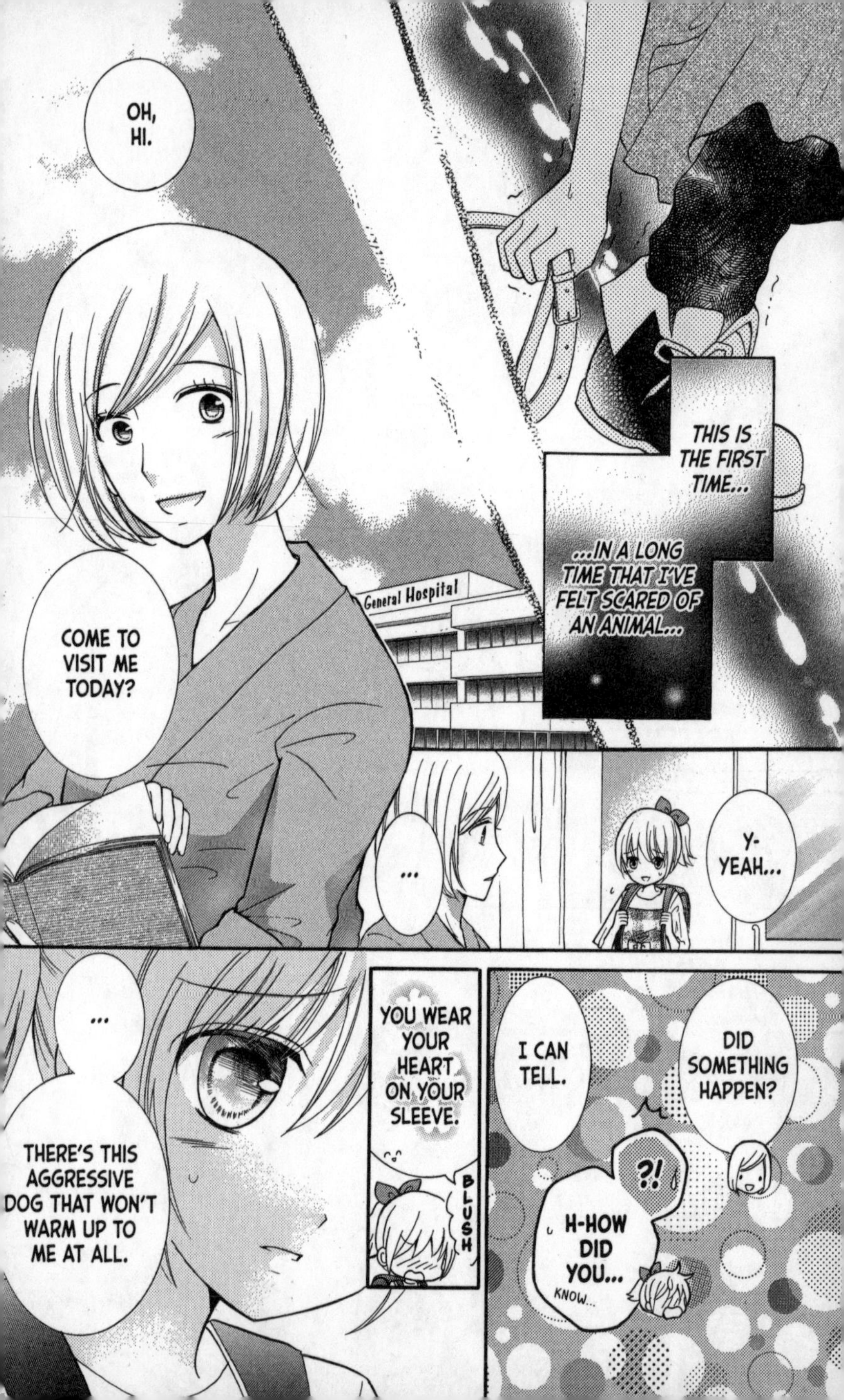
THIS IS THE FIRST TIME...
...IN A LONG TIME THAT I'VE FELT SCARED OF AN ANIMAL...
OH, HI.
General Hospital
COME TO VISIT ME TODAY?
Y- YEAH...
...
DID SOMETHING HAPPEN?
?!
H-HOW DID YOU... KNOW...
I CAN TELL.
YOU WEAR YOUR HEART ON YOUR SLEEVE.
BLUSH
...
THERE'S THIS AGGRESSIVE DOG THAT WON'T WARM UP TO ME AT ALL.

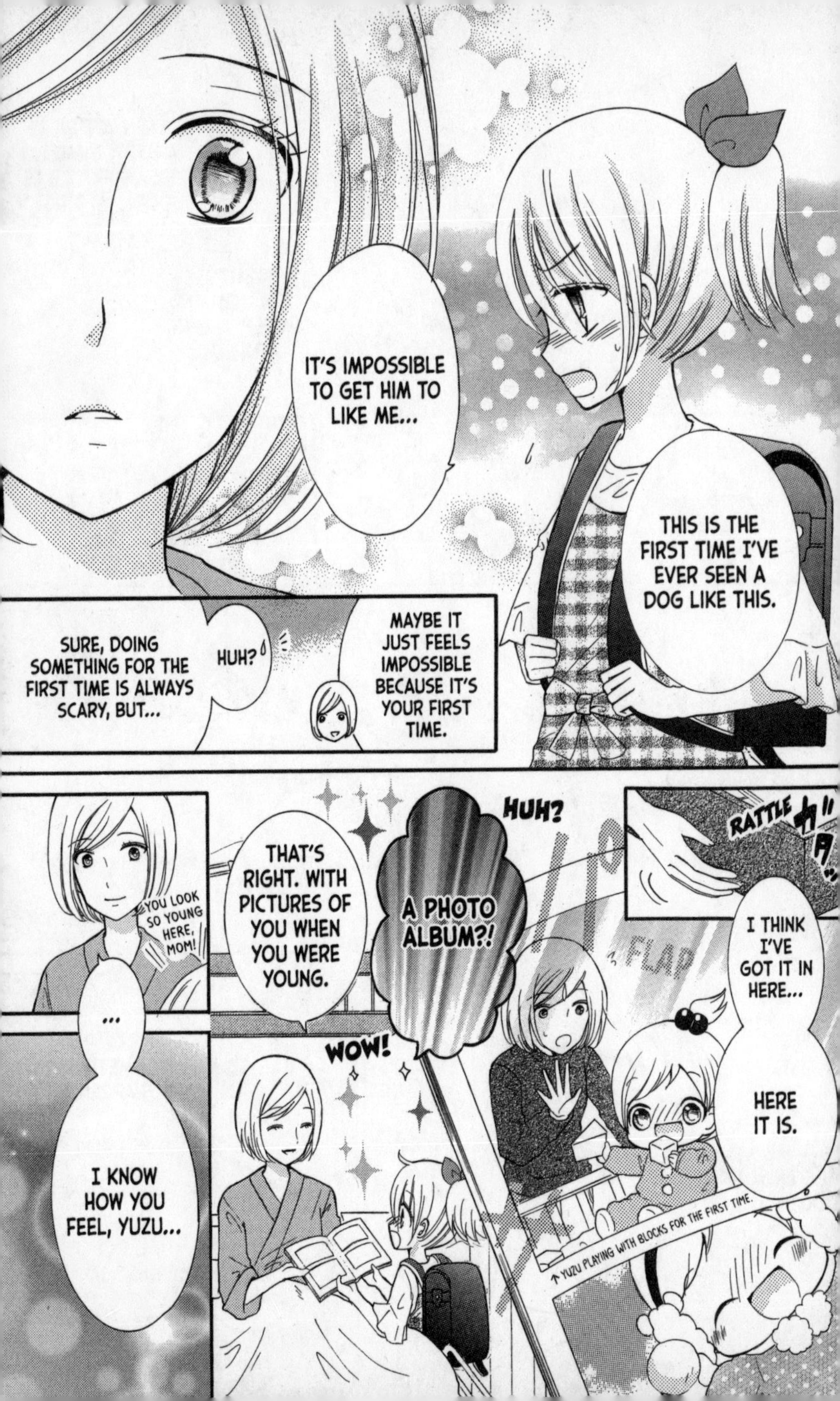
THIS IS THE FIRST TIME I'VE EVER SEEN A DOG LIKE THIS.
IT'S IMPOSSIBLE TO GET HIM TO LIKE ME...
MAYBE IT JUST FEELS IMPOSSIBLE BECAUSE IT'S YOUR FIRST TIME.
HUH?
SURE, DOING SOMETHING FOR THE FIRST TIME IS ALWAYS SCARY, BUT...
RATTLE
I THINK I'VE GOT IT IN HERE...
HERE IT IS.
HUH?
A PHOTO ALBUM?!
FLAP
↑ YUZU PLAYING WITH BLOCKS FOR THE FIRST TIME.
WOW!
THAT'S RIGHT. WITH PICTURES OF YOU WHEN YOU WERE YOUNG.
YOU LOOK SO YOUNG HERE, MOM!
...
I KNOW HOW YOU FEEL, YUZU...

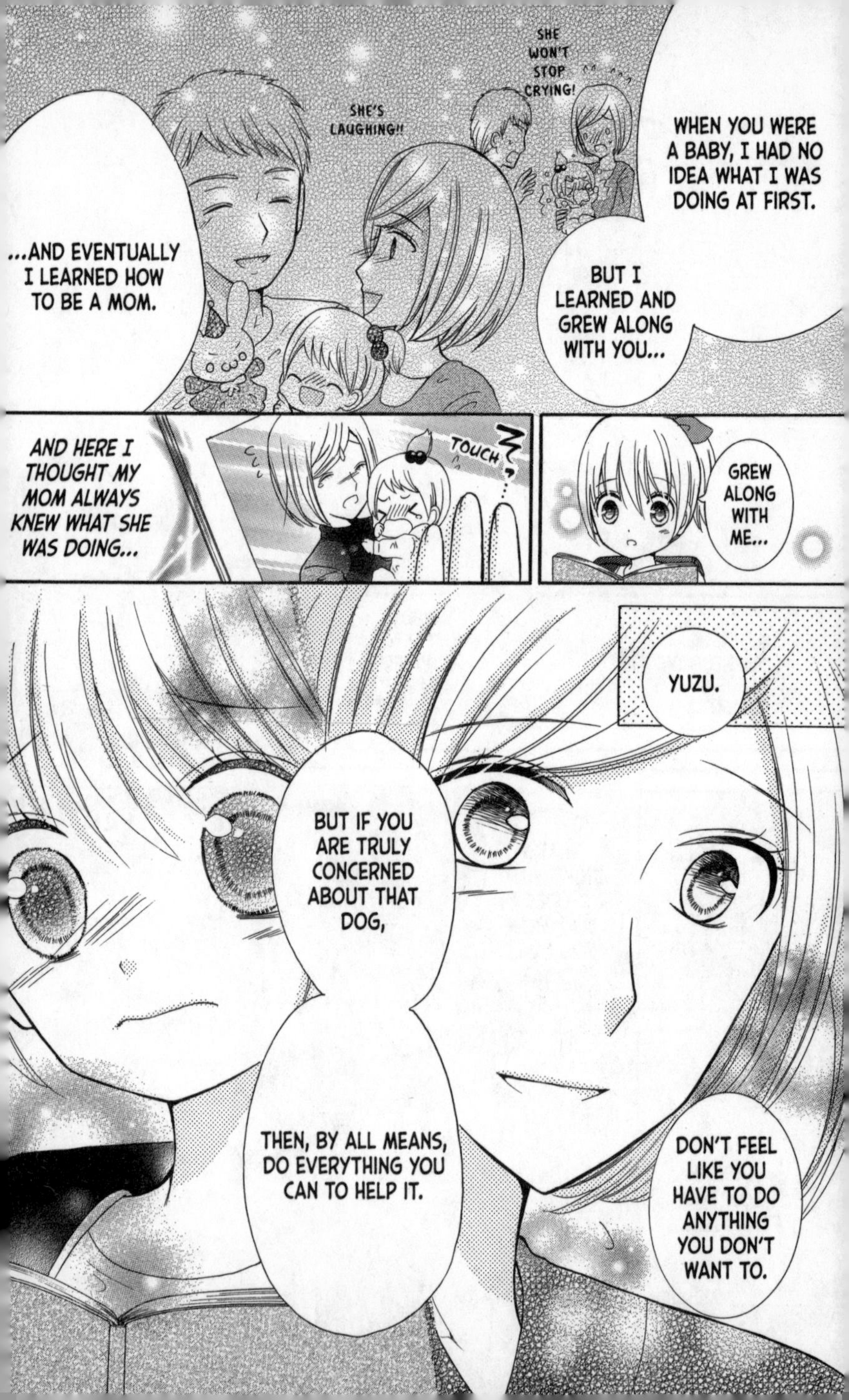
WHEN YOU WERE A BABY, I HAD NO IDEA WHAT I WAS DOING AT FIRST.
SHE WON'T STOP CRYING!
BUT I LEARNED AND GREW ALONG WITH YOU...
SHE'S LAUGHING!!
...AND EVENTUALLY I LEARNED HOW TO BE A MOM.
GREW ALONG WITH ME...
TOUCH
AND HERE I THOUGHT MY MOM ALWAYS KNEW WHAT SHE WAS DOING...
YUZU.
DON'T FEEL LIKE YOU HAVE TO DO ANYTHING YOU DON'T WANT TO.
BUT IF YOU ARE TRULY CONCERNED ABOUT THAT DOG,
THEN, BY ALL MEANS, DO EVERYTHING YOU CAN TO HELP IT.

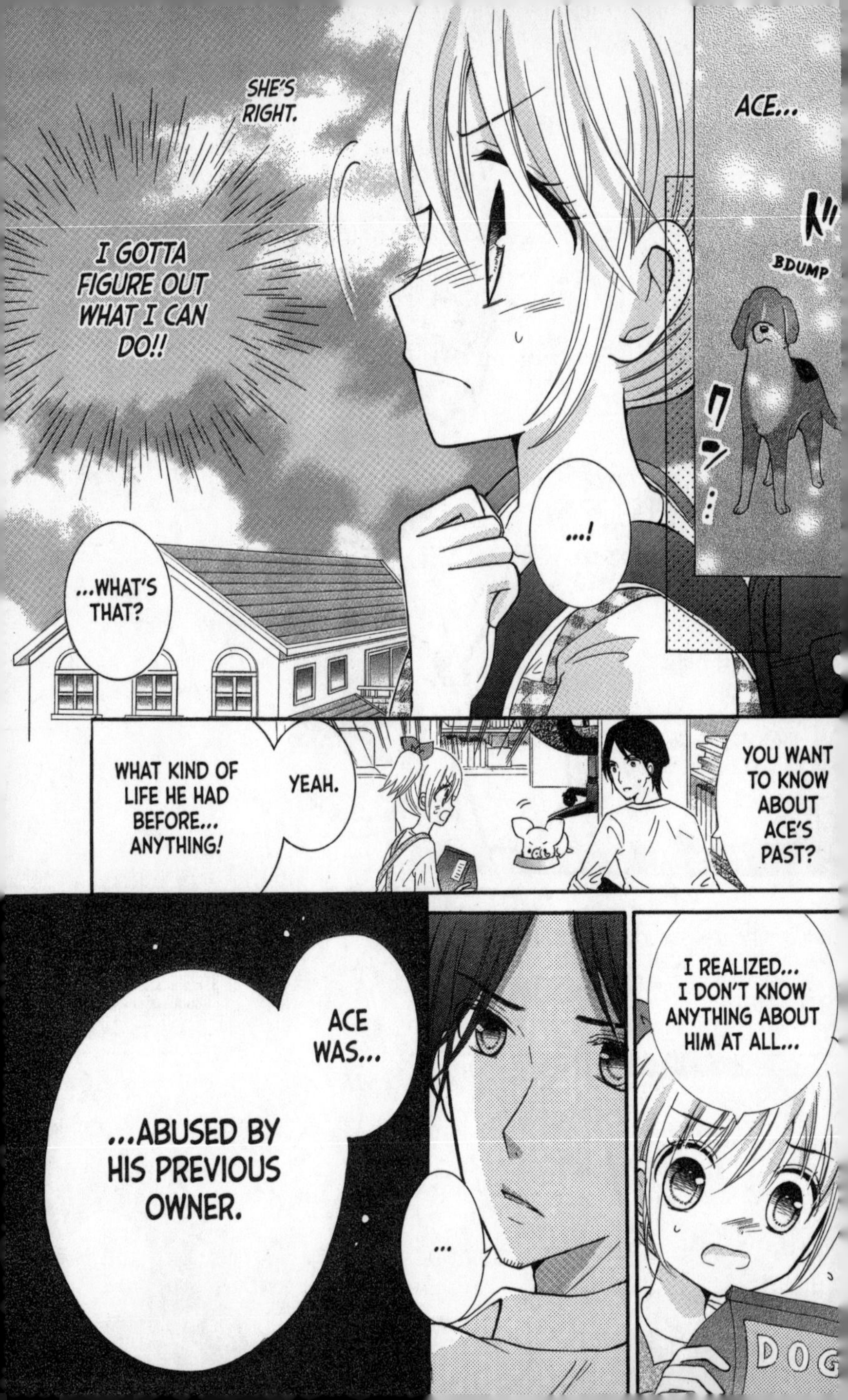
ACE...
BDUMP
SHE'S RIGHT.
I GOTTA FIGURE OUT WHAT I CAN DO!!
...!
...WHAT'S THAT?
YOU WANT TO KNOW ABOUT ACE'S PAST?
YEAH.
WHAT KIND OF LIFE HE HAD BEFORE... ANYTHING!
I REALIZED... I DON'T KNOW ANYTHING ABOUT HIM AT ALL...
DOG
...
ACE WAS...
...ABUSED BY HIS PREVIOUS OWNER.

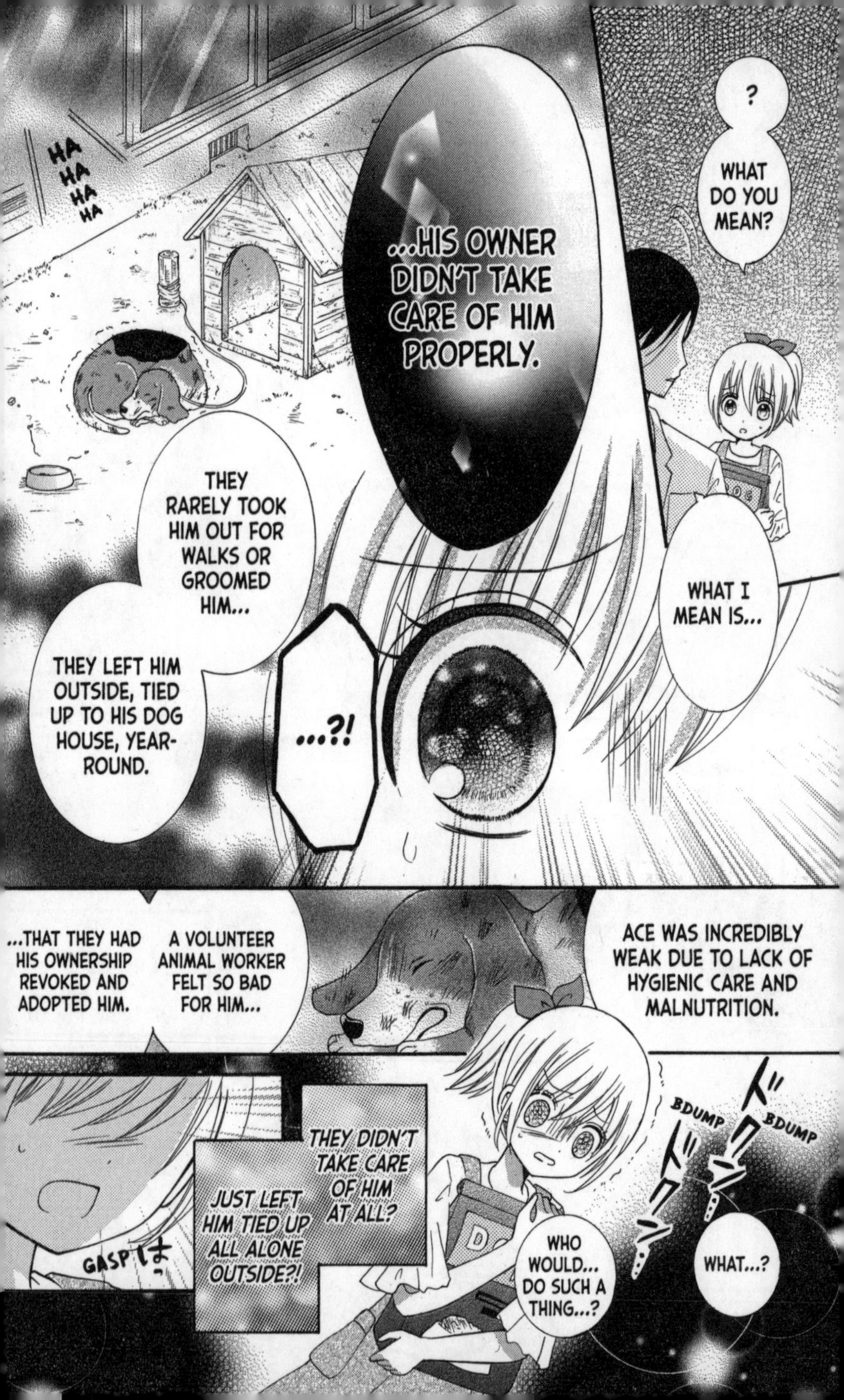
?
WHAT DO YOU MEAN?
WHAT I MEAN IS...
...HIS OWNER DIDN'T TAKE CARE OF HIM PROPERLY.
HA HA HA HA
THEY RARELY TOOK HIM OUT FOR WALKS OR GROOMED HIM...
THEY LEFT HIM OUTSIDE, TIED UP TO HIS DOG HOUSE, YEAR-ROUND.
...?!
ACE WAS INCREDIBLY WEAK DUE TO LACK OF HYGIENIC CARE AND MALNUTRITION.
A VOLUNTEER ANIMAL WORKER FELT SO BAD FOR HIM...
...THAT THEY HAD HIS OWNERSHIP REVOKED AND ADOPTED HIM.
BDUMP BDUMP
WHAT...?
WHO WOULD... DO SUCH A THING...?
THEY DIDN'T TAKE CARE OF HIM AT ALL?
JUST LEFT HIM TIED UP ALL ALONE OUTSIDE?!
GASP

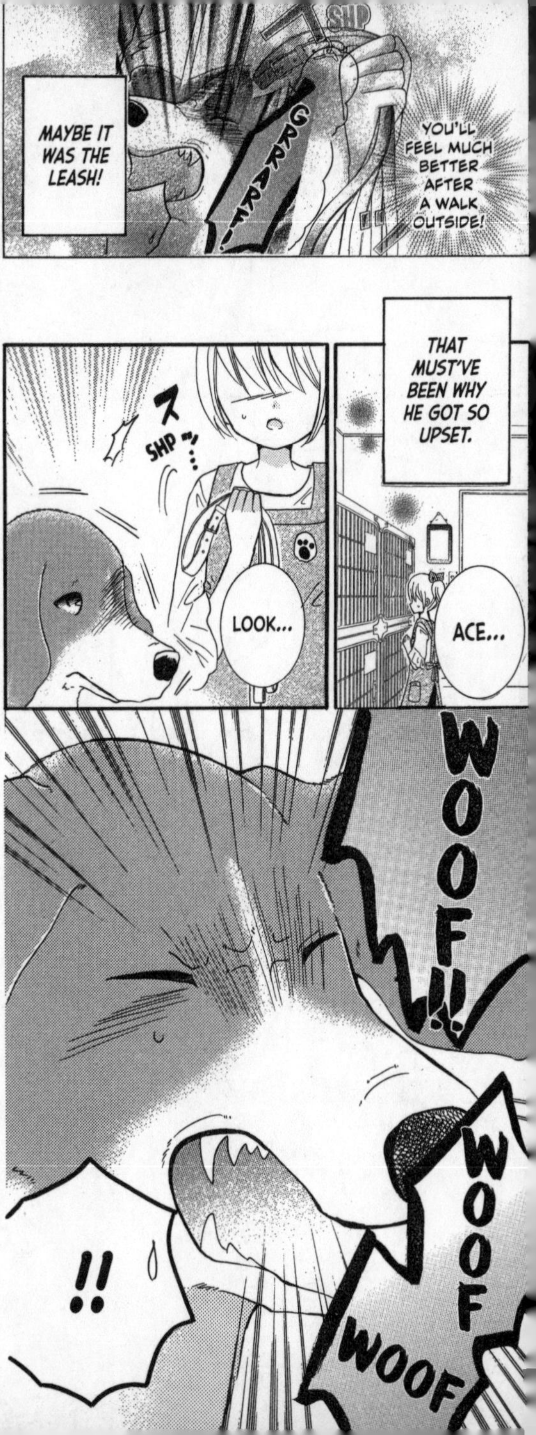
SHP
YOU'LL FEEL MUCH BETTER AFTER A WALK OUTSIDE!
GRRARF!!
MAYBE IT WAS THE LEASH!
THAT MUST'VE BEEN WHY HE GOT SO UPSET.
ACE...
SHP
LOOK...
WOOF!!
WOOF
WOOF
WOOF
!!

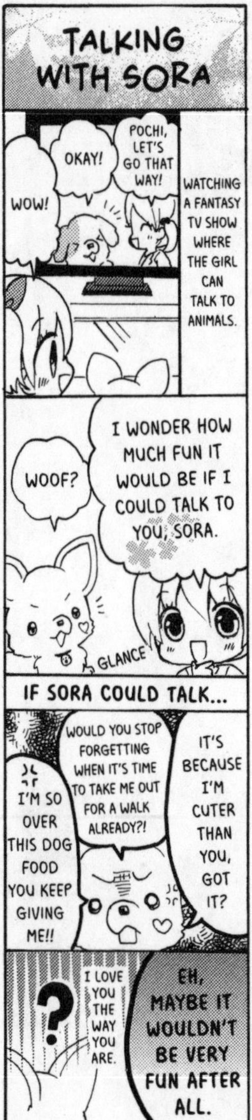
TALKING WITH SORA
WATCHING A FANTASY TV SHOW WHERE THE GIRL CAN TALK TO ANIMALS.
POCHI, LET'S GO THAT WAY!
OKAY!
WOW!
I WONDER HOW MUCH FUN IT WOULD BE IF I COULD TALK TO YOU, SORA.
WOOF?
GLANCE
IF SORA COULD TALK...
IT'S BECAUSE I'M CUTER THAN YOU, GOT IT?
WOULD YOU STOP FORGETTING WHEN IT'S TIME TO TAKE ME OUT FOR A WALK ALREADY?!
I'M SO OVER THIS DOG FOOD YOU KEEP GIVING ME!!
EH, MAYBE IT WOULDN'T BE VERY FUN AFTER ALL.
I LOVE YOU THE WAY YOU ARE.
?

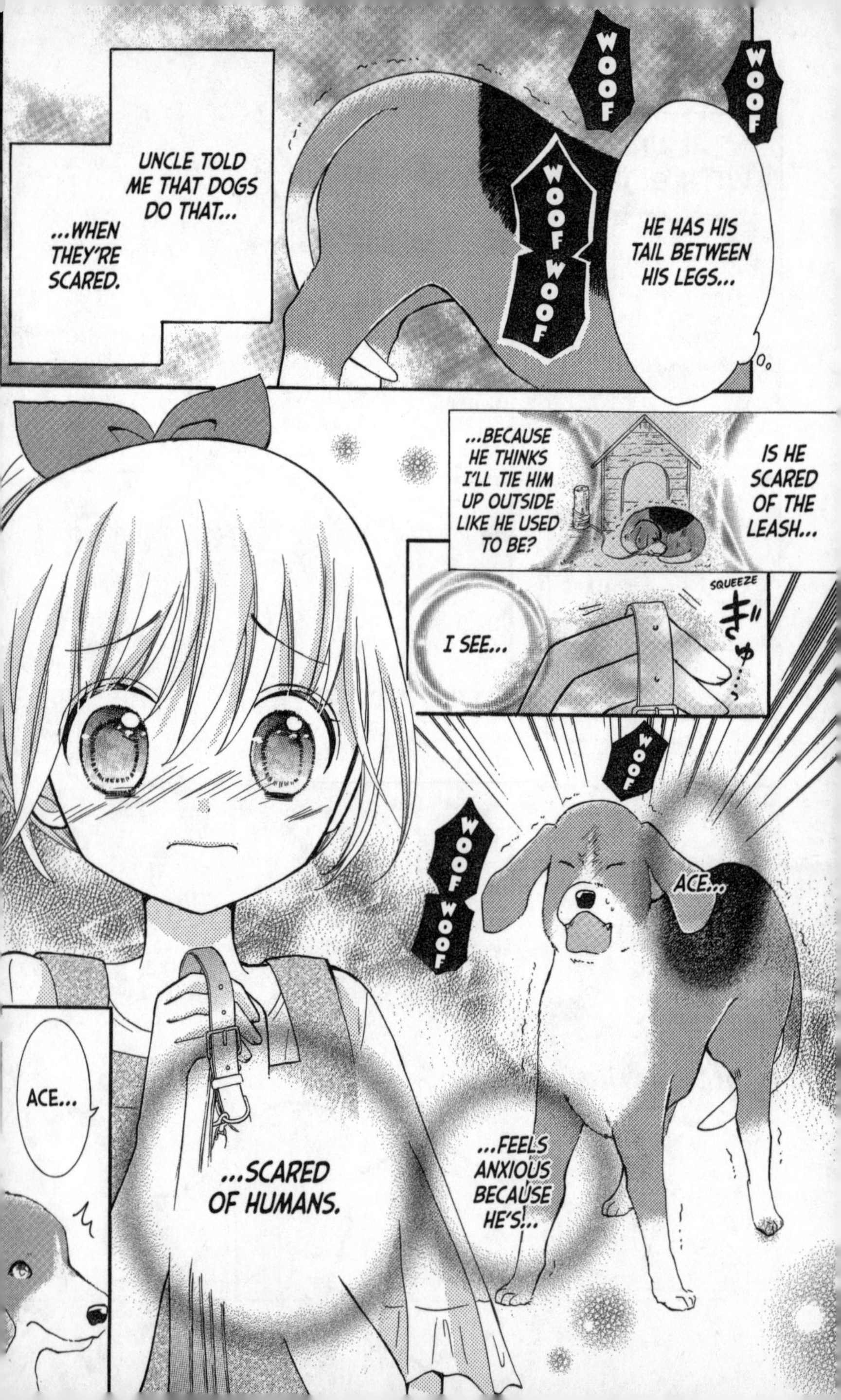
WOOF
WOOF
HE HAS HIS TAIL BETWEEN HIS LEGS...
WOOF WOOF
UNCLE TOLD ME THAT DOGS DO THAT...
...WHEN THEY'RE SCARED.
IS HE SCARED OF THE LEASH...
...BECAUSE HE THINKS I'LL TIE HIM UP OUTSIDE LIKE HE USED TO BE?
SQUEEZE
ぎゅ...
I SEE...
WOOF
ACE...
WOOF WOOF
...FEELS ANXIOUS BECAUSE HE'S!...
...SCARED OF HUMANS.
ACE...

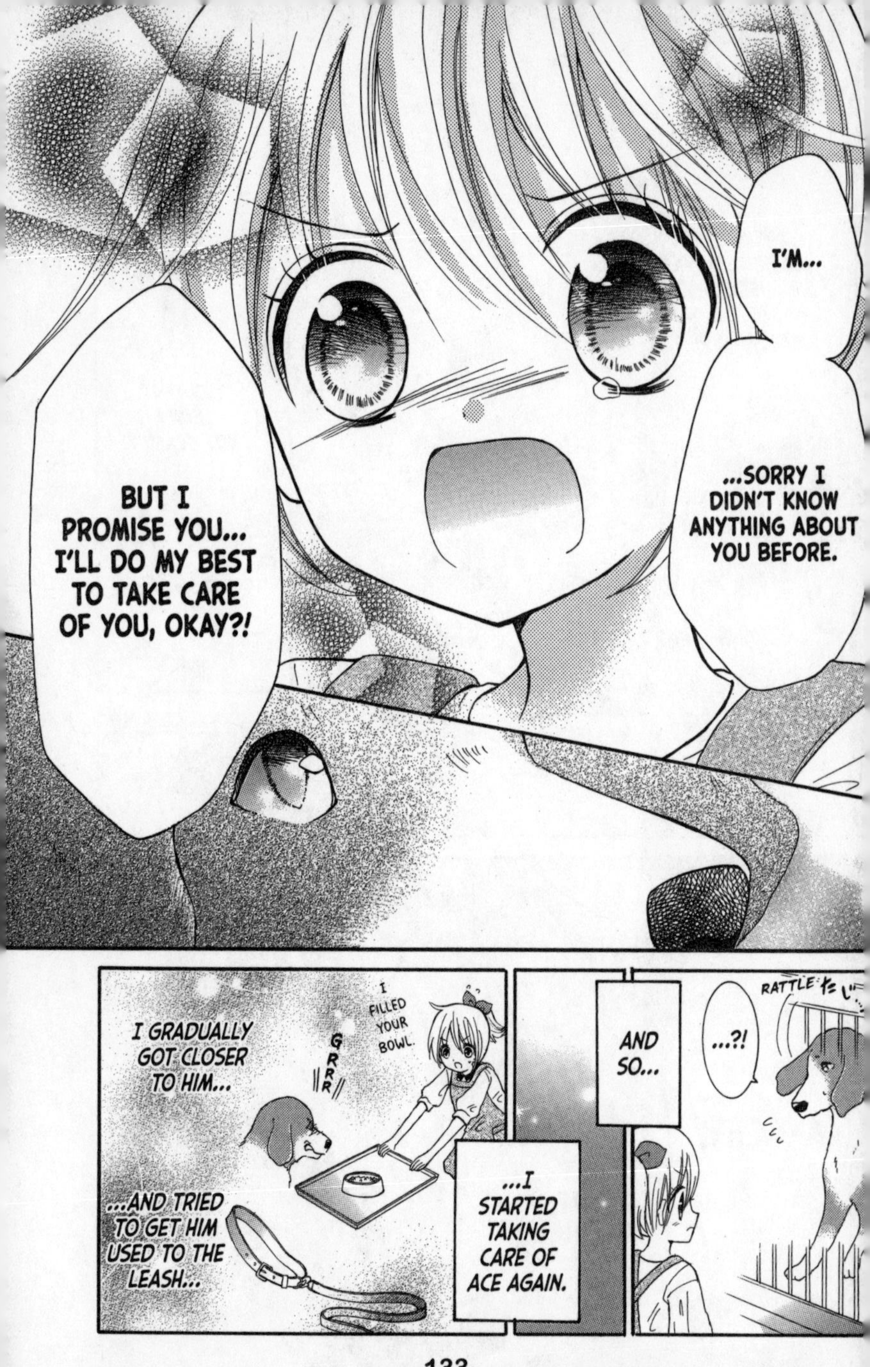
I'M...
...SORRY I DIDN'T KNOW ANYTHING ABOUT YOU BEFORE.
BUT I PROMISE YOU... I'LL DO MY BEST TO TAKE CARE OF YOU, OKAY?!
RATTLE
...?!
AND SO...
...I STARTED TAKING CARE OF ACE AGAIN.
I FILLED YOUR BOWL.
GRRR
I GRADUALLY GOT CLOSER TO HIM...
...AND TRIED TO GET HIM USED TO THE LEASH...

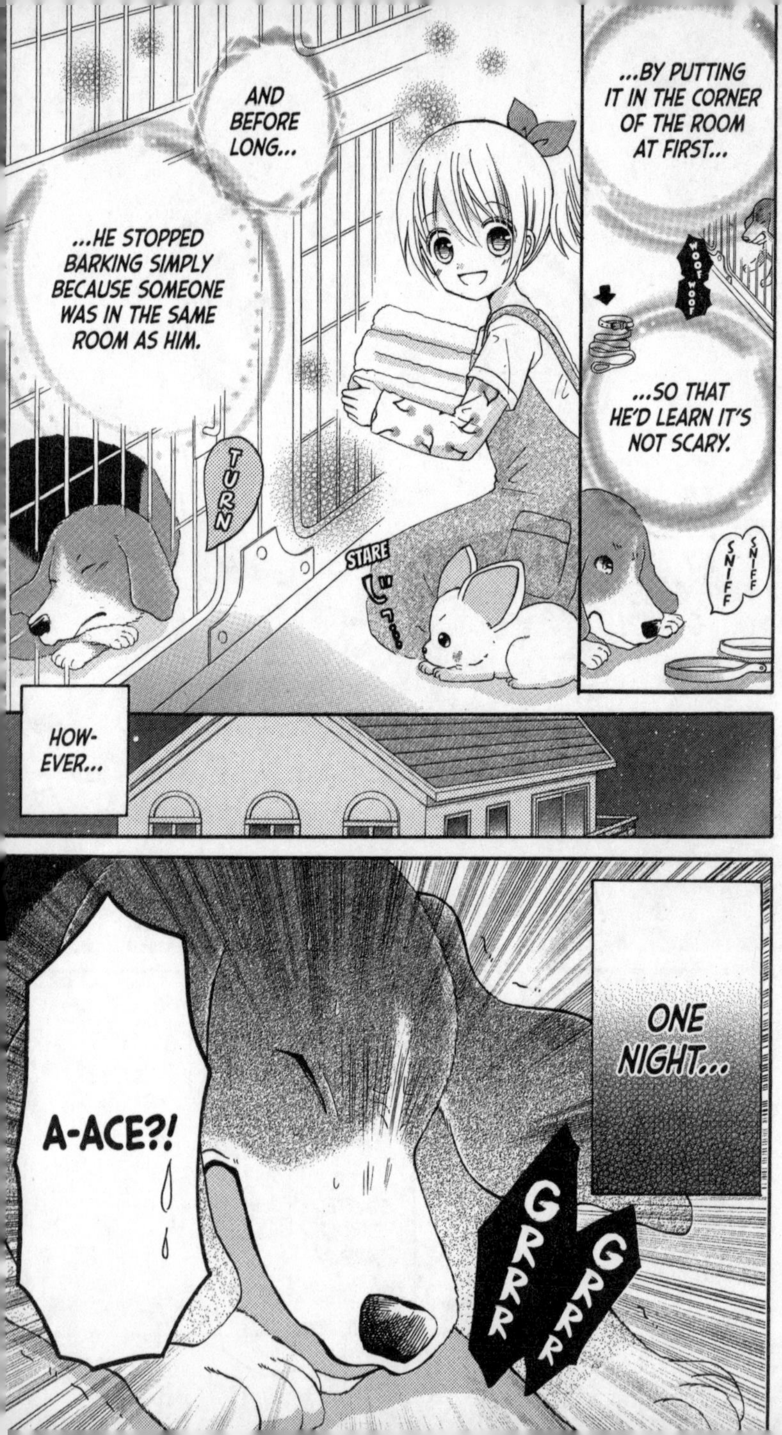
...BY PUTTING IT IN THE CORNER OF THE ROOM AT FIRST...
WOOF WOOF
...SO THAT HE'D LEARN IT'S NOT SCARY.
SNIFF SNIFF
AND BEFORE LONG...
...HE STOPPED BARKING SIMPLY BECAUSE SOMEONE WAS IN THE SAME ROOM AS HIM.
TURN
STARE
HOW-EVER...
ONE NIGHT...
GRRR GRRR
A-ACE?!

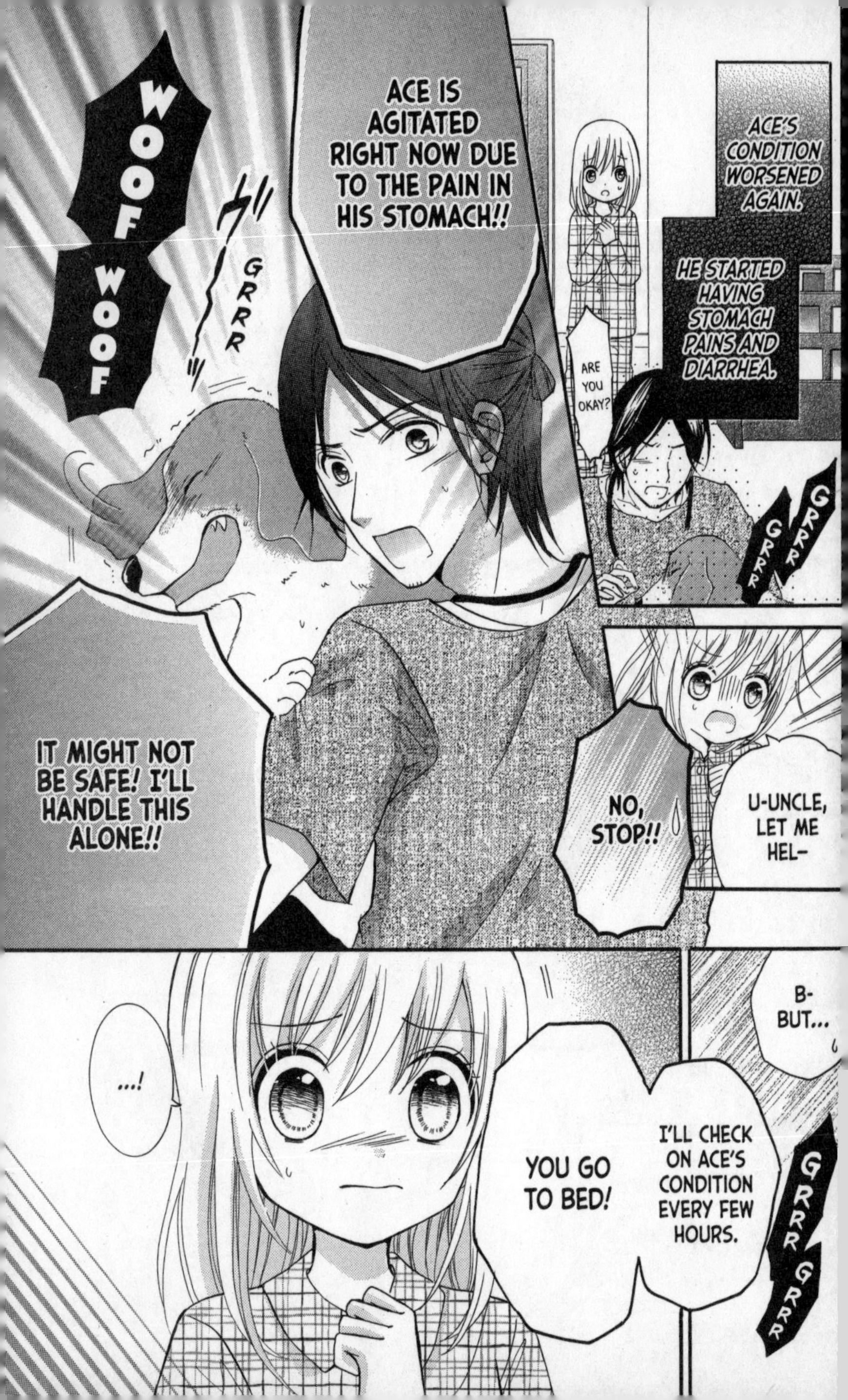

ACE'S CONDITION WORSENED AGAIN.
HE STARTED HAVING STOMACH PAINS AND DIARRHEA.
ARE YOU OKAY?
GRRR GRRR
U-UNCLE, LET ME HEL-
NO, STOP!!
ACE IS AGITATED RIGHT NOW DUE TO THE PAIN IN HIS STOMACH!!
GRRR
WOOF WOOF WOOF
IT MIGHT NOT BE SAFE! I'LL HANDLE THIS ALONE!!
B-BUT...
GRRR GRRR
I'LL CHECK ON ACE'S CONDITION EVERY FEW HOURS.
YOU GO TO BED!
...!

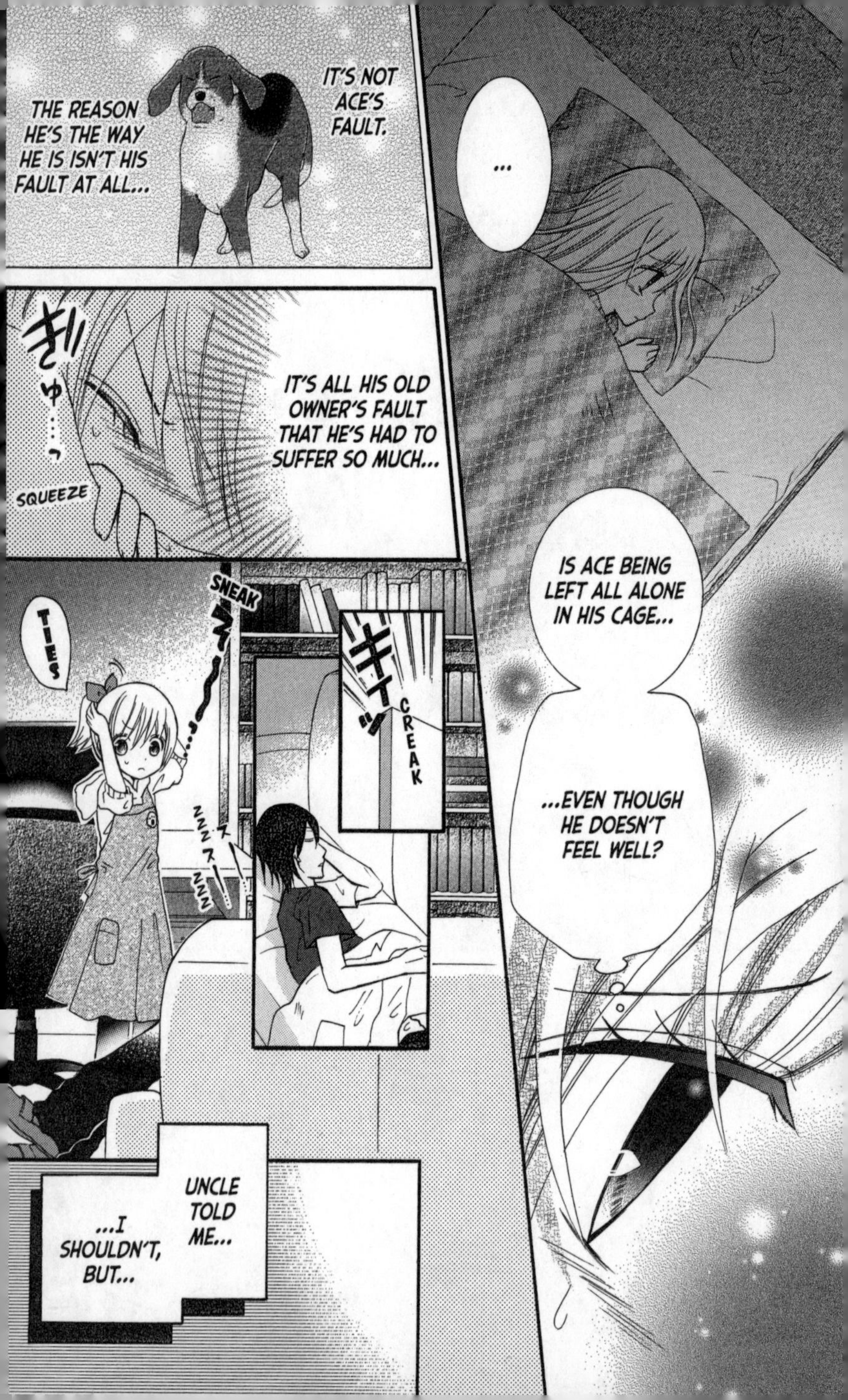
...
IS ACE BEING LEFT ALL ALONE IN HIS CAGE...
...EVEN THOUGH HE DOESN'T FEEL WELL?
IT'S NOT ACE'S FAULT.
THE REASON HE'S THE WAY HE IS ISN'T HIS FAULT AT ALL...
IT'S ALL HIS OLD OWNER'S FAULT THAT HE'S HAD TO SUFFER SO MUCH...
ぎゅ…っ
SQUEEZE
ギギ
CREAK
SNEAK
ZZZ
ZZZ
TIES
UNCLE TOLD ME...
...I SHOULDN'T, BUT...

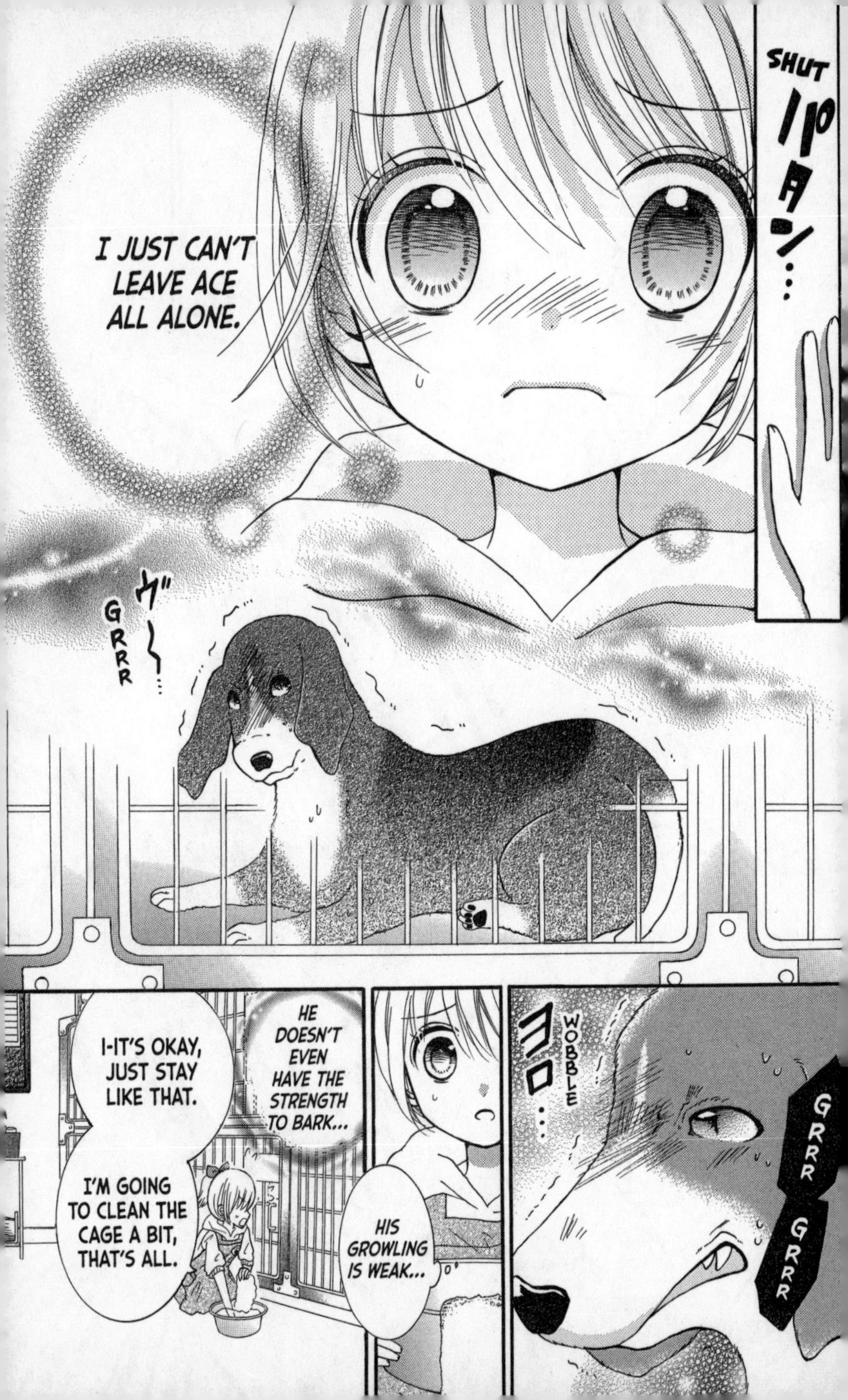
SHUT
パタン…
I JUST CAN'T LEAVE ACE ALL ALONE.
GRRR
ヴ〜…
WOBBLE
ヨロ…
GRRR GRRR
HIS GROWLING IS WEAK...
HE DOESN'T EVEN HAVE THE STRENGTH TO BARK...
I-IT'S OKAY, JUST STAY LIKE THAT.
I'M GOING TO CLEAN THE CAGE A BIT, THAT'S ALL.

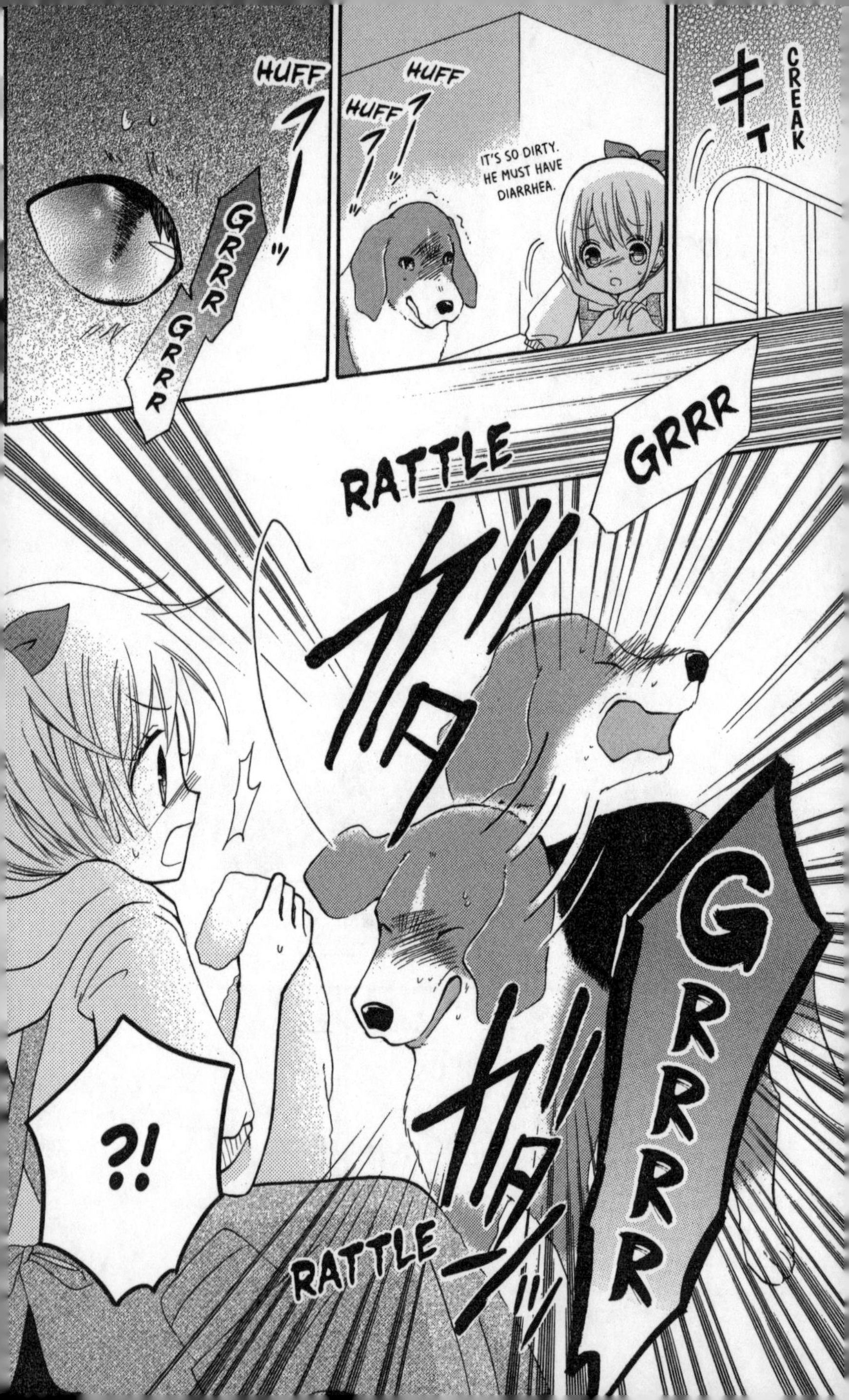

キ
CREAK
IT'S SO DIRTY. HE MUST HAVE DIARRHEA.
HUFF
HUFF
HUFF
HUFF
GRRR
GRRR
GRRR
RATTLE
ガタ
GRRRRR
ガタ
RATTLE
?!

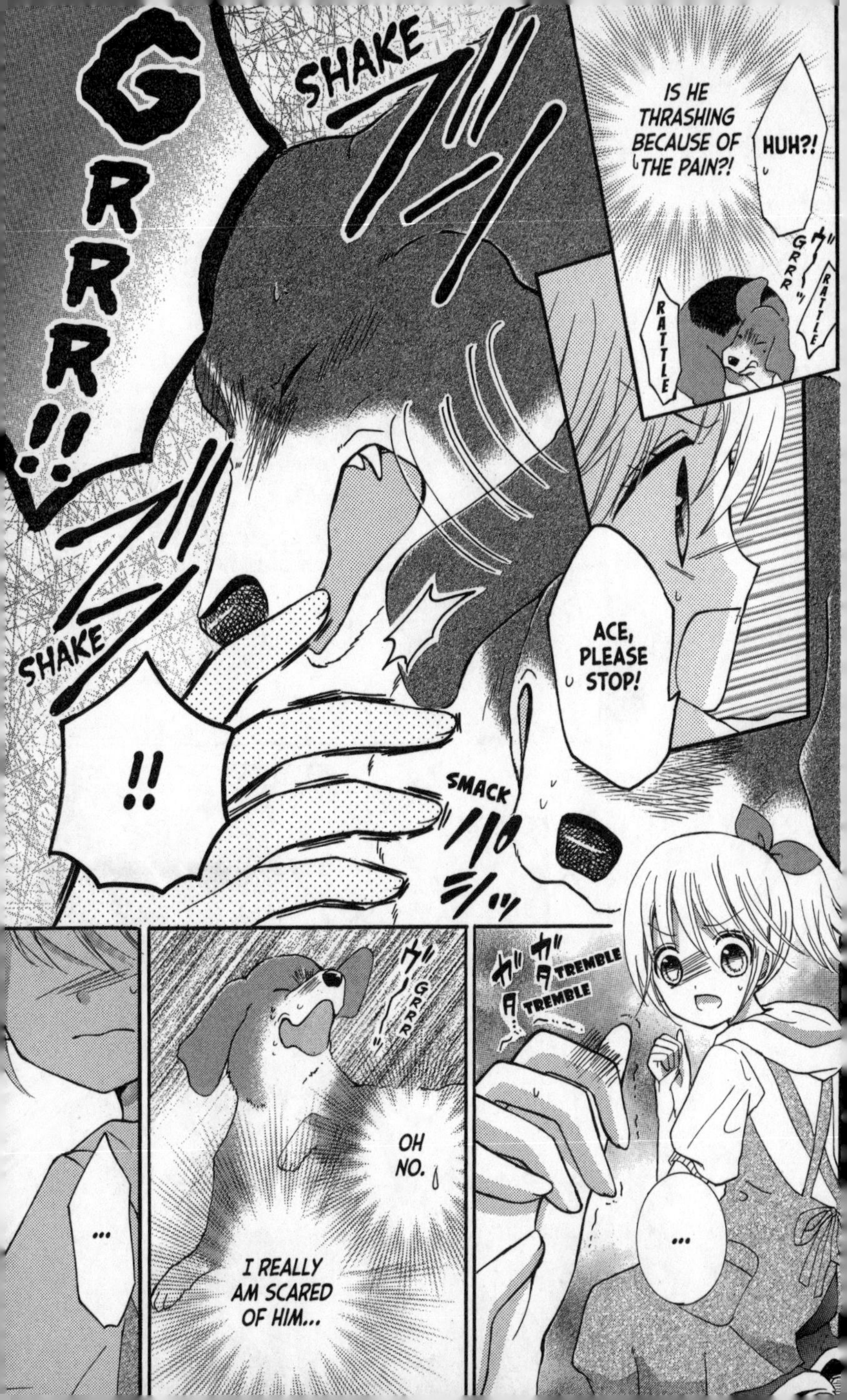
HUH?!
IS HE THRASHING BECAUSE OF THE PAIN?!
GRRR
RATTLE
RATTLE
ACE, PLEASE STOP!
SHAKE
GRRR!!
SHAKE
!!
SMACK
TREMBLE
TREMBLE
...
GRRR
OH NO.
I REALLY AM SCARED OF HIM...
...

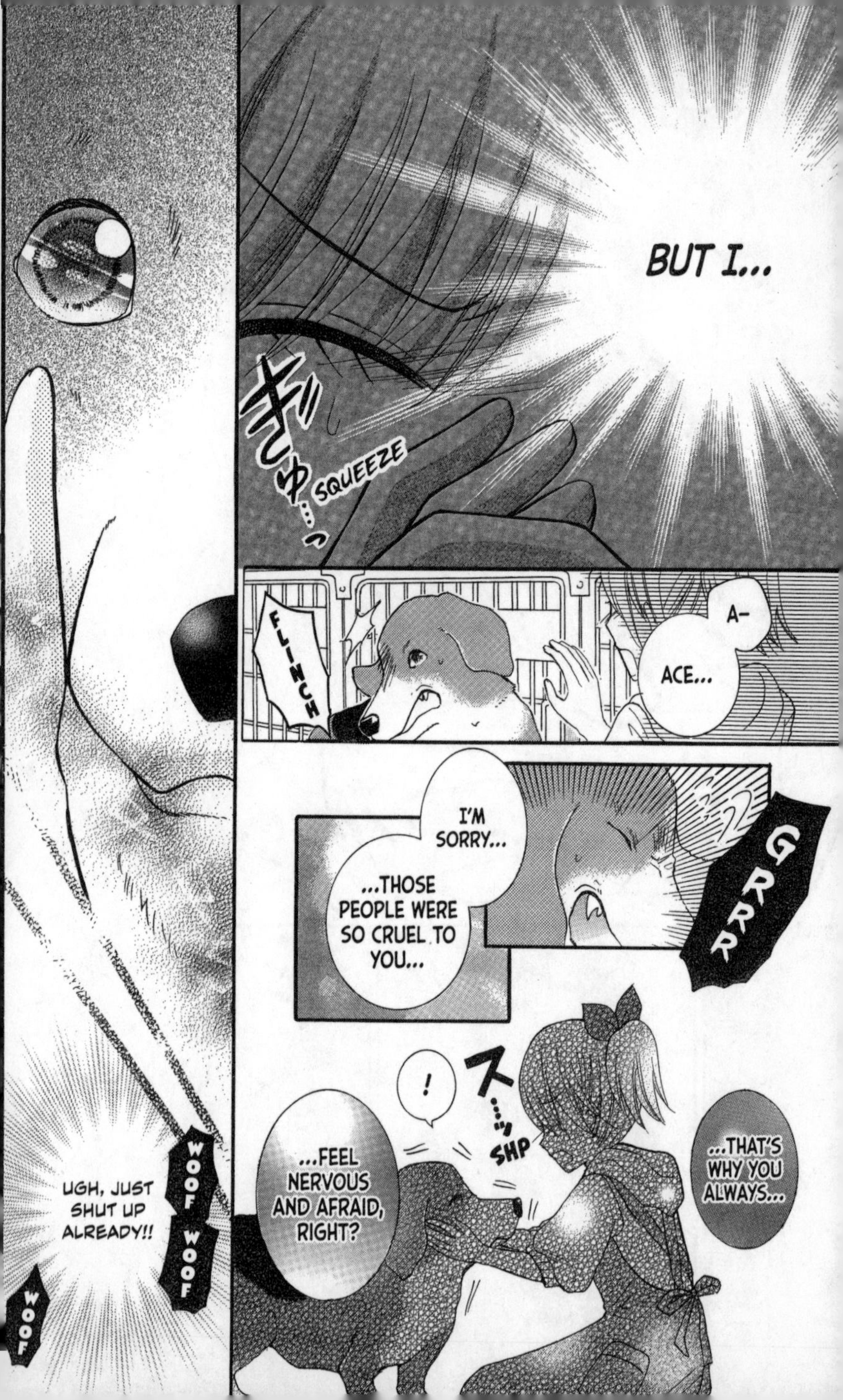

BUT I...
ぎゅ…っ
SQUEEZE
A-
ACE...
FLINCH
GRRR
I'M SORRY...
...THOSE PEOPLE WERE SO CRUEL TO YOU...
...THAT'S WHY YOU ALWAYS...
ス…ッ
SHP
!
...FEEL NERVOUS AND AFRAID, RIGHT?
WOOF
WOOF
WOOF
UGH, JUST SHUT UP ALREADY!!
WOOF

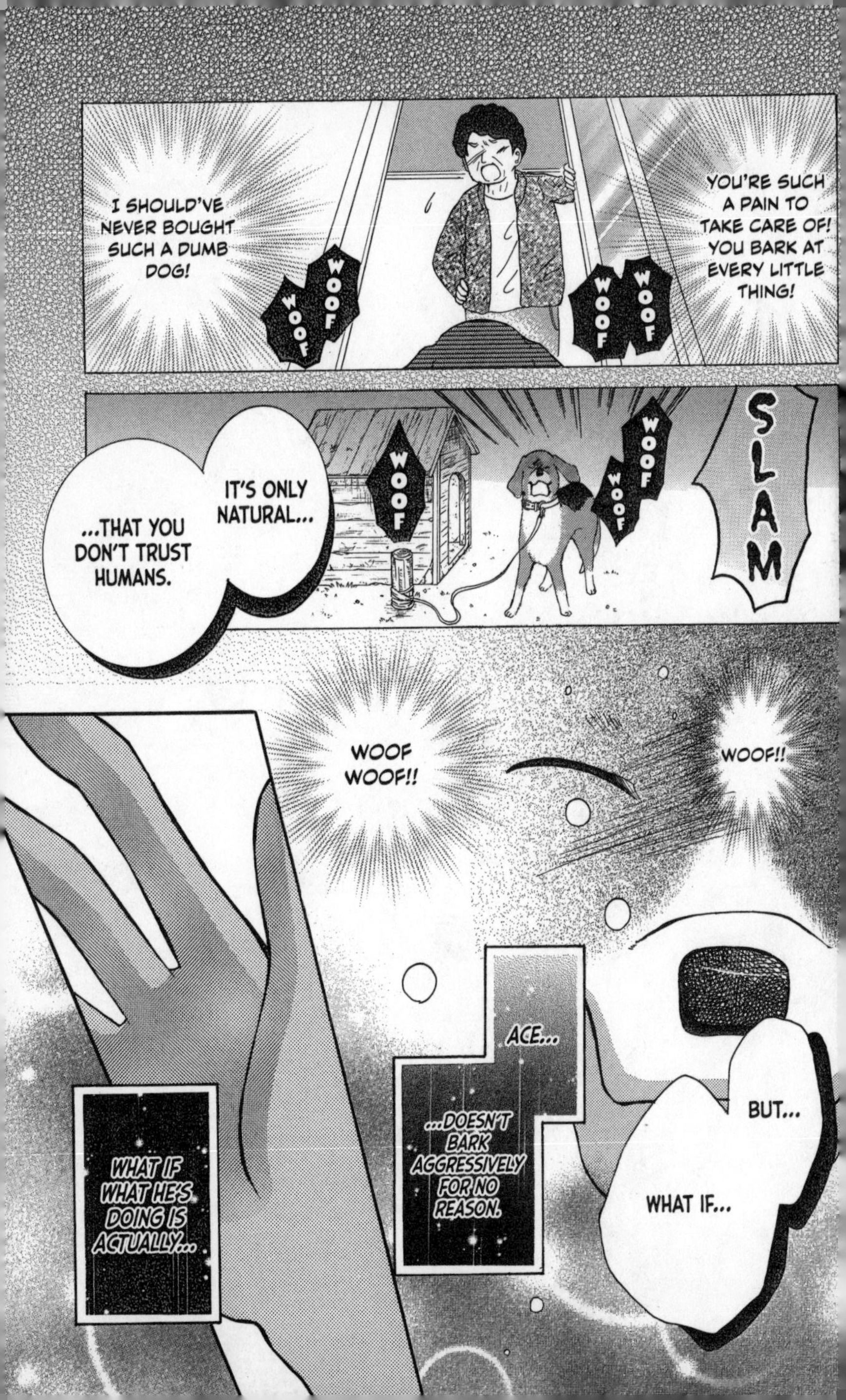
YOU'RE SUCH A PAIN TO TAKE CARE OF! YOU BARK AT EVERY LITTLE THING!
WOOF WOOF
WOOF WOOF
I SHOULD'VE NEVER BOUGHT SUCH A DUMB DOG!
WOOF WOOF
SLAM
WOOF WOOF
WOOF
IT'S ONLY NATURAL...
...THAT YOU DON'T TRUST HUMANS.
WOOF!!
WOOF WOOF!!
BUT...
WHAT IF...
ACE...
...DOESN'T BARK AGGRESSIVELY FOR NO REASON.
WHAT IF WHAT HE'S DOING IS ACTUALLY...

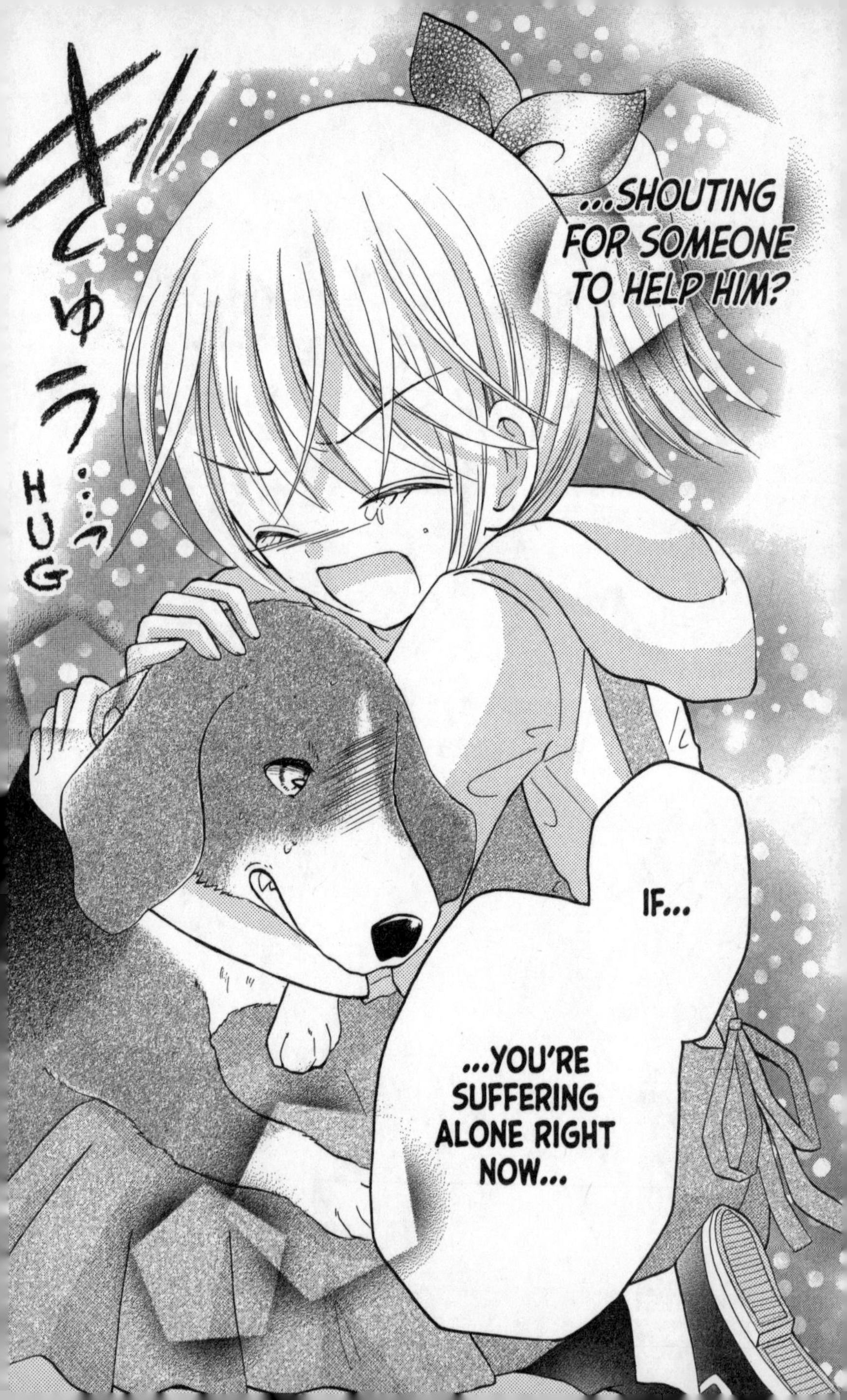
...SHOUTING FOR SOMEONE TO HELP HIM?
きゅう…っ
HUG
IF...
...YOU'RE SUFFERING ALONE RIGHT NOW...

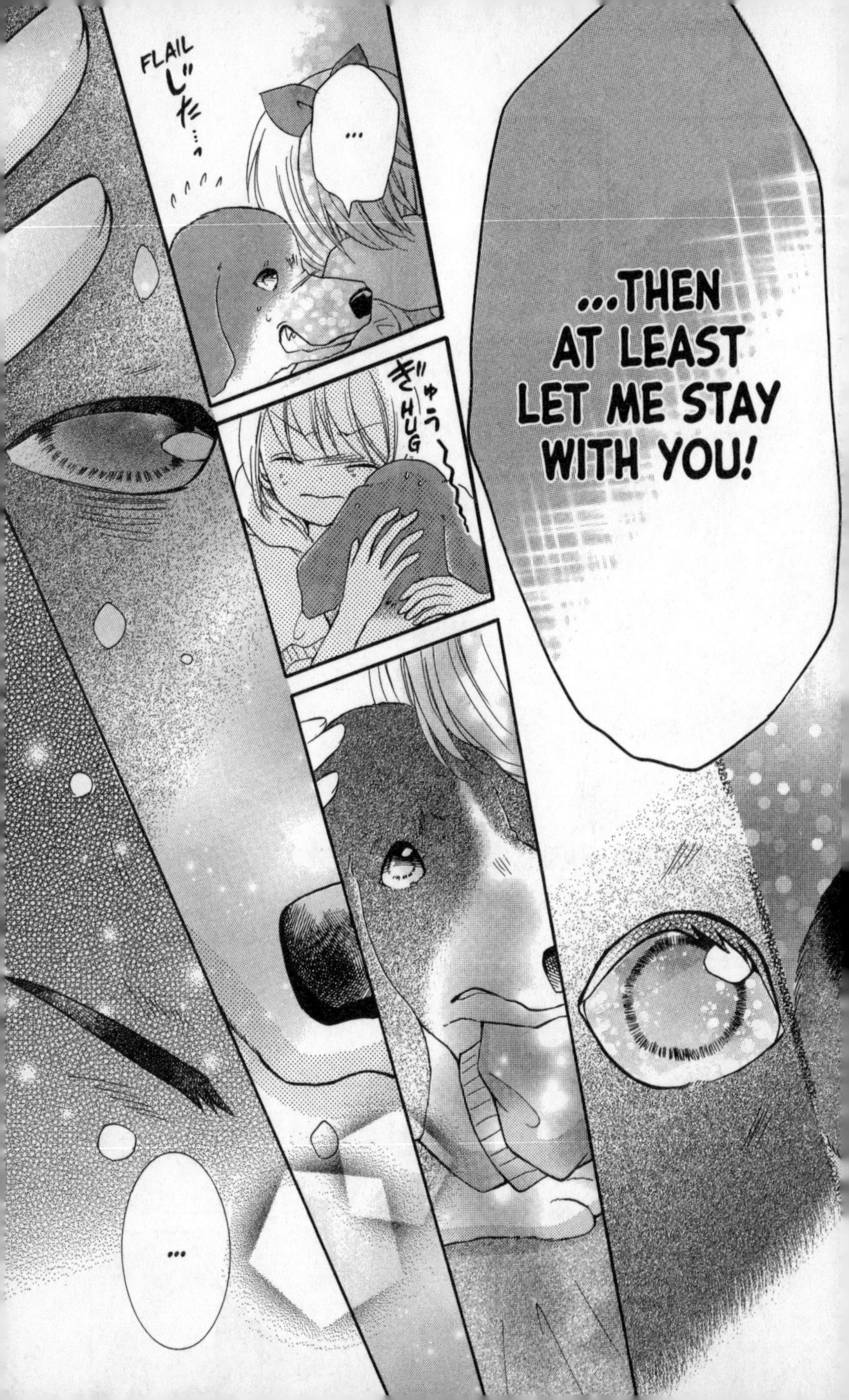
...THEN AT LEAST LET ME STAY WITH YOU!
...
FLAIL じた…
ぎゅう HUG
...

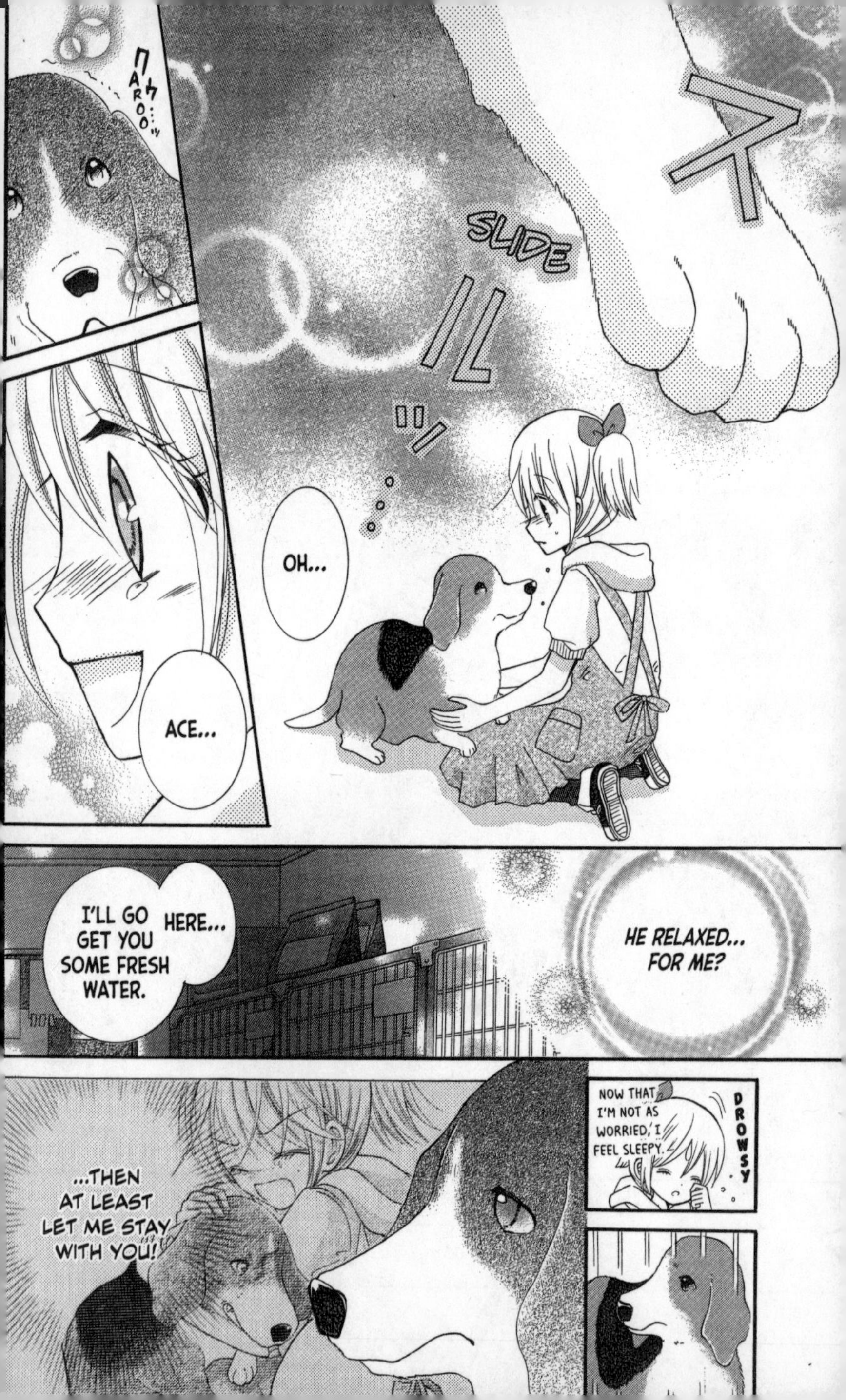
SLIDE
OH...
AROO...
ACE...
HE RELAXED... FOR ME?
HERE...
I'LL GO GET YOU SOME FRESH WATER.
NOW THAT I'M NOT AS WORRIED, I FEEL SLEEPY.
DROWSY
...THEN AT LEAST LET ME STAY WITH YOU!

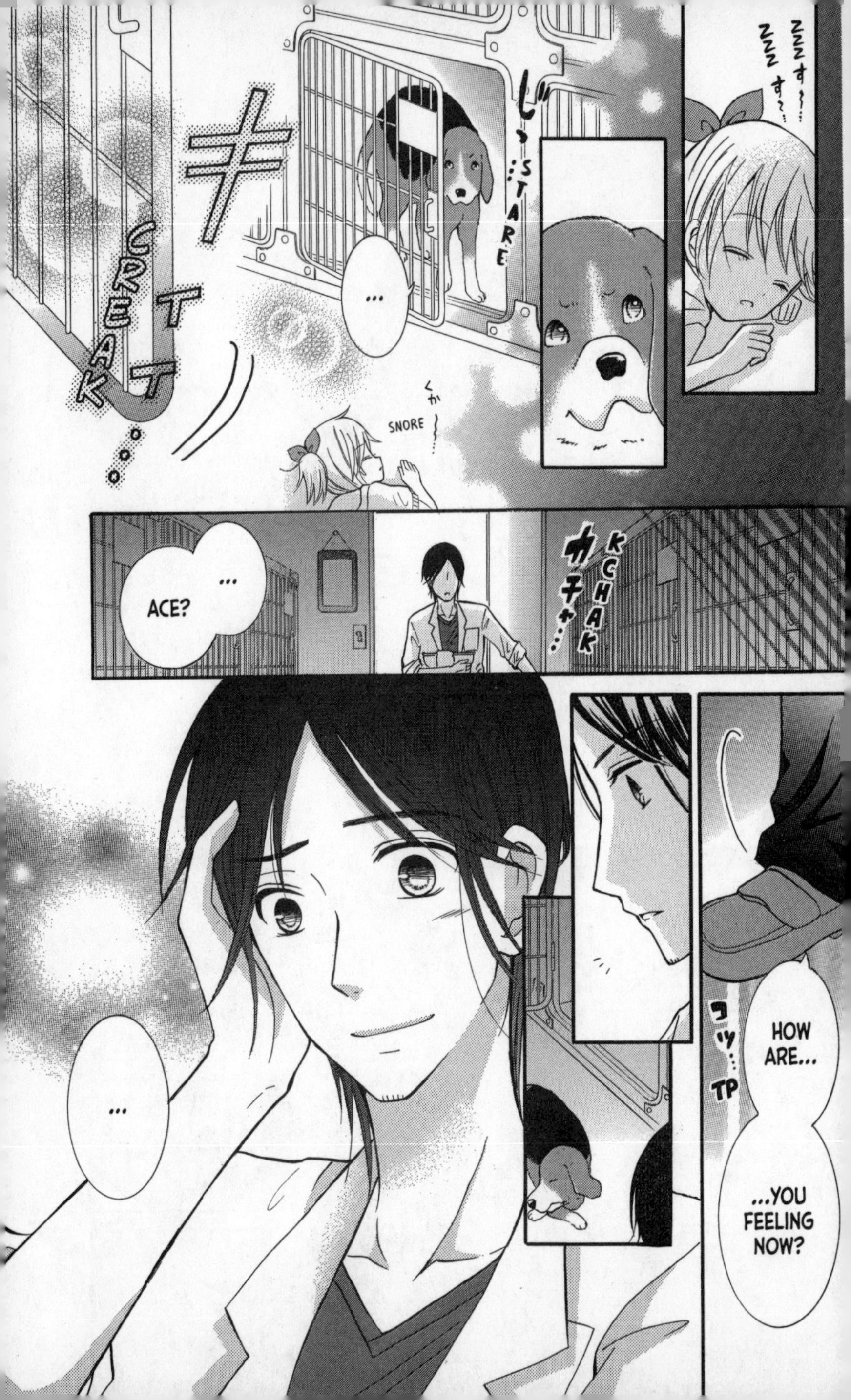

ZZZ す～… ZZZ す～…
じっ… STARE
…
CREAK
くか～ SNORE
カチャ… KCHAK
… ACE?
コッ… TP
HOW ARE…
…YOU FEELING NOW?
…

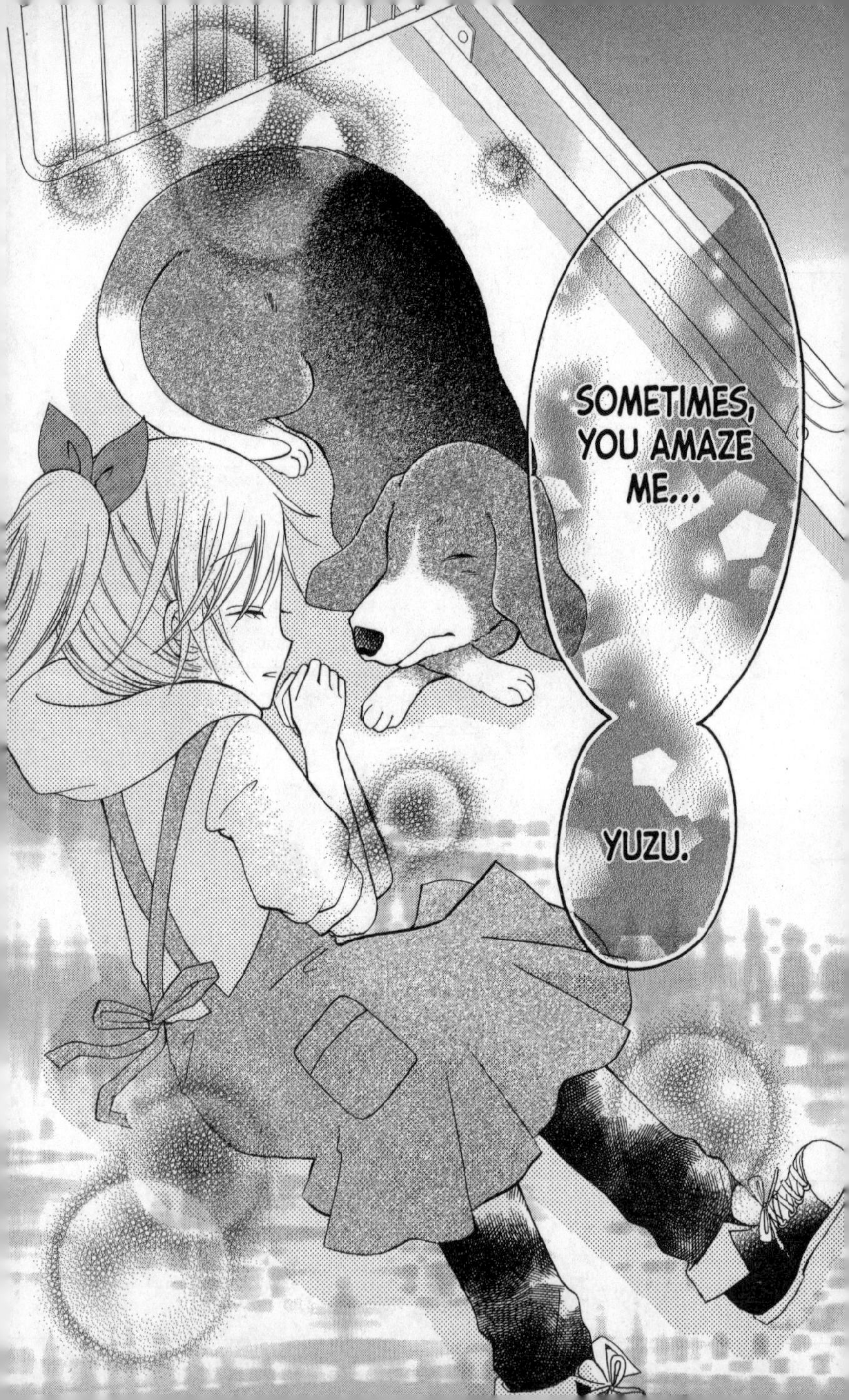
SOMETIMES, YOU AMAZE ME...
YUZU.

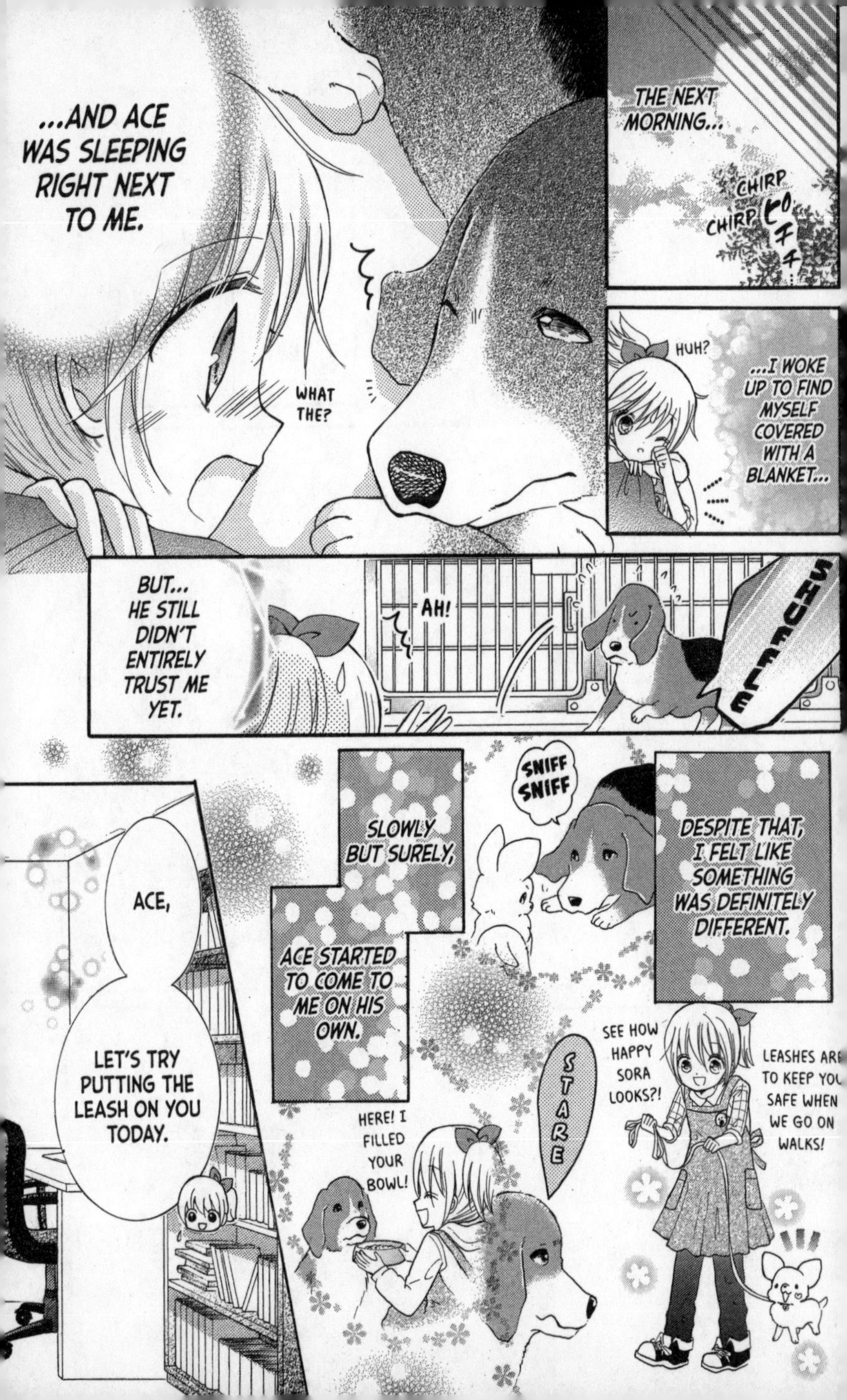
THE NEXT MORNING...
CHIRP CHIRP
ピチチ
HUH?
...I WOKE UP TO FIND MYSELF COVERED WITH A BLANKET...
......
...AND ACE WAS SLEEPING RIGHT NEXT TO ME.
WHAT THE?
SHUFFLE
AH!
BUT... HE STILL DIDN'T ENTIRELY TRUST ME YET.
DESPITE THAT, I FELT LIKE SOMETHING WAS DEFINITELY DIFFERENT.
SNIFF SNIFF
SLOWLY BUT SURELY,
ACE STARTED TO COME TO ME ON HIS OWN.
LEASHES ARE TO KEEP YOU SAFE WHEN WE GO ON WALKS!
SEE HOW HAPPY SORA LOOKS?!
STARE
HERE! I FILLED YOUR BOWL!
ACE,
LET'S TRY PUTTING THE LEASH ON YOU TODAY.

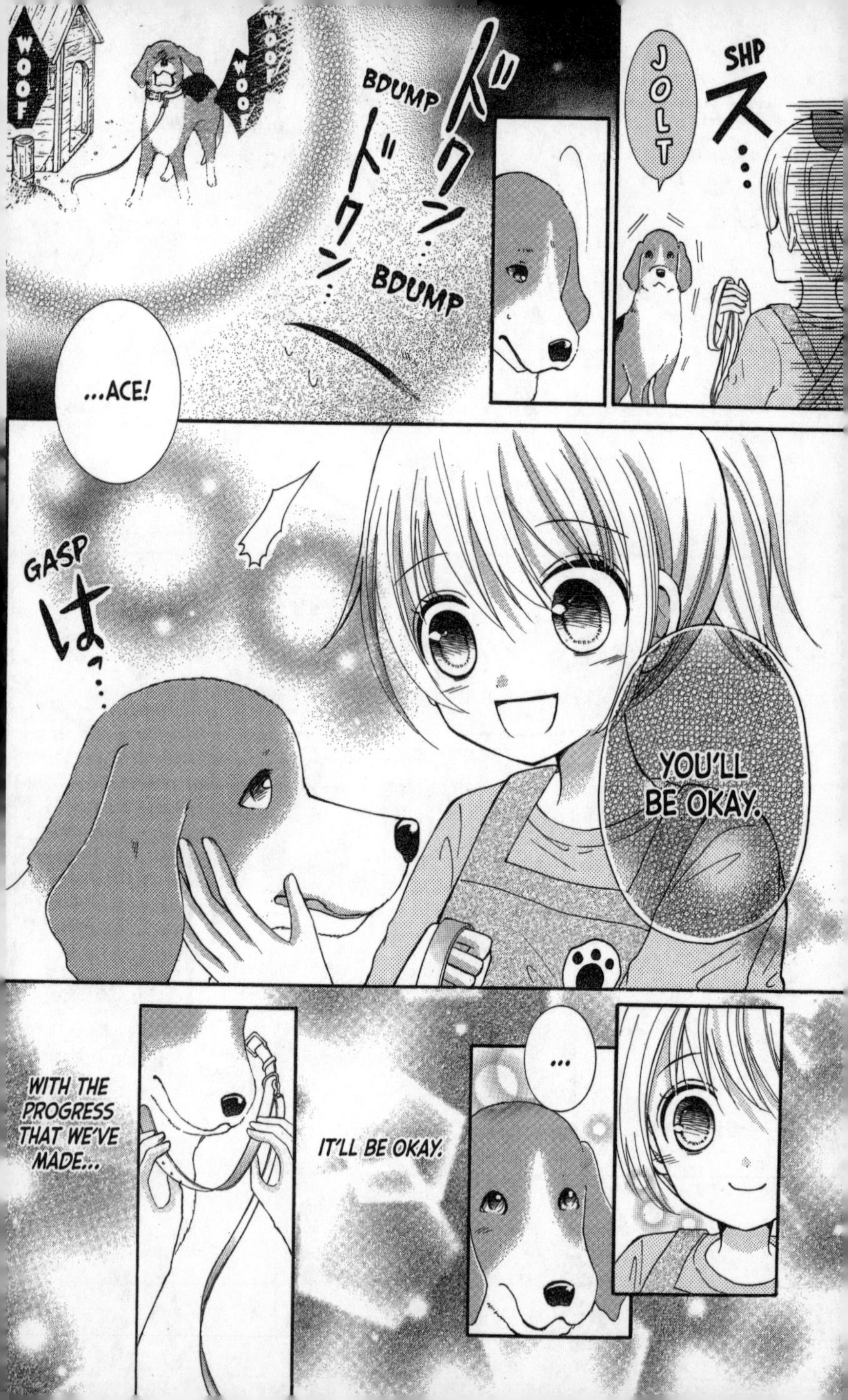
SHP
ス…
JOLT
BDUMP
ドクン…
BDUMP
ドクン…
WOOF WOOF
WOOF
…ACE!
YOU'LL BE OKAY.
GASP
はっ…
…
IT'LL BE OKAY.
WITH THE PROGRESS THAT WE'VE MADE…

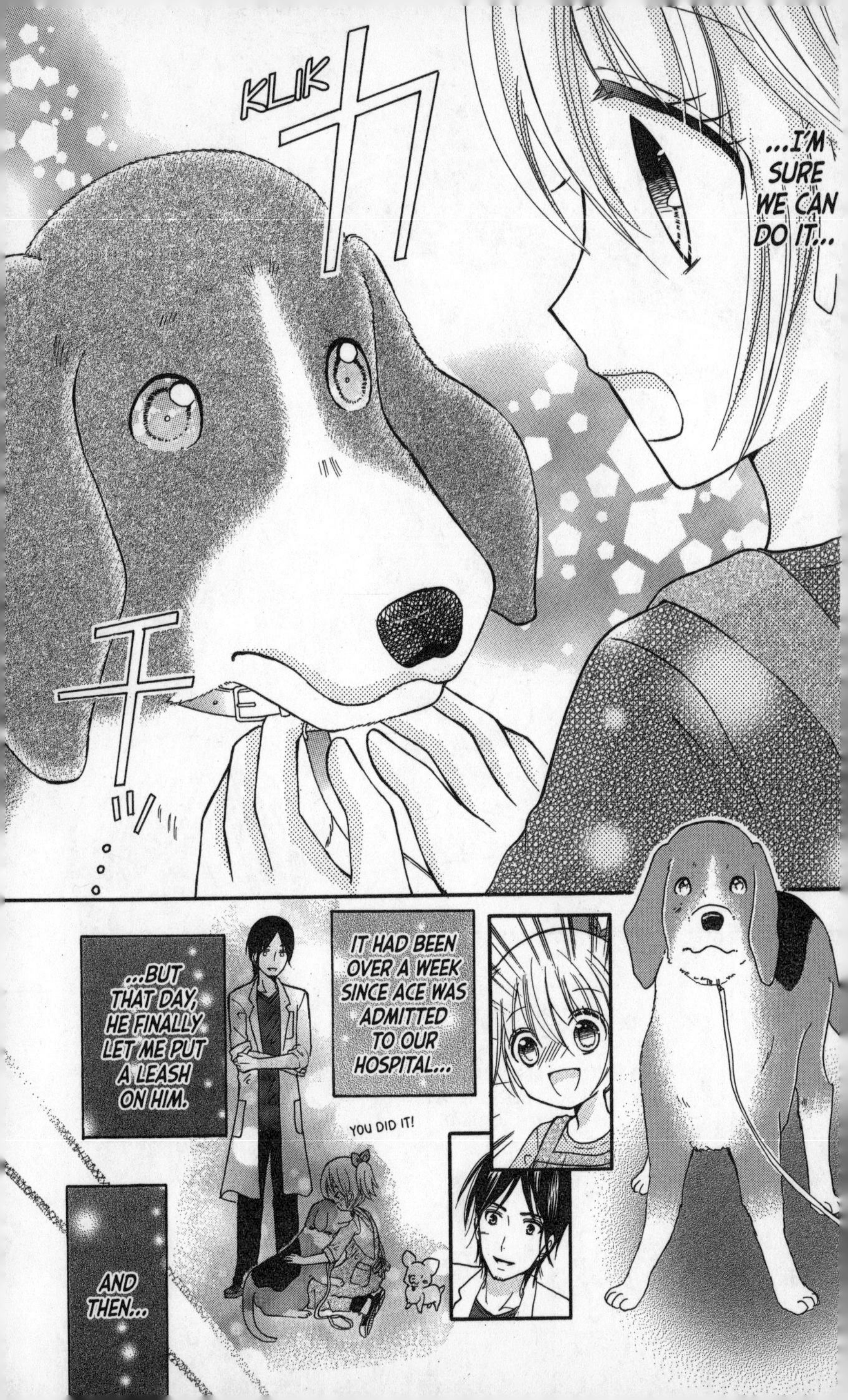
...I'M SURE WE CAN DO IT...
KLIK
IT HAD BEEN OVER A WEEK SINCE ACE WAS ADMITTED TO OUR HOSPITAL...
...BUT THAT DAY, HE FINALLY LET ME PUT A LEASH ON HIM.
YOU DID IT!
AND THEN...

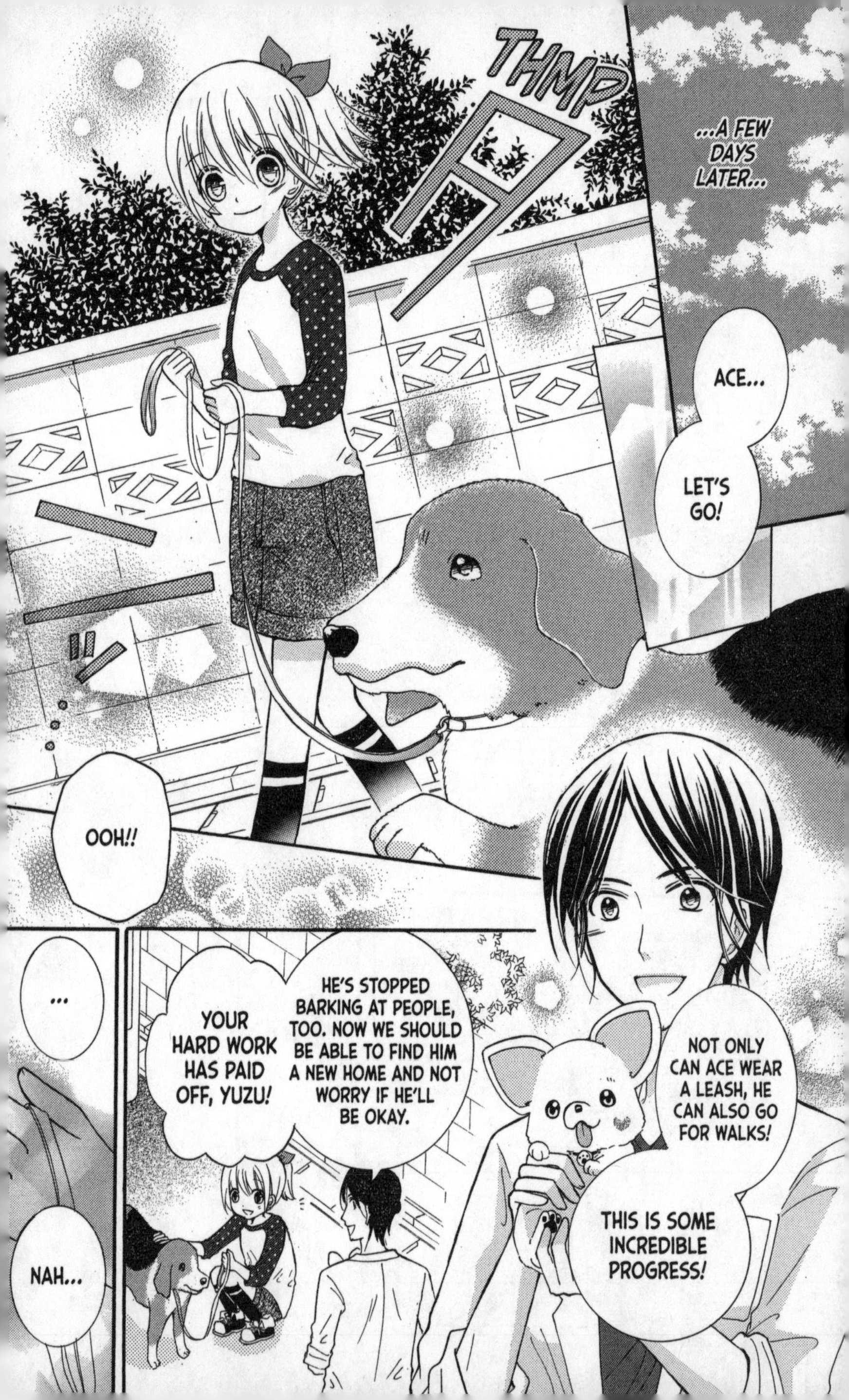
...A FEW DAYS LATER...
THMP
ACE...
LET'S GO!
OOH!!
NOT ONLY CAN ACE WEAR A LEASH, HE CAN ALSO GO FOR WALKS!
THIS IS SOME INCREDIBLE PROGRESS!
HE'S STOPPED BARKING AT PEOPLE, TOO. NOW WE SHOULD BE ABLE TO FIND HIM A NEW HOME AND NOT WORRY IF HE'LL BE OKAY.
YOUR HARD WORK HAS PAID OFF, YUZU!
...
NAH...

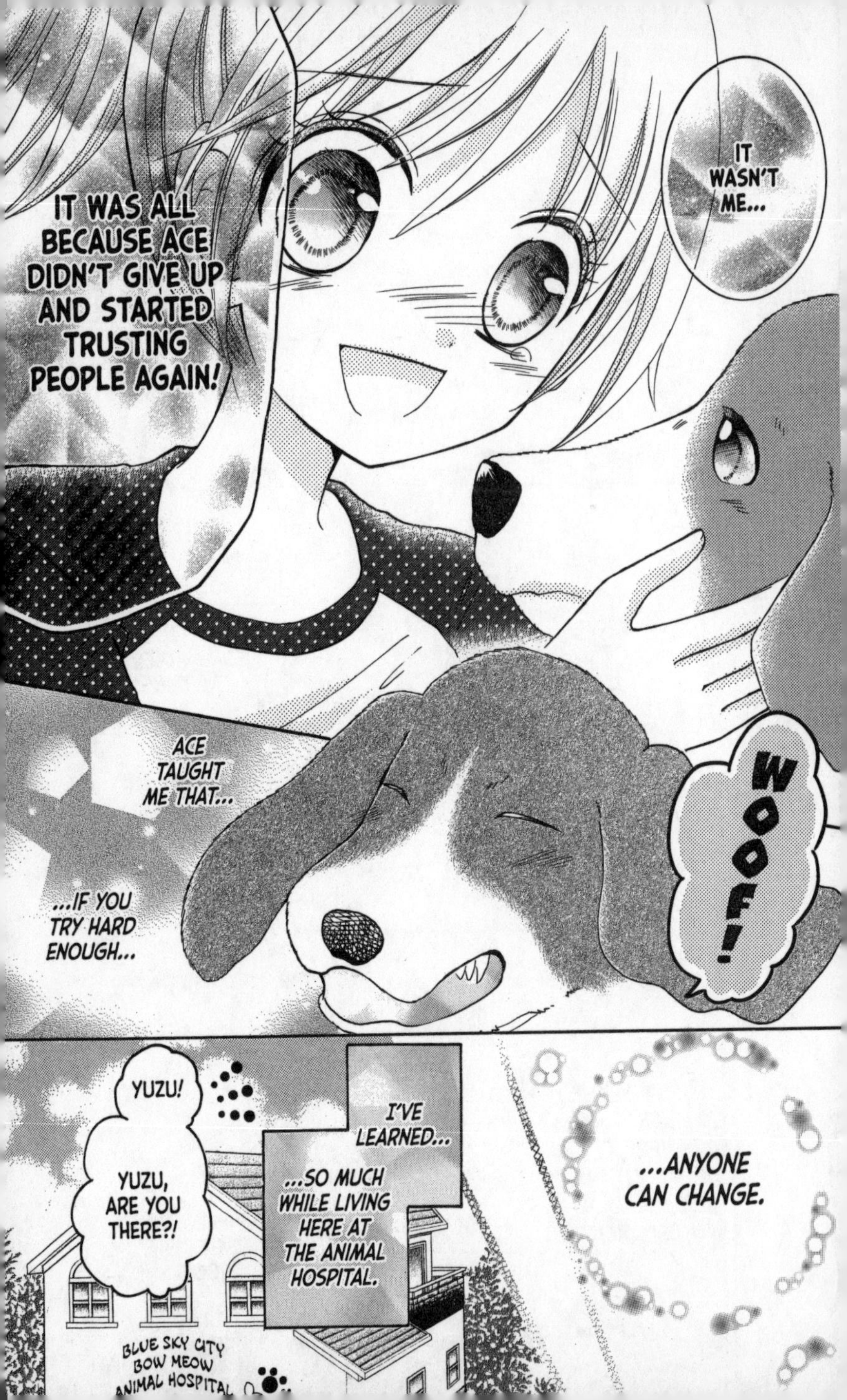
IT WASN'T ME...
IT WAS ALL BECAUSE ACE DIDN'T GIVE UP AND STARTED TRUSTING PEOPLE AGAIN!
WOOF!
ACE TAUGHT ME THAT...
...IF YOU TRY HARD ENOUGH...
...ANYONE CAN CHANGE.
I'VE LEARNED...
...SO MUCH WHILE LIVING HERE AT THE ANIMAL HOSPITAL.
YUZU!
YUZU, ARE YOU THERE?!
BLUE SKY CITY BOW MEOW ANIMAL HOSPITAL

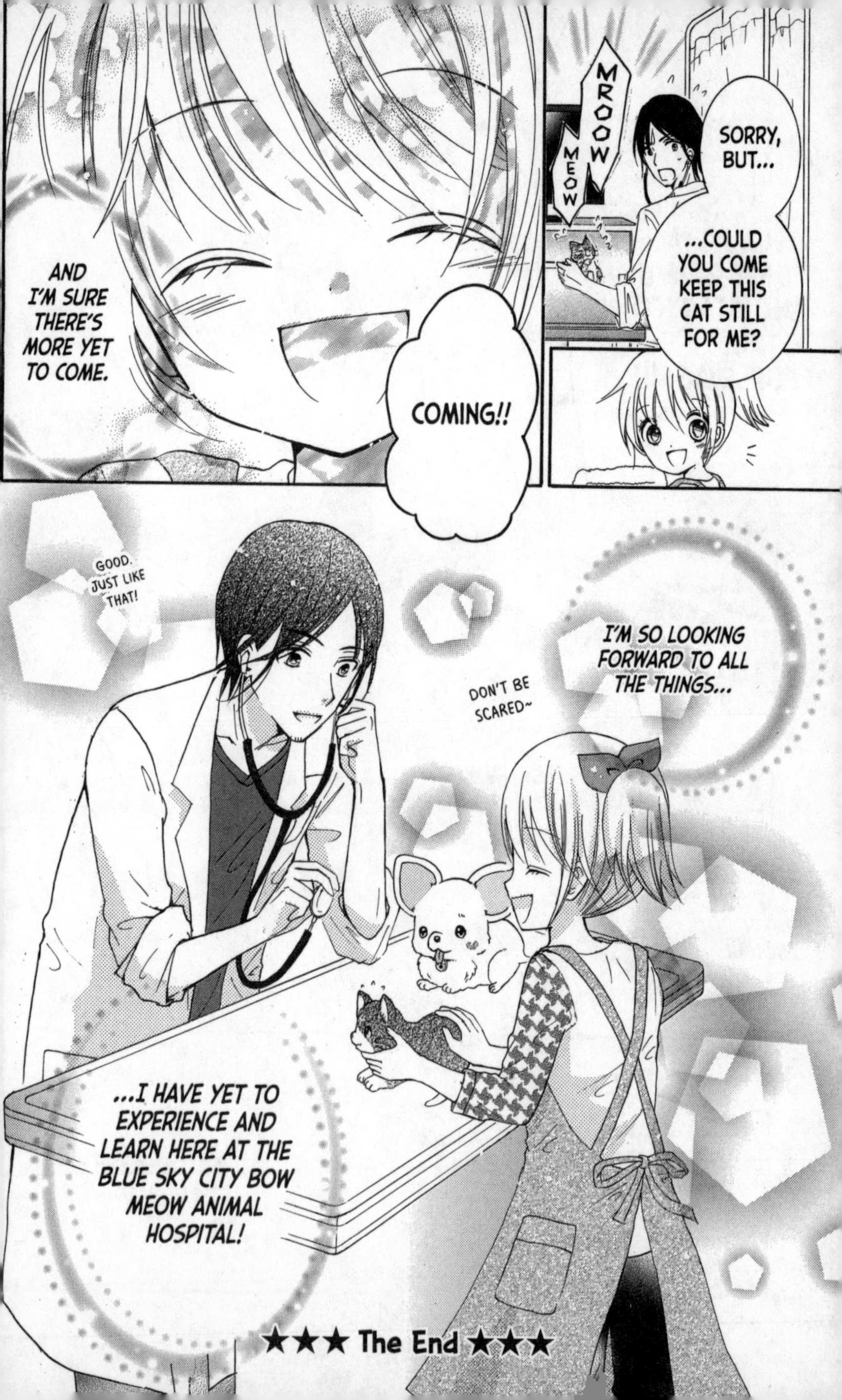
MROOW
MEOW
SORRY, BUT...
...COULD YOU COME KEEP THIS CAT STILL FOR ME?
COMING!!
AND I'M SURE THERE'S MORE YET TO COME.
I'M SO LOOKING FORWARD TO ALL THE THINGS...
DON'T BE SCARED~
GOOD. JUST LIKE THAT!
...I HAVE YET TO EXPERIENCE AND LEARN HERE AT THE BLUE SKY CITY BOW MEOW ANIMAL HOSPITAL!
★★★ The End ★★★

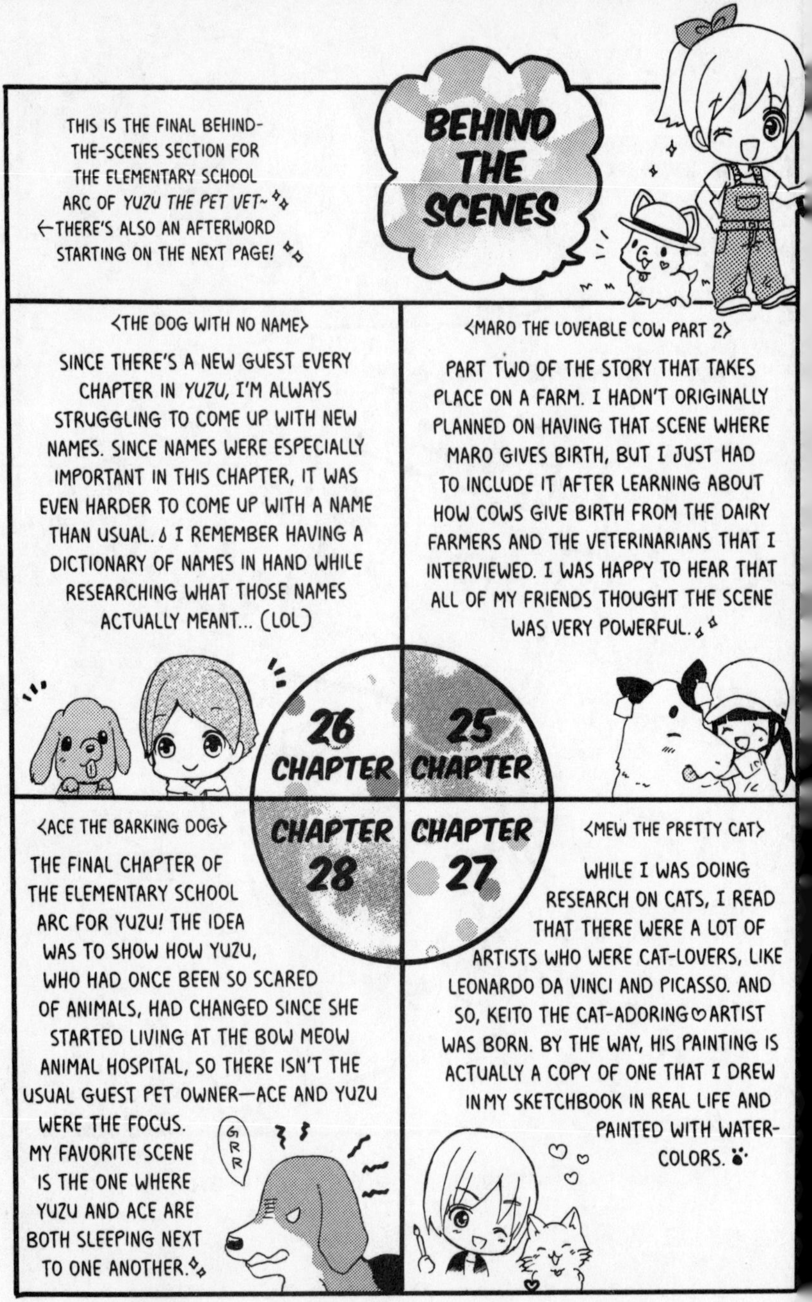
BEHIND THE SCENES
THIS IS THE FINAL BEHIND-THE-SCENES SECTION FOR THE ELEMENTARY SCHOOL ARC OF *YUZU THE PET VET*~ ←THERE'S ALSO AN AFTERWORD STARTING ON THE NEXT PAGE!
25 CHAPTER
<MARO THE LOVEABLE COW PART 2>
PART TWO OF THE STORY THAT TAKES PLACE ON A FARM. I HADN'T ORIGINALLY PLANNED ON HAVING THAT SCENE WHERE MARO GIVES BIRTH, BUT I JUST HAD TO INCLUDE IT AFTER LEARNING ABOUT HOW COWS GIVE BIRTH FROM THE DAIRY FARMERS AND THE VETERINARIANS THAT I INTERVIEWED. I WAS HAPPY TO HEAR THAT ALL OF MY FRIENDS THOUGHT THE SCENE WAS VERY POWERFUL.
26 CHAPTER
<THE DOG WITH NO NAME>
SINCE THERE'S A NEW GUEST EVERY CHAPTER IN *YUZU*, I'M ALWAYS STRUGGLING TO COME UP WITH NEW NAMES. SINCE NAMES WERE ESPECIALLY IMPORTANT IN THIS CHAPTER, IT WAS EVEN HARDER TO COME UP WITH A NAME THAN USUAL. I REMEMBER HAVING A DICTIONARY OF NAMES IN HAND WHILE RESEARCHING WHAT THOSE NAMES ACTUALLY MEANT... (LOL)
CHAPTER 27
<MEW THE PRETTY CAT>
WHILE I WAS DOING RESEARCH ON CATS, I READ THAT THERE WERE A LOT OF ARTISTS WHO WERE CAT-LOVERS, LIKE LEONARDO DA VINCI AND PICASSO. AND SO, KEITO THE CAT-ADORING♡ARTIST WAS BORN. BY THE WAY, HIS PAINTING IS ACTUALLY A COPY OF ONE THAT I DREW IN MY SKETCHBOOK IN REAL LIFE AND PAINTED WITH WATER-COLORS.
CHAPTER 28
<ACE THE BARKING DOG>
THE FINAL CHAPTER OF THE ELEMENTARY SCHOOL ARC FOR YUZU! THE IDEA WAS TO SHOW HOW YUZU, WHO HAD ONCE BEEN SO SCARED OF ANIMALS, HAD CHANGED SINCE SHE STARTED LIVING AT THE BOW MEOW ANIMAL HOSPITAL, SO THERE ISN'T THE USUAL GUEST PET OWNER—ACE AND YUZU WERE THE FOCUS.
MY FAVORITE SCENE IS THE ONE WHERE YUZU AND ACE ARE BOTH SLEEPING NEXT TO ONE ANOTHER.
GRR

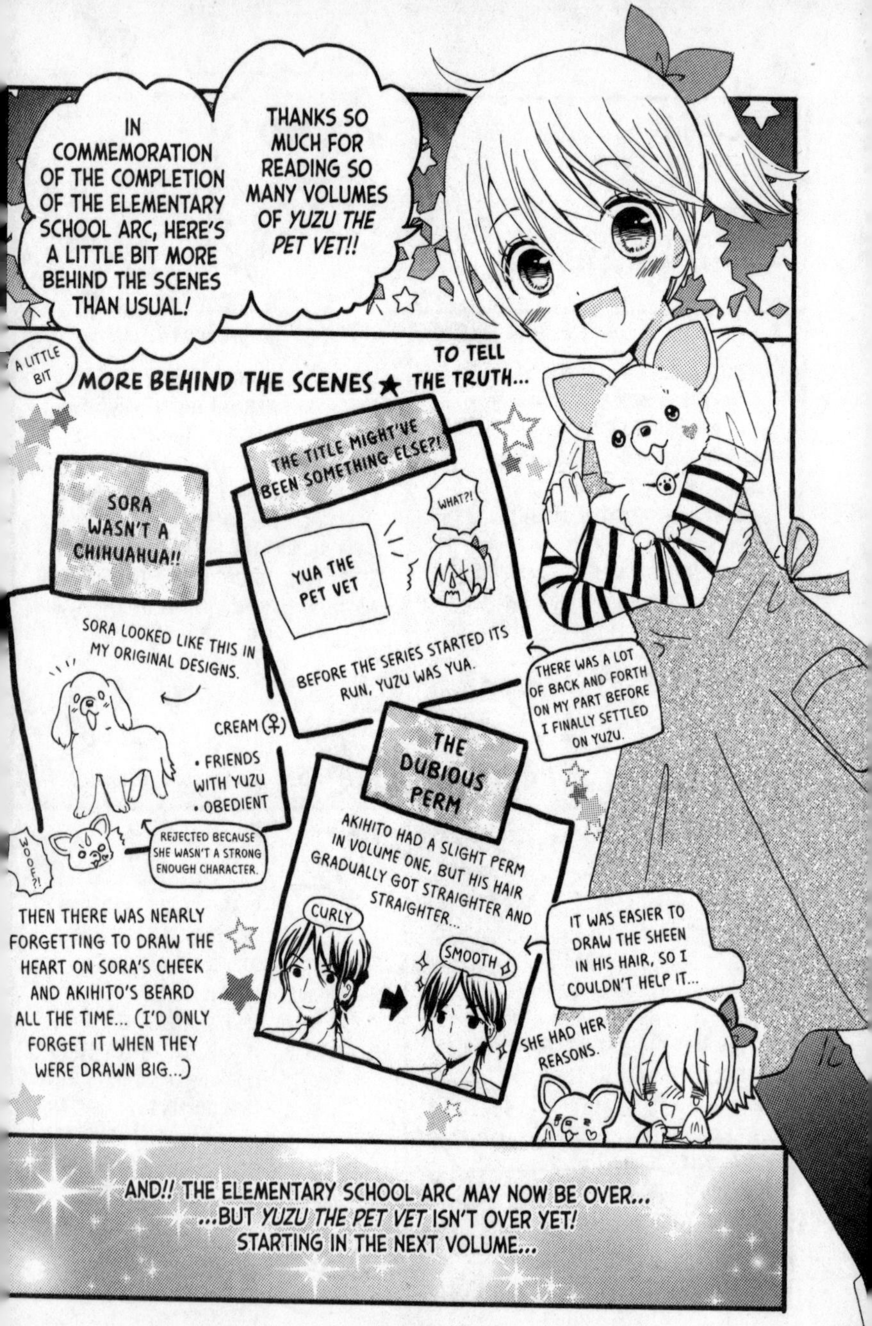
THANKS SO MUCH FOR READING SO MANY VOLUMES OF *YUZU THE PET VET*!!
IN COMMEMORATION OF THE COMPLETION OF THE ELEMENTARY SCHOOL ARC, HERE'S A LITTLE BIT MORE BEHIND THE SCENES THAN USUAL!
A LITTLE BIT
MORE BEHIND THE SCENES ★
TO TELL THE TRUTH...
THE TITLE MIGHT'VE BEEN SOMETHING ELSE?!
WHAT?!
YUA THE PET VET
BEFORE THE SERIES STARTED ITS RUN, YUZU WAS YUA.
THERE WAS A LOT OF BACK AND FORTH ON MY PART BEFORE I FINALLY SETTLED ON YUZU.
SORA WASN'T A CHIHUAHUA!!
SORA LOOKED LIKE THIS IN MY ORIGINAL DESIGNS.
CREAM (♀)
• FRIENDS WITH YUZU
• OBEDIENT
REJECTED BECAUSE SHE WASN'T A STRONG ENOUGH CHARACTER.
WOOF?!
THE DUBIOUS PERM
AKIHITO HAD A SLIGHT PERM IN VOLUME ONE, BUT HIS HAIR GRADUALLY GOT STRAIGHTER AND STRAIGHTER...
CURLY
SMOOTH
IT WAS EASIER TO DRAW THE SHEEN IN HIS HAIR, SO I COULDN'T HELP IT...
SHE HAD HER REASONS.
THEN THERE WAS NEARLY FORGETTING TO DRAW THE HEART ON SORA'S CHEEK AND AKIHITO'S BEARD ALL THE TIME... (I'D ONLY FORGET IT WHEN THEY WERE DRAWN BIG...)
AND!! THE ELEMENTARY SCHOOL ARC MAY NOW BE OVER...
...BUT *YUZU THE PET VET* ISN'T OVER YET!
STARTING IN THE NEXT VOLUME...

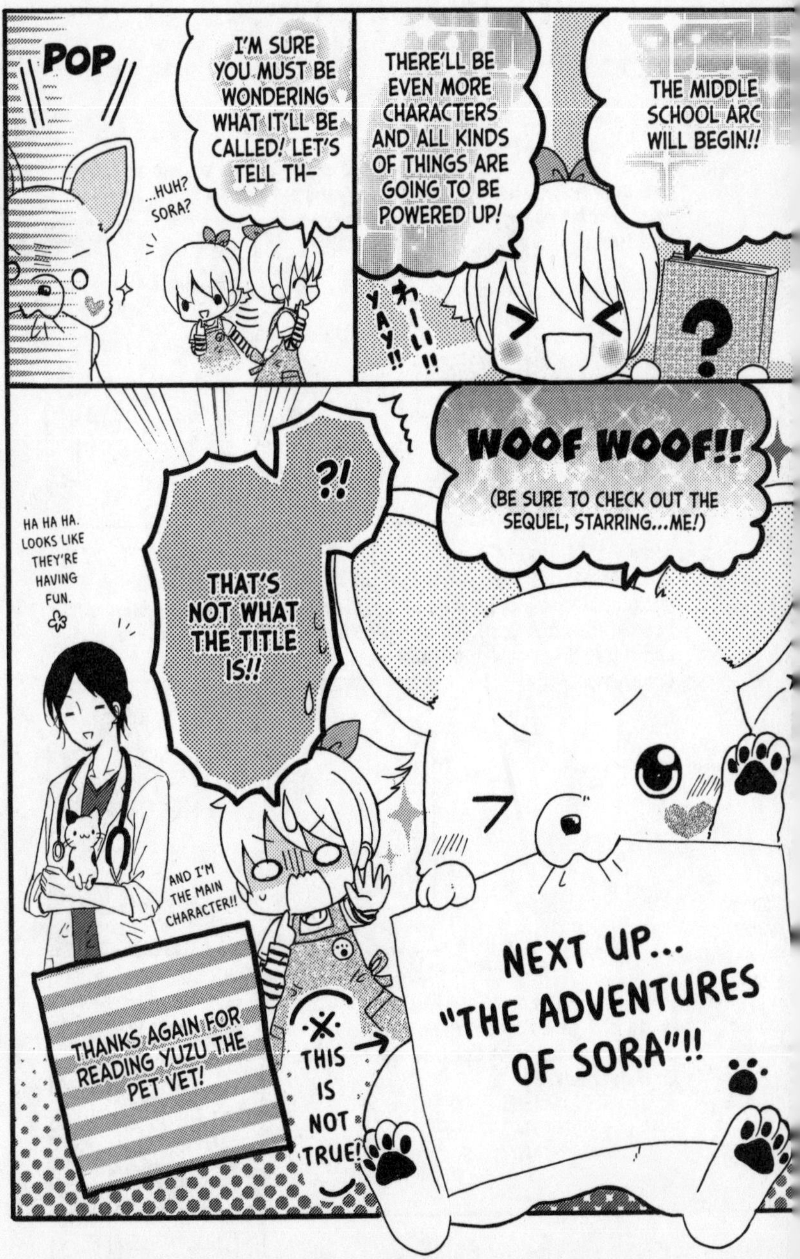
THE MIDDLE SCHOOL ARC WILL BEGIN!!
THERE'LL BE EVEN MORE CHARACTERS AND ALL KINDS OF THINGS ARE GOING TO BE POWERED UP!
わーい!!
YAY!!
I'M SURE YOU MUST BE WONDERING WHAT IT'LL BE CALLED! LET'S TELL TH–
...HUH? SORA?
POP
WOOF WOOF!!
(BE SURE TO CHECK OUT THE SEQUEL, STARRING...ME!)
NEXT UP... "THE ADVENTURES OF SORA"!!
※ THIS IS NOT TRUE!
?!
THAT'S NOT WHAT THE TITLE IS!!
AND I'M THE MAIN CHARACTER!!
HA HA HA. LOOKS LIKE THEY'RE HAVING FUN.
THANKS AGAIN FOR READING YUZU THE PET VET!

# Translation Notes

**10,000 yen bill, page 44**
Unlike in the US, it is actually quite common for people to carry around and pay using 10,000 bills (approximately $100) even at smaller stores in Japan.

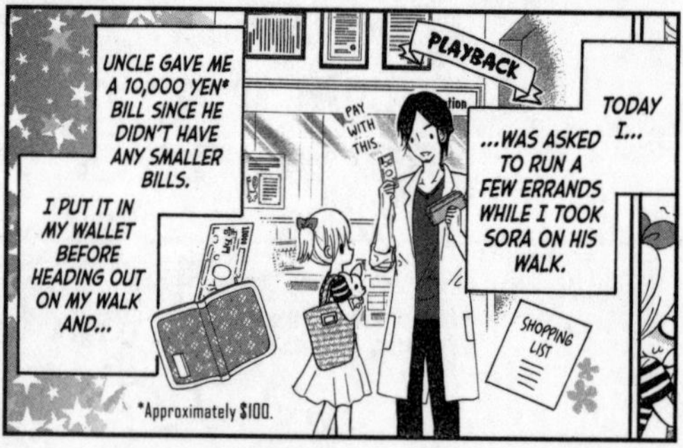

TODAY I...
...WAS ASKED TO RUN A FEW ERRANDS WHILE I TOOK SORA ON HIS WALK.
PLAYBACK
SHOPPING LIST
PAY WITH THIS.
UNCLE GAVE ME A 10,000 YEN* BILL SINCE HE DIDN'T HAVE ANY SMALLER BILLS.
I PUT IT IN MY WALLET BEFORE HEADING OUT ON MY WALK AND...
*Approximately $100.


**Yuzu fruits, page 57**
Yuzu fruits are yellow citrus fruits that are rarely eaten as fruits but commonly used as zest, juice, and in sauces, similar to how lemons are used. Its skin also has a very strong aroma and some people even float whole yuzu in their baths to enjoy their fragrance.

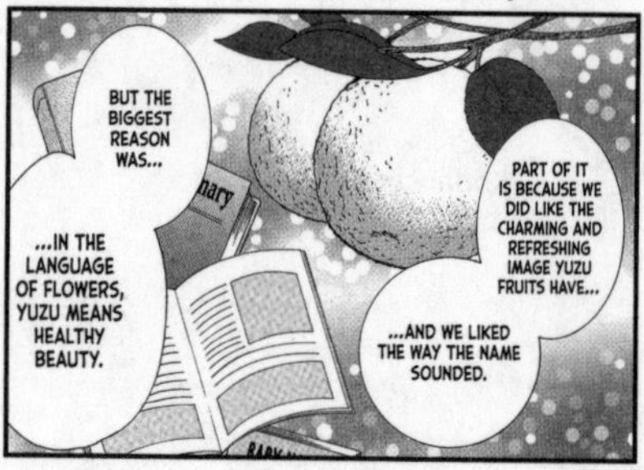

PART OF IT IS BECAUSE WE DID LIKE THE CHARMING AND REFRESHING IMAGE YUZU FRUITS HAVE...
...AND WE LIKED THE WAY THE NAME SOUNDED.
BUT THE BIGGEST REASON WAS...
...IN THE LANGUAGE OF FLOWERS, YUZU MEANS HEALTHY BEAUTY.


**Pochi, page 131**
Pochi is a generic name for dogs in Japanese, much like Spot or Rover is for English speakers.

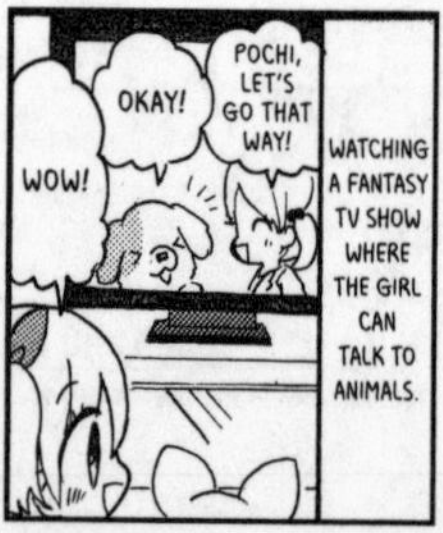

WATCHING A FANTASY TV SHOW WHERE THE GIRL CAN TALK TO ANIMALS.
POCHI, LET'S GO THAT WAY!
OKAY!
WOW!

A Kodansha Comics Trade Paperback Original
Yuzu the Pet Vet 7 copyright © 2019 Mingo Ito © 2018 NIPPON COLUMBIA CO., LTD.
English translation copyright © 2021 Mingo Ito © NIPPON COLUMBIA CO., LTD.

Published in the United States by Kodansha Comics, an imprint of Kodansha USA Publishing, LLC, New York.

Publication rights for this English edition arranged through Kodansha Ltd., Tokyo.

First published in Japan in 2019 by Kodansha Ltd., Tokyo
as Yuzu no Doubutsu Karute ~Kochira Wan Nyan Doubutsu Byouin~, volume 7.

ISBN 978-1-64651-098-6

Original cover design by Tomoko Kobayashi

Printed in the United States of America.

www.kodansha.us

1st Printing
Translation: Julie Goniwich
Lettering: David Yoo
Editing: Ryan Holmberg
Kodansha Comics edition cover design by Matthew Akuginow

Publisher: Kiichiro Sugawara

Director of publishing services: Ben Applegate
Associate director of operations: Stephen Pakula
Publishing services associate managing editor: Madison Salters
Production managers: Emi Lotto, Angela Zurlo
Logo and character art ©Kodansha USA Publishing, LLC

# HOW TO READ MANGA

Japanese is written right to left and top to bottom. This means that for a reader accustomed to Western languages, Japanese books read “backwards.” Since most manga published in English now keeps the Japanese page order, it can take a little getting used to—but once you learn how, it’s a snap. Here’s a handy guide!

Here you can see pages 24-25 from volume 1. The speech balloons have been numbered in the order you should read them in.

**Page 10**—read this one first!

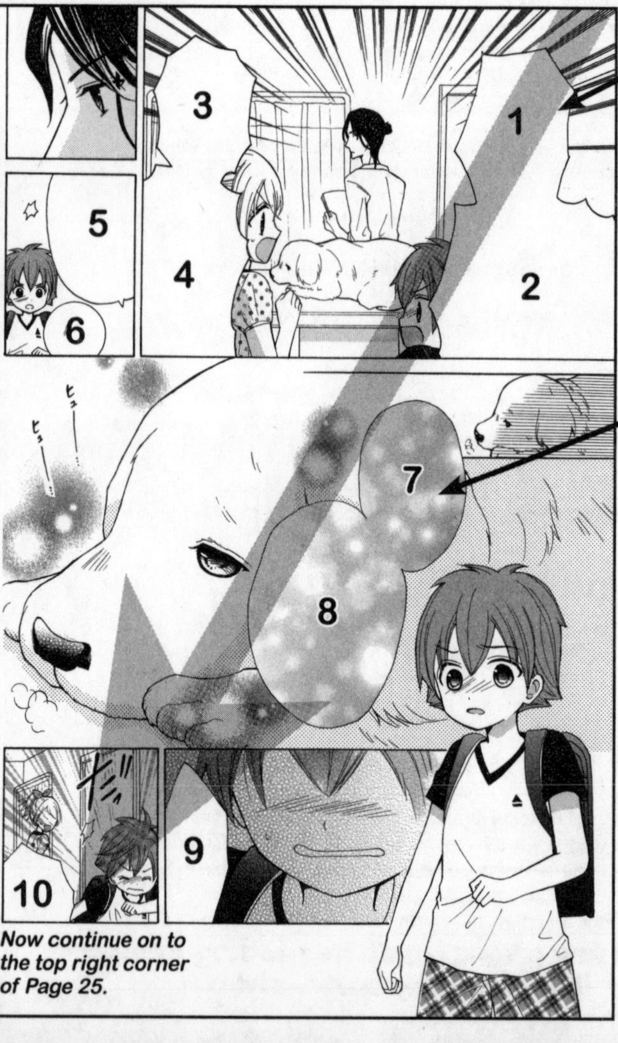
1
2
3
4
5
6
7
8
9
10

Start here, at the top right corner of the right hand page.

Read right to left, then top to bottom.

***Now continue on to the top right corner of Page 25.***

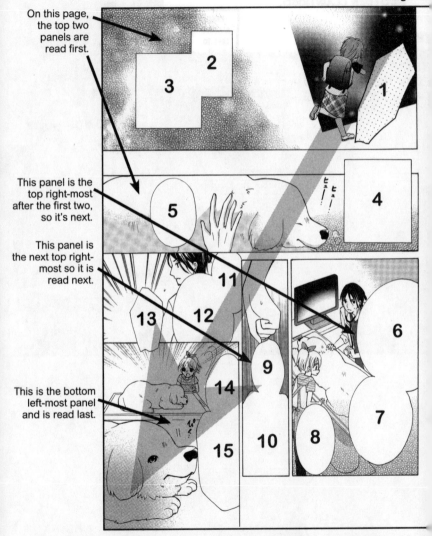

On this page, the top two panels are read first.

This panel is the top right-most after the first two, so it's next.

This panel is the next top right-most so it is read next.

This is the bottom left-most panel and is read last.

**After a few pages, you'll be reading manga like a pro-Japanese-style!**

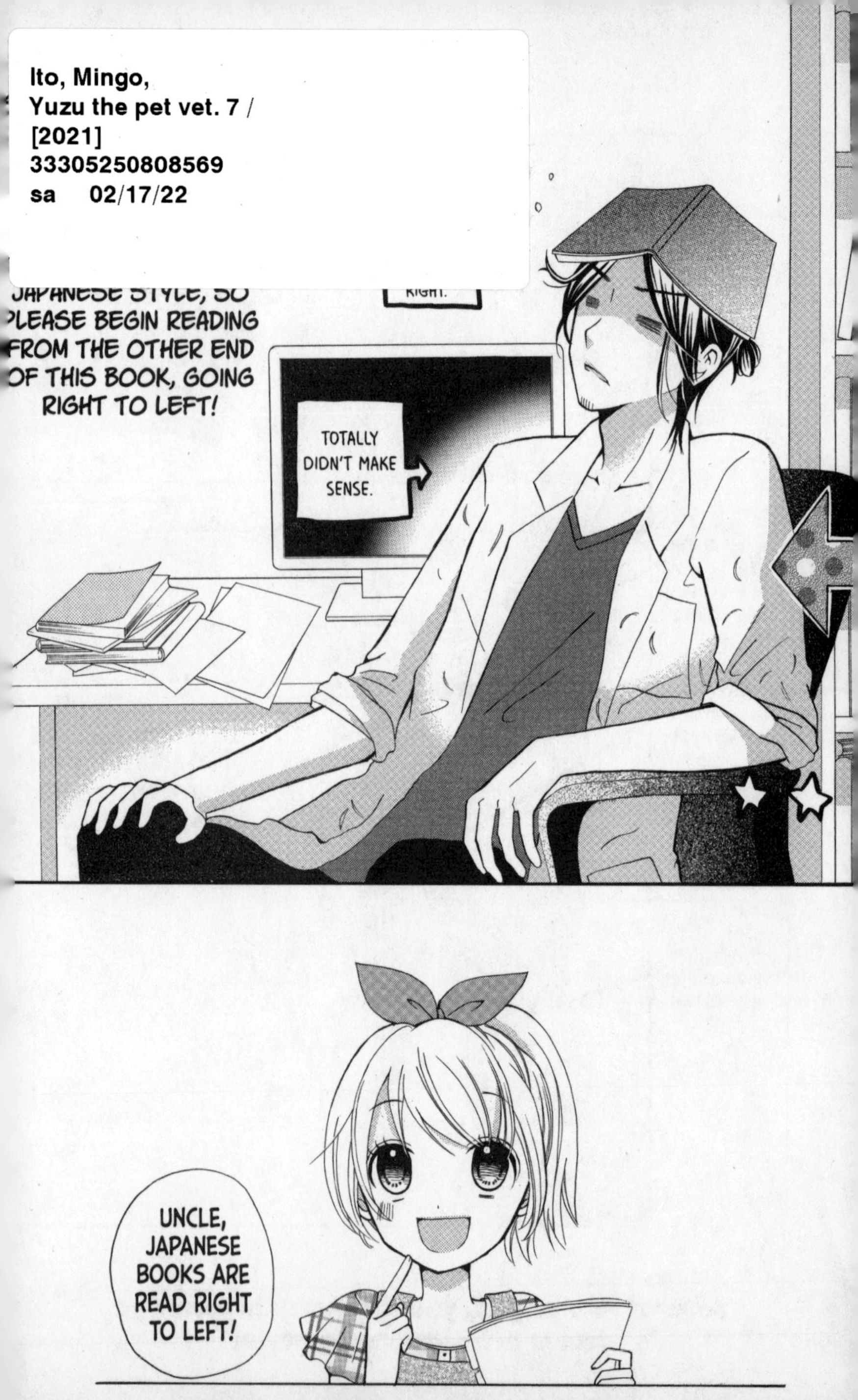
RIGHT.
JAPANESE STYLE, SO PLEASE BEGIN READING FROM THE OTHER END OF THIS BOOK, GOING RIGHT TO LEFT!
TOTALLY DIDN'T MAKE SENSE.
UNCLE, JAPANESE BOOKS ARE READ RIGHT TO LEFT!